Fiore dei Liberi's
SWORD IN TWO HANDS

Brian R. Price

A Full-Color Training Guide for the Medieval Longsword
Based on Fiore dei Liberi's Fior di Battaglia

Chivalry Bookshelf

Sword in Two Hands
A Full-Color Training Guide for the Medieval Longsword based on Fiore dei Liberi's Fior di Battaglia

Brian R. Price

Published in the United States by
The Chivalry Bookshelf, 3305 Mayfair Lane
Highland Village, Texas, USA 75077
tel. 866.268.1495 (US), fax 978.418.4774.
http://www.chivalrybookshelf.com

Copyright © 2007 Brian R. Price
Photography by: Ann Price, with contributions by Russell & Erika Kinder

ISBN: 1-891448-13-7

Price, Brian R. (1964-)

Subject: Martial Arts
    Fencing | Fencing History | Italy

Neither the author nor the publisher assumes any liability for the use or misuse of information contained in this book, nor do the author or publishers encourage the use of martial arts techniques other than for personal development and historical study. Study of historical martial arts can be dangerous and should only be practiced under the guidance of a qualified instructor.

Table of Contents

*I dedicate this book to the Schola Saint George
and our students, without which this book could not exist.*

Acknowledgements

A task such as this one is not less than Herculean. Not Fiore's material, difficult though it is in the original, but rather providing adequate and heartfelt thanks to the many, many people who have influenced this work or made it possible at all. Doubtless I will leave some out, and I would begin with sincere apologies to any who are not mentioned below.

First, my co-founder of the Schola, Dr. Robert Holland, who continues to pursue historical swordsmanship and to shepard the San Francisco Bay area Schola Branch. Robert's many years of patient and insightful thought contibuted a huge amount to my understanding of the core kinesthetics. Dr. Holland, an environmental engineer by trade, brings a piercing intellect and steadiness to the Schola that has inspired many. Currently he is working on his interpretation of the Royal Armouries MS RA I.33 sword and buckler treatise.

Next, to the "first class" of SSG students, most of whom are still with the school: Instructors Brian Keish and Instructor Colin Hatcher, who has grabbed Fiore's segno "by the tail" and gone further with it than any other student of Fiore's that I know. To the other Schola instructors, especially Juan Fajarado and Scott Thompson, together with our active cadre of study group leaders, most particularly Jason Willis (and the passionate Little Rock study group), Frank Petrino, Patrick Olterman and Brian Johnson.

To the current students of the DFW group, who have collectively had a great influence, including in particular Russell Kinder, Andy Borman, and Todd Richard. Not to be forgotten are Louis, Rob, Keanan, Dan, Edward, Cynthia, John and Alicia.

A host of Western Martial Arts members have also been influential, either through their works, through the late-night "after hours" sessions at seminars, or through sword-in-hand comparisons. On this list must go Gregory Mele, Christian Tobler, Bob Charron, Jorg Bellinghausen, Steve Hick, Tom Leoni, Guy Windsor, Stephen Hand, Andrea Sinclair, Bill Ernohazy, Jr., William E. Wilson, Gary Chalek, Ramon Martinez, Paul McDonald, Gus Trim, Jim Alvarez, Jeffrey L. Forgeng, Cliff Rodgers, Matt Galas, Paul Wagner, and Steven Muhlberger. Also to Professor Jeff Goodwin of the UNT Department of Kinesiology.

For the many readers of early drafts of the manuscript, including especially Clayton Towry, Steve Blazichevich, Charles Deily, William Adkins, and Tim Hardisty. Many typographical and key logic errors were caught by this able team, but any mistakes in the text remain my own.

A special thanks to Massimo Malipiero both for his early inspirational work, for his recent Italian edition of the Getty, and to a great deal of helpful personal correpondence, particularly with regard to the Friulian dialect. Paula Koerner, my Italian instructor at UNT, has done her best to reduce the number of errors in my understanding of this most beautiful of languages.

To the J.P. Getty Trust, for its kind supplying of images and permissions, especially Michaelle Keller. To our intrepid photographic crew, led by my timelessly beautiful wife Ann Marie, but also including Andy Borman, Russell & Erika Kinder and Dan Sepham.

The Author

Brian R. Price has been involved in medieval combat systems since 1981, fighting competitively within the Society for Creative Anachronism (SCA), reenactment, and since 1999 within the Western martial arts / historical swordsmanship community. He has experience in several martial arts and modern fencing as well as in jousting. He is an accomplished armourer, author of the influential *Techniques of Medieval Armour Reproduction*.

As an author, he has written numerous works in several fields, including the 1996 *Book of the Tournament*, Ramon Lull's *Book of Knighthood and Chivalry*, and the forthcoming *Ponderous, Cruel & Mortal: Martial Techniques with the Medieval Poleaxe*. He has contributed to numerous works including *King Arthur in Popular Culture* and *SPADA*.

He has made extensive studies of the medieval tournament, medieval armour, and knighthood, as well as holding interest in kinesiology, modern political systems, intelligence, warfare, and American political history. He holds a BA in political science from the Univesity of California, Los Angeles (UCLA), and is presently at work on a Ph.d in Military History University of North Texas as well as taking graduate courses in Kinesiology.

But his true interest has been in chivalric culture, which he has long exercised, first within the SCA, then with the founding of the Company of Saint George, the first American Tournament Society. He edited the journal *Chronique: The Journal of Chivalry* and has founded three companies: Thornbird Arms, the Chivalry Bookshelf and Revival Enterprises, Ltd., which supplies high quality leather goods, jewelry and Western martial arts equipment.

In 2000 he co-founded the Schola Saint George and began working on an interpretation of Fiore dei Liberi's text and on the medieval poleaxe. He has taught classes continually both to the Schola groups and at seminars in North America, in Canada and in Europe. Mr. Price studied with Theodore Katzoff at the Westside Fencing Center in Los Angeles and taught swordsmanship at the same location for two years. He has lectured at Stanford University and at the International Medieval Congress in Kalamazoo, Michigan. In 2003 he was admitted to the United States Martial Arts Hall of Fame.

Mr. Price makes his home in Highland Village, Texas, just north of Dallas with his wife Ann and his children, Elizabeth and Edward.

THE FIRST MASTERS OF BATTLE

he historical record has in recent years begun to offer profound, revolutionary insights into methods of personal defense practiced during the Middle Ages. The old way of seeing medieval combat as a disjointed, undisciplined and largely unrefined collection of brutal flurries has been challenged by a new appreciation for the sophistication of personal combat techniques available to professional masters-at-arms and their knightly counterparts.

Today's re-enactors, combat society members, fencing and military historians have rediscovered the treasure-trove of documentation for medieval fighting techniques as recorded in the *fechtbücher* or fight-books of the 13th – 16th centuries. These hand-drawn manuscripts detail German and Italian systems of combat which rival their Asian counterparts in terms of sophistication, efficiency, and knowledge of human combat principles. It is from these works that a new generation of scholars has looked to for clues as to how medieval and early Renaissance combatants may have fought.

A new kind of martial arts / fencing school has arisen in a symbiotic relationship with the old treatises. The manuscripts are the sources from which the schools draw their content, and the schools in turn interpret the works for the benefit of their students and for the wider "community" of enthusiasts. The interpretation of the old treatises is both challenging and rewarding, but it is also relatively new and as yet unformed in terms of accepted truths about the systems. The school leaders are passionate and serious about what they do, learning Italian or German, immersing themselves in the cultural context of the manuscripts, and striving to more clearly understand the seductive content recorded more than six centuries previously. By and large the published efforts of these early teachers have inspired and supported new generations of students and teachers who will reinterpret the works again and again, in the process taking into account new information and upsetting old assumptions. This a dynamic process which the young fight-schools of today are well-equipped to handle as they create a marketplace for martial ideas which are then tested, kept or discarded based on how well they actually work.

The Schola Saint George is one of these schools, and I am honored to be counted as its founder and leader. As a school our objective is to create scholars in the Art of Arms with foundations firmly rooted in the historical material. They can then study, practice, evaluate and analyze interpretations by Schola instructors and those advanced by others. We hope that our students will help to illuminate and showcase the works of the old masters, working in what Fiore dei Liberi called *concordia*—harmony—with other scholars in an ongoing effort to better understand what is written and what was perhaps intended by our forebears regarding the Art.

Our foundational text for the school, the place from which our core principles are derived, is the late 14th / early 15th century *Fior di Battaglia* (Flower of Battle) by the renowned master-at-arms Fiore dei Liberi. This seminal Italian text is consummately medieval in its outlook, even though published during the early Renaissance. As such, it is an amazing resource for students of medieval combat, however they practice it in today's world.

Fiore approaches combat rationally, underpinning his system with timeless principles of hand-to-hand combat recognizable to any serious student of the martial arts. Like other medieval texts, Fiore's art begins with a set of known guards or positions—*poste*—then highlights ramifications of the core principles in a series of techniques or set-plays with different weapon configurations. In the Prologue he articulates a sophisticated presentation of combat stages that are really a tactical algorithm, a combat model readily adaptable to any modern reconstruction of medieval combat.

The Schola's core curriculum is based on Fiore's system. Our foundational material is called the *First Masters of Battle* course, drawn from Fiore's longsword *poste* or *gaurdia*. Using this system, students gain insight into the movement and tactical framework—startling and elegantly simple—striving to learn how to fight from the *poste* and to strike their opponent in such as way as to reduce the chances of being struck in return. These basic combat skills do not require grappling and are rules-system agnostic, applicable to any hand-to-hand combat or combat sport environment. Our goal is to highlight these principles, building a foundation that strives to tie the *Fior di Battaglia*'s thematic elements into a simple, direct way to analyze encounters with swords or sword-like objects.

Most other schools looking at the Fiore tend to analyze the entire vertical history of Italian swordsmanship for clues as to how to proceed. This is a valid and important way of filling in the holes left in the text. However, we tend towards horizontal analysis, which means looking at parallel systems. In our case that means looking at the German systems, and trying to compare and contrast how other masters use similar weapons. Our theory is that similar weapons will result in similar optimizations of efficiency, and that over time, significant differences in the form and application of weapons and combat tactics produces dramatic changes in technique. As in other elements of language, the definition of a word (or a technique) can change over time, and I believe that this may have happened in the Italian tradition, even in the short space of time separating Fiore dei Liberi from his nearest descendent, Filippo Vadi. Continuity in Italian is important, to be sure, but there is perhaps more similarity to be gained in the contemporary German techniques than there are on Italian techniques which are recorded a hundred years later.

Using Fiore's **First Masters of Battle** a student of medieval combat systems can quickly gain a feel for how to achieve a first order of defense in a way that is both historically accurate and extremely effective. In a way, I hope that *Sword in Two Hands* is a **First Master of Battle** to our students, a guidebook and gateway to the world of historical combat.

For students already working within the Schola Saint George, this book should provide a comprehensive guide useful far beyond the *First Masters of Battle* course. The history, context and principles chapters attempt to articulate concepts that we hope develop throughout a student's study, while the technique chapters that follow in chapters 6-11 form the core content for the course. Our training techniques are covered in chapter 12, and the school's approach to the study and student advancement is covered in the closing chapter 13.

For students working with other schools or in other groups focused on medieval martial arts, my hope is to provide a useful resource providing context and martial insight into one of the most popular texts. By no means do I consider this book the final word in Fiore's technique, but I am confident that the interpretations work and they have been successful in developing students within our school.

For prospective students or to the curious, my hope is that this work will underscore the strength and sophistication of historical medieval methods of combat as illustrated by Fiore's book. Taken together with the German works in the Johannes Lichtenauer tradition, it becomes clear that medieval fighting was, at least in some quarters, highly developed and efficient. These arts qualify for and are being reconstructed today as martial arts systems capable of taking their place alongside their Asian counterparts.

Some prospective students may have or develop an interest in affiliation with the Schola Saint George. The School has, starting in late 2004, adopted a distributed model that encourages affiliation by members not only throughout North America, but in all countries where European historical combat has potential students. These Study Groups and Independent Scholars have contributed strongly to the Schola both in terms of our chivalric culture and our interpretations of Fiore's material. In 2006 we were both proud and pleased to admit our first European affiliate from Latvia, Riga. The most current information regarding affiliation is on the Schola website, www/scholasaintgeorge.org. and I would encourage prospective students to review what we are looking for and how individuals and new groups are approved.

Whatever the reader's interest, I sincerely hope that *Sword in Two Hands* rewards its students with the insights earned through research and through the perceptions of the great majority of combatants I have had the pleasure of working with and teaching.

There will doubtless be errors and flaws in the current work and I aggressively claim these as my own. What works and endures rightly belongs to Art, rather than to me.

A WORD ABOUT LANGUAGE

Perhaps the most confounding aspect of these arts brought up by new students is our heavy reliance on Italian terms. This trend has been carried over into *Sword in Two Hands*, so the same concern may be felt here and I am open to the charge of jargonism. But I have several good reasons why I have not translated the terms.

I have made a conscious choice *not* to translate many of the terms into English, not because there aren't loosely equivalent English terms, but because I believe that our present understanding of the original concepts is imperfect. Over time, I would hope that our understanding of these terms will deepen and in some cases, change. If the terms were translated, then they might then have to be retranslated, resulting in confusion.

Secondly, when students from different traditions or with different interpretations discuss Fiore's techniques and principles, they need a common language. Since a translation *is* an interpretation, students from different schools would have different translations, resulting in still more confusion.

Finally, I believe that having students learn the original Italian is no different than what many Asian martial arts have done. No doubt part of their objective is to create a jargon (with all of the accompanying sociological objectives), but a more important goal is to provide both connectivity with the original art and to preserve as much continuity as possible. I have the same objectives.

ITALIAN SPELLING

Fiore's text is in a vulgar (i.e, low) dialect of Italian. Like other Latin (Romance) languages, nouns carry a masculine or feminine denotation expressed both in the article and in the word's ending. The reader will also find archaic spellings throughout, as in the older form of *zhogo* (a play) versus the modern *giocco*. I have retained the older spellings in an effort to stay as close as possible to the original treatise.

Masculine nouns generally (but not always) have the ending –o, as in *magistro* or *zhogo*. The plural is indicated by changing the ending to –i, as in *magistri* or *zhogi*.

Feminine nouns generally (but not always) have the ending –a, as in *volta* or *spada*. The plural for nouns with the –a ending is expressed by changing the end to –e, as in *volte* or *spade*. This can be confusing, because some nouns end in –e in their singular form, and they can be either masculine or feminine, such as *fendente*. These nouns take the ending –i in their plural form, as in *fendenti*.

Verbs carry the endings –are, -ere and –ire, although –are is the most common form, as in *voltare* and *passare*. Nouns based on these verbs omit the participle and take an appropriate ending, depending upon their gender, as in *volta*, *passo*, and *rebatteimento*.

Because of these changes in word endings, the English reader might at first think that the inconsistencies within the words are due to carelessness or randomness: in fact they are just part of the Italian language.

CHAPTER ONE

INTRODUCTION

he City of a Hundred Towers—medieval Pavia—is situated not far south of Milan on the Ticino River just north of its confluence with the River Po. Pavia has a long martial history. It was an important military town to the Romans when it was known as the Ticinum Papiae. Under the Goths, it had become a fortified citadel, the last holdout against Belisarius. It was the capital of the Lombard kingdom, but was lost to Charlemagne in the Battle of Pavia in 773, after which it became the capital of his Regnum Italicum, a vassal kingdom of the Holy Roman Empire until the 12th century.

During the 12th century it adopted the Ghibelline (i.e. Imperial) position and became a self-governing commune, supported in large part through agricultural products, chiefly wine, rice, cereals, and dairy products. Traditionally at odds with its northern neighbor Milan, the Visconti family finally subdued it in 1359, and in 1361 founded a university around the famous and ancient School of Law.

The year is 1395, and the city sparkles with new construction, a burgeoning nexus of trade and artistic endeavor. The Certosa (a Carthusian monastery) has just been completed, and hundreds of narrow, finger-shaped towers rise on a tide of prosperity.

In the center of the city, a throng of townsmen crowd to see a procession. At the start of the procession there might have been two great beasts, followed by banner-carrying men-at-arms. After, two armoured men sit proudly upon their mounts bearing sharpened lances. Their helmets are polished bascinetti, bullet-shaped but elegant. Brightly colored velvet and shiny rivets hide the steel plates protecting their bodies, under which could be found mail and padded arming coats known as zuparelli. They are armoured from head to foot, and they look straight ahead, riding side by side. They are followed by other knights and damsels, ultimately by no less than the Duke and Duchess of Milan, newly invested with their titles from the Holy Roman Emperor, all en route to the imposing Castello Visconti on the north side of the city.

The two armoured men are both squires, one old and one young. The younger one is Zohanni de Baio da Milano. The other is a hulking old soldier from Germany known as Saam. Both remain sharply focused on the combat to come. Countless members of the lower nobility from the region have turned out to watch their combat, the Duke and Duchess to see how their Milanese squire will fare against the renowned Saam. While neither combatant is worried, confident in their skills and training, their deed of arms offers the very real possibility of injury or worse, since today they will fight a oltranza—with sharpened weapons—with every intent of "giving offense" to their able opponent.

As they pass through the wall and into the colonnade-encircled park-like scene for the upcoming battle, the two might have noticed the Castello's four massive towers standing like old Roman gods commanding the field. A platform has been erected for the Duke and Duchess, raising them above the throng of minor nobility which stretched "nearly to infinity," each trying to find a place to see the famous combat.

The preliminaries are dispensed, and the horns cry their shrill report. Arrayed at opposite sides of the lists, both men spur their mounts. The field is undivided, and the men drive hard at one another, their sharpened lances unmoving as the horses careen towards one another. Both men are visored, their faces hidden, but a hint of apprehension is clear, which serves only to increase their demonstration of courage. Most passes with the lance on horseback are tipped with a special crowned tip known in France as the coronel, but today the two men wield lances of war, sharp and hungry for flesh.

In seconds, the two men are together, seemingly blended for an instant in a mesh of horseflesh, steel, bright velvet, pennants and lances. A collective gasp is heard from the gathered spectators as both lances are broken against each man's helmet. But the men continue their ballistic trajectory as each horse reaches the ends of the lists where a man-at-arms is quick to provide another sharpened lance.

In seconds they turn again and are once again in flight towards one another like some crazy game of chicken in which both men know the other will not swerve. Again both lances find their way home against the combatant's bodies, and once again there is the collective gasp and a shattering of lance on plate. Both combatants say a silent prayer of thanks to God and to their armourers, for they remain unpierced, if not unbruised.

They are again armed and begin the third pass. With each pass the danger increases, each combatant knowing a bit more about their opponent's strategy of defense. But as the spectators hold their breath, the Milanese champion Zohanni drops his point on the left side of his horse's head. There is a premature gasp as the gathered nobility realize that the German's spear alone will land. Inside the German's visor, the old soldier smiles, his victory near at hand.

Not even a whole second before impact, however, Zohanni brings his lanza sharply upward. His timing is perfect, and in a single motion he lifts the German's lance, propelling it off its line. Simultaneously, Zohanni's own lance remains steadfastly on-target, pointed directly for the center of the German's chest. Microseconds later, the lance strikes and skips upwards towards the throat, where it lodges against the rolled edge meant to deflect such attacks. But the lance also catches on the roll, and Saam is lifted up and out of the saddle while Zohanni's lance splinters into a thousand pieces. Saam is propelled up and back, at long last crashing to the ground, where he rolls head over heels, finally coming to a stop in a heap of armour and dust.

Zohanni and his elated mount continue, raising his lance in celebration as the spectators roar their approval. The Duke himself applauds, standing in appreciation for the exceptional skill. Zohanni rides before the Ducal platform and salutes with his broken lance, his head bowed but his spirit soaring. He has opened his visor and his smile shines like a warm summer day, rekindling the audience's cheer of approval.

The old soldier Saam is bruised and bumped, but he is not beaten. As the crowd showers his opponent with honor, the German rises, shaking the cobwebs from his head and casting aside a broken spaudler, armour designed to defend the shoulder. The fight is not yet finished, and there are more exchanges to come. With gathering strength, he strides up to Zohanni's mount and offers his hand. The Milanese squire shakes it, riding then over to his men-at-arms, who take his lance and provide him with a six foot warhammer, its slender but potent head surmounted by a sharpened spike. Zohanni takes a duplicate in his left hand, proceeding to the center of the field to meet Saam, where he offers the choice of either weapon.

Saam pauses for just a moment, finally selecting the one in Zohanni's right hand. He tests its heft and balance, grunting in approval. With his left hand he closes his visor once more, nodding in salute to his surprising young opponent. The squire likewise dismounts and closes his own visor, striving again to concentrate after the flush of success with the lance. As his old mentor said time and time again, he must guard himself against underestimating his opponent, always entering into combat with the audacity of the lion.

But the poleaxe was a dangerous tool, the medieval equivalent of an assault weapon, capable of smashing, piercing, tearing, tripping, hooking or binding. It was really three weapons in one—the most obvious one at the head above the right hand, the end below the left hand, and the haft between the hands. It would be very, very difficult to control the opponent's axe, for if one end was bound, the other could immediately and powerfully be brought to bear. His magistro called the azza "ponderous, cruel & mortal," and the squire dearly hoped that today his azza would prove to be none of the three. He worried.

Old Saam loved his weapon. His teachers, not far to the north of Italy in the Holy Roman Empire, had a long tradition with the weapon. Old Johannnes himself barely mentioned the weapon, but its nature perfectly suited the German's combat style, usually a powerful, dizzying rain of blows that would eventually force an opponent off-balance or out of guard. He could wield the axe like an armoured staff, smashing with each end and trying to hook his opponent around the neck or at the knee, driving him to the ground. He would recover much of the ground lost in the equestrian encounter, possibly even ending the fight altogether.

Like the exchange with the lanzi, this bought was to be fought until one combatant landed three telling colpi—blows—upon the other. Even given the sophisticated and highly mobile defenses of plate and covered plate armour, there was a good chance that one of the two men would earn honor and renown because their courage was laid bare for all to see, and it was highly unlikely that either would shrink from the challenge, difficult though it was.

Once again, the men stood in the center of the sbarra, the wooden enclosure that surrounded the fighting field. Both hands on their axes, they offered each other a sincere salute of respect, raising the axe and bowing their heads just a little. For a few eternal moments, nothing seemed to happen.

With a roar, the German seemed to explode at the younger squire, seeking to drive right through him. He launched blows one after the other from the left and right, striking at anything that even hinted at presenting itself: Zohanni's head, body, knees, arms or even his hands.

It was all Zohanni could do to cover himself, and several of the blows came in, their stinging report announcing his failure to cover many different points on his body. His defenses didn't so much crumble as they failed to materialize, and suddenly, before he knew what had happened, he felt a wrenching from behind his neck and he was propelled forward at his opponent's feet, striking the ground with an explosion of sound that must have been louder than the one his opponent had made after he was catapulted from the saddle. Dust swirled inside his visor, and he tasted blood.

It all went as Saam had hoped. His younger opponent was overwhelmed, just as the zettel or mnemonic verse fighting verse had suggested, and he had retreated under the pounding of blows. Eventually, after a telling blow to the squire's head, he was able to slip the beak forward and hook him behind the neck, stepping back then and pulling him to the ground with great force. "There, that should do it," he thought.

Indeed it was a long moment before Zohanni moved. The spectators were quiet, the Duke's head bent slightly forward with concern, sure Milan's young champion had been defeated.

"What still works?" Zohanni felt his thoughts moving reluctantly. Chiefly, his head hurt. No, more precisely it rang, the thousand bells an unwelcome and sadistic cacophony. He shook his head, and a very few of the bells were silent. One of his ribs was probably broken, as was at least one finger. No, make that two fingers. The steel lames and gatlings of his gauntlet had provided some protection, but the azza was just too powerful, and he wanly remembered that he had managed to hold onto his weapon at least until he met the ground. At that point…well, there was no telling where it was now. Also, walking would be a challenge, if the swelling in his left knee was any indication. He had been paid back in martial coin for his pride. "Nice," he thought dryly.

But the very youthfulness that caused him to hesitate also helped him to rise. And rise he did, getting up to a thunderous roar of joy that did nothing to help his head, even as it lent him additional strength at a high rate of interest. The spectators were pleased.

Saam looked on with respectful assessment. It would have been foolhardy and he would have lost renown to have continued the attack after he had his man on the ground, and it was clear that he had without question won that pass. As the younger man tried to clear his head, it was Saam who made his way to the edge of the sbarra, accepting two long swords—what his countrymen would know as langenswerten. As Zohanni had done before him, he strode confidently to the center of the sbarra and offered the partly recovered squire his choice of weapons.

"Nicely offended," the young man offered a shaky hand.
"Stoutly taken," the German returned the gesture, shaking his hand and smiling. "Shall we?"
"Indeed."

The two walked a few paces apart before turning to salute one another, raising the sword in a gesture that left no doubt about their mutual respect.

Even after the drubbing Zohanni had just received, his confidence was again high. He gripped the spada in two hands, not adopting any guardia, holding himself ready with easy grace. The German did the same, the blade resting casually over his right shoulder and his left hand seemed to wander near his left hip. The two combatants eyed one another, calculating, measuring, thinking. Although nothing appeared to happen, those with combat experience well knew that the combatants were already engaged in a mental contest, a contest of wills that raged as they very slowly closed the distance as if strolling through the market. But the effected grace, what the Duke and Duchess thought of as sprezzaturra, was deceptive. Both men's bodies were coiled and ready to strike, a ready reserve of power stored in of the body's large muscle groups. As they circled ever closer, their grips tightened imperceptibly.

For his part, Saam had raised his own weapon above his head, letting the point rest in the center of his face, the hilt held high in the right side in a position or leger his fechtmeister called Ochs, "Ox." It was a strong guard that rained powerful blows from above. When the time

was right, he would employ the same strategy that had worked with the streitaxst, driving forward to unbalance the young squire.

Zohanni kept his posta, but as the German closed the tiniest amount, he shifted his guardia, sliding his point forward into a position his magistro called porta di ferro mezana, the "half-iron gate." This would give Zohanni time at the expense of power and would allow him to be late, in case his opponent caught him unawares. He would have to work harder to develop enough power to wound his opponent, but he was sure he could do it.

It was not long after that Saam found his moment. As the young man shifted his point, it looked almost exactly like the German guard Alber, the "fool." Saam had always thought of the guard as foolish, and with relish he drove his hilt downward, turning his blade so that the tip whipped around viciously, driving for his opponent's helmet. He stepped forward also, adding still more power to the attack.

The young squire immediately pulled his guard up, seeking cover. It was his intent to increase his stability by seeking posta breve—the short guard—which simultaneously provided cover and would, hopefully, bring his point to bear not far from his opponent's visor. From there it would take just another step to drive that same point into the aventail or linked wire defense for the throat, and the fight would be done. It was excellent, and it was near!

Unfortunately, the blow came in with far more power than Zohanni anticipated, and the German redirected the blow, concentrated his force on the squire's sword at the middle, what the Italian magistro had called the mezza spada. This drove Zohanni's point far out of line and even pushed his body so that his weight transferred to the outside of his right foot. His balance was now compromised, and he was forced to step quickly backwards to recover himself. But the German followed, striking immediately and powerfully on the other side, having raised his sword high and rolling it using leverage in what the German fechtmeisters called a zwerchhau. He then repeated this to the other side, hammering first on one side and then the other, all the while forcing the squire further and further back.

Space disappeared quickly. Zohanni was behind, fighting in what his opponent would call nach, or "after." He was merely responding to what Saam was doing, while the German enjoyed fighting in the vor, the "before" where he controlled the action. Zohanni was forced to step backwards again and again, and suddenly, the world turned.

Saam had lost count of how many blows he had thrown at the young squire, stepping with each blow. But he was impressed that the squire had managed to make cover, although to do so he had been forced to give ground with every step. Before either of them knew it, the squire's back was to the fence, and as the last blow rained down from the right—a particularly powerful oberhau aimed at Zohanni's helmet— his sword made cover but his feet were stopped by the fence. His upper body, however, kept going, and he did a backwards flip over the waist-high fence of the sbarra. He landed with another crash.

In all of the fury of the attack, no blows had found the young squire's body. Surprised at finding his opponent no longer before him, it took a couple of seconds or so for the German to lower his head so that he could see downwards. The squire was already rising, dusting himself off. Saam offered him his hand and the squire bounded over the fence, an impressive feat in complete harness. In silence, the two men centered themselves once more in the field, saluted, and started again.

This time Saam was less certain of how to proceed. None of his attacks had landed, but he adopted the familiar and comfortable guard Ochs once more, since that had more or less worked, Zohanni, however, found a new confidence determined not to allow himself to be so overwhelmed again. He once more adopted the mezana porta di ferro, hoping to draw his opponent into making the same attack. It worked.

As Saam stepped forward, determined this time to make his first strike count and gain a large advantage by placing the squire more off-balance, he roared forward, striking for all he was worth.

With lightening speed, Zohanni drew his point back and added power, moving through tutta porta di ferro, the Full Iron Gate, then bringing his sword up to meet the attack once more.

But this time, he allowed the swords to cross—incrosare—with more subtlety. The blades met and the force of the German's blade pressed inexorably against his own, threatening to send him not only pff-balance, but flying like a discarded apple core. As his point crossed the center of the fight, he now allowed the pressure of the contact to push the sword, and, coupled with gravity, his sword rotated in a tutta volta, a complete turn. Simultaneously, he made a passing step to his left—a passo ala traversa—and brought his sword down from the left in a manroversa. It crashed down on the German's helmet.

The older man barely perceived what happened. One moment, his attack was driving through the young man's defense, but the defense yielded unexpectedly and with startling efficiency his opponent's swords found its mark with power against his helmet.

It was a solid strike, and while it most assuredly accounted for one of the three agreed upon blows, it hardly affected the German. He was lucky, indeed, that the young Italian did not follow-on with a telling finale, since he certainly had the time. Another youthful mistake.

As the men separated and reestablished themselves, they repeated an abbreviated version of their salutes and were almost immediately back in range. This time, the German held his sword conservatively at his side, the hilt at his right hip and the blade menacing directly at his opponent's face in a guard his opponent would have thought of as Pflug, or "the plow." His opponent was cleverer than he'd thought, and he would have to be careful. But Saam was well trained and well experienced, the victory of many such fight, and thus very hard to rattle.

Zohanni could feel the tide shifting his way. He progressed through different poste, tasting his opponent's guard and looking for an opening. None were immediately apparent, and the German remained stubbornly in his guard, comfortable and calculating. It made Zohanni uncomfortable, and he knew he had to act.

Zohanni extended his sword into an instabile or unstable position, the posta longa, his arms extended out front, nearly but not quite extended, the sword directly at his opponent's face. It was good bait, but tasting his opponent's defense and intention in this way was risky, a fickle proposition that could as easily be turned against him as it could be to his advantage.

Saam took the bait, seizing immediately upon it, striking to bind the weapon. This time, however, Zohanni simply lowered the point slightly and watched the German's sword go sailing by. He then brought it up quickly, and thrust for the head using a passing step.

He missed.

The older man had not quite committed to the attack against his blade; instead he had changed through, moving to the other side. The center of the fight was not clear, and, stepping slightly to the side, he sent his own thrust home.

And missed. Zohanni brought his sword quickly back, covering himself near the hilt, on the forteza of his own blade. He coiled his hips and prepared to strike.

But Saam stepped back, flicking his sword with a shietelhau for his forehead, and the blow landed nicely on the Italian's helmet, adding a small, longish dent on the forehead. It was a good blow.

It was only a few seconds before the two were again in range, for their salutes were even less obvious—many held that there had been no salute at all—and neither retreated out of distance before starting again. Instead, the German immediately drew his sword high towards the sun in an appropriately-named guard called vom Tag, "from the day," or "from the roof," and brought it crashing down.

Zohanni was by this time now close enough to his core guard, the tutta porta di ferro. As the sword came in, he too stepped forward, attempting to drive his opponent's sword back. But this time his force was late, and he found his own sword driven to the ground on the right side, his energy expended.

The two men were now close enough that they could easily reach one another's heads with their gauntleted hand, could hear one another's breath. The German's sword was atop of his, the older man had a clear shot at his opponent's head. He quickly brought the sword in a direct strike for the Italian's head grunting not with a lack of air but with exaltation, as there was nothing between his sword and his opponent's head.

But the young squire had also brought his own sword up just behind the German's, and just before he was struck, his sword added a little extra energy to his opponent's attack. Accompanied with a very small step, it was enough to propel it safely upward and away using the German's own power against him. The squire let go of his weapon with his left hand, taking the sword up again at the middle—the mezza spada—and effectively turning it into a short, vicious poleaxe.

He stepped forward, pressed by the spirit of the lion, and slid the point

He stepped forward, pressed by the spirit of the lion, and slid the point forward. It tore upwards along the velvet of his opponent's breastplate, however, and continued on into the space under his arm. With an uncharacteristic shout, the Italian stepped traversely and used the sword like a lever between the German's upper arm and body, effectively locking the arm into a ligadura. The effect was immediate.

Pain shot through his opponent's body like a lightning bolt, nearly paralyzing him. But in anger, the man dropped his sword and tried to make a grip—a presa—against his captor. With just a little further pressure, however, the effort was immediately halted, and the man cried out. The fight was over, and the young Italian very slowly relaxed the pressure.

Several of the ligaments in Saam's rotator cuff were stretched and one let go altogether, an injury which would plague him for the rest of his life. But in the moment of victory neither the spectators nor Zohanni were aware of this, and the cries of exhortation and joy covered both men with the thunderous roar of victory. Both men had earned a wealth of renown on that day. The young squire smiled.

Under the platform, in the quiet shade housing the servants, the young man's scrimatore—fighting master—watched with approval, his arms crossed. Few present knew who he was, as he eschewed attention, preferring the precision of his Art to the intrigues afforded by people. But today his Art had won another victory, and he allowed himself to indulge in the small luxury of a hinted smile. His name was Fiore dei Liberi, and his memory would, as he hoped, survive long after the day's fight was forgotten, because the Italian swordmaster recorded his Art in a book, the Fior di Battaglia, the "Flower of Battle."

Fiore's art is a complete personal combat system encompassing unarmed grappling, strikes with and defenses against the dagger, sword in one and two hands, spear and poleaxe, in and out of armour. This plate shows a seated defense using a short baton from the Getty, fol. 11d.

Today most people believe that medieval fighting was crude, based more on luck and power than on training and precision. The idea has been ensconced for so long that few scolars or enthusiasts question it. Indeed, the only people to look further into the matter for several centuries have been fencing historians, who largely viewed swordsmanship as "developing" or "evolving" over time, a point of view based on scientific advancement.[1] What was older was or is generally considered to be cruder, imperfect; the product of people who were somehow less intelligent and less refined than the people of "today."

The danger in this view is that it takes fighting technique—like so many other things—out of context and applies modern rules to the analysis of a historical problem. While medieval people possessed much less knowledge about the physical laws of the universe than we do today, and commensurately worked a much lower level of technology, within the constraints of their time they seem to have been as enterprising and as intelligent as we are today. Applied to swordsmanship, this idea suggests that medieval swordsmanship, insofar as it was an art practiced by soldiers and a portion of the civilian population to keep themselves alive and intact, was probably as refined and effective as any martial art has ever been.

Students of medieval and early Renaissance military culture have long had access to tournament treatises, princely handbooks, romance literature (as in the Arthurian and related romance, not modern fantasy), and historical chronicles. From the text and illuminations or illustrations in these texts, historians, storytellers, and reenactors have built up ideas about how medieval men fought. Some of these ideas are silly—like armoured men being lifted into the saddle with a crane—while others are less obvious and more widespread, like the idea that armour was excessively cumbersome.

One counter to this trend has been the examination of surviving arms and elements of armour. By using reproductions of these surviving pieces, students of medieval culture and experimental archeologists have been able to put on the armour and fight, seeing something of what was possible.

Many of these experiments by reenactors, combat society members (such as the SCA), and live-action role-players (LARPS) seem to bear little fruit, their clumsy efforts largely reinforcing the evolutionist's claims. Modern martial artists and high level fencers, watching such displays, are often amused at the lack of efficiency and effectiveness of reenactors and their kin. Although some of these groups have developed their own highly effective martial sports (practiced as martial arts in their own right by a significant minority), by and large they are constrained by rules structures based both on perceptions of safety needs and on tradition. This is not to take anything away from these groups, for whom combat serves largely as an end for chivalric, social or entertainment objectives, but it may bear only a passing semblance to what medieval combatants actually did.

We now know, or strongly suspect, that medieval fighting was, at least in some quarters, a highly refined and effective martial art. Since the 1990s, an increasing body of evidence supports this theory as a host of fighting treatiscs—*fechtbücher*, in the German—have become more widely known, translated, and interpreted. Like the tournament books and romances that informed earlier generations of scolars and reenactors focused on knightly culture, the fighting treatises offer a new window into the murky world of medieval fighting technique.

The picture that is forming is exciting: organized systems of personal combat equal to anything practiced today, combined with sophisticated teaching methods designed for quick recall that produce elegant models for the encounter. These systems—essentially martial algorithms—demonstrate a keen understanding of the principles of combat on the individual level and give the combatant an extremely efficient analytical model which allows him to make critical combat decisions quickly. Emerging we see combat which was not only on power (power becomes less important as later styles emphasize the sword's point), but also on speed, precision, and position, all tempered by measured judgment.

And so we can talk today not so much about fighting styles *evolving* or improving as *changing*. These changes seem to have been driven more by technological necessity and fashion, rather than by increasingly well understood principles of combat. It akin to saying that Alexander the Great was as good a general as Rommel, even though he didn't have tanks.

Indeed, the medieval methods, in their simplicity, are in many ways much more effective for the casual student than are the highly sophisticated and complex geometrical analyses of the revered Renaissance masters. By studying these systems in an organized way modern students and schools have begun to add a new dimension to our understanding of the medieval fighting man, whether a noble knight or a man-at-arms.

Our Schola Saint George First Master of Battle course introduces Fiore's art through the sword in two hands using just six pages of Fiore's fighting treatise. Intermediate modules cover the plays in the zhogo largo (long play) and zhogo stretto (close play) sections, and the other weapons are included as advanced curricula.

ABOUT THIS BOOK

Sword in Two Hands is the first part of my interpretation of Fiore dei Liberi's increasingly well known treatise on personal defense known as the *Fior di Battaglia*. I say it is the first part because it covers the fundamentals of medieval fighting technique inferred from the original manuscript, but it only goes as far as fighting from the twelve longsword guards, what Fiore refers to as the **First Masters of Battle**.

The material in this book also represents the first module of training within the Schola Saint George, what we now call our **First Masters of Battle** course. Although the Getty version of the text is comprised of 78 leaves, this first course is based solely on just five leaves (fol. 22, 23, 23v, 24, 24v, and the *segno*, fol. 32). We have been in development of this material since 1999, and surprisingly, the technical material has not changed greatly, although it has been very much more streamlined and refined as the years have passed.

Since the Schola is a distributed school with study groups, independent scolars and affiliated dojos in North America and Europe, there was a need for us to expand on our hodge-podge of notes, class outlines, and background essays for the benefit of our student body. The production of this book is thus a direct result of the support and community which is developing within the Schola Saint George (SSG). It makes commensurate sense to dedicate this book to them.

Chapters 1-5 are background, extra material useful for both novice and intermediate students. Our classes quickly survey these chapters, but the bulk of the material is left for outside study by interested students—especially those interested in testing and advancement within the school.

Chapters 6-11 are really the core of the First Masters of Battle course, focused on developing a solid fighting platform from which the more advanced plays are done. Chapter 6 focuses on foundational aspects of stance and movement. Chapter 7 talks about the core guards and their properties. Chapter 8 introduces the concept of transitions between these guards, while chapter 9 discusses the development of power and kinesthetic efficiency for both blows and thrusts. Chapter 10 represents what I think of as the keys to understanding the First Masters of Battle as a combat system, the tactical principles involved in striking the opponent without being struck in return in the absence of a blocking device, such as a shield. Chapter 11 discusses specific ways of dealing with opponents who, objecting to being hit, cover themselves with their swords, thus adopting what Fiore calls the Second Masters of Battle. Taken together, these chapters encapsulate the essence of Fiore's system and should enable the novice or intermediate combatant to defend themselves with a sword in two hands using Fiore's fundamental tenets.

Chapters 12 and 13 discuss training and advancement within the Schola Saint George. The content of these chapters is subject to considerably more development and potentially radical change over time as the school and our teaching techniques continue to evolve.

WHAT DO WE CALL THIS ART?

Today the study of medieval and Renaissance arts is known by different names. The fencing community calls the medieval and Renaissance arts *ancient* and *historical* fencing, respectively. This follows the lead of the **Association for Historical Fencing** (AHF), but the moniker historical fencing has also taken root in other fencing communities I've had the pleasure of working with.

The term *fencing* comes from the French, *de-fense*, or defense. To make defense is to defend one's self, and it is from this idea that the term fencing seems to derive. The term fencing has a decidedly civilian connotation, at least to modern students. For the study of the rapier, a consummately civilian weapon, fencing makes very good sense and seems to fit both the historical and modern connotations of the word's use. *Historical fencing* thus

works reasonably well (contrasted with the later *classical* fencing tradition), although the label "historical" in many ways implies outmodedness or, as in the term *academic*, without use.

Treatment of the medieval systems is more difficult. I don't find the term *ancient fencing* to be particularly evocative of the whole corpus of weapons employed, including the dagger, spear and poleaxe. The image of *fencing* in plate armour seems discordant. This dissonance seems to be present in the modern fencing community itself: medieval forms of swordsmanship are by and large considered by the modern fencing community to irrelevant to the *sport* of fencing. While the complex defensive theories of the Italian or Spanish masters holds the interest of some classical fencers,[2] the medieval material is usually considered to be far to crude to include as it has no analogue to the modern three-weapon weapon suite of foil, saber and epee. With limited exceptions, there seems to be no place for medievalists in the fencing community, and there is no route available to study pre-1500 weapons within formal fencing instruction systems.[3] Sport fencing has traveled quite far from the dueling green, although it enjoys a rich lineage and can carry much of the sword's richness to successive new generations of fencers.

Literature on medieval combat talks more often of combat as *fighting*, which carries a military or at least a survival connotation. In the French, the term normally applied to sword contests within the lists or in battle is *combat*. In the German, the term *fechten* can either be translated fighting or fencing,[4] in the Italian *combattamento*.

The extent to which professional teachers of combat techniques had traffic with the professional soldiers remains to be demonstrated. Historical teachers of fighting techniques were known in England as masters-at-arms, in Italy as *scrimatore*, and in Germany as *fechtmeisters*. Most of these *scrimatore* or masters-at-arms, as we will see in the next chapter, taught paying students, although most of them cloaked their presentations in the accepted chivalric language of the day, claiming to have traveled and studied with famous knights and masters-at-arms, so it is possible that the techniques presented at least resemble those in use by the military classes.

MEDIEVAL MARTIAL ARTS

I believe that medieval martial arts are those that might have been practiced during the Middle Ages, including the span of weapons usual to a knight or traveler on the road: unarmed fighting (wrestling, pugilism, baton, staff, knife or dagger, sword with or without a shield, spear or lance, and poleweapons), in and out of armour, on foot and on horseback.

While some medieval martial arts are based solely upon experimentation and practice, there is a growing body of reconstructed arts revived from the surviving fighting treatises, primarily of England and France. When these arts are practiced in a regular or systemic way, they can transcend entertainment and become martial arts.

Like other martial arts, there is a spectrum of disciplines ranging from form-only (like Tai-Chi) distillations of combat techniques to the brutal *simulacra* which might sometimes become real fights. Within the Medieval Martial Arts, there are groups that focus primarily on technique, those that are primarily sparring or competition oriented, and those who extract only what will be useful for "modern" self-defense.

THE MMA COMMUNITY TODAY

The Schola Saint George strives to distill historical technique from Fiore's treatise, and our emphasis is on developing technique and a tactical algorthym that will hold up under a sparring or competitive encounter. All of this strongly emphasizes functional, increasingly efficient technique in service of character development through the chivalric virtues. Showcased on the tournament field, we exercise ourselves in a *pas d'armes* format where there is competition but in which chivalric deeds are expected. It is our hope that through this practice our scolars will enrich themselves through the arts of self defense to the higher aspects of character that will make them good citizens.

Our focus within the SSG is on Fiore's material, although we encourage and practice, to a limited degree, systems from other traditions, including the German, English, and Burgundian traditions.

Today there are several schools of historical or medieval martial arts working with the Fiore material. The best known in the English-speaking world is Bob Charron's **Saint Martin's Academy**, but there are other students of the Art working across the United States, in Canada, and in Europe, such as Gregory Mele's **Chicago Swordplay Guild**, Maestro Sean Hayes' **Northwest Academy of Arms**, the **Academy of European Medieval Martial Arts** (in Toronto), Guy Windsor's **School of European Swordsmanship** in Helsinki, Massimo Malipiero's Italian **Compagnia Malipiero** and also in Italy, the **Nova Scrima**. Finally, our own **Schola Saint George**, based in Dallas-Forth Worth (TX) and the San Francisco Bay Area (CA), with study groups in many other cities.

RECONSTRUCTION, REINVENTION, REENACTMENT: HISTORIOGRAPHY OF MMA

The surviving treatises are incomplete. Reading on the various Internet fora one will find, however, many who present a great number of "facts" based on insubstantial data and inference. These are in reality interpretations of scanty evidence based on varying degrees of research and related knowledge. They are made both about the technique itself and about the masters who taught them. There is nothing inherently wrong with an interpretation, so long as it is not presented as the "one true way," or a "fact." The historical systems are perhaps not so much incomplete as they assume a great deal of knowledge that has been lost. Filling in the lost pieces takes a great deal of work, and today's generations of scolars and practitioners are working to fill in the gaps.

With regard to the historical context, there are a few researchers who strive to place the treatises in context.[5] Figuring out what these treatises mean involves fascinating questions. How representative are the manuscripts for military combat techniques employed in the region or throughout Europe? What was the purpose of the treatises? Who financed them? What purpose did the author intend for them? How influential were they? Who were their authors; how were they employed, who influenced them, and who did they influence? These are interesting questions whose answers require painstaking research into archives, accounts, court records, chronicles, letters, and the like. This is work for interested scolars, professional and amateur.

Similarly, there is much foundational material and basic technique either not included in the treatises or encoded within the common cultural context now lost to us. Therefore, reconstruction of these arts requires expanding the interpreter's knowledge of the period, the locality, and of related arts and books. The "gaps" within the original texts must be filled in with what Greg Mele has aptly termed "frog DNA."[6]

The art of interpreting historical fighting treatises is complex but can be rewarding. It is complex in that the original treatises are written in old Italian, Latin, German or French. They are rendered more difficult as they are both dialect and in old forms of each language, making them difficult even for modern speakers of those languages. We do not know how accurately the author encoded his meaning in his language: these were teachers of fighting technique, not literary giants. Did they succeed in conveying their meaning to their contemporaries? We don't yet know, unfortunately.

The images are rendered with varying levels of accuracy and much of the information within the manuscripts is tied to regional culture at the time the manuscript was produced. They were generally produced by artists working within various schools of style that relied on convention for the rendering elements of a figure, which could further distance the drawing from the author's intent. Fortunately, these books were produced at the time when realism had begun to blossom in European art, and this attention to detail is abundantly clear in several of the Fiore treatises.

Depending upon how much and from what source interpreters infuse "frog DNA" into their interpretation will dramatically influence the interpretation of the art. In essence, there are three available routes: *vertical* organization where trends within an evolving system changing over time are the primary references; *horizontal* organization where the arts of contemporary nations outside the tradition are consulted (this could be as near as referring to the German system in Fiore's case to looking at modern arts or sports); or *modern* references that do not refer to the other two, but instead draw from other sports or arts more distantly removed in place and time. Many interpreters have little historical research in their background, so are necessarily driven to the modernist approach.

Since the surviving treatises remain incomplete, in the Schola we strive to bring in material from the horizontal temporal plane more than from the vertical: what this means is that we look for clues within contemporary German tradition first, since my assumption is that these weapons are most similar in use and form to those

Fiore employs. While it is possible, and sometimes necessary, to look at later Italian styles (for example, Fiore himself does not discuss time, but Filippo Vadi, who follows fifty years later, and Angelo Viggiani, who follows 160 years later, both do), I believe this should approach must be employed with caution, not only because weapons and armour change dramatically during the 15th and into the 16th century, but also the uses for the sword in general change, suggesting also a change in the methods through which they are employed. For this reason, we try to avoid including material that is too far removed in time from Fiore (for example, it is fairly common to employ di Grassi's footwork in Fiore, as it is the earliest clear articulation available, but we expressly don't do this in the SSG).

Most other schools approach the material differently, although none are purely one way or the other. The Chicago Swordplay Guild, for example, conducts their training according to the corpus of Fiore and later Italian masters. The Nova Scrima in Italy do essentially the same thing, going so far as to think of their art as a new iteration of the long Italian rich martial tradition of combat with swords. Sean Hayes and his Northwest Academy of Arms informs their instruction with accepted and well proven of classical fencing, drawn from the better known rapier and later masters. Similarly the successful and well-trained students in Guy Windsor's school base their interpretations on a blend of Fiore and Vadi.

I mean these comparisons to be observational rather than judgmental. Excellent results are achieved by all of these schools, as I believe we do within the Schola Saint George. I count it a very good thing that the different approaches create essentially a marketplace of ideas where interpretations can be tested. Within the Schola, we keep those interpretations that 1) do not conflict with the text in some major way and 2) seem to work the best in terms of sparring and flow within the rest of the system.

INTERPRETATIONS

Because Fiore dei Liberi and the other medieval masters have been dead for more than 600 years, it is impossible to know for certain what they meant in their writings and illustrations. Fiore's Art does not have an unbroken lineage, so any approach to it or to any "historical" art must of necessity be interpretative. These interpretations are based on the information available to the interpreter at the time, and since we continue to unearth new information, the interpretations likewise change and grow. Or at least they should.

Added to this, any translation of an historical text is itself an interpretation. Some will disagree, although it is impossible to simply render an ancient dialect of a language into modern English and have it carry the same connotations and meaning as it had for its original audience, if only because the audience's culture and experiences are dramatically different. I have often said that we cannot be 14th century people, no matter how hard we try. I mean this not in a negative way, for certainly the ideas we find in history can and should inform us about our own time. Although some of our students will engage real enemies in combat, it will likely be with the weapons of today, not with the weapons of Fiore's day.

But if the hand-to-hand principles inform their tactical choices in a positive way—and I think they can—then from a technical standpoint the interpretation will have added something to their toolkit.

I hope that our interpretation of Fiore's Art continues to grow and develop over time, but I am confident that the core principles have been well-demonstrated and vetted by our aggressive and talented student base. There are many, many more things to learn, however, and it is my hope that this book will inspire others to contribute to the pool of knowledge we have begun to explore.

Books like *Sword in Two Hands* strive to present interpretations that free novice and intermediate students from the burden of having to do the original interpretations. Advanced students are strongly encouraged to go back to the original texts, but in the main the interpretations provide a very solid base from which to begin. The oldest such work, John Clements *Medieval Combat*, is largely out of date. In the Italian context, Mr. Guy Windsor's *Swordmans' Companion* was the first. Videotapes and a new book by Massimo Malipiero and books by the Nova Scrima group provide for an interesting survey of the Italian systems. In the German, Christian Tobler's *Secrets of the German Longsword* (and *Fighting with the German Longsword* have done a similar service, while the Ochs videotape *Longsword of Johannes Liechtenauer* provide an excellent motion study. It is my hope that *Sword in Two Hands* will provide a similar level of background for modern students, and that this will in turn draw more scolars to the Art who can improve and document it still further.

TRANSLATION

Fiore's material was written in Friulian, a northern dialect of Italian. Although this book presents a broad and integrated interpretation based on Fiore's text, I have included both the original text (as drawn from Massimo Malipiero's fine transcriptions) and my own translations of the text for intermediate or advanced students.

As I mentioned previously, I consider any translation an interpretation. There are words and problematic aspects to translating Fiore's work, not the least of which is translating from the Italian. Some words have a meaning that is different in the dialect than in the central Italian or Tuscan dialect that became modern Italian.

Like most English translators, I have relied chiefly upon Florio's fine dictionary, *A Worlde of Words*, the closest Italian-English dictionary dating from 1598. But I have asked for assistance from both native speakers of Italian and other scolars working with Fiore's material. Even so, any errors are my own responsibility. I do not consider my translations to be in any way definitive, but I hope they are helpful. The reader will find copious footnotes where problems in translation or various interpretations are suggested.

USING THIS BOOK

The first five chapters of this book are optional historical and technical background which will hopefully help the student to place the rest of the material in context.

The technique chapters, 6-11, are designed to guide the student through the fundamentals that I believe underlie the system and which follow modules within the Schola Saint George curriculum. With the kind assistance of the J.P. Getty and Morgan museums we have been able to reproduce plates from the original manuscripts in color, and we have augmented these with photographs of students and teachers executing our interpretations of those same techniques. Alongside the images I have provided transcribed text from the manuscript and my translation, followed by what might be considered a *glosa*, or my explanations of what the techniques might mean. Exercises, drills and games are provided as a starting point for skill development.

Because our intent is to build a solid foundation, we begin with the core of Fiore's system, the twelve *posta* or *guardia*. These anchor points represent places from or through which a fight progresses, key points of advantage. Fiore describes these positions as the **First Masters of Battle**, and from these positions it is hoped that the scolar or combatant can find a point of advantage and strike under cover to win the fight. All of this is contained on a relatively few numbers of leaves—six, including the *segno* ("teaching diagram")— a surprising amount of material distributed in just a few pages. All of the plays or techniques we teach in the core material are drawn from Fiore's descriptions of these *poste* or which illuminate core principles needed by students in order to use the material effectively. The order of our presentation follows my in-class presentation, building one skill upon another. Students in those classes can use the book to expand or clarify what is said in class, while non-SSG students may find the explanations interesting, stimulating discussion and debate if nothing else.

THOSE BLOODY ITALIAN NAMES

One point of difficulty for new students is the seemingly endless stream of untranslated Italian names. I do not feel that any scolars of Fiore's Art yet have a deep enough understanding of the Art to render it completely into English while carrying all of the connotations of the original text (indeed, I believe this is an impossible task). In order that modern students of the art preserve their ability to communicate with one another, to freely exchange ideas about the system, I have elected to leave the main terms in Italian. I have also done this to assist the more serious student in distinguishing what in the interpretation we consider to be "frog DNA" from what is printed in Fiore and also to more fully connect students with the historical material.

THE COLORED FIGURES

The original figures are done in ox-gall ink which turns red over time because essentially it rusts on the paper or vellum. When we started our study of the art in 1999, few resources were available and the Pisani-Dossi figures were of a very low quality. In order to present our students with a more graphically educational structure, I cleaned up and colored the figures in 2003, encoding within them Fiore's Getty classification of *pulsativa*, *stabile*, or *instabile*. Figures that are red and white represent the Guardia which are *Pulsativa*. Those which are solid red and blue (not party-colored) are *Stabile*, while those who are party-colored red and blue are *Instabile*. We have included those figures here because our posters use these figures and we want to ensure continuity between the classroom and the book.

-Notes-

[1] The most famous quote cited is by Edgerton Castle, where he describes medieval combat as "rough and untutored." He was followed almost slavishly by a host of 20th century authors: Arthur Wise, 1971, p. 34, "There was here a continuous tradition of sword and buckler play, but it was a tradition that relied very much on personal tricks and personal ability." C.L. de Beaumont, 1978, p. 256, "In the Middle Ages swords were heavy and clumsy, and more strength than skill was required for their use." Richard Cohen, 2002, "The sword was used primarily to bludgeon the opponent... Parries with the sword were avoided and knights either evaded blows or used their shields for protection. Swords which could weigh well in excess of three pounds, were heavy affairs requiring strength to wield as much as skill."

[2] Maestri such as William Gaugler and Theodore Katzoff, to name but two.

[3] Maestro Sean Hayes, student of William Gaugler, must be considered as a unique exception in this regard within the United States. While the Association for Historical Fencing has recognized three instructors in "ancient" fencing, the AHF's approach remains rooted in the study of modern and classical systems, trying to route interested students of the ancient arts through modern and classical weapons first. Maestro Hayes teaches students concepts from the *Fior di Battaglia* and from Royal Armouries MS I.33 directly, but as I mentioned, he is the only recognized fencing maestro I know who takes this approach.

[4] The earliest reference I have found is in the 8th century, *fehten*, which is the same word in the old Saxon and *fiuchta* in the old Frisian, *ve chten* in Middle High German. It is unclear to me when the word comes to mean "fencing" as we understand it today.

[5] Professor Sydney Anglo is perhaps the only professional scolar now working in the field, but talented amateurs Matthew Galas, Steven Hick, Gregory Mele must also be mentioned.

[6] After the concept developed within Michael Crighton's 1990 book *Jurrasic Park*, where gaps in the ancient DNA sequence were filled in with modern frog DNA. The case made by Crighton was that this importation by definition changes the organism, that a *new* creature based on a historical one resulted.

CHAPTER TWO

FIORE'S WORLD

"Io Fiore sapiando legere, e scrivere, e disegnare, e habiendo libri in quest'arte e in ley o studiato ben xl anni o piu..e vogliando che di mi sia fatta memoria in ella, io faro un libro in tua larte…segundo l'ordene lo quale ma dado quell alto Signore [Getty F.1]."

"I, Fiore, knowing how to read, to write and to draw, and having books in the art [of combat], studied the art for 40 years or more…and desiring that I should be remembered in it, I made a book of the whole art… according to the order which my noble lord [Niccolò III] gave to me."

The rich Italian tradition of martial combat with swords has survived for more than six and a half centuries. Owing to the production and survival of at least three books detailing his fighting system, Fiore dei Liberi stands as the great-grandfather of this art, the producer of a stunningly rich and effective approach to personal combat whose techniques transcend their place and time of origin and which may be applied to any martial encounter fought hand-to-hand, with or without weapons.

Today the Italian tradition survives in a highly regarded school of sport fencing. It counts amongst its heritage some of the greatest names in the history of fencing: Achille Marozzo, Salvator Fabris, Ridolfo Capo Ferro, Angelo Viggiani. But sport fencing bears only a dim semblance to the original deadly art, which included and integrated the arts of grappling (*abrazzare*), encounters with and against the dagger (*daga*), the baton (*bastoncello*), the sword in one hand and in two (*spada a una mano e due mani*), spear (*lanza*), the poleaxe (*azza*), on foot and on horseback, in and out of armour. This was a holistic martial art based on simple, sound biokinesthetic principles. As with most high-quality martial arts, dei Liberi's system was easily adaptable to circumstance and was governed by judgment.

L'ARTI MARZIALE IN NORTHERN ITALY DURING THE 14TH AND 15TH CENTURIES

Martial arts are the arts of war practiced by a single man against his adversaries, usually in the context of hand-to-hand combat, although they need not be practiced in war. During the Middle Ages and into the Renaissance, the martial arts of Italy included such things as wrestling, grappling, forms of boxing, and the use of weapons, including the dagger, sword, baton, spear, and poleaxe. The shield was also in use, as was its smaller civilian

version, the buckler or target. Men fought in and out of armour, on foot and on horseback, with hand-arms and with missile weapons.

It has been often commented that warfare on the Italian peninsula took on a rather different character from the rest of Europe: its internecine character caused by political, religious and economic fragmentation—coupled with local jealousies and outright crime. This meant that conflict escalated to combat was a common aspect of Italian culture, even as Italy advanced culturally in the arts, letters and sciences. Not surprisingly, this patchwork character of war brought many different classes of men into conflict, a rich mixture of noblemen, mercenaries, and footsoldiers. Knights and Lords fought in companies of mixed men, largely hired for specific campaign objectives

There were a wide number of forms that the combat could take. On one end of the spectrum, personal defense in town and during travel would suggest some skill-in-arms for any male traveler or town-dweller. Judicial duels were fought to a limited degree in Italy (although they seem to have been far more common in Germany), while duels based on honor and rights seem to have been more common in Italy than elsewhere. War was endemic to the region as city-states vied with one another for influence, and during this period the Great Schism added a religious aspect to the Byzantine system of alliances, familial conflict, and clash of interest that fed local war on a large scale.

But war in Italy during the time was not fought with the large hosts of Northern Europe employed during the Hundred Year's War. Instead, the great families, cities and religious lords employed companies of men, often including or based wholly upon mercenaries. These men, known as *condottieri*, were to become famous, as did the Englishman Sir John Hawkwood and his White Company. These were skilled men-at-arms, professional soldiers who served not for the forty days customary under the feudal system, but according to a written contract that governed in detail the soldier's relationship with his captain and his employer. Such men were drawn from all parts of society, a genuine alloy of martial culture where ideals and the chivalric culture could blend with the rougher and stoically practical world of the common soldier.

We might expect that the men of Italian cities would grow war-weary, but in fact the cities were fiercely proud of their martial traditions and local histories. Civic festivals that featured various forms of combat, from the theatrical to the brutal, were common. Landowning noblemen continued their interaction with the "international" chivalric class, traveling to far lands to participate in wars and other deeds of arms, and hosting grand feats of arms in their rich *palazzi*. As the wealthy of both town and country created lavish courts, collecting poets, musicians, horse- and dance-masters, an opportunity was created for sword-masters. Fiore dei Liberi capitalized on at least one such opportunity as he secured notice from one of the most powerful men of his day, Niccolò III d'Este, Lord of Ferrara.

The full spectrum of martial encounters, from those we read as "à plaisance,"[1] (including highly staged round tables, carousels, jousts and civic festivals) to those we think of as far more dangerous or "à outrance," (It: *oltranza*, which included duels, street fights, and war) were found in Italy. The traditional dominance of war management and tournament (*hastiludium*, *ensiludium*)[2] participation by the gentry of Northern Europe was far less pronounced in Italy, possibly because the commercial classes held far more influence and even participated in the management of war through communal government. As such, the precise role of arms and their use in Northern Italy is difficult to understand with clarity because all kinds of encounters took place, from friendly celebrations to deadly duels and war, both local and national.

In the surviving accounts we find that festivals, jousts and martial demonstrations or games were an integral part of civic life during the 14th and 15th centuries.[3] Noble weddings and gatherings were punctuated with such displays, as are recorded in Italian chronicles (especially those of the Este Chronicles—*Chronicon Estense*—and others). For example, in 1377 we find the usual preference for a tournament followed by feasting and jousting at the wedding of Francesco Novella da Carrara and Taddea d'Este.[4]

The Visconti and Gonzaga were particularly fond of such celebrations, and there are well-recorded instances in Padua, Verona, and Venice. Indeed, one of the feats of arms Fiore cites is to have taken place within the Visconti castle at Pavia. As these contests where sponsored by princely families, they took on the character of those practiced in France, Burgundy and in Savoy, where the princes vied with one another for the more ornate, elaborate and thus expensive displays. Noblemen and members of the gentry were the participants in these encounters, including those from Italy and from other nations, including England, Spain, France, and the Holy Roman Empire (Germany). Such encounters are mentioned directly in Fiore's Prologue:

"So that the mentioned Fiore was many times requested by Lords, knights and squires, so to teach this art of fighting and combat *à outrance* within the lists. This art he has demonsrated to Italians, Germans and other great Lords who had to fight within the barriers. And also to infinite numbers who did not need to fight. And of some of them, my scholars, who have had fights within the lists, I name and give memory of some of them here:
First amongst them was the noble and gallant knight **Messer Piero del Verde** (Morgan: *piero dal uerde*), who had to fight against Messer Piero de la Corona (Morgan: *piero dala corona*), and both were Germans. The duel was supposed to be in Perugia.
Also the valiant knight **Messer Nicolò Wàizilino** (Morgan: *nicholo vnriçilino*),[5] a German, who had to fight against Nicolò Inghileso (Morgan: *nicholo Inghlesio*).[6] The field was set in Imola.
Also the notable, valiant and gallant knight **Messer Galeazzo de Capitani da Grimello** (Morgan: *galeaz delli capitini de gremello chiamado da mantua*),[7] called *da Mantova*,[8] who had to fight against the valiant knight Messer Buzichardo de Fraza (Morgan: *briçichardo de Franza*; French: Boucicaut – Jean II il Meingre).[9] The field was set in Padova.

*15th century map of Imola, where Fiore's scolaro **Nicolò Wàizilino** fought the German Nicolò Inghileso*

Perugia main gate in a photo from 1908.

12

Also the valiant squire **Lancillotto de Becharia de Pavia** (M: *Lanzilotto de Boecharia da Pavia*),[10] who inflicted six thrusts [strikes] with sharp-ironed [sharp headed] lance, against the valiant knight Messer Baldassarro (M: *Baldesar todesco*), a German, who had to fight in the barriers in Imola.

Also the valiant squire **Zhioanino**[11] **da Bavo** (M: *Zohanni de Baio da Milano*), from Milan, who, in the castle in Pavia,[12] achieved three thrusts [strikes] with sharp-ironed [sharp headed] lance, against the valiant squire Sàam, a German (M: *Sram todesco*). And then on foot he gave three axe strikes, three sword strikes and three dagger strikes, in presence of the very noble prince and Signore Messer the Duke of Milan, and Madonna the Duchess, and infinite other Signori and Donne.

Also the cautious knight **Messer Azzone da Castell Barco** (**M:** *Azo da Castelbarcho*), who one time had to fight against Giovanni di Ordelaffi (M: *Zohanni di li Ordelaffig*). And another time, against the valiant and good knight Messer Giacomo da Boson (M: *jacomo da besen*), the field had to be chosen by the Duke of Milan.

Of these and of others, whom I, Fiore, have taught, I am very proud, because I have been well rewarded and I obtained the esteem and the affection of my students and of their relatives."[13]

Although such encounters were lavish and expensive, that does not mean they were necessarily safe. Injuries, both intended and otherwise, accompany most feats of arms, especially those conducted *à outrance*. Frequently individual encounters *à outrance* were loosely regulated duels, sometimes national in character, that resembled the chivalric and classical traditions of single combats fought between champions. Although regulated, such duels were in many ways more dangerous than open warfare, since a nobleman on a European battlefield often enjoyed the benefit of ransom: he was essentially worth more alive than dead. No such mechanism functioned in a duel, public or private. Many of the encounters Fiore notes seem to belong to this category.

In Florence, Pisa, Perugia and in Sienna, amongst other cities, the contests took on more civic character. Citizens and townsmen competed using padded armour and clubs or other weapons. In Pisa, the *massascudo* involved the use of the club and shield, the face of an inspirational consort was often painted on the shield. The *ponte, battaglia de'sassi, elmora* and *pugna* were other localized forms of civic combat[14] that culminated in the Venetian *battagliola dei pugni* (War of the Fists)[15] or today's *Carnivale d'Ivrea*, where the "battle of the oranges" celebrates a popular revolt whose origins have been lost to the fog of history. Many of Italy's civic festivals mirror this one, in that they celebrate an historical event of importance to the city or town.

Prior to Fiore's time, the master swordsman in Italy appears from time to time in civic records that suggest a tradition of inny- ard-based teachers who earned a little money teaching what they knew to those who would pay.[16] The Italian tendency to hire military expertise in the form of *condottieri* captains perhaps

Perugian Palazzo from the early-mid 15th century.

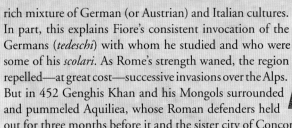

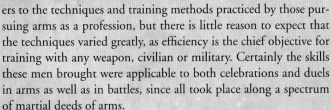

Italian cities still hold civic festivals like the Carnavale in Ivrea, many of which commemorate significant local events.

made such a profession steady, if not terribly lucrative. The very presence of martial companies suggests a role for the swordmaster, especially if he was also a respected captain in his own right, as Fiore may have been.

As discussed in the last chapter, we do not know about the relationship of these informal teachers to the techniques and training methods practiced by those pursuing arms as a profession, but there is little reason to expect that the techniques varied greatly, as efficiency is the chief objective for training with any weapon, civilian or military. Certainly the skills these men brought were applicable to both celebrations and duels in arms as well as in battles, since all took place along a spectrum of martial deeds of arms.

Fiore's techniques, suitably tempered with wisdom, are appropriate in virtually any form of martial encounter of the period, *à plaisance* or as Fiore seemed to prefer, *a oltranza*. We see this in the sections that detail defenses with a cap or with gloves, or with a simple stick. Ultimately, martial competence requires each of the qualities Fiore discusses, tempered by judgment and grace, as denoted by the figure atop Fiore's *segno*, the Lynx, which we'll discuss in the next chapter.

FRIULIA AND CIVIDALE

Fiore was born in and active in the north-eastern region of Italy known as Friuli, a region bordered by the Alps to the northwest and the Adriatic Sea to the south that has a long and turbulent history. Early Illyrians were attacked and conquered by the Celts, who descended from Bavaria and the Tyrol. In 222 B.C. a long and bloody conflict with Rome ended in a Roman victory, later consolidated by Julius Ceasar as he Romanized the region through military colonization based around a new city called Aquiliea, destined to become one of the most prosperous and important cities in the Empire based on its location along major trading routes.[17]

The name *Friulia* comes from a contraction of the the *Forum Julii*, which was based during Roman development in what was to become Cividale. Conflict threatened the whole region from across the Alps for its entire history, which resulted in a

rich mixture of German (or Austrian) and Italian cultures. In part, this explains Fiore's consistent invocation of the Germans (*tedeschi*) with whom he studied and who were some of his *scolari*. As Rome's strength waned, the region repelled—at great cost—successive invasions over the Alps. But in 452 Genghis Khan and his Mongols surrounded and pummeled Aquiliea, whose Roman defenders held out for three months before it and the sister city of Concordia were mostly razed. Although there are records of Aquiliea as late as 625, the city never recovered her importance or vitality. From the 5ᵗʰ – 9ᵗʰ centuries Friulia was dominated by the Lombards, who fought more or less incessantly with the Slavs and Avars, but control of the region was more importantly debated in ecclesiastical circles, as the Bishop of Aquelïea vied with the Bishop of Grado for sovereignty over the bishops of Venice, Istria, Como and Mantua. The late 9ᵗʰ and 10ᵗʰ century saw yet more fighting, as the Hungarians (Magyars) destroyed much of the region, bringing a darkness that characterized it for the whole of the 11ᵗʰ century. During the 12ᵗʰ and 13ᵗʰ centuries, the German system of feudalism gradually spread throughout the region, evolving a commercial hybrid under the protection the very powerful Patriarch of Aqueliea and the various communes (small cities with specific commercial rights and generally republican in local governance). By the 13ᵗʰ century the region was an open door between Italy and Germany through which commerce flowed bringing the commensurate economic prosperity. In the 12ᵗʰ century Cividale became the seat of the Patriarch, and it gained the expected cultural and social prestige that it would retain through and beyond Fiore's lifetime.

With the death of Patriarch Bertoldus in 1251, the Germanic nature of the Patriarchiate became Italian, a character it sustained until 1331. Some clearly Germanic possessions remained, most notably those of the powerful Count of Gorizia, whose holdings would seep war into the region. But the change did not bring peace; small wars between feudal lords, communes and ecclesiastical figures were legion during the period. But most "wars" were based not on issues of state, but rather on feuds, fed by the exceedingly warlike character of the local lords. These feuds sometimes lasted for generations and as much as a century, a cycle of revenge that proved exceedingly difficult to quench. During this time the first encounters of the Guelphs against the Ghibellines were fought, as Ghibelline lords sided with the German interests of the Count of Gorizia against the Guelphs, who backed the Patriarch. The labyrinthine character of these complex conflicts reflected perhaps the relative locality of Byzantium; "byzantine" is an accurate modern adjective that describes the overlaid webs of intrigue and betrayal perfectly.

GUELPHS & GHIBELLINES

During the 12th century Frederick Barbarossa, Emperor of the Holy Roman Empire, attempted to increase his influence into northern Italy. In the process, he imported an old conflict begun during the Investiture Conflict of the 11th century which pitted the Emperor against the Pope in a titanic struggle for power. Those who supported the expansion of Imperial power, mainly the landed nobility, became known as the Ghibellines, while those who resisted the encroachment and who sided with the Pope were known as the Guelphs.

Throughout the 13th century the struggle plagued northern Italy, dividing it sometimes even withn a single city. In general, Ghibelline families were tied to agricultural wealth while the Guelphs based their wealth on mercantile operations. Guelph cities tended to be found in areas where incroachment by the Empire was the greater threat, while Ghibelline cities tended to be found where expansion of Papal influence was more likely an issue.

Allegience to one party or the other was often a cause for violent hatred, and by the 14th century allegience to one party or the other seems to have been as much a matter of local politics as ideology. Smaller cities tended to affiliate the the opposite party as their larger neighbor, as in the case of Ghibelline Siena in the shadow of its larger rival the Guelph Florence. In Florence itself the Black Guelphs struggled and sometimes fought against the White Guelphs, with factions breaking down guild by guild. This was not unique to Florence.

As political parties the Guelphs and Ghibellines represented the larger struggle for power between the landed nobility and the mercantile commercial classes as much as between the German and Papal influences. At times the Guelphs--or a sub-party--stood opposed to Papal interst and at times Ghibellines defended Papal interests.

The conflict continued to afflict the region through the 15th and 16th centuries, as the Guelphs supported Charles VIII's invasion of Italy while the Ghibellines supported Maximilian I.

In Fiore's day the battle-lines of Guelph and Ghibelline provided just one front for local conflict as the communes competed amongst one another, each city potentially itself divided between familial and guild affiliations.

The d'Este family were ardent Guelphs, papists, who in recognition of their loyalty became papal vicars in 1332. As a soldier, it is unlikely that Fiore himself had an affiliation, but if he did, his association with the d'Este family would suggest a Guelphic allegience.

These conflicts continued throughout the century, and were exasercbated by new conflicts that accompanied the Great Schism and the struggles between Udine, Cividale and Venice. Each of these urban centers was jealous of the influence of the others, and a great tripartite struggle between the three of them characterized the century. But commerce and people still flowed between Germany and Friuli, and we can see evidence of this flow in Fiore's Prologue, where he cites several *tedeschi* who trained with him and at least two Germans with whom he studied.

The cauldron of Italian fortunes during the late 14th century was brimming with wealth and economic prosperity owing to trade with the Orient and the complicated relationships between the communes of the cities (city-states) and the older feudal establishment. The result was wide-spread warfare, war that would have made for a ripe audience for students of the military arts. It was into this cauldron that Fiore dei Liberi was born and in which he made his reputation.

THE D'ESTE FAMILY

Ferrara, where many students of Fiore believe he spent some years, is a city and region in Northern Italy, south-west of Friulia. Since the 12th century the Este family—named for Castle Este in the region—were the city's *Signori* or lords, as they were for the city of Modena,[18] which sits not far to the west.

In 1264 Obizzo d'Este defeated a rival Ghibelline family, the Salinguerra, clearing the way for consolidation of family power

The river alongside Cividale, showing the beauty of the region.

in the region. They reigned as *signori* over Ferrara (1264) and Modena (1288). As Ferrara was held from the Pope and the family members were prominent in the Geulf party, they became papal vicars in 1332. For nearly three centuries, the family brought relative stability and prosperity to the region, which enabled the d'Este court to be renowned throughout Europe for splendor and patronage of the arts. During Fiore's time, it was dominated by uncle and nephew, both named Niccolò (II & III).

Niccolò d'Este II (1361-1388), uncle of the Niccolò III whom Fiore names in the Pisani-Dossi and Getty versions of his manuscript, consolidated much of the family's holdings in the region. But in 1385 a devastating famine struck, and the populace of Ferrara rebelled. After putting down the rebellion, Niccolò II consulted with his architect, Bartolino di Novara, and the result was the beginning of the great Ferraran castle that remains today, the Castello di San Michele (see the photo on the following page). It is generally held that this castle provided a symbol and a practical tool that enabled the family to repel successive enemeies and maintain their strict authority over the region. It would have been under construction for much of Fiore's active career, and as Fiore was thought to have been in Ferrara during at least part of this time, it would have been familiar.

After Niccolò's death in 1388, he was succeeded by his able brother Alberto, under whom the University of Ferrara was founded in 1391-2. Niccolò III was Alberto's illegitimate son (by Isotta Albaresani), and his keen sense for the political enabled him to further consolidate the family power in the region, setting the stage for the splendor that was to follow. Alberto died in 1393, placing the 10-year old Niccolò under the protection of the republics of Florence, Venice, Bologna and the lord.

15

of Padua—troops were even dispatched immediately to Ferrara to help defend the young signore. This was prudent, for the forces of the Milanese Visconti were quick to take advantage, sending a force in 1394 led by a relative, Azzo d'Este, aided by a coalition of Ferraran and Modenan families, and led by the able *condottieri* captain Giovanni Barbarino, who the Ferrarans tried to in vain to bring to their side (when this failed, he was assassinated). The force was defeated and Azzo was captured, effectively diffusing the challenge to Niccolò's reign.

In 1397-8, Niccolò married the daughter of the powerful *signore* of Padua, Gigliolà da Carrara, binding the two powerful Geulf families together and drawing Niccolò still closer to the Papal cause. By 1402 he was in part of the league that opposed the Duke of Milan and was declared Captain-General of the Pope's armies.

In 1407 Niccolò was involved in a military dispute over Reggio against Ottobuono Terzo, a tyrant of the region who, acting under the protection of the powerful Duke of Milan, practiced many acts of brigandage, rapine and torture in the region of Lombardy. At this time the famous *condottieri* captain Muzio Attendola served as a general under Niccolò, eventually defeating, capturing and killing the tyrant Terzo (by 1409). It was Niccolò's captain who gave him the nickname, *sforza*—"the strong"—and at whose court the young Francesco Sforza was educated. Francesco would go on to become a great *condottieri* captain in his own right, eventually becoming the Papal governor of Milan, founding a splendid court, and becoming close friends with his Florentine contemporary, Lorenzo da Medici. It was the 1407-09 action against Ottobuono that earned for the d'Este family the signory of the city of Reggio, in 1409.

Niccolò had more than twenty children, both legitimate and illegitimate, hence the popular saying of the time: "On this and the other side of [the river] Po, everywhere are the sons of Niccolò." In 1416 wife Gigliolà da Carrara died childless of the plague, and in 1418 he married the daughter of Andrea di Malatesta, the ill-fortuned Madonna Parisina Malatesta, who according to several accounts loved horses and was the consummate medieval lady. Unfortunately, she became overly familiar with her son-in-law Ugo, and being caught in the act by the Marquis himself, was beheaded several days later along with her lover. It is is the subject of a poem by Byron, entitled *Parisina* (see Appendix D).[19] Four years later, in 1429, Niccolò named Ugo's younger brother, Leonello, his heir, and sent him to be educated in war under the *condottieri* captain Braccio da Montone as well as liberal arts under the famous humanist Guarino Veronese.[20]

Fiore dedicated one of the three surviving works to the Marquis, Niccolò III, and this books is recorded in the library records from 1436-1508. There are many other works listed as well, 279 in all,[21] including a large number of classical authors, French romances, and numerous books by "contemporary" men such as Boccaccio and Dante. The extensiveness of the library helps to underscore how the wealth and stability of Niccolò's court helped to foster the splendor that the court would achieve during the 15th century under his sons Leonello and Borso.

Castello di San Michele, the d'Este family stronghold in Ferrara begun in 1385 and probably familiar to Fiore.

CONDOTTIERI

During Fiore's lifetime, Italy was rich from trade with the Orient, but it was also patchwork of city-states that vied with one another for economic and political ascendancy. Feuds between communes, families, and factions fomented a state of constant warfare as civic life clashed with the older feudal establishment. The papal schism added froth to an already rich brew as the infinately complex political maneuverings spawned countless military engagements.

At the same time, England and France competed in what has become known as the Hundred Year's War, which transformed military practice in favor of the English combined arms approach piloted by Edward III, and created roving bands of unemployed, experienced and competent soldiers. These soldiers at first roamed over French territory, and were comprised of English, French and German troops led by a captain elected from their ranks. Such bands were hired by both sides during the conflict, but during periods of truce maintained themselves both by banditry and by fanning local conflicts.

Many of these bands came to Italy, where they became known as Great Companies or *condottieri*. The opportunity for war was an obvious invitation, especially given the wealth and fragmented nature of the Italian political structure, since each city stood on its own.[22] At first hired in by factions for use against their enemies, the companies stayed, earning reputations as a scourge for their infidelity—switching sides before, or even during a battle—and for their extortion of cities and even whole regions. Their self-interest was sated only temporarily by huge sums of money paid by the communes to keep them away, sums that taxed even the fiscal resources of the rich trading societies of the city-states. Operating on their own, the companies were a demon for cities such as Florence, Siena, Perguia, and Pisa, and their heinous crimes were amongst the worst excesses known in all of medieval Europe. Efforts to counter them militarily met with even higher expenses, so there was little the Italians could do and the companies devastated the peninsula throughout the 14th century. Their presence was decried by the famous 14th century Italian poet Petrarch, Niccolò Machiavelli and Pope Urban V:

> "A multitude of villains of various nations associated in arms by their greed to appropriate the fruits of labor of innocent and unarmed people, let loose to every cruelty, to extort money, methodically devastating the countryside."[23]

But the Great Companies thrived in Italy also because they were hired into the internecine warfare between the cities. The White Company, led by Sir John Hawkwood, was hired and led over the Alps by the Marquise of Monteferrat in a struggle against Milan. Sir John himself is perhaps one of the most celebrated of the captains, an Englishman who is thought to have fought at both Crècy and Poitiers, and who took part on both sides of the struggle between Milan under the Visconti and Florence. The White Company and many others were employed in the myriad struggles by the Pope, and by communes in an effort to defend themselves against each other and against roving companies. The feudal nobles, quick to realize the potential of the *condottieri*'s military power, sometimes joined their ranks. Military capitulation and the plunder available through the commerce-rich region meant that the prize for success of a

company could allow for some commanders to raise their social and political stature even to the point of taking over the states they threatened.

In response, some Italians formed companies of their own, desperate perhaps to reduce the destruction by the foreign companies. Alberico da Barbarino is perhaps the most successful of these native-born captains. Alberico began his career as part of Sir John Hawkwood's White Company, but, disenchanted with the slaughters of Faenza and Cesena in the 1370s, he formed his own company, the *Compagnia di San Giorgio*, or Company of Saint George in 1378, through which he attempted to better arm his mounted troops and improve their training. Companies like Amberico's eventually reduced the influence of the foreigners, but the depredations continued. Interestingly, Alberico would have been a contemporary of Fiore's, dying in the same year (1409) on his way to Udine. It is possible that the two knew or knew of one another.

Another of these Italian captains was Muzio Attendolo Sforza. Muzio began in the service of Alberico da Barbarino—who gave him the nickname "Sforza" (the strong)—and founded his own company which fought against and lost to Alberico's company at the Battle of Casalecchio in 1402. Active in the conflict around Naples, one of his illegitimate children, Francesco, fought alongside him and earned a reputation for being able to bend iron bars by hand. It was this same Francesco who established his own dynasty in Milan, building a splendid court which was to shape Italy during the late 14th and early 15th centuries.

Most if not all of the men named in Fiore's prologue were *condottieri* captains, and it is perhaps interesting that it was with the professional soldiers that Fiore seems to have gained his immediate acceptance, prior to his affiliation with Niccolò d'Este III. The region of Friuli, caught in a struggle for power between Cividale, Udine, Venice and the Austrian Counts of Gorizia, was probably a plentiful recruiting ground and hosting center for many of the mercenary companies. And we know that being a successful *condottieri* was a possible route to political power. It is possible that this was this the route that Fiore, claiming to be the son of a gentleman affiliated with the House of Liberi, used to come to the attention of his eventual patron, Niccolò d'Este III.

Portrait of Muzio Attendolo Sforza, condottieri capitan and founder of the Sforza family of Milan.

17

FIORE'S LIFE & WORKS

Fiore dei Liberi was active in the second half of the fourteenth century[25] and into the early fifteenth. We know him primarily from the content of his three works, two of which are associated with Marquis Niccolò III, Lord of Ferrara and Modena. There are a scant handful of historical records that mention Fiore as well, and there is some documentation about the *condottieri* he names in the Prologue. The survival of his three books offers the modern student of medieval and early Renaissance fighting techniques a wealth of material, an integrated system that is at once efficient and documentable from the 14th century, a likely distillation of contemporary martial techniques which can be used today in medieval tournament societies, reenactments, or as a martial art in their own right.

What we know of Fiore himself, however, comes to mostly from the Prologues that open his three works, but we must look at the information provided with caution, as one of the purposes of a Prologue is to establish legitimacy both for the author himself and for the work in general.[26] To be certain of what is written we must corroborate as much as possible from other historical records, but sadly scholars have been unable, thus far, to document most of what Fiore writes, although efforts are ongoing.

FIORE'S BIOGRAPHY

According to his account, Fiore was born in Friulia, probably in Premarriacco, a small village not far from Cividale,[27] the son of the "noble"[28] *messire* Benedetto. He claims attachment to the dei Liberi family of Premariacco, and notes that the region lies within the diocese of the Patriarch of Aquelia:

> "Fior furlan de Civida dostria che fo di missier Benedetto de la nobel casada deli liberi da Premeryas dela diocese dello Patroarchado de Aquileglia…"[29]

> "Fiore Furlan of Cividale, of Austria, that is of messer Benedetto of the noble house of dei Liberi from Premaraccio, of the diocese of the Patriarch of Aquelia…"

We do not know when Fiore was born. Francesco Novati, writing about Fiore in 1902, believes him to have been born between 1340 and 1350, but there is no documentary evidence to suggest the earlier of these dates, as the first mentions of him are not until 1383, when we find him listed in the city accounts of Udine as a *magistro*.[30] We know that he lived at least until 1410—since that is the date given in the Novati as to when it was begun—but I believe that, since the Getty version is almost certainly later, that he probably lived until the 1420s (see the later section on dating the manuscripts). If he was old at this time, we can perhaps think of him as born between 1350-1360.

Nothing else is known about Fiore's young life, except that he had a natural desire, from a young age, to learn the art of arms in and out of armour, with all manner of weapons, as he writes in each of his three prologues:

> "…In sua zouentu uolse imprendere ad armizare e arte de combater in sbara zoe a oltranza. De lanza, azza, spada e daga e de abrazar ape e a cauallo in arme e senza arme…e fateza de zascuna arma a cosi a defendere como a offendere e maximamente cose da combatere a oltranza. Anchora alter cose meraueglose e occulte che a poche homeni del mondo sono palese. [Morgan Fol.1v]."

> "Who in his youth wanted to learn the art of armoured fighting and the art of combat *a oltranza* within the barriers (or lists). Of the spear (lance), [pole]axe, sword, dagger and wrestling on foot and on horseback, in and out of armour…and the qualities of each weapon in the defense and in offending, and most of all, for fighting *a oltranza*. Also other marvelous and secret things known to few other men in this world."

Fiore also says that he had a desire to learn the "temper of steel," which, given the lyrical nature of Italian in general and the Friulian dialect in particular, could either mean that a literal interest in iron and steel or a metaphorical interest in things pertaining to steel. Or, put another way, the Arts of War:

> "anchora uolse sauere tempere di ferri [Getty Fol. 1]"[31]

This idea is reinforced by the specific mention of fighting *a oltranza*, and for fighting conducted *sbarra*, literally "within the barriers"—the notation that describes feats of arms conducted in a duel or other feat of arms where few rules apply.[32] This does not mean that Fiore's art is restricted to encounters where a mortal outcome is expected, but it does seem to suggest that these were his special areas of interest. His techniques and the emphasis on controlling his opponent's options strongly reinforces this suggestion.

Wanting to know more about these arts, Fiore claims to have traveled and studied—at great expense—with diverse German and Italian experts in arms, masters, scholars and noblemen:[33]

> "Et lo ditto Fiore sia imprese le ditte chose da molti magistri todeschi, e di molti italiani in piu prouincie et in molte citade cum grandissima e cum grandespese. E per la gracia di dio da tanti magistri e scolari. E in corte di grandi Signori principi duchi, marchesi, e conti chaualleri e schedieri in tanto a imprese questa arte. [Getty Fol. 1]."[34]

> "And the above-said Fiore learned these things from many German masters, and from many Italians in many provinces, in many citadels with great effort and at great expense. And by the grace of God from many masters and scholars. And [he] learned this art in many courts of great Lords, princes, dukes, marquises, counts, knights and squires."

Above: The arms of Premarriacho still carry a sword, very likely commemorating Fiore as a local hero.

It is interesting that Fiore is careful, in all three works, to note first that he studied with German masters, a hint perhaps at the probable highly regarded reputation held of the German *fechtmeisters*, especially in northern Italy, where commerce between Austria and the Italian states was strong. Many *condottieri* were *tedeschi*—German. Recall also that Fiore refers to himself as an Austrian in his first paragraph, *dostria* ("of Austria"). Taken together, it is a powerful suggestion that the German martial arts where, prior to Fiore, ascendant, as Fiore is careful to invoke them, probably to add weight to his legitimacy. In the Latin section of the Pisani-Dossi, Fiore even names a specific German master, *Suveno*, with whom he claims to have studied.

Whether or not Fiore actually traveled or studied in Metz or anywhere else is presently unknown, and more research is needed in this area. But we do know from other sources that Fiore took part in at least a few actions during the course of his lifetime.

Francesco Novati, writing in his presentation of Fiore's material for his 1902 reprint of the Pisani-Dossi, provides some good research drawn from city records to conclude that Fiore was present at Udine for the 1384-5 conflict with Cividale, appealing to be included as a "citizen" on the side of Udine. He is included in the city records as taking care of the crossbows, and possibly artillery and firearms.[35,36] We know from other sources that Fiore was in Padua in 1395, and in Padua in 1399.[37]

It has been assumed by many writers that Fiore eventually met and entered the service of Niccolò II and / or III, based on the dedications of both the Pissani-Dossi and the Getty manuscripts. Indeed, both are at least associated with Niccolò III d'Este, Marquis of Ferrara and Modena, Lord of Reggio and of Parma:

"Anchora lo libro istoriado de figure dipento e fato appeticione de lo Illustrio et Excelso Meser Nicholo Signor Marchese dela cita de Ferara de la cita de modena e de reço citade [PD Carta 2A]."

"Also the historical book of figures drawn and made at the petition of the illustrious and excellent Sir Niccolò, Lord Marquis of the city of Ferrara, of the city of Modena, and of Patma and the citadel at Reggio."

"Considerando io predetto Fiore che in questarte pochi almondo sen trouano magistri e uoglando che di mi sia fatta memoria in ella io faro un libro in tuta larte e de tutte chose le quale iso e di ferri e di tempere edaltre chose segondo lordene lo quale ma dado quallalto Signore che sopra glaltri per marcial uirtude mi piase piu epiu merita di questo di questo mio lbro per sua nobilita chaltro Signore loquale uedessi may e ueder poro çoe el mio illustro et ecelso Singore possente principo Missier NICOLO Marchese da Este Signore de la Nobele Cita di ferara di modena Reço e Parma etcetera a chuy dio dia bona vita e ventura prospera cum victoria degli inimisi suoy. AMEN [Getty Fol. 3v]"

"Considering that I, the forementioned Fiore, find few masters in this art and wanting to make my memorial, I make this book which will contain the whole art and all that I know of iron—it's temper and other things that follow—in the order in which my high Lord, who is above others in martial virtue and who is more deserving of my book for his nobility than are other Lords who I may encounter, that is my illustrious and excellent Lord, the powerful prince Sir NICOLO, Marquis d'Este, Lord of the noble city of Ferrara, of Modena, Reggio and Parma, etc., who God gave good life and future prosperity with victory over his enemies. AMEN."

Unfortunately, there are as yet no corroborating documents placing Fiore at any of Niccolò's courts. We have fairly good records for many others who were present there, but puzzlingly, there is nothing about Fiore. There is a hint, buried at the end of the PD

Municipal records on Fiore

"1383: Die 30 Septembris in consilio Terri Utini deliberatum fuit supra balistris grossis et sagitamentis magister Flor, qui fuit de Civitate Austria (sic), qui examinet et ponat ad ordinem omnia existential in camera comunis et eciam que habent Fraternitates."[38]

"1383: Die lune terito Augusti. Utini in consilio. Magister Flor de Civitate dimicator ieceptus fuit in vinicum Terre, cum capitulis alias obvervatis et D. Federigus de Savorgnano fuit fideiussor."[39]

"Anno 1384, ind. VII. Infrascripti sunt qui iuraverunt astare dominion Capitaneo pro bono et tranquillo statu Terre quod contra quoscumpque delinquents et excessores fiat iusticia criminalis secundum laudabiles consuetudines Terre Utini et deliberations consiliarias maioris Consilii et Consilii Secreti: omissis: In Burgo Glemone: Magister Florius scarmitor."[40]

prologue, that perhaps Fiore was by this time old, between fifty and seventy years old, depending upon the accepted date for his birth. We know that he lived at least until 1410, when the Pisani-Dossi manuscript was written and since, in 1409, Niccolò III became master of both Parma and Reggio, both mentioned in the Getty and PD manuscripts. He claims at the end of his prologues that he had, at this point, studied for more than forty years, which strongly suggests 1360 or 70.

So we know little if anything about Fiore's later life, except that several of his books made their way into the d'Este library. My own belief is that Fiore led a humble life, punctuated with some success and at least limited access to the court of d'Este. It is likely, perhaps, that like the other *scrimatore* mentioned in various accounts, he taught his art in the inn-yards.[41] His attempt to secure a more stable and comfortable retirement within the d'Este court, around the Castello di San Michele, may or may not have been successful. But we are fortunate that at least three of his books have survived, and it is with these three books that we'll begin.

In the prologue of the Getty, Fiore states that he has studied the arts of arms for forty years, so these books represent a lifetime's worth of work, but that he still had more to learn, as he was as yet "an imperfect master:"

> "Che io Fiore sapiando legere e scriuer e disignare e abiando libri in questa arte e in lei o studiado ben XL anni e piu. Anchora non son ben perfecto magistro in questa arte [Morgan F. 2v]."[42]

> "That I, Fiore, knowing how to read, write and draw, and having books on this art, have studied in them for more than forty years. But I am [still] not a perfect master in this art."

We know by this declaration that Fiore claims to have been at least fifty years old at the time when the Morgan and the Getty were written. He writes in the final paragraph of the PD that he recommends himself to the Marquis because it tooks six months to compose and because he is now old, and did not want to undertake another similar effort.[43] Did the rich Marquis perhaps convince Fiore to produce more works, perhaps improvements on the relatively rough Pisani-Dossi?

THE TREATISES

Two of Fiore's works survive today and are in the United States, while the other resides in private hands. Each begins with an introductory prologue that contains biographical points, mentions Fiore's more famous students who engaged in feats of arms, and provides the "keys" for understanding the manuscript. The prologues of the Morgan and Getty are very similar except for the Morgan's missing dedication to Niccolò III, while the Pisani-Dossi is quite different but includes some of the same information. The introductions are generally illuminated, though not heavily and not at the highest quality, which seems to suggest a concern with economy.

The prologues are followed by the technique sections, which include three or four figures, each page divided roughly into quarters. In the PD, space is saved by including six figures per page. The accompanying text appears above each figure, a paragraph in the case of the Morgan and Getty and a rhyming couplet in the case of the Pisani-Dossi. The language is in a dialect of Italian—Furlan—the dialect of Friulia. The paragraphs in the Getty and Morgan are generally complete and very informative, but somewhat difficult, as the dialect is not quite modern Italian and there are places where there is potential confusion between things like front and back. The Pisani-Dossi has a Latin pre-prologue, followed by a near-repetition in a "vulgar" Italian dialect.

The figures are generally very well drawn, showing artistic training, likely by a student of the late 14th century artist Altichiero.[44] The style is definitely Veronese, and it captures details of armour and costume as well as precision in the rendering of the techniques demonstrated. We'll discuss the artistic connections for the illustrations later, but for now it is important only to note that we believe them to be very accurately portraying what Fiore intended.

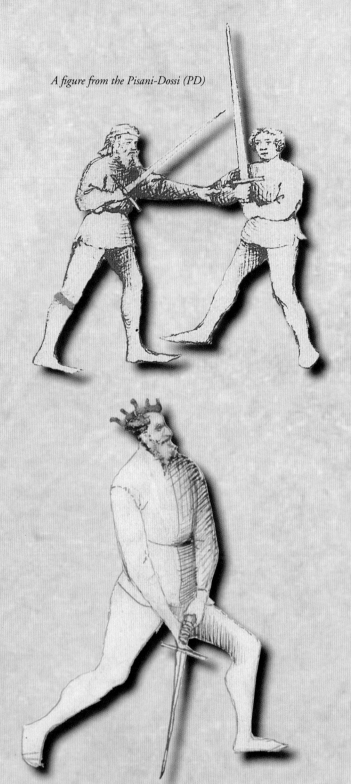

A figure from the Pisani-Dossi (PD)

A figure from the Getty, Fol. 23v Courtesy J.P. Getty Trust, Inc.

The Pisani-Dossi (Novati) Manuscript

Recent research has located the original manuscript, apparently still in the Pisani-Dossi family collection.[45] It is considerably different than the other two, featuring different (and I believe earlier) styles of armour and with much abbreviated rhyming couplets. It has two prologues, the first in rudimentary Latin and the other in Italian, and the figures appear far more roughly drawn than the fine figures of the Getty or Morgan copies. We know very little about the manuscript's history, although the contents are the most well known, owing to the facsimile reprint and study made in 1902 by Francesco Novati (the mss. is sometimes called the Novati, rather than the Pisani-Dossi [PD]). The 1902 is presumed out of copyright and has been circulated widely on the Internet.

The PD version, is difficult and the language far less descriptive than in the Morgan or the Getty, but there are sections that do not appear in either of the other two treatises. Owing to the styles of clothing, armor and more rudimentary nature of the figures, my own belief is that the PD represents the earliest of the three works, that the best example we have is actually in the Getty, where technique, illustration and descriptions are all fuller and far more efficiently rendered. But the PD version is widely available, and the illustrations in particular have great value for the community as they are frequently reproduced.

When Francesco Novati examined the original, presumably around 1900, it consisted of 36 leaves, with 281 drawings, and it was unbound. We do not know if it has since been bound, but research is ongoing and there is s ome hope that one of the current generation of scholars will be able to examine the treatise first-hand for the first time in a century.

The Morgan Manuscript

The Pierpoint Morgan library in New York holds the second treatise, this one consisting of just 15 leaves[46] and featuring just 108 drawings. It is known as M.0383. It could well be an abridged version of the Getty, or of the larger 58-leaf version noted in the d'Este library inventory of 1436.[47] Presumably this manuscript is also on vellum, probably with the same ox-gall ink and gilding as the Getty. The text of the prologue is substiantially the same as the Getty, with only dialectic variance and a few content differences. The Morgan is not dedicated to Niccolò III, nor does it mention him. The order is also different; there are few *poste*, no *abrazzare*, no spear, and no poleaxe plays. There is very little play in armour; one has the impression that the Morgan is but an incomplete collection of tricks, either a few favorites of a student/patron, or perhaps a teaser, or a section of a larger work, now lost. There is evidence that it is unfinished, as there are several penciled illustrations mentioned in the Morgan card catalog. It is not a small volume, measuring 10 7/8" x 7 5/8", very close to the modern 11 x 8 ½"" size common in the United States.

The Getty Manuscript

Within the United States, the larger and assumably more complete copy survives in the Getty collection, where it is known as the Ludwig XV 13, because it was acquired from the collection of Peter & Irene Ludwig, purchased through the agency of H.P. Kraus (New York), but the sale date is unknown. A physical description taken from the sale catalogue follows:

> "Manuscript on vellum, written in a clear Italian Gothic book hand. 2 cols. 47 leaves (ff. 3-5 blanks). With 291 splendid pen drawings, by the author: one full-page (f. 32); one half-page (f. 47); the rest mostly quarter-page; many burnished with gold details on the figures, and a few with silver details. Folio. 280 x 205mm. Italian blind tooled light brown calf (c. 1800). From the libraries of Niccolò III d'Este, Marchese of Ferrara, with his name in large gold letters, with penwork decoration, in the dedicatory passage, f. 1 verso; Niccolò Marcello di Santa Maria; Apostolo Zeno (1668-1750); Luigi Celotti (c. 1789-1846); his sale, London. 14 March, 1825, no. 134; and Sir Thomas Phillipps (ms. 4204)."[48,49]

The Getty is the most complete of the three surviving manuscripts. It has descriptive paragraphs, written in the Friulian dialect, that accompany the ox-gall[50] pen-and-ink illustrations. The combination of the longer descriptive paragraphs with the detailed, highly precise drawings make the survival of this manuscript a treasure for modern students and it is the one that the Schola Saint George uses as our base text for advanced work.

Other Manuscripts – The Este Library

Two manuscripts attributed to Fiore were definitely kept within the d'Este library during the the fifteenth century. Fortunately several inventories survive,[51] and they include not only a listing but a brief description of the volumes included. Most interestingly, there is a tantalizing reference to a volume of 58 leaves, larger by 11 leaves than the most complete one now known, the Getty. There is also another one mentioned, also attributed to Fiore, that consisted of 15 leaves, which was still in the collection as of 1508 and which may be the Morgan.

The larger volume is thought to have been to be dedicated to Niccolò III because it is thought to have included on the frontispiece an escutcheon featuring a double-headed, helmeted eagle. It was number 84 in the d'Este collection, but is now presumed to be lost,[52] but what material might have been included on those eleven other pages? Perhaps the manuscript will surface eventually in a private collection.

The smaller version is known to have held 15 leaves, the same number as we find on the present Morgan treatise. It is recorded as number 110 in the d'Este family collection (now held at Modena), and it too disappears after 1508.[53]

And so we are left with three surviving manuscripts, one of which might be traced to the d'Este library. In his prologue, Fiore makes an interesting mention about one of the *condottieri* captains, Galeazzo da Mantua (the man who fought with and twice defeated Boucicault, believed to be the one-time Marshal of France, or his younger brother):

> "Anchora digo che nesuno de questi scolari aqui anommandi non aue may libro in larte de combater altro che miß galeaz di manthoa. Ben chello diseua che senza libro non sara zamia nesuno bono magistro ne scolaro in questa arte. [Morgan F.2v]"

> "Also I say that no other scholars of those named had my book in the art of combat other than messire Galeazzo di Mantua. Well that he said that without books one will not be a good master or scholar in this art."

This would indicate that at least one other book belonged to Galeazzo di Mantua, but it is unlikely that the book was the Pisani-Dossi or the Getty, as these were dedicated to to Niccolò III (although it is possible). It is also possible that Galeazzo had the Morgan at one time—the 15-leaf version—and that it somehow ended up in the d'Este family library by 1436, where it became catalogued as number 84. But this seems unlikely[54]—as the paragraph above is from the Morgan prologue—so we now find five or six copies recorded:

1. The now-lost 58-leaf version featuring the double-headed eagle on the frontispiece, in the d'Este family library from 1436-1508+, probably Fiore's copy meant for Niccolò III himself. This is d'Este family library no. 110.

2. The 47-leaf Getty edition, which is dedicated to Niccolò III but which does not appear to have been in the d'Este family library. It is also possible that when this edition was rebound, pages were lost,[55] including the frontispiece and 10 other leaves. This is the "main" version usually followed by modern students of the art as it is the most complete.

3. The 15-leaf version, which is not mentioned as being dedicated to Niccolò, and could be the copy surviving in the J.P. Morgan library. It would be the d'Este family volume no. 84.

4. A 20-leaf version, which currently resides in the J.P. Morgan library in New York, M.0383. This could possibly be one and the same with #3 above.

5. The 36-leaf Pisani-Dossi version, also termed the Novati. This is the most commonly reproduced copy, as it was printed in facsimile in 1902 by Francesco Novati. It is accompanied with voluminous notes, a second prologue in Latin, and features short rhyming couplets instead of the descriptive paragraphs that appear in the Getty and Morgan.

6. An unspecified copy belonging to Galeazzo di Mantua, mentioned in the Morgan and Getty prologues.

My personal belief is that Fiore perhaps wrote one or two treatises himself, which took him six long months to complete, and that subsequent variations were made at the behest of his new patron, Niccolò III. I find it likely that the PD is the one he wrote, and he may have written the one owned by Galeazzo da Mantua. These variations would have been professionally written and illustrated, probably by a Veronese artist of the school of Altichiero. It is likely that Niccolò himself commissioned the works and perhaps that Fiore oversaw the production of new variations.

DATING OF THE MANSCRIPTS

Based on the content of the manscripts, as well as their artistic aspects and the events noted in the prologues, I offer the following dates for the three treatises:

PISANI-DOSSI (PD): Probably composed, as Fiore mentions, in 1409. I believe this was an early effort that was possibly similar to the copy that Galeazzo di Mantua might have had, but it is not his, as there is a paragraph near the end recommending the book to Niccolò III.

GETTY: I believe this edition represents a junior copy to the larger 58-leaf edition, or perhaps it is the 58-page one that belonged to Niccolò, but pages are now missing. I believe its dating to be later than for the Pisani-Dossi, based on the increased sophistication of the techniques and the dating of armour and costume included within. My own guess is that it dates from the 1420s.

MORGAN: This copy is probably contemporary with the Getty, and there are no specific dating clues as to its production. The text is substantially similar to the Getty, saving that the dedications to Niccolò are missing. This is curious, as it is likely the 15-leaf version recorded as being in the d'Este library from 1436-1508+. I believe this text likely dates from 1415-1425.

The community of scholars and students of Fiore do not agree on the dating of the treatises. Many, if not most, have taken Fiore at his word and said that the PD manuscript, dated 10th Feb. 1409, is the last work.[56] But I find that my consideration of the evidence suggests that the PD is the first of the surviving manuscripts, followed by the Getty and Morgan, both of which may be derived from another manuscript now lost.

To arrive at this conclusion we will look at the text and the art of the manuscript itself, returning to the question of dating at the end of the section.

Text – Clues in the material
Using clues from the prologues we can gather the scant dating information. In each of the treatises Fiore includes a prologue or introduction in which some traceable information has been provided.

The PD begins with a declaration that Fiore began the work on February 10th, 1409, *De*

Fresco by Altichiero
Oratory of S. Giorgio, Padua.

mille quatrocento e nove a dix X de lo mese de febraro.... And the treatise ends with another interesting paragraph:

"Io predicto Fior prego el mio signor marchese che lo libro li sia arecomandado perche Voy non trouariti may uno parechio de questo pero che magistri non se trouaria che saueseno far si facti libri ne anchora intendere in lo libro pocho o niente et etiam per lo longo tempo che io sonto stato a farlo non sonto per fame piu nesuno de tanta quantita como e questo che per mia fede io li sonto sta meço anno a farlo si che io non uoio piu de queste brige per lo tempo uechio che me incalça. Dio guardi lo segnore Marchese Nichollo da este signore de la cita de ferara de la cita de modena de la cita de parma e de la cita de reço. [PD C.2b]".

"I, the previously mentioned Fiore prays that my Lord the Marquis, to whom I recommend this book, because you cannot find it's equal, nor can you find [other] Masters who know how to make books. In this book there is little or nothing that I have not made myself; I worked on it for a long time and I cannot make it longer—it took me half a year to make. I don't want more of the troublesome [work] that it has caused me, for I am old. God watches the Lord Marquis Niccolò d'Este, lord of the city of Ferrara, of Modena, of Parma and of Reggio."

Fiore states boldly that he could read, write and draw:

"Che io Fiore sapiando legere e scriuer e disignare e abiando libri in questa arte e in lei o studiado ben XL anni e piu…considerando io preditto che in questa arte pochi al mondo son touano magistri e uoglando che de mi sia fatta memoria in questa arte io faro uno libro in tuta larte de tute cose chio so e di ferri e de tempere e d a;tre cose segondo che nuy saueremo fare per lo miglore e per piu chiareza. [Morgan F.2v]"[57]

"That I Fiore, knowing how to read, write and draw, and having books on this art, and having studied in them more than forty years…and considering that I have said before that in this art there are few masters found in the world and wanting to make my memory in this art, I have made a book of the whole art and other things I know of steel and its temper, and other things following that we know to make the art better and more clear."

He claims to have written and drawn his text, but it is more likely that he did preliminary work and had the art and calligraphy professionally done.[58] Certainly Fiore oversaw the work at the very least.

Beyond the prologue,[59] which provides the clues, each technique is described. In the Getty and Morgan these paragraphs are almost exactly the same for the included elements (although the Morgan is both incomplete and contains far less material than the Getty, and is presented in a much different order.), but in the PD, the accompanying text is restricted to less expert verse couplets that don't offer very much information but which are more like what modern youngsters would think of as "trash talking."

The text itself is written in a beautiful flowing Italian gothic hand, and it is for this reason that many suspect that the hand was professionally written, rather than being Fiore's own. We have no signature or other writing sample to correlate, unfortunately. The

PD prologue refers to "text written in red," and the illuminated capitals that accompany each page of the Getty are made in red and blue,[60] but the text itself is written in black ink. The style of the letters and floriated ornament suggests a date between 1380 and 1400, but at present this doesn't add much to the dating question.[61]

While the language of the text is dialect—something close to the Venetian—it is not particularly difficult for speakers of Romance languages, akin to reading Middle English for speakers of modern American English. But understanding the text is critical to deciphering the techniques and principles included in the text.

By looking at the text there is a great deal that can be guessed at regarding Fiore's dates and his intent, but the truly interesting material is in Fiore's description of the techniques and principles involved, which accompany each illustration.

Considering the Illustrations – Artistic connections

Alongside the text are included very finely drawn illustrations—drawings—in iron-gall ink. These drawings, called by art historians "pen and ink," have turned a pleasant brown given the iron present. They are uncolored, but are finely wrought and are exquisitely detailed. I have had the pleasure of examining the Getty edition in person, and was struck by the incredible delicateness of the lines, combined with an obvious precision

and attention to detail. Truly these are masterpieces of the drawing art of the period in their own right!

Art historians largely agree that there is a strong resemblance in the figures to those drawn by Altichiero (active 1330-1384, died c.1395),[62] student of Martino di Verona (d.1412) and teacher of Jacopo da Verona (1355-1432). He is often credited with founding the Veronese school, although he worked mainly in Padua, where he produced stunning frescos in the Basilica of Saint Anthony (between 1372-79) and the Oratory of Saint George (between 1377-84), working with an unknown artist by the name of Avanzo. Some of Altichiero's drawings survive and have been compared with those of Fiore, although given how early Altichiero himself stopped working (considered to be 1384, upon completion of the Oratory of Saint George), this seems unlikely.

There is a common belief that Fiore drew and wrote the *Fior di Battaglia*, but it seems unlikely that he was both a talented student in Altichiero's school and a preeminent sword-master. What seems more likely is that the d'Este family, either Niccolò II or Niccolò III, tapped into the artistic community and contracted to have Fiore's drawings and text formalized into a multiple beautiful works recorded in the d'Este family library. This is rendered more likely given that the PD drawings are far less expertly executed, and probably represent a less wealthy client—perhaps even Fiore himself. I do find it credible that Fiore perhaps executed the PD drawings himself, but it is more likely that they, too, were done by a hired artist.[63]

Each drawing does contain precise information about each technique, and a student of Fiore's art should note well such subtle details as the position of each foot and hand, the distribution of weight, and so on. The Veronese school seems to have excelled at

Two anonymous works, "after Altichiero." The one above is from the British Museum, while the one to the left is from the Musuee Louvre. Below, A page from Fiore's treatise, Getty fol. 33v, is shown for comparison.

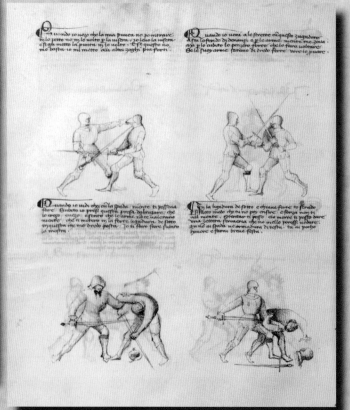

Hüyb Midrag

Fiore's later work appears to have been done by a student of the Veronese artist Altichiero. It is likely that Fiore's patron for these works, Nicollo d'Este III, commissioned the work and hired the artist while Fiore oversaw the production. Above: Anonymous Veronese battle scene by an anonymous Veronese artist, courtesy the Trustees of the British Museum. Above right, two figures from the Getty copies of the Fior di Battaglia showing figures remarkably close in posture, dress and drawn with very closely related drawing techniques.

capturing such minute details of movement. There are clues to aid the student, such as shading made on the limbs, used to denote which limb is in front and which is behind.[64]

In addition, the illustration also detail elements of costume and armour from the period, and by these it may well be possible to add support to theories about the manuscript's date, but also to shed light on the development of armour in the region.

Lombardy and the areas between Lombardy, Milan and Venice were strong producing centers for armour during the period, but in this respect the the Getty and the PD manuscript are quite different, as we'll look at in more detail in Book II.

SECRECY & FIORE'S MOTIVATION TO WRITE THE *FIOR DI BATTAGLIA*

The "secrets" of arms have long been seductive, the generalized fascination with superior, surprise techniques have probably been sought by soldiers and men-of-arms as long as their have been arms. Fiore states boldly that he taught in secret:

"Digo anchor che questa arte iolo mostrada sempre oculta mente siche non gle sta presente achuno alamostre se non lu scolaro et alchuno so discreto parente e se pur alchuno altro gle staper gracia o per cortesia cum sagramento a fede de non palentare alchun çogo veçda mi Fiore Magistro. [Morgan F.3r-3v]"

"E marzormamente me o guardado da magistri scarmidori e da suoy scolari. E loro per inuidia çoe gli Magistri mano conuidado açugare a spade di taglo e di punta in çuparello darmare sençaltrarma saluo che un paro di guanti de Comoça. E tutto questo e stado per che io non o uogludo praticar cum loro ne o uogludo insegnare niente di mia arte.

"E questo accidente e stado V uolte che io son stado requirido. E V uolte per mio honore ma conuegnu çugare in luoghi strany sença Amisi non habiando spreança in altruy se non in dio in larte et in mi Fiore e inlamia spada. E per la gracia di dio io Fiore son rimaso cum honore e sença lesione di mia persona. [Morgan F.3v]."

"Also I say that this art I have always demonstrated in secret, with none present at the demonstrations save for the scholar and other discrete relatives. Others, if they were allowed to stay, were sworn in grace and with courtesy with a pledge in faith not to reveal any of the plays they saw from Master Fiore.

"And I have been wary of other masters of the sword and their scholars. But they, out of envy, demanded that I play with edge and point, in but a *zuparello* (arming cote)[65] and gloves of chamois. All of this because I did not want to practice with them, and did not want to teach them anything of my art.

"And this collision happened five times, as they required it of me. And five times for my honor I met them, but in foreign places, without friends or relatives, and without hope from anyone but God, myself, my art, and my sword. And by the grace of God, I, Fiore, kept my honor without a mark on my person."

The Getty has very similar information, but it is not metioned in the PD. Fiore claims to have offered his knowledge only to his scholars and certain of their courteous and discrete relatives. But he says that he avoided other masters of the sword (*scrimatori*) and their scholars, but that from envy he was challenged five times in an arming coat and soft leather gloves, and that each time he emerged from the contest unscathed.

As yet we have found no record of these contests, but as these were duels amongst *scrimitori*—not gentlemen—they would probably have been held in secret, back-of-the-inn duels that telegraphed the dueling craze that would envelope Italy from the 15th – 18th centuries.

HONOR & QUARRELLING

"*Then, both for his own sake and for that of his friends, he must understand the quarrels and differences that can arise and he must be quick to seize the advantage, always showing courage and prudence in all things. Nor should he be too ready to fight except when honor demands it; for besides the great danger that the uncertainty of fate entails, he who rushes into such affairs recklessly and without urgent cause merits the severest censure even though he be successful. But when he finds himself so far engaged that he cannot withdraw without reproach, he ought to be the most deliberate, both in the preliminaries to the duel and in the duel itself, and always show readiness and daring.*"

Book of the Courtier, F. 21, p. 30-31.

Indeed, Fiore goes as far in the PD as to implore his students not to share his art, reserving it instead for those with a sense of nobility:

"Therefore every man of a generous mind, who loves and hides his work nearly like a treasure, so that it should never be divulged to rural thugs, in which heaven created an obtuseness and inadequate agility, carrying weights like beasts of burden. Therefore, I decree that to this precious mystery must Kings, Dukes, Princes and Barons be invited, and also other courtiers and others skilled in the duel, secondly to those who said, 'the majesty of the Emperor must be adorned with arms.' [PD Carta 2A, Latin prologue]"[66]

This is a textbook invocation that usually proceeded books on princely arts and other aspects of chivalric literature, representing, I believe, an effort by Fiore to elevate the art from the red-light district of the inn-yard to the noble halls of the courtiers and nobility, but I have written about this more extensively elsewhere.[67]

Fiore's book must be considered, in addition to being a practical treatise on arms, a piece of chivalric literature, an effort to infuse and invigorate the soldiers, knights and noblemen of his day with an appreciation for the value of training and study in arms. It is a theme that resonates across the centuries with other chivalric literature in that it represents a recognition of knighthood's failings, yet also a hope for the humanizing impulse of the chivalric ideal.

Within the Schola Saint George, this chivalric expression is one of the most important aspects of our development of combatants. Through technique we strive to develop prowess, prowess that conveys confidence and excellence in multiple facets of the combatants' lives. In a chivalric sense, the use of this prowess is tempered by judgment and nobility—elements that can elevate the art from the merely physical into the spiritual.

Fiore says that he wrote his book for several reasons. First, that he was old (and a little tired), and that he was no longer terribly interested in the physical performance of the art's mysteries. Second, he wrote, as in previous quoted passage, that he did not want the art to be lost to noble men who must rely upon the use of arms. Third, he wanted to be recommended in his old age to the most powerful man he likely knew, Niccolò d'Este III, in hopes of securing perhaps a pension or attachement to his household or court. Fourth, so that his own memory was not lost to the world, he decided to write a book on arms, since having met with thousands of men who called themselves *magistro*—and finding few worthy of the title—he wanted to create a book in which the art could be both readily understood and passed on, for no one can be called master who knows less than a quarter of the art, and no one can remember more than a quarter of the art without books.

It is a noble thing to have done, and I think Fiore succeded in his objective, creating a book that is close to complete, a masterwork preserving a martial art from nearly six hundred years ago, an art he kept secret from other masters but which he illuminated for future generations. It is an art anchored in the Western world, one of a very few martial arts to have survived in some form after the widespread adoption of gunpowder and reliable firearms. And it survived not because it was passed down from master to student, but because Fiore, who could "read, write and draw," recorded it in the *Fior di Battaglia*.

CONNECTION TO GERMAN MATERIAL

As discussed in the last chapter, the German corpus of material is overwhelming in this period. There is clear German influence in Fiore's *poste*, and he claims to have traveled in Germany and to have trained with a John Suveno in the diocese of Metz.

Whether Fiore actually traveled to Metz—or anywhere else—is unknown. The community of historical swordsmanship has gone back and forth comparing the Italian and German systems. In the beginning, the trend was to see connections everywhere, as between some of the German *leger* and the Italian *poste*. And in truth there *are* many similarities (starting with the numerous German fighting books), probably owing to Fiore's interaction with German combatants, but there are also important differences. Here are a few of my observations:

The potent German school has similarities to the Italian, but there are also important differences. The figure at right is from Paulus Kal's 15th century treatise, showing the arm-based leger or guard vom Tag. This is almost, but not quite, like Fiore's posta frontale. Kal's treatise is am important source for information on the German medieval tradition.

1. Fiore associates stability with the ground, hence the majority of his *poste* are well anchored, and he has a preference for the low *guardia*. In the German systems, by contrast, much of the fighting seems to take place above the shoulders.

2. Fiore's system uses the whole body to propel the blows. Cuts are not much used, and the flicking motions using the wrists and arms common in the German plays are not found in Fiore.[68]

3. Fiore seems to evince a preference for *mezzo tempo*, while the German masters seem to favor *stesso tempo*. This could be because, as I believe, Fiore might have found the fight safer by first securing information and control using the blade contact or expenditure of this opponent, then turning the sword to take advantage, rather than committing to a simultaneous attempt to make cover against an incoming strike and attack in the same moment, as is done in the German *meisterhau*.

LEGACY: THE ITALIAN SCHOOL

Fiore dei Liberi's *Fior di Battaglia* was an important book. He succeeded in getting at least two copies into the possession of Niccolò d'Este III. While the lineage of the later Italian *scrimatori* are complex, it is clear that many of Fiore's explorations were either reflective of martial techniques then practiced in his day, or his work was sufficiently influential to resonate through the centuries.

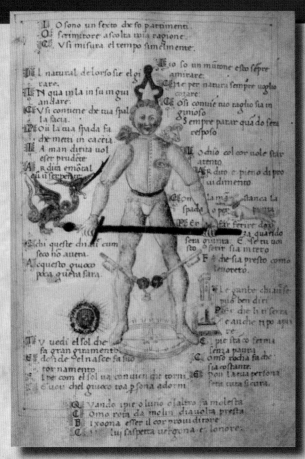

Three plates from the next survivng Master's work in the Italian tradition, Fillipo Vadi. Vadi's De Arte Gladiatoria Dimicandi is valuable for students because there are explanatory chapters that discuss such tactical questions as when to thrust, and how to feint or false. However, Vadi's style is also very different: higher, more oriented on the thrust, and it includes much narrower stances. All in all, less based on power than position.

Filippo Vadi followed Fiore's writing with a book of his own, written in the 1470s, probably fifty years after Fiore's work. It is a small and beautiful book, *De Arte Gladiatoria Dimicandi*,[69] that shows much in common with and very likely a close familiarity with Fiore's books. But by 1470 the art of swordsmanship was starting to undergo its tectonic shift, and we see within Vadi a narrower stance, circular footwork, and an emphasis on maintaining distance and a greater reliance upon the *punta*. Whether Vadi inherited anything from Fiore's *scolari* is unknown, but Vadi's work laid the groundwork for the flowering of Italian swordsmanship that would explode under Pietro Monte, Achille Marozzo, Antonio Manciolino, Giacomo di Grassi, Ridolfo Capo Ferro, Salvatore Fabris and the rest.

Today the Italian medieval arts are undergoing a resurgence. Within the United States, the Schola Saint George, Chicago Swordplay Guild, Academy of Saint Martins, the Northwest Academy of Arms and others are pursuing Fiore's art with vigor and passion. In Europe, the Exiles, Scuola Gladiatoria, The School of European Swordsmanship in Helsinki, Nova Scrima, Sala d'Armi di Achille Marozzo, and the Malipiero Company in Italy—amongst others—are all working to build a new generation of *scolari* trained in different interpretations of Fiore's art, and it is an art that holds great promise for the resurgence of Western martial arts in general both for those with an interest in history and for those looking for an art based in Western culture and secured with the Western value set. It is a fine journey.

[1] Martial engagements have been roughly distinguished by their intention: those which were *à plaisance* tend to be more celebratory in nature, contrasted with those which were *à outrance*, where the outcome of the fight was of more importance. These are medieval French terms (which we retain since the literature on the Tournament is based mainly on French accounts), and Fiore himself mentions his interest in *chose de combater ad oltrança* in the first paragraph of his Prologue. By this interest it might be suggested that he is not particularly interested in jousts, pas d'armes or civic contests, but rather in the duel, in personal defense and in war. This is not to say that Fiore's techniques are any less valid in circumstances where less force is expected, but Fiore's interest seems to have focused on fights *à outrance*, and this is borne out by the potential lethality of his techniques.

[2] The *hastiludium* was a contest with spears. The *ensiludium*, by contrast, may have used swords. For more on these terms, see Juliet Barker, *The Tournament in England, 1100-1400*, and Barber & Barker, *Tournaments*. Francesco Novati also discusses the two in note 55. Both terms are loosely grouped under the modern word *tournament*, although the tournament itself should be more properly understood as an encounter between groups of mounted men in something like mock combat.

[3] See especially Pietro Gori, *Le Feste Fiorentine: Attraversa i secoli* and Duccio Balestracci, *La Festa in Armi: giostre, tornei e giochi del medioevo*. The Italian tradition of sometimes baffling civic festivals is a rich vein of study that resemble, in many respects, those of the Low Countries, where similar civic festivals took place. For these see Evelyn van den Neste, *Tournois, Joutes, Pas d'Armes Dans les Villes de Flandre a la Fin du Moyen Ages* (1300-1486). A brief survey can be found in Barber Barker's landmark survey work, *Tournaments*. This last entry is probably the most accessible treatment on the whole topic, and I highly recommend it for casual students of the medieval feat of arms.

[4] Barber & Barker, *Tournaments*, p. 83.

[5] Transcription and translation of the name courtesy *The Exiles*. Bob Charron has rendered this as *Urrizilino*.

[6] *Inglese* means "English," so Nicholas was probably British.

[7] A very interesting General of Venice who seems to have been highly regarded for his military acumen.

[8] Known more commonly as Galeazzo Cattaneo dei Grumelli, Galeazzo Gonzaga) Di Mantova. *Secondo alcune fonti, di Grumello nel pavese*. He appears as #997 on the very fine web resource, **condottieri di ventura**, http://www.condottieridiventura.it, where author Roberto Damiani adds, "*Si batte una prima volta a duello a Padova con il Boucicaut: costui, infatti, trovandosi a mensa con lui, accusa di viltà gli italiani; da qui ne segue la sfida, che si svolge davanti al signore di Padova Francesco Novello da Carrara ed a Francesco Gonzaga, signore di Mantova. I due cavalieri combattono a piedi e si colpiscono vicendevolmente con le lance. Intervengono i due signori a rappacificare gli animi.*" He writes that he was, "*Piccolo di statura. Fortissimo. Di grande forza. Robustissimo.*" One of the great captains of his day.

[9] Some researchers have postulated that this is perhaps the famous Marshal Boucicaut, but it could also be his younger brother Geoffrey. Most of the research pertaining to the Marshal stems from the *Le Livre des Faites du Bon Messire Jehan le Maigre, dit Boucicuaut, Mareshal du France et Gouveneur du Jennes,* although a fine biography was done in 1988 by Denis Lalande, *Jean II Le Meingre, dit Boucicaut,* Librarie Droz. He is also mentioned in various chronicles and records from Italy. Boucicaut was in Italy at the time and was an active participant in the conflicts involving Venice around the very times mentioned.

[10] Lancilotto Beccharia, as he is known in modern references, served together with his brother (Castellino the Younger) in a long career documented in the fine *Condottieri di Ventura* website.

[11] This is my own moderninzing of the name to be consistent with the use of the sound in *zhogo* (modern Italian: *gioco*).

[12] This is undoubtedly the famous Castle Visconti in Pavia, which was begun in 1360 and has survived to the present day as one of the most important attractions in Pavia. As a Visconti palace it was both a military stronghold and a cultural center, a impressive 180m x 180m square structure featuring four guard towers and enclosing a massive space. I find it likely that the famous encounter between Zhionino da Bavo and Giovanni di Ordelaffi may well have taken place within this beautiful courtyard.

[13] The original transcription: "…che lo ditto fiore à stado più e più volte richiesto da molti Signori e chavallieri e schudieri per imprender del ditto fiore sifatta arte d'armizare e d'combatter in sbarra a oltrança la quale arte ello à mostrada a più sori ytaliani e todeschi e altri grandi Signori che àno debudo combattere in sbarra, e ancho ad infiniti che non àno debydo combattere, e de alguni che sono stadi miei scolari che àno debudo combatter in sbarra de' quali alchuni qui ne farò nome e memoria. Como de loro si fo el nobele e gagliardo chavaliero Misser piero del verde el quale debea combattere cum Misser piero d'la corona i quali forono ambidoy todeschi. E la Bataglia debea esser a Perosa. Anchora a lo valoroso chavaliero Misser Nicolò ??? thodesco che debea combatter cum nicolò Inghileso. Lo campo fo dado ad Imola. Anchora al notabele valoroso e gagliardo chavalliero Misser Galeaço di Captani di Grimello chiamado di Mantoa che debea combattere cum lo valoroso chavalliero Misser Briçichardo de fraça lo campo fo a padoa. Anchora al valoroso schudiero Lancilotto da Becharia de pavia el quale fe' VI punti de lança a ferri moladi a chavallo contra lo valente cavalliero Misser Baldassare todescho i quali ad Imola debea combatter in sbarra. Anchora al valoroso schudiero çoanino da Bajo da Milano che fe' in pavia in lo castello contra lo valente schudiero Gram??? todesco tre punti di lança a ferri moladi a chavallo. E poy fe' a pe' tre colpi d'aça e tre colpi d'spada e tre colpi di daga in presença del nobilissimo principe e Signore Missier lo Ducha di Milano e d'Madona la duchessa e d'altri infiniti Signori e donne. Anchora al cauteloso chavalliero Missier Açço da Castell Barcho che debea una volta combatter cum çuanne di Ordelaffi. E un'altra volta cum lo valente e bon chavalliero Misser Jacomo di Bosom??? e 'l campo debea esser al piasere de lo Signore ducha di Milano, di questi e d'altri i quali io fiore ò magistradi io son molto contento perché io son stado ben rimunerato e ò aibudo l'onore e l'amore di miei scolari e di parenti loro digo anchora che questa arte io l'ò mostrada sempre ocultamente sì che non glie sta' presente alchuno [3v] a la mostra se non lu scolaro et alchuno so discreto parente e se pur alchuno altro glie sta' per gracia o per cortesia cum sagramento gli sono stadi prometendo a fede de non palesare alchun çogo veçudo da mi fiore magistro E mazormamente me ò guardado da' magistri scrimidori a da' suoy scolari e loro per invidia çoè gli magistri m'àno convidado a çugare a spade di taglio e di punta in çuparello d'armare senç'altra arma salvo che un paio di guanti de (camoça?) e tutto questo è stado perché io non ò vogl(i)udo praticar cun loro nè ò vogliudo insegnare niente di mia arte." Transcription courtesy Sala d'Arme Achille Marozzo.

[14] Ibid., p. 83-4.

[15] See especially Robert C. Davis, *The War of the Fists: Popular Culture and Public Violence in Late Renaissance Venice*, Oxford, 1994.

[16] This tradition of the teaching of fighting and fencing in Cividale, explored briefly by Francesco Novati in his exposition on Fiore, are discussed in detail on pp. 18 and 19, and documented in notes 37-39.

[17] The original colony consisted of just three thousand under the command of Caius Famimius and Lucius Manlius Acidinus, and was strengthened in 169 B.C. with the arrival of one-hundred sixty nine more families. See P.S. Leicht, *A History of Friuli*, for excellent details on Friuli's early history.

[18] Modena is also the place where the famous Italian car marker, Ferrari, is based.

[19] Poem to Scrope Bedmore Davis, Esq.

[20] This artistic connection with Verona is interesting, as the consensus amongst art historians who have examined Fiore's figures in the Getty and Morgan treatises, is that they are quite definitely Veronese in influence.

[21] The contents of the library are noted in two studies: in A. Capelli's study of the 1467 inventory and in the 1903 study by Bertini. Mr. Matthew Galas, Mr. Steven Hick and Mr. Brian Stokes have pushed forward and are working on even more detailed accounts of the manuscripts in the Este collection that may shed light on whether there are three or five known treatises by Fiore.

[22] On the efforts to reduce these incursions and the lackluster results see William Caferro, "Slaying the Hydra-Headed Beast: Italy and the Companies of Adventure in the Fourteenth Century" in *Crusaders, Condottieri, and Cannon: Medieval Warfare in Societies around the Meditteranean*.

[23] Bull issued by Pope Urban V, 1364. Drawn from *Storia d'Italia*, ed. Nino Valeri.

[24] Frizzi, *Storia di Ferrara,* unattributed translation on the Internet alongside Byron's poem, http:photosspects.com/chesil/byron/parisina.html.

[25] What the Italians refer to as the *trecento*, as the dates are within the thirteen hundreds (1300-1399).

[26] Some biographical work was done by Luigi Zanutto, *Fiore di Premariacco ed i ludi e le feste marziali e civili in Friuli nel Medio-evo, drawn from various civic records* (1907) but even in this work very little corroboration was established.

[27] Different scholars working on Fiore's background attribute his origin to Cividale or Premariacco, both of which are in the region of Friuli. Premariacco is not mentioned in the Pissani-Dossi version, but it is included in both the Morgan and Getty.

[28] The question of Fiore's claimed nobility is not clear. Most scholars have translated *messire* to mean "Sir," although I have seen no civic records that correlate the knightly rank of a Benedetto dei Liberi. Indeed, it is not clear that Fiore himself is indeed part of the ancient and noble dei Liberi family of Premariacco; we do not find any records that Fiore himself was knighted during his lifetime, nor does he claim the title knight anywhere in his known writing. Additionally, we find in his prologue several of the *condottieri* captains he mentions as *cavaliero*, titles which seem to accurately reflect corroborating records relating to these men. I suspect that Fiore claims the noble family on very loose terms as a method of establishing legitimacy, although there is a chance that we may discover something more concrete.

[29] Getty MS Fol.1.

[30] I know of no records that state at what age a *scrimatore* might expect to receive such a title during this period, but it would be an excellent thread for the next generation of students to research.

[31] The same phrase is mentioned in the Morgan, Fol. 1v.

[32] To my knowledge no satisfactory definition of the phrases *à plaisance* or *à outrance* have yet been offered within the literature on the medieval tournament.

[33] This same claim is made by nearly every author of a fighting treatise from the 14th and 15th century, so I wonder if perhaps it is a legitimizing tool or if Fiore truly did travel to learn his art. It is possible, if "messire" Benedetto had some small holding of land, a trade or business, that Fiore could have had the means to travel and study, but I have seen no evidence that he did so. One interesting clue is that he specifically names a German master, in the diocese of Metz, a John called *Suveno*, a "scholar of Nicholai of Toblem." With luck, future researchers can shed more light in this reference, which is included only in the Pisani-Dossi Latin prologue, Carta 2A.

[34] The Morgan treatise differs very little and may be considered essentially the same.

[35] The direct citations are given in the sidebar, but mention is also made in Matt Easton's 2003 article and on various websites that describe Fiore's early life.

[36] Francesco Novati claims that Fiore came back to Friulia midway through the year in 1383, but unfortunately he offers no further evidence beyond the city annals cited. I do not believe it has been established where Fiore was between 1384, when the last annal record was made, and the next mention of him, made in Padua (1395). Luigi Zanutto (p. 197) claims, also without evidence, that Fiore became a wandering *magistro* after this time, but there is precious little fact upon which to make a conclusion. As Matt Easton asserts, this agrees with Fiore's claim made in his own prologue that he traveled to study with masters and scholars, as well as noblemen, but this cannot, regrettably, be considered evidence.

[37] Luigi Zanutto, *Fiore di Premariacco ed i ludi e le feste marziali e civili in Friuli nel Medio-evo*, p. 212.

[38] Municipal Archive of Udine, *Deliber. Consoli Civit Utini*, v. VII, c. 239, cited in Novati, note 48.

[39] Municipal Archive of Udine, *Deliber. Consoli Civit Utini*, v. VII, c. 208, cited in Novati, note 47.

[40] Municipal Archive of Udien, *Annales*, vol. VOO, c. 78, cited in Novati, note 49.

[41] Francesco Novati discusses the location of Italian fencings schools near to the taverns (see note 39), and Sydney Anglo makes the same assertion for the English masters at arms in his *The Martial Arts of Renaissance Europe*, p. 7-8.

[42] The Getty text is essentially the same.

[43] There is a note at the end of the martial poem in the PD, that claims Fiore studied for fifty years, rather than forty, *Che cinquanta anni in tal arte ostudiado, Chi inmen tempo piu so elne bon mercado* [PD Carta 2B]. I believe this is perhaps a boast, since he claims earlier in the prologue to have studied for more than forty years, not fifty. It is also possible that the verse was added sometime later.

[44] Mr. Gian Lorenzo Mellini, writing in 1962, attributed several of the Morgan illustrations (2v-8v) to Altichiero himself. "Designi di Altichiero e di sua scuola, 1" in *Critica d'Arte*, LI, May-June 1962 and "Disegni di altichiero e della sua scuola, 2," *Critica d'Arte*, LIII-LIV, September-December 1962, 9-19.

[45] Mr. Steve Hick, personal communication.

[46] The bibliographic card catalog from the J. Pierpont Morgan library lists 20 leaves.

[47] From the Morgan card catalog, the manuscript's history gives a list of owners: Giacomo Soranzo (no dates); Matteo Luigi Canonici (1727-1805); Walter Sneyd (1809-1888); J. Pierpoint Morgan.

[48] From the sale description of Ludwig XV 13, obtained from the Getty Museum by the author.

[49] After this the manuscript was sold to Peter and Irene Ludwig, from a Sothebys auction in 1966. This information was provided by Matt Galas, personal communication. It seems likely that the current leather binding, c. 1800, was done at the behest of Luigi Celotti, probably in London.

[50] Iron gall ink is primarily made from tannin (most often extracted from galls), vitriol (iron sulfate), gum, and water. Because of its indelible nature, it was the medium of choice for important papers and many drawings. When new, the ink created a velvety, deep, appealing black. Through age, however, it turns a warm iron oxide brown, and it begins to interact with the medium—in this case vellum—in an acidic and destructive manner. Much research is being carried on to protect important documents and manuscripts from the Middle Ages. See especially *The Ink Corrosion Website*, http://www.knaw.nl/ECPA/ink/index.html.

[51] The 1436 inventory has been studied by V. Camera.

[52] Francesco Novati gives inventory records from the d'Este library that show that this book was in the library until 1508, at which point it disappears. In note sixty-six Novti includes all of the original citations, which I reproduce here for the convenience of modern students:

"1436: Libro uno da insignare de scremia afigurado et cum lettere per vulgare in membrane compilado per M° Fiore Furlan coperto de chore roso. [V. Camera c.65]"

"1467: Liberi Bellicosus vocatus Florius friuiloensis docens forma actgorum dimicandi in duello litteris cursivis in membranis forma parga figuratus diversis modis in pluribus et diverssis cartis cum litteris super figures cum Aquilla alba et doubus Cimeriis pictis super prima carta chopertus montanina alba cum brochis et uno azullo. Cartarum inter scriptas et non scriptas 58, Signatus numero 84. [V. Cancelleria c.1]"

"1474: Item uno libro de bataglie ditto fiorio n° 84. [V. Camera c. VI]"

"1508: Florius firliviensis figuratusin membranis numero 84. [V. Cancelleria c.15]"

[53] Francesco Novati again gives the useful original citations in his notes, but there is a curiosity. The final entry lists the number not as 110, but 111, which Mr. Novati has taken to be an error by Bartolomeo Silvestri, when he mixed up the reference with *another* treatise on war, #111, which was in the library. Investigation on exactly what manuscript 111 was remains to be published.

"1436: Libro uno de fati de arme fato per M° fiorio et da combatiere in membrane couerto de una carta senza alueu. [V. Camera c.39 & Capelli, p. 18]"

"1467: Liber in Arte Duelli in cartis membranis forma parua littera cursiua in columnis editus per Florium Friuiolensem cohopertus carta pecudna sine tabullis cartarum 15. Singatus numero 110. [V. Cancelleria, c.4]"

"1480: Libro da combatere, no. 110 [V. Camera, c.7]"

"1508: Item liber Florii Furliani sine albis. In papiro numero 111 (sic) [V. Cancellerita c. 15]"

[54] There are a couple of other problems with this theory, too. First, Francesco Novati refers to No. 84 as a "small" volume, which the Morgan's 10 7/8 x 8 5/8" measurement hardly lines up (if Novati's assertion is correct). Second, Galeazzo is mentioned in the Morgan prologue in the third person past, so it is unlikely that it was intended for him. Third, the Morgan is probably an unfinished manuscript, as it contains one or more penciled illustrations. And finally, the current record at the Morgan has the treatise at 20 leaves, rather than the of-cited 15, and was bound in the early 1800s by J. Clark. However, it is an interesting theory and there are possibilities for error: Are any of the 20 leaves fillers designed to make even signatures? Could Novati's information about the measurements be incorrect? More research is needed to answer these and many other questions, but the idea remains intruiging.

[55] There is good evidence for this as there is at least one error in the previous bindery that has been convincingly argued for by Mr. Bob Charron according to the letter he forwarded to me and to the Getty Museum making the case for a reordering of an aborted translation facsimile project.

[56] Robb Lovett, Mark Lancaster and Matt Easton have both taken this position, and I find it viable. It is certainly possible that the PD was later than the other two treatises, but that the artist retained to do the drawings had been trained earlier and was not familiar with the cutting-edge equipment shown in the Morgan and Getty treatises. However, the problem remains that several elements of armoured harness present in the Getty are unknown to have been developed before 1415-1420, and the PD is dated 1409.

[57] The content of the Getty is essentially the same.

[58] It is highly unlikely that he did the work, although F. Novati has made a little of the case in his notes, believing that Fiore perhaps studied with Altichiero himself.

[59] The first prologue included in the PD is in Latin, but its contents are substantially repeated in the second prologue, in the "vulgar" or common Italian language, albeit in dialect. The reason for the inclusion of this first Latin prologue is not clear, but it is not a direct repeat or translation of the Italian that follows.

[60] I have handled the original manuscript, and there could be some sort of encoding that accompanies the red and blue letters, but this awaits further investigation.

[61] A likely route of inquiry would be into the floriated ornament and paleography of the specific hand used to write the treatise. It is likely that studies of these two elements in all three surviving manuscripts would add valuable data to the dating and point of origin questions.

[62] The Getty Museum lists in their card catalog for the *Fior di Battaglia*, "The style is very reminiscent of the drawings of armed men attributed to the Veronese artist Altichiero. While it is clear that Altichiero could not have made the drawings c. 1410, since he died in c. 1385, it is evident that Fiore must have studied under him or in his school, as the resemblance to his style is close."

[63] A needed avenue of research would be to look into the potential relationship between Altichiero and Nicollo II and III, and to find other Veronese or Paduan artists listed as being commissioned by them during 1380-1420.

[64] This keen observation must be credited to Schola Saint George *scolaro* Scott Thomas, and I am thankful for his comments made at the Western Martial Arts Workshop, Dallas, TX, October 2006.

[65] The *zuparello* seems to have been very similar to the gambeson or arming cote of Northern Europe. It was quilted, fitted at the waist, and seems to have been closely related to, or a synonym for, *farsetto*. One possibility is that the *zuparello* might refer to the military version, but it is more likely perhaps that the two words were used interchangeably. In any event a *farsetto* is agreed by numerous scholars to have been a quilted garment with probable military origins, made of wool, linen and fustian, lined and stuffed to make a kind of quilting. See especially Jacqueline Herald and Rosita Levi-Pizetski.

[66] Translation based upon a modified version of the Exiles work, used by permission.

[67] See my paper on this topic, *Birds of a Feather*, delivered Summer 2005, at the SCA's Known World Rattan Symposium, Kansas City, MO.

[68] One possible exception is the *butte di punta*, what I translate as "casting the point," which relies on a levered motion similar to that employed when casting a fishing rod to propel the tip forward with a great velocity—but without much force. The result is generally a strike with the point that can either be a thrust or a cut, depending upon how it lands.

[69] Also published by Chivalry Bookshelf as *Arte Gladiatoria: Master 15th Century Swordsmanship of Master Filippo Vadi*, translated by Luca Porzio & Gregory Mele, 2002.

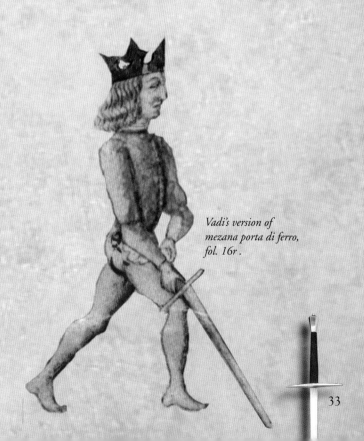

Vadi's version of mezana porta di ferro, fol. 16r .

[F]iurlan de Ci
uida dostria
che fo di chusi
Benedetto de
la nobel casada
deli liberi da
Premeryas d
la dyocesi dilo
patriarchado
de Aquilegia
in sua conuentu
uolse imprender ad armizare
e arte de combatter in sbarra
De lanca Acca Spada e da
ga e de abrazare a pe e acaual
lo in arme e senca arme
Anchora uolse sauere tempere
di ferri E fatecce d caschuna
Arma tanto a defendere quato
ad offendere e maxima mente
chose de combatter adoltranca
Anchora altre chose merauegliose
e oculte le quale a pochi homini
del mondo sono palese E sono
chose uerissime e d grandissima
offesa e de grande deffesa e chose
che cio si po fallare tanto sono
lude a fare La quale arte e
magisterio che ditto di sopra
E lo ditto fiore sia imprese le
ditte chose da molti magistri
todeschi E di molti Italiani
in piu puince in molte citad
cu grandissima e cu grand spese
E p la gracia a dio da tati ma
gistri e scolari E in corte di
grandi Signori principi duchi
Marchesi e conti chaualieri e
Schudieri in tanto a ipresa gsta
arte Che lo ditto fiore a stado
piu e piu uolte richesto da molti
Signori e chaualieri e schudieri
p imprender del ditto fiore si fatta
arte darmizare e d combatter i sbarra
a oltranca laquale arte ello a mon
strida a piusori ytaliani e todeschi
e altri grandi Signori che ano de
budo combattere in sbarra E
Ancho ad infiniti che non ano debu
do combattere E de alguni che

sono stadi miei Scolari che ano dbudo
cobatter in sbarra De quali alchuni
qui ne faro nome e memoria Como
de loro si fo el nobele e gagliardo cha
ualiero Missier piero del verde el qle
debea conbattere cu a Missier piero
Sla corona iquali feruno ambi doy
todeschi E la Batugla debea esser
a perosa Anchora alo ualoroso
chaualiero Missier Nicolo voricilino
thodesto che debea cobatteré cu Nicolo
Inghleso Lo campo fo dado ad Imola
Anchora al notubele ualoroso e
gagliardo chaualiero Missie Galeazo
di Captani di Grimello chiamado di
Mantua che debea cobattere cu lo ua
loroso chaualiero Missier Bucichar
do de fraca lo campo fo a Padua E
Anchora al ualoroso sthudiero Lan
calotto da Becharia de pauia el qle
se in punti de lanca a ferri mola
di a chauallo contra lo ualente ca
ualiero Missier Baldassaro todesho
iquali ad ymola debea cobatteré in
sbarra Anchora al ualoroso
Schudiero Coanino da Bayo da mi
lano che se in pauia in lo castello
contra lo ualente Schudiero Sram
todesto tre punti di lanca a ferri
moladi a chauallo E poy se a pe
tre colpi d Acca e tre colpi d Spada
e tre colpi di daga ipresenca del
nobilissimo priapo e Signore Mis
ser lo Ducha di Milano e d Madona
La duchessa e altri infiniti Signo
ri e donne Anchora al caute
loso chaualiero Missier Acro da
Castell Barcho che debea una uolta
cobatter cum Cuanne di Ordelaffi
E un altra uolta cu lo ualente
e boy chaualiero Missier Iacomo
da Boson el campo debea esser al
piascre delo Signore ducha di ai
lano di questi e daltri iquali io
fiore e magistradi io soy molto
contento p che io son stado ben rimu
nerito e o habudo lonore e lamore
di miei Scolari e di parenti loro
Digo Anchora che questa arte io lo
mostrada sempre oculta mente
siche no gle sta presente alchuno

CHAPTER THREE

THE FIOR DI BATTAGLIA

"Io Fiore sapiando legere, e scrivere, e disegnare, e habiendo libri in quest'arte e in ley o studiato ben xl anni o piu..e vogliando che di mi sia fatta memoria in ella, io faro un libro in tua larte…segundo l'ordene lo quale ma dado quell alto Signore [Getty F.1]."

"I, Fiore, knowing how to read, to write and to draw, and having books in the art [of combat], studied the art for 40 years or more…and desiring that I should be remembered in it, I made a book of the whole Art… according to the order which my noble lord [Niccolò III] gave to me."

n this chapter we'll focus on Fiore's superb books, their content and the keys to understanding the *spada a due mani,* "sword in two hands," as well as Fiore's other weapons. We will survey the book's title, examine his ordering of the contents, and look in detail at the sections of the Prologue in which Fiore explains how to interpret his drawings. The books were meant to be easy to understand, and his stated goal was to make the Art of Arms understood *per piu chiareza*—"for more clarity." Fiore's system may be unlocked using the keys he offers in the Prologue. Once unlocked, the *Fior di Battaglia* is a rich mine from which to draw knowledge about medieval and early Renaissance fighting technique.

WHAT'S IN A NAME

Fiore's book is called *Fior di Battaglia*—the "Flower of Battle."[1] Because the PD version is preceeded by a Latin prologue, it carries its title in Latin, the *Flos Duellatorum.* The translation is essentially the same.

It is uncertain why Fiore might have called his text the *Flower of Battle,* although it may represent a play on Fiore's name (which means "flower") and the "flower of knighthood" imagery popular in chivalric literature. Taking his claims to have traveled widely at face value, Fiore would have developed his system based on the best and most effective techniques and principles he observed. I believe that he meant the title also as the "flower" of the age's finest techniques for battle, gathered together. As with other surviving treatises, each of Fiore's techniques or "plays" is an illustration of a martial principle, more than a depiction of a technique. The system is thus taught by example, with variations on core principles according to the performance characteristics of each weapon.

CONTENT OVERVIEW

While the content of all three treatises is not identical, they are so strongly similar that they are clearly of a group. The Getty and Morgan treatises contain near identical phraseology, save that the Morgan is much abridged and probably incomplete. The PD is, as I have posited in the previous chapter, probably earlier and may represent a rougher and less refined expression of the techniques and their underlying principles expressed in the other two versions.

All three include an informational or legitimizing Prologue that contains biographical information, a summary of the included techniques, and an introduction explaining his motives for writing the book, a mixture of a modern preface and introduction.[2] He discusses the manuscript keys, the visual references that explain how the figures in the technique sections should be understood. Next follows the weapon-specific segments, starting usually with the *guardie* or *poste,* flowing then into a series of techniques or plays. The *daga* and *spada* sections are further prefaced by plates with drawn figures depicting the angles and targets of the primary *colpi* (strikes or blows) and *punte* (thrusts).

Fiore's plays are illustrated pairs of combatants drawn with some detail, accompanied by an explanatory paragraph, a *glosa,* or in the case of the PD, a rhyming rubric. As discussed above, the plays themselves represent principles illustrated by specific techniques. These techniques are employed in a particular context where Fiore has shown, I believe, his optimium execution for a particular place and time and in response to a specific set of movements by the opponent.[3] In order to understand, internalize and integrate these techniques into a fighting repertoire, the combatant must be able first to comprehend the play or *zhogo* itself, but more importantly, he must grasp the concept *underlying* the play. These underlying principles represent the core combat fundamentals—and are expressed as Fiore's tactical framework.[4] When interpreting or learning these or any play recorded in an historical treatise, I believe that is far more important to internalize this essence and then to be able to apply it in to any appropriate sitation under the stress of a fight. This is not easy, but as it turns out there are nowhere near as many principles expressed as there are plays, so once they are internalized, a senior *scolari* will in fact be able to discover the later plays on their own—because they make tactical sense—or to innovate within the framework of Fiore's tactical sensibilities. The Schola's objective is to provide a foundation upon which our students can grow and to make their

Sample text from two of the three manuscripts. Above, from the PD section on the colpi *and below from the Getty. One of the challenges for a modern interpreter is deciphering the handwriting of the original, including the many abbreviations. This is the art of* paleography. *From the original hand, a* transcription *is made. The language of the* transcription *may then be translated into a modern language, taking into account the local dialect and changes in word meaning in the intervening centuries.*

own solid contributions to the evolving reconstructions of this ancient art.

Indeed, the principles that bind Fiore's art together are a simple, effective and coherent system applicable to any form of hand-to-hand combat. Fiore presents techniques grouped together by weapon type, illustrating variants on core principles based on the nuances and performance characteristics of each weapon. But as a system the modern student could begin with any weapon, so long as the core principles are internalized. But as Fiore does not articulate the principles clearly within the text, their identification is open to considerable interpretation.

Another important element of the text is what is *not* said. There is very little discussion of time, feinting or falsing, or about the fundamentals of footwork and nothing about the development of power or even how to hold the sword, leaving much that must be inferred. The modern student of Fiore's work must interpret these foundational elements or rely on their interpretations of their instructors. Within the context of the Schola, we have done this by testing our assumptions and interpretations in many open and focused sparring encounters, striving to continually improve our understanding of what might have been intended.

THE FORMS OF COMBAT

Fiore's art encompasses techniques in and out of armour, on foot and on horseback. It includes unarmed combat, *abrazzare*, which is similar to Japanese Ju-jitsu with its reliance on control through joint manipulations (*abrazzare* means, literally, "to the arms"). It includes work with and against a single rondel dagger, *la daga*. There is a limited amount of transitional material that focuses on a baton, and some staff or stick material. But the use of the sword in one hand, *spada a una mano*, and two, *spada a due mani*, comprises a significant portion of each manuscript. There are also some plays with the spear, *lanza*, and the polehammer or poleaxe, *azza*. Finally, there are applications of Fiore's principles to fighting on horseback.

While the material in all three treatises is very similar, it is not quite the same. There are techniques in some versions which are omitted from others, but there remains a very strong concordance. The order varies, and indeed we do not really know how Fiore taught the material, as he suggests that the ordering of the material in the Getty and PD may have been directed by the Marquis himself:

> "Começamo lo libro segondo lordinamento del mio signore Marchese e façemo che non gli manchi nienti in larte che io mi rendo conto che lo mio Signore mi fara merito perla sua grande nobilita e cortesia. [Getty F.3v]"

> "We start this book following the order of my lord the Marquis, and I will make it so that he lacks nothing in my rendered Art, and that my Lord will make it good to me due to his great courtesy and nobility."[5]

As I have argued, I see the presentation of the Getty and Morgan manuscripts as more evolved and refined than those of the PD, and indeed we can see that there is an evolution in some aspects of the system between the two treatises.

Although we do not know how Fiore taught his art, but we do know that he applied his techniques to a wide variety of weapons in common use at the time in all manner of personal defense situations, in deeds of arms and in war.

In each section, the figures begin with a series of *guardie* or *poste*, core fighting positions. There is continuity of these positions from weapon to weapon, but there are also important variations according to the properties of each weapon type. Sometimes, as in the case of the *lanza* and *azza*, not all of the *poste* possible are given—only those that take into account the weapon's special capabilities are depicted, but the slight variations on the core *poste* are implied.[6] Indeed, in each *posta* description Fiore generally offers a core movement or technique that epitomizes that position and it is from these descriptions that the six plays offered in chapter 11 are largely drawn.

CONTENT COMPARED FOR THE THREE SURVIVING COPIES OF THE FIOR DI BATTAGLIA

	Getty	Pissani-Dossi	Morgan
Prologues	F. 3r-4r (3 pages)	C. 2a-2b (2 pages)	F. 1v – F. 2v (3 pages)
Abrazzare - grappling	F. 6 – F. 8 (5 pages)	C. 4a-5b (3 pages)	--
Bastoncello and/or staff	F. 8v, 31, 31v (3 pages)	C. 15a (1 page)	18v
Daga - dagger	F. 9-19v, +38,38v (22 pages)	C. 6a-12b (14 pages) C. 35a-36a (2 pages)	18v, 19r, 17v
Spada a una mano - sword in one hand	F. 20-21 (3 pages)	C. 13a-14b (4 pages)	10-11v, 18r
Spada a due mano - sword in two hands	F. 21v-31 (19 pages)	C. 17b-24b (15 pages)	F. 12-17, 18v
Segno	F. 32 (1 page)	C. 17a (1 page)	--
Spada en arme - sword in armour	F. 32v-35 (6 pages)	C. 25a-26b (4 pages)	19v
Azza - poleaxe	F. 35v-37v (5 pages)	C. 27a-28a (3 pages)	--
Lanza - spear	F. 39-40 (3 pages)	C. 15b -16b (3 pages)	--
Equestrian	F. 41-47 (13 pages)	C. 29a-34b (12 pages)	F. 2v-9v (17 pages)

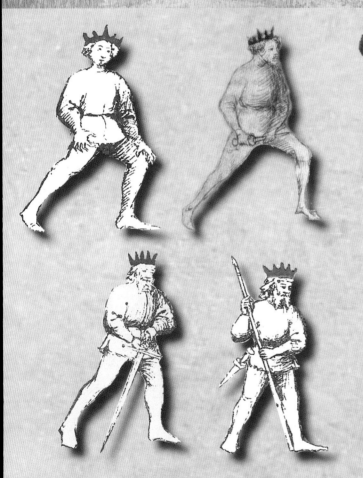

Poste porta di ferro from the abrazzare, daga, spada and lanza compared. Note the continuity of positional integrity—the same poste can be seen throughout the system and applied to any hand weapon. Although the relationships in the PD manuscript are evident, they seem far more refined in the Getty, represented by a single example (upper right). The three other figures are from the PD.

Abrazzare—unarmed combat

As noted above, *abrazzare* means "to the arms." In Fiore's system, the grappling or *abrazzare* is a method of increasing control over the opponent through his body, especially by manipulating the joints. The combatant may also make a *presa*—a grapple—against the body or against the opponent's weapon. This strikes many practitioners of Asian martial arts as familiar, a fact which should be no real surprise, as the human body has changed little in the six hundred intervening years, and not at all between East and West.

This section is often called "wrestling," by modern students, but it is more akin to the lightning-quick seizure of control in Ju-jitsu or Aki-jitsu[7] than with modern collegiate or Greco-Roman wrestling. The idea seems to have been to seize and establish control immediately, and to thwart the opponent's attempt at the same. Colin Hatcher, our instructor for grappling and dagger work, has highlighted the distinctions between wrestling and grappling, strongly suggesting that a better term for what Fiore teaches is *grappling*, rather than *wrestling*.

It has been offered by many modern interpreters that Fiore's system is based upon wrestling, and that it cannot be learned without first learning wrestling. Clearly, Fiore was a stunningly effective grappler, and the tactical principle of maximizing control runs as a constant thread through all of his plays. But Fiore was a realist, and he tempers his favor for *prese* with the following:

"Lomo che uole abraça se lo compagno e piu forte o sello e piu grande di persona e sello troppo zouene o uero troppo uecchio. Anchora de uedere se mette ale guardie dabraçare e de tutte queste chose si e de preudere. [Getty 3v]."

"The man who *abrazza* (comes to the arms) wants to note whether the *compagno* is stronger, larger, younger or older. He wants to note all of these things and to see if he takes the *guardie d'abrazzare* (guards of wrestling); all of these things may be observed [before engaging]."

First play of the *abrazzare* play from the Getty manuscript showing an arm bar, fol. 6v.

Within the Schola we generally introduce the wrestling plays later in the curriculum, based on our desire to keep the material compelling and to increase safety. Many beginning students are uncomfortable with body to body contact, but they are comfortable and well pleased to wield a sword. If they are serious and stay with the training over time, they will see the *abrazzare* integrated with a module that focuses on the *zhogo stretto*—close play—building from the grappling, through the *daga*, and coming finally back to the sword in two hands.

The *abrazzare* opens the PD and Getty manuscripts—the two "ordered" by the Marquis—but it is absent entirely from the Morgan, although the mounted *abrazzare* techniques are depicted. There are not many grappling plays offered, but what is included is a simple, effective system of hand-to-hand combat reminiscent in many ways to modern krav maga—just a few techniques that can be mixed and matched to meet any hand-to-hand defense situation.

"Anchora digo che labraçare uole auere viii chose çoe forteça presteça sauere çoe sauer prese auantiçade, sauere far roture çoe romper braçi e gambe, sauer ligar braçi permodo chel homo non habia piu defensa ne se possa partire in sua liberta, sauer ferire in luogo piu periculoso. Le quale tutte chose scriuiro e poro depinte in questo libro de grado in grado chomo uole arte [Getty F.4v]."

"Also I say that the *abrazzare* requires eight things: **strength** (*forteza*), **speed** (*presteza*), **knowledge** (*sauere*); knowing how make **grips** (*prese*), knowing how to **anticipate** (*auantiçade*), to make *roture*, namely **breaking** (*romper*) the arms and legs. Knowing how to **bind** (*ligar*) his arms so the opponent has less defense and cannot freely move. [Finally], knowing how to **injure** (*ferire*) at the vulnerable points. [All about] which I write and depict in this book step by step, as the Art requires."[8]

The *abrazzare* begin with just four *poste*, which we'll examine later in this book as they form the foundation for our stance and footwork. By transitioning through these four *poste* and seeking to control the opponent through his arms—if available—or by throwing him to the ground, the idea is to gain and maximize control.

"Noi auemo ditto ço che uole labraçare si po fare per diuersi modi. E un modo e migliore del altro. Ma queste iiii guardie so le migliore in arme e sençarme auegna dio che le guardie non a stabilita per la prese subite che se fano [Getty 4v]."

"We have said that he who wants to *abrazzare* can do so in many ways and that one method is better than the others. But these four guards know how to best come against me in and out of armour. [Other] guards do not have stability for the *prese* that these can make."

"Elli primi quatro Magistri che uederiti cum le corone in testa per quegli in testa per quegli si nostra le guardie del abraçare çoe posta longa e dente di çengiaro le quale fano una incontra laltra, e poy fano porta di ferro e posta frontale luna incontra laltra. [Getty f.4v]"

"The first four *magistri* that are drawn with a crown on their heads show the guards of *abrazzare* named **posta longa** and **dente di zenghiaro**, each encountering the other, which can then make **porta di ferro** and **posta frontale**, one encountering the other."

One of two types of throw within Fiore's system. In this variation, the upper body is pressed while the lower body is pulled. The resulting "push-pull" is effective even against a larger opponent. The original figures are on fol. 6v of the Getty manuscript.

Throws are made simply and effectively simply by extending to *posta longa* and stepping through and casting the opponent over the knee or hip, or counter-balancing him with a push above paired with a simultaneous pull below. In all cases the combatant remains standing, his stance upright and his head alert. This is required because multiple opponents are always a possibility. There is no ground-fighting, as there is in the German material or in modern Brazilian Ju-jitsu.

> "Anchora saue mettere uno in terra sença periculo di si instesso. Anchora sauer dislogar braçi e gambi per diuersi modi [Getty f.4v]."

> "Also knowing how to take one to the ground without peril of the same. And knowing many ways to dislocate the arms and legs."

The system is meant both for unarmoured opponents—*disarmado* or *senza arme*—and for those *en arme*. In all cases there is an emphasis on the control of the joints using *ligadura* (binds), *roture* (breaks)—which are really binds or locks—and *dislogatura*, dislocations. Fiore's art is highly developed in this regard, although many of the techniques are shown only the *daga* section that follows and they are possible with all weapons.

Similarly, combatants must know how to strike at the delicate points, *ferire in luogo piu periculoso*, and:

> "E se lo tuo inimigo e disarmado attende a ferirlo in lo loghi piu doglosi e piu periculosi çoe in glochi in lo naso inle femine sottol mento e in li fianchi. E niente meno guarda si tu puo uegnire ale prese dele ligadure o armado o disarmado che fosse luno e laltro [Getty 3v]."

> "...If your enemy is unarmoured, wait to injure in the places more grevious and vulnerable, namely in the eyes, on the nose, in the soft under the chin and in the groin (hips). And if nothing else watch to see if he can come against you with a *prese* of the *ligadura*, armoured or not, which is one against the other."

Bastoncello / first transitions

Following the *abrazzare* section in the Getty and PD are a very few techniques with the short baton or *bastoncello*. These techniques serve as transitional material[9] to the much larger *daga* section that follows, illustrating how the principles can be generalized and applied to short sticks—or to gloves or a hat—while standing or even while sitting!

Daga or dagger from the first page of Fiore's text. The spike at the pommel is not known to be something that was actually made or used, but an imaginative adaptation.

La daga—dagger

By far and away the most numerous plays in the Getty and PD[10] are with and against the rondel dagger or *daga*. This long, acutely tapered blade generally did not feature an edge during Fiore's time, and it was the weapon most likely to be encountered by a man in a personal defense context, as they were worn ubiquitously at the belt by men of all stations.[11]

Daga poste from the Getty, fol. 9

Long and pointed—like a sharpened screwdriver—the *daga* would have been capable of punching through defenses of mail and being worked into the spaces between armour, such as at the armpit, elbow, neck or waist.

In the Getty, Fiore first presents his *daga poste*, the five *magistri della daga*,[12] which also follow in the way of the *poste*:

> "Como noy auemo parlado qui dinançi de le guardie debrazare…Et perlo simile cum la azza, ecum la spada duna mano e de dey mani. E perlo simile cum la daga [Getty F.4r]."

> "As we have spoken before with the guards of the *abrazzare*, similarly for the axe, for the sword in one and two hands, and for the dagger."

Within the dagger plays, many of the deflecting motions (*rebattemento* and *redoppiando*) which form the core of his methods of controlling the opponent's sword are found. Indeed, Fiore also demonstrates how to counter a sword with just a dagger. Many of these plays focus on countering a dagger attack while unarmed, smoothly blending techniques introduced in the *abrazzare* section, building on and extending the same principles.

Within the Getty manuscript there are more than eighty dagger techniques, compared to the three with the *lanza* (spear) or the perhaps twenty-five with the *spada* (sword). There are a similar number in the PD, but only a few in the Morgan.

It has been said that Fiore's *daga* work is merely, "*abrazzare* with the *daga*," and this is at least partially true, at least in close work (what the Germans refer to as the *krieg* and which Fiore seems to denote with the phrase *zhogo stretto*). Some have extended this cogent observation to work with the *spada*, *lanza*, and *azza*; but I think this overlooks Fiore's keen insight into the properties of these weapons and oversimplifies his approach, even though it is true with a subset of the plays, the *zhogo stretto*. Much of Fiore's art takes place at a wider distance (*zhogo largo*), not only because some weapons are more effective at that range, but since it is also not tactically sound to always close with an opponent, especially if there is a possibility of intereference by his companions and because as one closes, the opponent's options for attacks multiply because he can both strike more of the companion's body and use more of his secondary weapons (feet, hands, head, pommel, secondary *daga*, etc.).

Many of the *daga* techniques involve first checking the opponent's dagger—capturing it or stopping it and then controlling it if he strikes first—then extending this control with *prese* of the *abrazzare*:

Daga play from the Getty, fol. 10v, demonstrated by Schola compagni.

ligadura, *disligadura*, or taking him to the ground with a throw (*mettere in terra*). This pattern of arresting the opponent's attack or his ability to attack, fixing his weapon(s), and then following-on with a potentially devastating final attack characterizes the system as a whole, but it reaches its most thorough expression in the eighty-odd plays of the *daga* section.[13]

La spada a una mano—sword in one hand
The Italian word for sword during Fiore's time was simply *spada*, and that this kind of sword could be wielded either in one or two hands. While the majority of Fiore's sword material focuses on the sword in two hands, there are sections in all three surviving manuscripts on one-handed methods. This moderately long-handled weapon is what collectors or reenactors would call a "bastard" or "hand and a half" sword, and Fiore's text covers fighting with it without a buckler:[14]

"Poy trouariti uno magistro contra iii scolari chef e el zogho de la spada d'una mane sença bucolero [PD Carta 2a]."

"Next we find a *magistro* opposite three chief *scolari* and the play of the sword in one hand sans buckler."

Fiore's uses the single-handed sword to set aside attacks. In this plate, Getty fol. 20, the magistro (right) does not face three opponents; but he will meet all kinds of attacks—each represented by a single opponent—including thrown weapons (left), strikes or colpi (center), and thrusts or punte (right).

Fiore's approach to the sword in one hand is simple. The weapon is held low, in what must be considered a *pulsativa* position,[15] well-wound and ready to strike. If there is no way to strike safely with cover, incoming attacks are met with a sweeping motion that sets the blow aside and either maintains the dominance with the *punta* by expending the opponent's weapon (see chapter 10). Essentially Fiore does both the *redoppiando* and the *rebattemento* using the single sword, downplaying its lack of strength against other weapons and extending the combatant's control once the *incrosa* has been established. These techniques are very similar to those shown in the *spada a due mani*, although they are also excellent auxiliary sources for some of the *zhogo largo* and *zhogo stretto* plays.

For each technique shown in the *spada a due mani* section, there are certainly analogues of how the underlying principles can be applied to the sword in one hand, since the kinesthetics of the movements are based on similar physics.[16] Schola students often select *spada a una mano* as the first "secondary" weapon they study as an application exercise, and those within combat societies such as the SCA find that this is immensely useful to their tournament skills.

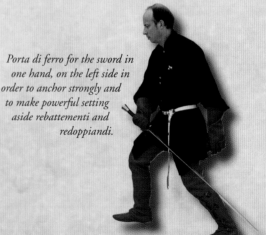

Porta di ferro for the sword in one hand, on the left side in order to anchor strongly and to make powerful setting aside rebattementi and redoppiandi.

La spada a due mani—sword in two hands

For the Schola, the sword in two hands is the core section of the treatise. Our students usually begin by studying swordwork, although there are variant syllabi whereby students begin with another weapon, but cover the same core principles examined in this book.

Fiore's *spada a due mani* sections comprise the bulk of non-dagger material included, starting again with the *poste* or *guardia*. Next follows the *zhogo largo*—the "wide" or "long" play—where combatants meet outside the distance that enables grappling. As we will see, I firmly believe that Fiore's presentation of the *zhogo largo* offers students a solid tactical framework that guides the dangerous entry phase of a fight. The object during this phase is to first "taste" the opponent's guard to see if there is an opening, striking if one is present. Then a *volta* or turn will bring the sword to the other side. If either of these actions are countered and the opponent finds cover, the swords will be crossed—*incrosare*—in the Second Master of the Crossed Swords. From this point, the other plays of the *zhogo largo* and *zhogo stretto* are made depending upon the circumstance. In general, the section begins with very long-distance play and works towards closer, more dangerous encounters.

This close play is the *zhogo stretto*, a far more dangerous state to enter if a corresponding increase of control does not accompany it. For this reason an increase in the level of control is sought, first by contact in the *incrosa*, next through various elements of the *abrazzare*, essentially "wrestling with the sword." All of the *ligadure* (binds), *dislogature*, and throws (*mettere di terra*) are available, along with secondary strikes from the hands, feet, pommel, etc.

Together, the *zhogo largo* and the *zhogo stretto* provide a holistic tactical framework through which combat with the sword in two hands may be understood. They make an algorithm of "if-then" statements that simplify the analysis necessary to ascertain an appropriate, safe, and effective follow-on action. The framework will be more fully presented in Book II as it comprises the foundation of our second level actions, to be studied once the core elements in this book are well understood.

Fiore presents this material in another way, encoded into *magistri*, *magistri remedi*, *contra magistri remedi*, with as many as four levels of action/reaction/reaction/reaction, stating however that most plays will go no deeper than three, *ben che pochi zogi passano lo terço magistro in larte. E si piu sin fano se fa cum periculo.* "Although few plays go beyond the third master of the art; more than this he does with peril."[17] This is the encoding that we will decipher in the next section (*The Fiore dei Liberi Code*) and which our students employ throughout their study.

La spada en arme—sword in armour

Immediately following the *segno* (discussed in the last section of the chapter) is Fiore's *spada en arme* (sword in armour) section. As with the German system, Fiore's treatise seems to prefer grasping the sword in the middle—at the *mezza spada*—and using the sword like a short, vicious axe.[18]

As with the other sections, this one begins with several *poste*. Next follow a series of plays that are very different from the *zhogo largo* or *zhogo stretto* sections that preceed it, in that all three sections of the sword are employed at close range into a thorough integration of the *abrazzare* and *zhogo stretto*.

Within the Schola we have placed the *spada en arme* as module #5, to follow the work with the *abrazzare*, *daga* and *zhogo stretto*. This method has the side benefit of giving new and enthusiastic combatants the chance to assemble the armour they will need to execute these plays with confidence and relative safety.

La lanza—spear

Overall the spear work in Fiore is limited to just six special techniques:

> "Poy trauariti le guardie de la lança che sono vi magistri li primi iij magistri çogano de parte drita, li altri tri che segueno zogano de parte stancha [PD Carta 2a]."

> "Next we will find the guards of the *lanza*, which are first six masters who know the right side, and those who follow play on the left."

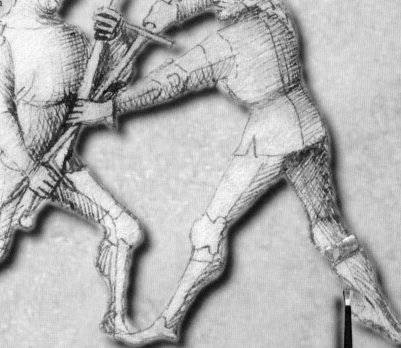

Essentially these plays are all iterations of a basic principle, that thrusts can be effectively countered by exchanging (*scambiare*) or breaking (*rompere*) them.[19] These plays are well articulated in the *zhogo largo* section of the sword in two hands, and they form the best example of Fiore's approach to dealing with thrusts. Exchanges with the lance on horseback are dealt with in the same way, either by exchanging or breaking them. These techniques are covered in Book II, as they are plays #7 and #8 of our *zhogo largo* curriculum.

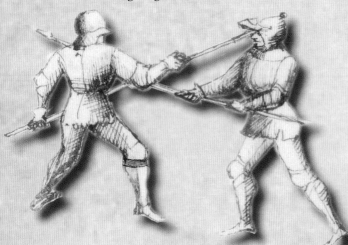

Above: *In Fiore's lanza or spear play, the idea is to "exchange" (scambiare) the thrust, controlling the opponent's weapon and dominating the center of the fight to clear the way for an attack with the combatant's own point. Getty fol. 39v.*

L'azza—poleaxe

Similarly, Fiore's approach to the poleaxe applies the core principles while taking into account its special features. The axe is the assault weapon of the period, a rending, piercing, smashing, thrusting, and crushing weapon designed for use against plate.

"Poy trauariti quatro magistri cum iiij açça in guardia e una guardia contra laltra li qualli magistri pono far cinque zoghi ed altri zoghi che sono in lo çogho de la spada che ben faro mentione [PD Carta 2a]."

"We will find four masters in guard with the *azza*, one against the other. These masters can do five plays and some other things, which are the plays of the sword already mentioned."

Fiore is saying here in the Prologue to the PD that the *azza* can do these five special plays, but that it can also do the plays of the *spada in arme*, which as we recall are primarily wrestling plays. But he also recognizes the danger inherent in a staff weapon such the *azza*: the control techniques he employs with the longsword are far more difficult with the *azza*, because the axe is essentially three weapons—the portions above and below the hands as well as the section between the hands,[20] which makes it very difficult to establish meaningful control over the opponent's weapon. His solution in the five plays is therefore to eliminate the axe, if possible, and to rely on the student's advantage in *abrazzare* to establish control. Commensurately, the objective is to pin the *azza* to the ground and then to move in for a *presa*. Another solution is to attempt the pressure-based control techniques of the *spada en arme*. The poleaxe was an important weapon for combat within the lists (*sbarra*), and it appears in all three treatises.

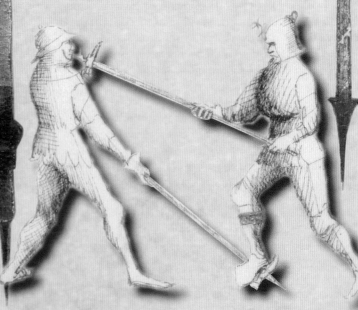

Above: *Fiore also plays with the poleaxe or azza in armour, as shown in the above plate Getty fol. 36v.*
Left: *Leader of the New Jersey study group Frank Petrino uses tutta porta di ferro with the lanza in 2005.*

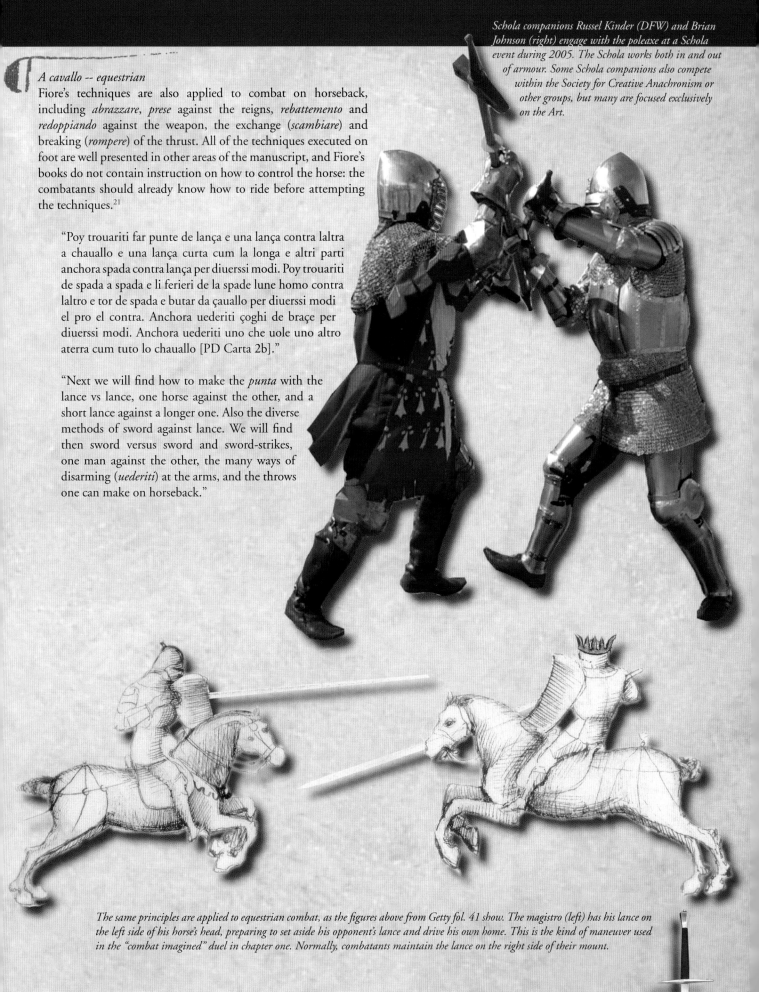

A cavallo -- equestrian

Fiore's techniques are also applied to combat on horseback, including *abrazzare*, *prese* against the reigns, *rebattemento* and *redoppiando* against the weapon, the exchange (*scambiare*) and breaking (*rompere*) of the thrust. All of the techniques executed on foot are well presented in other areas of the manuscript, and Fiore's books do not contain instruction on how to control the horse: the combatants should already know how to ride before attempting the techniques.[21]

"Poy trouariti far punte de lança e una lança contra laltra a chauallo e una lança curta cum la longa e altri parti anchora spada contra lança per diuerssi modi. Poy trouariti de spada a spada e li ferieri de la spade lune homo contra laltro e tor de spada e butar da çauallo per diuerssi modi el pro el contra. Anchora uederiti çoghi de braçe per diuerssi modi. Anchora uederiti uno che uole uno altro aterra cum tuto lo chauallo [PD Carta 2b]."

"Next we will find how to make the *punta* with the lance vs lance, one horse against the other, and a short lance against a longer one. Also the diverse methods of sword against lance. We will find then sword versus sword and sword-strikes, one man against the other, the many ways of disarming (*uederiti*) at the arms, and the throws one can make on horseback."

The same principles are applied to equestrian combat, as the figures above from Getty fol. 41 show. The magistro (left) has his lance on the left side of his horse's head, preparing to set aside his opponent's lance and drive his own home. This is the kind of maneuver used in the "combat imagined" duel in chapter one. Normally, combatants maintain the lance on the right side of their mount.

CODE

Within the treatises, there is a dizzying array of figures, directed if not depicted directly by Fiore himself. The figures wear different forms of martial dress, from the starkly efficient *zuparello* to more flamboyantly dagged *cottes*. Some of the combatants wear crowns, while others are adorned with a gold-gilded garter on one leg. For years students have attempted to study these drawings, but the work is difficult to interpret without the foundational passages that explain how the figures are ordered which is present in each of the three Prologues.

In the Getty and Morgan there are, fortunately, descriptive passages which accompany the skillfully drawn figures. In the PD, the figures are accompanied by short, roughly-wrought rhyming couplets that attempt to summarize the figure's action or the effect of that action. All three treatises feature text in the Prologue that tells the reader how to read the manuscript and how the figures relate to one another, all designed to make the system easy to learn:

"E per questo modo porite uedere tuta larte de armizar in questo libro che non se pora falar niente tanto dirano bene le glose sopra le figure depinte [Getty F.2v]."

"And in this way you will see the whole art of arms in this book, an art that cannot fail while well executed, explained in the text above the figures depicted."

PERFORMERS AND PORTRAYERS— EACH ANOTHER'S AUDIENCE

First Fiore discusses the identities of the characters who will demonstrate his techniques, the *magistri* (masters), *scolari* (scholars), *zugadori* (players). The Masters of Battle, *magistri*, may be easily identified in the treatise by their crowns. His *scolari* demonstrate the plays and are known by their gold-leafed garters, while everyone else is a *zugadore*, a player.

In addition to these basic figures, there are also the *magistri remedi* and the *magistri contra-remedi*. By learning to identify these figures as depicted the plays are easier to decipher and multiple layers of relationships between the techniques are revealed.

"Mo bisogna fare per modo che le guardie sen cognosca delli Magistri zugadori, elli scolari da zugadori, elli cugadori de Magistri, e lo remedio del contrario ben che sempre lo contrario e posto dredo al remedio etal uolta 'lo remedio' dredo o dredo tutti li soy zogi e di questo faremo [Getty f.4r]."

"He needs then to take the form of the guards known by their Master players, by the scholars of the players, and the players of the Masters, and the remedy of the contrary well always contrary to them, and positioned after the remedy, behind all the plays that we make."

Magistri

Magistri are the crowned figures that form a starting point for the plays that follow. He begins by showing the key guards or *poste*. They wear crowns to distinguish them and the guards are so named because great defense can be made from these positions (in the right circumstance).

The figures in the *poste* or guards are *magistri*, as are certain of the figures that follow in the chapter. But there is a whole parade of "remedy masters" and "counter-remedy masters" and "counter-counter remedy masters" to be contended with, and Fiore only discusses their relationship in a complex series of confusing paragraphs in the Prologue.

Fiore's *Magistri* (masters), are shown wearing a crown (*corona*). *Magistri* shown in a *guardia* or *poste* (see ch. 7) and are also the First Masters of Battle.

Fiore's *Scolari* (scholars) do the plays or techniques described in the text. They are denoted by a gold-leafed garter worn below the knee. This scolar finishes a *tutta volta* of the sword in the Getty fol. 26v.

GARTER

All figures are players—*zugadori*. They are the copperative companions, *compagni*, the training partners.

Magiſtro   **Scolaro**   **Zugadore**

THE FOUR KINGS

First Master of Battle (*Magistro*): The first masters are the crowned figures in the *poste*.

"E questa sono chiamade poste ouero guardie ouero primi Magistri de la Batagla E questi portano corona intesta perche sono poste in logo e per modo di fare grande defesa cum esso tale aspetere. E sono principio di quellarte çoe di quallarte delarma cum la quale li ditti magistri stano in guardia [Getty F.4v]."

"And these are called *poste*, *guardia*, or the First Masters of Battle. And they wear crowns on their heads because positioned like this they can wait with good defense. And it is a principle that in the art of arms the abovesaid Masters stay in guard."

The *magistri* demonstrate superior positions adopted in an effort to enable striking the opponent without risk to one's self, as we will explore in chapters 7 and 10:

"E tanto e adire posta che modo de apostar lo inimigo suo per offenderlo sença periculo di se instesso [Getty F.4v]."

"And it is as much to say that a *posta* is a way of gaining position on the enemy to offend him without being in danger yourself."

The **First Master of Battle seizes the initiative by acting first**, forcing the opponent to respond or to be struck. It is this objective that forms the core of our first module of training within the Schola.

Second Master of Battle (*Remedio*): To make a **remedy** against this attack is to adopt a different *poste*, in the process covering yourself against the incoming attack. The figure who does this in Fiore's plays is the *remedio*, or the Remedy Master, the Second Master of Battle. Essentially the *remedio* is the fellow who for some reason doesn't want to be hit, so he covers himself, spoiling the attack made against him. He also wears a crown, but has made cover:

"Laltro magistro che seguita le…guardie[22] uene ad ensire dele guardie e si uene adefender dun altro zugadore cum gli colpi che esseno de le…guardie che sono denançi. E questro magistro porta anchora corona, e si e chiamado secondo magistro. Anchora sie chiamando magistro remedio perche ello fa lo remedio che non gli siano dade de le feride ouero che non gli sta fatta inçuria in quellarte che sono le ditte poste ouero guardie [Getty F.4r]."

"The masters that follow the…guards come also from the *poste*, coming so to defend themselves from another player who comes to try an attack from the [same] guards that came before. And this master wears another crown, and is called the Second Master [of Battle], also called the Remedy Master because he remedies the attack which is made [against him] and is not injured. In the Art these are the said *poste* or guards."

When the *remedio* makes cover, he thwarts the incoming attack simply by adopting another *posta*, one of the key positions shown at the beginning of the section. The *remedio* can be thought of, very loosely, as the defender.[23] Once he has made cover, the swords are crossed, a state known as the *incrosa*, from *incrosare*, "to cross."[24] From this point the plays of the *zhogo largo* and the *zhogo stretto* follow, although this will be treated in much more detail in Book II. Good examples are the First and Second Masters of the Crossed Swords from the *zhogo largo* section, where the swords are crossed at the tips and middle respectively.

All of Fiore's plays follow from an *incrosa* position. In the case of the *zhogo largo*, one play is illustrated for the crossing at the sword's *punta* or tip, while there are many that follow from a more usual crossing at the *mezza spada*, the middle of the sword. This crossed state is generally a neutral position, as the **First Master of Battle** has started in a *posta*, and attempted to strike. He has been thwarted by the **Second Master of Battle**, who adopts a new *posta* and in the process makes his cover. The result is an *incrosare*, generally the First or Second Master of the Crossed Swords shown on the following page. From this point the plays that follow will begin.

The *zugadore* (player) who first takes advantage of the *incrosare* is the **scolaro**, denoted in Fiore's treatises by a garter worn below the knee of burnished gold, like the crown. The result is a clear visual distinction on each page regarding which of the two *zugadori* was executing the technique described in the text—the reader had only to look for the burnished gold.

"E questo segondo zoe rimedio si a alguni zugadori sotto di si i quali zugano quello zogi che poria zugare lo magistro che deuanti zoe lo rimedio piglando quella couerta ouero presa che fa lo ditto rimedio. E questi zugadori portarano una diuisa sotto lo zinocchio [Getty f.4r]."

"And these following, called *rimedio*, has other *zugadori* under him who play the techniques that the *magistro remedio* taking his cover or *presa* done by said *remedio*. And these *zugadori* wear a device (garter) below their knee."

Hence, to decode many of the plays, the reader would look first to the foundational *poste* that begin each weapon-section. Here he will find the **First Masters of Battle**, the *poste* or *guardia*. From these positions will follow various attacks and covers. Each *zugadore* will move between the *poste* using transitions, seeking an advantage. When one is found, the strikes (*colpire*) against the opponent will be made also as *posta* transitions, but this time with power. The opponent will naturally attempt to make cover against an attack if he does not attack first, and if cover is made, then we have the **Second Masters of Battle**, usually but not always resulting in an *incrosare*. The first *zugadore* to take advantage of the situation becomes the **scolaro** as he executes one of the plays or a play based on Fiore's principles. The **Second Master of Battle** is thus **responsive**, having lost the initiative by having his opponent striking first, he quickly responds and makes cover, hopefully following-on with one of his *scolari* to make an immediate attack.

Variants on the *scolaro's* play would be done by "his" players, or *zugadori*, just as there are multiple *scolari* (plays) from the Second Masters of Battle. All of the *scolari* who follow their *magistri* are executing variants based on circumstance, and all *zugadori* who belong to their *scolari* execute variants based on their situation.

"E farano questi zugadori tutti li zoghi de lo rimedio infin tanto che si trouara un altro magistro che fara lu contrario delo rimedio e di tutti suoi zugadori [Getty f.4r]."

"And these *zugadori* make all of the plays of the remedy until is found another master who makes the counter of the remedy (*contra-remedio*) and of all of his players."

Third Master of Battle (*Contra-Remedio*): There are, of course, always counters. If one of the plays is countered, checking the *scolaro's* action, then the roles change. This counter to the remedy is termed the *contra-remedio*, the Third Master of Battle. Within the sword in two hands section there are only a couple of instances where this *contra-remedio* is depicted (such as on the *punta falsa*, Getty f.27v-b) although there are cases where counters are mentioned in the text but not depicted or where the figure appears in the black-and-white copies available to be devoid of the stated badge.[25] Overall there are few *contra-remedio* depicted in the sword sections sections, but there are many in the *daga* section.

"E perço chello fa contra lo rimedio e contra soy zugadori ello portera la diuisa de lo magistro e desoi zugadori çoe lacorona in testa ela diuisa sotto lo zinocchio E questo Re echiamado magistro terço ede chiamado contrario perche sara contra glaltri magistri e contra asoi zogi [Getty f.4r]."

"And because I make the counter to the *remedio* and his *zugadori*, I wear a crown, the device of the *magistro* and his *zugadori* on my head *and* a device (garter) below the knee. And this King is called the Third Master [of Battle] and *contrario* [*contra-rimedio*] because he is against the other masters and their players."

punta falsa

Fiore's famous zhogo stretto (close play) technique known as the punta falsa, the "false thrust," shown here from the Getty fol. 27v.

Fourth Master of Battle (*Contra-Contrario*): Fortunately, Fiore says in the Getty that there are only a few places where there is a *contra-contrario*, the Fourth Master of Battle, because if the encounter has gone this far then it is really spinning out control. The *contra-contrario* will not be seen in work with the sword, so for now we will set it aside after including Fiore's description:

"Anchora digo che in alchuni loghi in larte si trova loquarto magistro zoe Re che fa contra loterço Re, zoe lo contrario delo rimedio. E questo Re e lo magistro quarto chiamado magistro quatro. E de chiamado contra contrario. Ben che pochi zogi passano lo terço magistro in larte. E si piu sin fano se fa cum periculo [Getty f.4r]."

"Also I say that in some places in the art are found a Fourth Master [of Battle], called a king, a king called the counter of the *rimedio*. And this king is the Fourth Master, called *contra-contrario*. Well is it that a play seldom passes the Third Master of the Art, as he who does this often places himself in danger."

ZUGADORI, COMPAGNI, CORTESIA & CONCORDIA

Another way that we can think about the combatants who study Fiore's art as as he refers to them in general, as *zugadori* (singular: *zugadore*). This can be a generic term used in place of combatants, or something similar. *Zugadore* comes from the verb *zugare* (modern Italian: *giocare*), meaning "to play." Another variant is *zhogo* (modern Italian: *giocco*), meaning game.

Although Fiore's techniques are clearly meant to be practiced in earnest and can be deadly, there is a spirit of harmony and cooperation (*concordia*) that runs through his text, a companionship between the *scolari* that was reflective of the common bond felt by men of the chivalric and noble classes, or to the more local community around one of the Italian communes. Fiore often refers to his combatants as *zugadori*—players—and we see the *zhogo largo / zhogo stretto*, the long and short *play*, respectively.

In addition, Fiore uses another important term, *compagno*, to refer to the bond that ties his *scolari* together. Although *compagno* is not defined as the other words are within the Prologues, it is used in the text.

Within the Schola we use the term *comnpagno* to define both a level of accomplishment—completing and testing the material in this book—and as a notation of companionship for those who study with us. We are all *compagni*; the mutual respect is what keeps these techniques from becoming dangerous.

This is an important concept for safety, as Fiore mentions. Many of the *abrazzare* techniques could be dangerous if practiced without concern for the *compagno* or without diligence and control (it is for this reason that we typically do not teach these techniques to the newer students).

"Che zoghi che se piglia de concordia, le prese se fa damore e non da ira. E sopra larte de la braçar che se fa a guadagnar le prese tal uolta se fa da ira e alunga uolta per la uita e sono prese e zoghi che non se po çugar de cortesia anche sono çoghi pericolusi [PD carta 2a]."

"These plays must be taken with harmony, the *prese* made with love and not from anger. [As in] the above art of the *abrazzare*, which gains the *prese* at certain times from anger and other times from good spirit. And there are plays that the player cannot make with courtesy because they are dangerous."

These techniques must be practiced with harmony—without anger or *ira*—and with superior control. The mutual respect that is held between the *compagni* or *zugadori* is the most important safety rule a group can have, more important by far than all of the necessary attention to detail in terms of equipment and training, although these are also important.

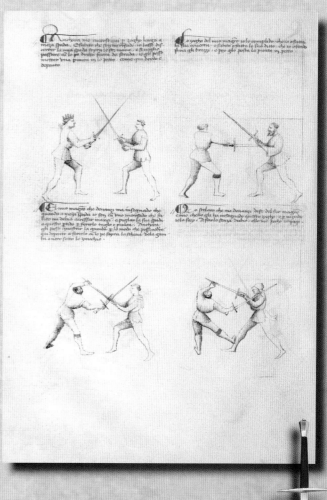

Fol. 25v of the Getty manuscript shows, starting in the upper left, how an attack is made from the magistro remedi, or the Second Master of Battle. In the first figure, the swords are crossed as the master covers himself. In the next plate—right—he senses insufficient pressure from his opponent and drives through the defense. The third plate —lower left—gives another option for an opponent who has committed to a firm cover. The fourth play (lower right) shows another available option once the sword has been captured in the prese.

SEGNO

One of the most important drawings in Fiore's manuscript is the *segno*. In Italian, *segno* simply means "drawing," but, intersingly, to teach something is to *insegnare*. There is broad agreement that the *segno* is a teaching tool, a profound, compact and layered presentation of condensed information that grows in meaning as the students increase their knowledge of Fiore's art.

In the center of the drawing is a clothed man, over which are superimposed seven swords[26] and around which four animals are arrayed. Each of the swords represents an attacking angle, and each of the animals a martial quality that the combatant must have in order to be successful. As Fiore writes in the PD Prologue:

"Poy trouariti uno homo incoronadi cum septe spade adosso cum iiij figure intorno e si se pora uedere zo che a asignificar le dicte figure spade [PD Carta 2a]."

"We will find a crowned man with seven swords adorned with four figures around him, to see if he can see the significance of the said figures and swords."

The *segno* appears on carta 17a of the PD manuscript, where it preceeds the section on the sword in two hands, and on folio 32 of the Getty, where it follows the the odd little baton/*daga* section immediately before the section on *spada en arme*. Curiously, it does not appear in the Morgan at all.

The Getty *segno* opens with a short declaration explaining its purpose:

"Questo magistro cum queste spade significa gli setti colpi de la spada. Et lli quatro animali significa quatro vertù, zoè avisamento, presteza, forteza, e ardimento. A qui vole esser bono in questa arte questa vertù conven de lor aver parte [Getty f.32]."

"This master with the seven swords signifies the seven *colpi* of the sword. And the four animals signify four virtues, known as *avisamento* (judgment), *presteza* (speed), *forteza* (strength), and *ardimento* (ardor). He who wants to do well in the Art, of each virtue must he have part."

THE SEVEN SWORDS REPRESENT
THE SEVEN PRIMARY ATTACKS

Turning our attention first to the swords, as Fiore writes, there are seven, one for each of the attacks he discusses earlier in the treatise (which we will introduce in chapter 9). There are no words that accompany the swords in the Getty version of the *segno*, but there are words written around the swords on the PD describing nine of the key *poste*: **poste di donna destra**, **posta di donna sinestra**, **posta di finestra destra**, **posta di finestra sinestra**, **posta longa**, **posta breve**, **tutta porta di ferro**, **mezana porta di ferro**, and **dente di zenghiaro**. From these places the seven attacks are efficiently made, a quick-reference for the most important *poste*.

The two downward-sloping swords traversing the shoulders represent the blows called *fendenti*, those to the middle the *mezani*, and the two angled rising strikes the *sotani*. The one in the center represents the *punta*, or thrust. The primary attacks in the system are comprised of these strikes, an efficient summary that strongly resembles similar attack series in later Italian swordplay[27] and in modern stick combat systems.[28]

THE ANIMALS REPRESENT
MARTIAL VIRTUES HELD IN BALANCE

What is perhaps more important are the four martial virtues Fiore offers, embodied through his four animals. They are arrayed around the *magistro*: the *ellefante* at the bottom, the *tigro* at his right, the *lione* at his left, and the *cervino* (lynx) above his head. Each animal symbolizes well understood qualities, and taken in balance, a man must possess all four if he is to do well in the art. In the PD version, Fiore writes:

"Noy semo quarto animali de tal conplesione;
Chi uole armiçar de noy faça conpartatione;
E chi de nostre uertù harà bona parte
In arme hauerà honor chomo dise larte."
[PD 17a]

"We are the four animals of such contemplation;
Who the combatant wants to make a part;
And our virtues must he have in good measure.
Thus armed will a man have honor in the Art."

This is substantially the same as in the Getty's script, but it has perhaps a different tone. Interestingly, there is a slight variance in the naming of the virtues within the manuscripts, but their desciptions remain remarkably constant. Perhaps these are teaching rubrics similar to the Johannes Liechtenauer's *zettel*.

Queſto maġro cū queſte ſpad ſignifica glī ſetti colpī de la ſpada. Ell quatro anīmalī ſignifica quatro uertū, zoe auiſameto, preſteza, forteza, e ardimento. Echi uole eſſ bono in queſta arte de queſte uertū conuen de lor auer parte.

Meglio d'mi louo ceruiero no uede creaſa. Eaquello mette ſemp a ſeſto e a miſura.

· Auiſa · mento ·

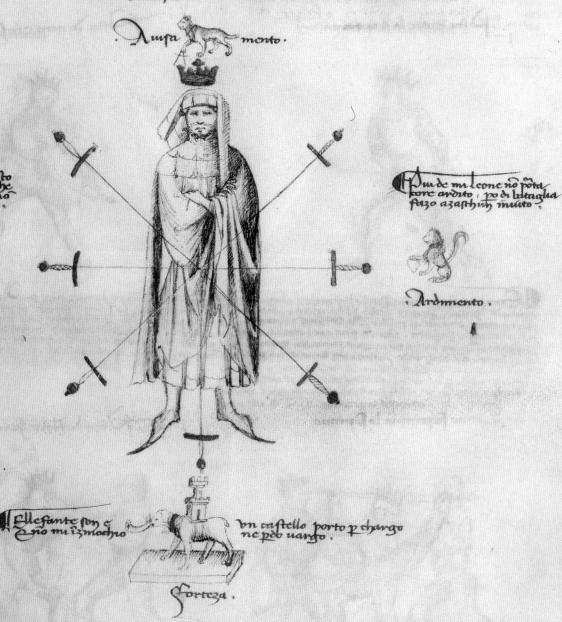

o tigro tanto ſon pſto a correr euol pare che la ſagitta del cielo no mi poria auanzare.

Preſteza.

Piu de mi leone no porta core ardito, po di bataglia fazo a zaſchun multo.

· Ardimento ·

Ellefante ſon e no mi izmoehno un caſtello porto p chargo ne pto uargo.

Forteza.

Fiore's segno from the Getty, fol. 32.

SEGNO

We are the four animals of such contemplation;
Who the combatant want to make a part;
And our virtues must he have in good measure.
Thus armed will a man have honor in the Art.

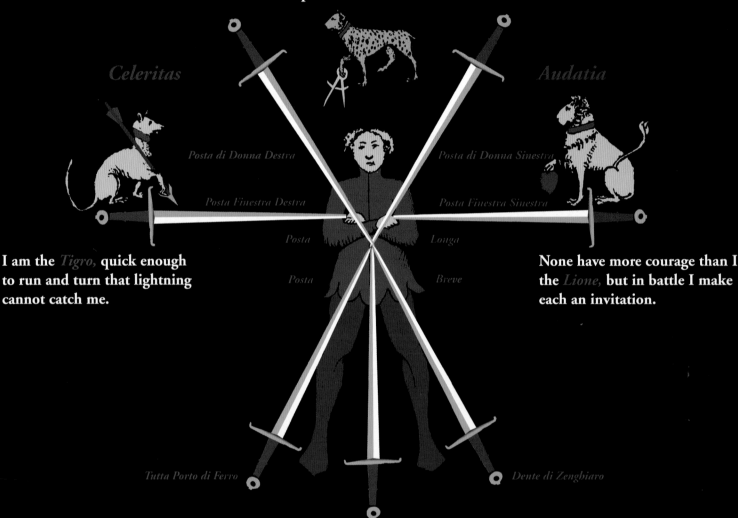

Prudentia

Better than the *Cervino's* **(lynx's) eyes does**
no creature see, with which I always make
with a compass and measure.

Celeritas

Posta di Donna Destra

Posta Finestra Destra

Posta

Posta

I am the *Tigro,* **quick enough**
to run and turn that lightning
cannot catch me.

Tutta Porto di Ferro

Mezana Porto di Ferro

Audatia

Posta di Donna Sinestra

Posta Finestra Sinestra

Longa

Breve

None have more courage than I
the *Lione,* **but in battle I make**
each an invitation.

Dente di Zenghiaro

Fortudio

I am the *Ellefante,* **and a castle I am burdened by.**
I do not kneel, nor do I lose my way.

FORTUDIO

FORTITUDO – *ELLEFANTE* [GETTY–*FORTEZA*]

"Ellefante son e uno castello ho per cargho,
"E non me inçenochio ni perdo uargho." [Getty]

"Ellefante son e un castello porta per chargo.
E non mi inzinochio nè perdo vargo." [PD]

"I am the Elephant, and a castle I am burdened by.
And I do not kneel,[29] nor lose my way."

Fiore's elephant stands at the foot of the diagram, positioned upon a small, flat base-plate. It forms the base upon which the rest of the art rests, the art's foundation. The elephant represents stability, strength, and an ownership of the combatant's ground.

In a medieval context, according to the Aberdeen Bestiary, the Elephant was one of the greatest of beasts. It was a common belief that the elephant did not rise if he fell. This parallels Fiore's lack of ground-fighting, and his strong preference to put the opponent onto the ground, without being taken to the ground himself.

The elephant may have carried other great symbolism for Fiore's audience. The Aberdeen Bestiary adds that the Elephant represents innocent goodness (for he represented Adam), a creature who cared for the wounded, who knew nothing of adultery, and who defended his mate. The Bestiary also records the Great Elephant as a symbol for the civilizing law that stands as a bulwark against sin. They were (and are) thought to be of a very high intelligence.[30]

Fiore associates the Elephant with *Fortudio* and *Forteza*, or strength. His steadfast nature supports a citadel upon his back, and combined it is a potent fighing platform, known to the Italians of the day as a weapon employed by the Persians and Indians.

In practical terms, a man's body supports his fighting efforts, and indeed the image of the elephant carrying the tower should be strongly internalized. The combatant's weight should be carried low, but not too low. The back—like the tower—should be straight (I have often instructed students who have a tendency to lean to imagine wearing a coronet behind which miniature archers are poised: they must take care that these small soldiers aren't spilled out of a "leaning tower.").

When an elephant moves, it cannot afford to misstep. When modern humans walk, we tend to step towards the heel in what is essentially a semi-controlled fall. But when elephants step, they first distribute their weight evenly between the three other feet, then move the front foot with surprising grace and gentleness—but also with confidence, placing it upon the ground. Occassionally, having tested the ground, he wishes to change his mind, but as he has his weight still on three other legs, moving the leg is no problem. In the same way, a combatant is well-served to keep his

weight upon his back foot while he moves the front foot, in case he has to reevaluate owing to combat conditions. As Fiore says of the *Ellefante*, he strives to keep himself from the ground and does not kneel.

For a combatant, it is important to maintain the elephant while pursuing other martial tasks. He must maintain his balance, his connection with the ground, his fighting platform. It is common for beginning students to lean, to leap, to slide, or to cast their balance to the wind in an effort to gain a small momentary advantage. But these temporary advantages are usually low-probability gambles that risk the critical stability that supports all of the combatant's efforts and should be avoided or trained out.

We call the first course of the Schola class the Elephant module, because the focus is on building fundamentals appropriate to further study. As such, we build balance, focus, awareness, and core movements that comprise the system. The combatant will seek the first and most advantageous First Master of Battle, securing victory through superior position such that the opponent cannot easily remedy his attack. He is then ready to apply this martial intelligence to more complex situations, the inevitable case where the opponent makes cover.

Elephant from a Bestiary. Bodliean Library, Univ. of Oxford. MS Bodl. 764, fol. 12r

CELERITAS – *TIGRO* [GETTY–PRESTEZA]

"Yo tigro tanto son presto a corer e uoltare,
Che la sagita del cello non me pò."

"Io tigro tanto son presto a correr e voltare che la
sagitta del cielo non mi poria avanzare."

"I am the tiger quick enough to run and turn that
arrow from the sky (lightning)[31] cannot catch me."

Fiore's tiger may not be Giotto-like in its realism,[32] but
the tiger's association with lightning stands for initiative,
physical and mental speed, the benefits of natural speed and/
or training. The *tigro* clutches an arrow in his paw, the *satiga del
cello* or "arrow of the sky," a metaphor for lightning.

Medieval and early Renaissance writers had little direct experience
with tigers, often confusing them with other big cats, such as
panthers or cheetahs. But the idea of the tiger seems well represented
within the most famous medieval Bestiary, the Aberdeen:

> "The tiger is named after its swift flight: the Persians, Greeks
> and Medes call it, 'the arrow.' It is a beast with colorful spots,
> of extraordinary qualities and swiftness, after which the River
> Tigris is named because it is the swiftest of all rivers."[33]

*Tiger from the Aberdeen Bestiary.
Permission courtesy the University of Aberdeen.*

In addition to speed, medieval legend held that tigresses could be
captured through the use of a mirror or reflective sphere by taking
advantage of their extraordinary devotion to their cubs—their
fidelity. Real tigers stalk their prey and then ambush them in a
lightning attack. They are silent, deadly killers.

Combatants must leverage speed through the development of
highly efficient motor control programming. Some are fortunate
and are gifted with natural speed, but all combatants can develop
speed through training. The purpose of drills and plays is to
establish patterns of movement based on sound principles that
can be manipulated under the quickly changing environment of
movement in a fight.

Fiore's tiger rests near the right hand, the hand that controls the
sword. Like the *sagita del cello*, the sword can strike like lightning—
fast, unpredictably, and with unerring precision.

More basically, combatants must immediately seize upon their
opportunities in order to capture or hold the iniatiative. When
the time is right, a lightning-quick decision and movement are
necessary for success—or else the opponent may well have time
to act.

Tigro from the Getty, Fol. 32

"Più de mi lione non porta cor ardito,
Però de batalia faço a zaschaduno inuito."

"Più de mi leone non porta core ardito, però di bataglia fazo a zaschun invito."

"None have more courage than I, the Lion, but in battle I make each one an invitation."

Audiacious courage is symbolized by the lion, who, at the left side, holds a heart in his paw, the symbol for strength and character. As he says, none have more courage than the lion, but in battle the lion invites each to combat. He does not rush in head over heels, but he tempers his audacity with wisdom. He invites, and then pounces in a frontal assault. He is the king of beasts, full of pride, but noble and merciful.

In medieval lore the lion emerges much as he is now. He was believed to eshew the killing of women, children and the ill. It was believed that they ate in moderation. That his commanding roar dominated all other beasts, and that he could be killed through deception and falsehood (such as a snake's bite or a scorpion's sting).

For the combatant, the lion symbolizes martial courage, the fine place between rushing into an entry and seizing the initiative. I remind combatants to move with the boldness and courage of the lion, seizing ground with a calm surety borne of both *ellefante* and *lione*. But the combatant must take command of the fight, not hang back and negotiate the outcome. The boldness, tempered by nobility, will drive him strongly forward and with audacity at the right moment to seize the quickest and most efficient outcome appropriate to the encounter.

Many beginning students will hang back at *misura larga*—wide distance—in their encounters, subconsciously fearful of entering the fray. While this can be a tactic of good judgment, it is frequently accompanied with overcautiousness, or what in the school we think of as insufficient lion in the attack. At the other end of the spectrum, other combatants will rush to the fray, seemingly without caution, certainly without adequate judgement. We can think of this approach as the lion's pride—or vainglory—but it can also be a symptom of fear—the combatant subconsciously hopes that by rushing in he can drive past both his fear and the opponent's guard. Both are costly mistakes.

Lions from a Bestiary. Bodliean Library, Univ. of Oxford. MS Bodl. 764, fol. 2v

PRUDENTIA – *CERUINO* (LYNX) [GETTY–AVISAMENTO]

"Meio de mi louo ceruino non uede creatura;
E aquello meto sempre a sesto e mesura." [Getty]

"Meglio de mi lovo[34] cervino non vede creatura.
E aquello mette sempre a sesto[35] e a misura." [PD]

"Better than my lynx's eyes no creaturc does see,
And with which I always make with a compass
    and a measure."

The medieval lynx, *cervino*, was associated with alertness, keen eyesight and hearing. Unlike the domestic lynx, the Eurasian Lynx is a big cat, with bold eyes and a beautiful spotted coat, like Fiore's depiction. In his paws he holds a set of dividers—a measuring tool. The *Cervino* or Lynx stands for measure, insight, knowledge, and that most important quality, judgment.

In the Middle Ages the lynx was associated with sharp vision, but there was also a sense that it was not a big cat but a member of the wolf family,[36] and as such it was sometimes associated with envy. But more commonly, it became an image for the all-seeing nature of Christ, who knew the wicked thoughts of his listeners (Matthew 22:8), and as we find in Paul: "there is no creature hidden from His sight, but all things are naked and open to the eyes of Him to whom we must give account (Heb 4:13)." It is far more likely that this all-seeing nature was what Fiore intended.

Within its paws the *cervino* grasps the compass or divider, a measuring instrument familiar to masons and artisans of all kinds. Using a divider, distance could be measured. The sextant, derived from the *sesto*, was used by navigators to locate their position with precise measurements of the stars in celestial navigation.[37] The lynx thus measures not only physical distance, but the whole nature of the fight, arriving at a sound judgment through which he may govern the other animals.[38]

The combatant must temper the other qualities with sound judgment, and he must accurately measure both the physical aspects of the fight—time and distance—and the qualitative measures such as his belief about the opponent's plans and intentions. In a broad sense this is expressed by the phrase *sentimento di ferro*, or "feel of the steel," the feel of the opponent's blade when the weapons are crossed, but it is much more than that. In the German, this is

Lynx from the Bodley Bestiary, MS 764, fol. 11r.
Photo courtesy Bodliean Library, Univ. of Oxford

expressed as *fühlen*—feeling.

First the combatant must use his senses to accurately measure time and distance, and he must then arrive with good judgment at a solution within the tactics taught within the system. I believe this is the most important of the four virtues, if there is one, because all of the other animals ought to be held in balance, in equal measure, the quality governed by the *cervino*. A keen eye and a keen brain are crucial to this or to any combat system. Being able to "see" through the Fog of War has driven military theorists for hundreds of generations—the ability to notice the small details upon which a martial encounter can turn. The obvious things are usually (but not always) traps, so there is a substantial benefit to "seeing" and "measuring" what is important and what is dangerous.

*Cervino or Lynx
from the Getty, Fol. 32*

THE MAN HIMSELF

At the center of the *segno* is the combatant himself. Medieval beasts were thought to be ruled by their wills, free to be led whereever their instincts willed them to go. But man is different than beasts because he is ruled by reason, and through both reason and enlightenment he can become moral, and through morality he is fit to rule.

Each of Fiore's beasts wears a collar, symbolizing that the creature is captured, harnessed, controlled by the man in the center. It is the man himself who must tame or harness the beasts, directing them to do his will. As the first part of the *segno* says, he must have a part of each. Stepping further from the written text, they must be in balance and brought to bear with judgement. A strong combatant must possess each animal with appropriate measure.

European Lynx.
Photo © Tatiana Morozova

FOR INTERMEDIATE COMBATANTS

What's Your Animal?

Gathering the students, the teacher asks which animal the student fights from as a position of strength, and which is his weakness. Allow the discussion to run around the group in order to deepen their knowledge of the animals. Alternatively, have each of the students evaluate each of the other students, assessing what they perceive to be their strengths and weaknesses. One trick is to have each student write down what he thinks his are before the circuit begins, then compare during the analysis.

Another technique is to ask the combatants following a fight what animal he and his opponent's fought with in primacy, and ask them to talk about how the two interacted.

APPLYING THE SEGNO

The *segno* is much more than an abstract teaching tool. Even for a modern student, it can be a potent reminder of the core martial qualities or virtues. For example, a combatant working through fundamentals of the system or intermediate plays may find himself off-balance—physically or mentally—and in need of tending to his *ellefante*. Or he may be rushing into the fight, or holding back, too much or too little *lione*. Or he may be missing his opportunities to attack with undeveloped attacks or slowness as he tries to recognize a situation for which he is not yet trained or experienced, an understrength *tigro*. Or he may make poor judgement, or mis-time a movement, failing with the *cervino*. Or his opponent may provide an opportunity based on these common errors.

Fiore's *segno* provides an easy-to-remember presentation of core combat qualities. Internalizing the *segno* and the characteristics of the beasts shown will offer the combatant an advantage in that it simplifies the complex variance of skills, mistakes and opportunities that arise during a fight. It is a fine, well-wrought model.

But the *segno* is also like an onion. The more experience a combatant brings, the more he will see. Intermediate combatants may notice that their opponents have one of the animals as their totem, fighting from the Elephant, Lynx, Tiger or Lion. But they are also weak in one—and that weakness suggests lines of attack. As Colin Hatcher has ably noted, individual plays may be done emphasizing any of the four, with different results. Certain plays rely more on one animal than the others, and if this animal is a place of strength for the combatant, then he should be able to take exceptional advantage of the technique and hopefully it's underlying principle.

EXERCISE

ANIMALS AT PLAY
Brian R. Price & Colin Hatcher

Once the students have worked with all six plays presented in chapter 11, have them analyze which animal seems to govern each play. This should yield insights about how and why the principle works.

Next, have them attempt to execute the play emphasizing each of the four animals to see how differently the play can be made. Not all of the attempts will be successful, but in the process the students should begin to see how the qualities govern a fighting context.

MOVEMENT: THREE CATS, AND AN ELEPHANT

One of the common ways the *segno* assists in general is in its suggestions about movement. The three figures above are all big cats. Just as big cats move with graceful power, picking their way with calculated precision as they stalk their prey, so too should combatants move like cats, but with the elephant's precision and calculated balance.

Seen from above, the "seven swords" can be thought of as a footwork diagram, showing a preference for *passi a la traversa*. Yet other combatants, especially Paul MacDonald, have peered deeper into the *segno* to find connections with other groups of four: the elemental natures of Air, Earth, Fire and Water; the Christian symbolism of Father, Son and Holy Ghost in the form of a cross, and a dizzying number of other permutations. Other researchers have striven to find connections with Kabalistic secrets, Masonic iconography or esoteric elements, but I'll leave those potential connections for others to write about. Whether or not these things are actually in Fiore, it is astounding that all of this can be fit to such a simple, elegant diagram. But the very simplicity of the diagram is in itself a mirror of the whole system: a simple, efficient model easily adapted to circumstance.

Status of an Ellefante from Northern Italy, depicting classical events.

MEDIEVAL BEASTIARIES

Medieval books on the natural world, known as bestiaries, were the most common books available after the Holy Bible. Every library would have had at least one.

The Bestiary is a pre-science account of the modern world, a compendium of knowledge which probably originated in Egypt but was recorded in Greek as the *Physiologus*, an immensely influential volume interpreting knowledge through the lens of the Christian religion.

Bestiaries usually contained thirty to forty animals, giving traits of each drawn from other sources, mainly the aforementioned *Physiologus* and other sources of local history and myth. Each entry usually included an illuminated plate of the animal itself, followed by explanatory text. The text is based in part on the observations of Aristotle, Pliny and others, but they extended the descriptions into what are almost morality plays, using aspects of the animals in question to add sermonic reminders from Scripture.

That beastiaries were influential is not in doubt. Within the context of the Christian educational system, they were powerful teaching tools insofar as they presented important information—the moral questions—through animals both exotic and familiar. By remembering the qualities of a particular animal, such as a lion, members of a diocese could recall something important from scripture, a powerful learning tool based on symbology. The most famous but by no means dominant beasitary known today is the Aberdeen Bestiary, a compendium of 13th century knowledge and belief, available on the web or in a polished print form. Fiore's text uses symbology that appears right out of a medieval Bestiary. The elephant, lion, lynx and tiger are all included. By further study of the use of animals as symbols, the student can gain a greater understanding of what Fiore may have intended with his immensely useful *segno* illustration.

1 One possibility is that Fiore took the pseudonym "Fiore" as a *nom de guerre*, or a pen-name, and that his real name is unknown. His name might be translated as "flowers of liberty," a possible reference to the strength needed to defend freedom. Certainly *Fiore, magistro* is recorded in the 1385 records at Udine and elsewhere. The taking of such names was common amongst *condottieri* of the time, and all of those captains mentioned in the Prologue were *condottieri*.

2 I have discussed these Prologues, and the Prologues of other treatises, as elements of chivalric literature in a paper I presented for the 2005 SCA Rattan Symposium, held in Kansas City, MO, entitled, *Reaching for the Stars: Fighting Treatises as Chivalric Literature and Thoughts on Motivations of their Authors.*

3 There is a tendency in the Western Martial Arts community for scolars of Fiore's work to become very concerned with replicating every detail shown in the drawings. While this precision is laudable because it produces important insights, I believe it also creates an inherent rigidity in many interpretations that is alien to Fiore's system. Within the Schola, we teach our *scolari* to study the play as presented, but we focus much more on the operational principle underlying it. In some cases, we have found a more universal principle inherent in the drawing that is unexpressed in the text. An example would be Fiore's third play of the *zhogo largo*, the blade grasp and kick to the knee (examined in detail in Book II). In the text Fiore discusses kicking, but in context of the second and fourth plays, it is the blade grasp that represents the seizure of control over the opponent, and I believe this is far more important than the kick itself, which is merely a follow-on attack chosen at this point because it is particularly effective—but many follow-on attacks at this point would be equally effective. There are many examples of this kind of unspoken principle in the text, and it is also the reason that a community of interpreting scholars will be better at sorting possible interpretations over time.

4 This framework is the subject of Book II in this series and forms the basis for our curriculum for students who have been recognized as *compagni*.

5 This could mean that Fiore ordered the specific weapons according to the wishes of the Marquis, or simply that the Marquis ordered that the book be created. I suspect that the meaning is the former, because the PD and the Getty both begin with the *abrazzare*, which is not even present in the Morgan, which also does not mention the Marquis at all. But for lack of proof we shall have to hold this as a possibility rather than as a fact. This can be seen in such things as the more compact carriage of the figures and the anchoring of the sword at the power points of the hips in the Getty and the Morgan, as well as in the change in the guardia *posta di donna sinestra*, which we will examine in more detail in chapter 7. This is a theory at the moment, but it is one I am doing more work on.

6 This too is a research topic in need of further exposition, but it has been well demonstrated in our free play and sparring tests using all the core *poste* with weapons such as the *lanza* and *azza*, as well as analyzing other forms such as the German sword and buckler of RA MS I.33, where the core poste can be very effectively used with virtually any medieval or even improvised weapon, greatly simplifying the combat calculus necessary when using a new and unfamiliar weapon.

7 Schola instructor Colin Hatcher has highlighted the distinction between Aikido and Aki-jitsu, distinguishing the modern Aikido (the modern peaceful art) against Aki-jitsu, the medieval battlefield art.

8 This paragraph's translation owes much to Colin Hatcher, its final form a blend of my original and his suggestions.

9 The idea that these techniques are transitional was first articulated and continues to be championed by Mr. Bob Charron. Indeed, in an interesting *daga* encounter shown in a video on the Schola website, Mr. Charron faces a dagger wielded by Mr. Keith Jennings of the Chicago Swordplay Guild, where he attempts to apply this play.

10 The material in this section focuses on the Getty and PD alone.

11 I feel it is this that expresses the practical reason that there are more techniques with the *daga* than with the other weapons. Fiore seems to have been eminently practical, and if a man would be more comfortable with a dagger and more likely to encounter one, then that is where much of his training should perhaps have been directed.

12 In the PD, he offers four masters of the dagger, *Poy serano iiij magistri incoronadi che serano magistri de la daga*, [PD Carta 2a], "We will find four crowned masters of the dagger who are the masters of the dagger."

13 I say "eighty odd" because the plays are not numbered in Fiore's treatise, and it depends how you count *magistri*, *magistri remedi* and *contri magistri remedi*. This will be addressed more fully in Book II.

14 This is curious, since the record seems to suggest that fighting with a buckler (a small shield, usually less than 12" in diameter) and a single-handed sword would have been very common all across Europe.

15 The concept of *poste* which are *pulsativa* is analyzed in chapter 7.

16 Although there is no counter-balancing lever on the single-handed version, and this does have implications for how some of the blows are done.

17 Getty F.4r.

18 The reason for this is an extension of the reason sword handles were elongated during the late 14th century—to create more leverage in an attempt to defeat the plate armours of steel which had recently come into fashion, especially in Germany and the armour-producing centers of northern Italy. By gripping the sword like a short axe, leverage is dramatically increased, but at the expense of distance (and thus potential safety). But since the combatants depicted are fully or close to fully armoured, they could withstand an occasional strike. Their accuracy with the *punta* and the leverage gained enables a considerable variety of throws and prese of the *abrazzare*. These actions are commonly called "half-swording," by members of the WMA community, although Fiore does not appear to use *mezza spada* as any kind of verb; instead he simply states that the sword must be grasped in the middle to make these plays.

19 Plays on Carta 20b & 21a of the PD and Fol. 26v of the Getty.

20 Which the French call the demi-hache, as drawn from one of the most important poleaxe treatises and the only French contribution to medieval weapons treatises, the anonymous *Jeu de la Hache*. I have a translation of *Le Jeu* and an accompanying study of poleaxe technique in the final stages that focuses also on the important German material entitled *Ponderous, Cruel & Mortal: Techniques of the Medieval Poleaxe*, Chivalry Bookshelf 2008.

21 Mrs. Kristi Charron, a talented *equestrienne* and the wife of Mr. Bob Charron, has done some excellent work with Fiore's mounted techniques. We do know something of of near-contemporary horsemanship from the surviving Portuguese work by King Dom Duarte of Portgual, whose work Bem Cavalgar has been recently published in English by the Chivarly Bookshelf, ably translated by Antonio Preto, the *Royal Book of Jousting, Horsemanship and Knightly Combat*.

22 I have taken this text from the Getty Prologue, where Fiore is using the example of the *magistri della daga* to illustrate how the masters will work in all of the other sections. I have contracted the original text to remove the number of guards and the specific references to the *daga* only so that readers are less likely to be confused.

23 As we will see, I do not encourage using the term "defender" or "defense" because they carry connotations of reaction rather than being the initiator of the action. Within the English tradition of the 16th century this idea seems to have been in mind, as certain English masters chose "agent" and "patient-agent" titles for their players. Within the Schola we use *scolaro* and *compagno* to clarify roles during drills.

[24] *Incrosare* is, of course, a regular Italian –are verb. The noun is *il croce*, but common usage amongst WMA practitiones treats incrosare also as a noun, as Fiore does with the verb *abrazzare*.

[25] Such as on the counter to the *scambiar de la punta*, the exchange of the thrust. This is a confusing case, because the *zugadore* would have had to make a thrust from the *incrosare*, which the *scolaro* depicted sets aside (exchanges) while placing his own point on target, qualifying him as a *contra-remedio*, but the figure is not so denoted. Worse, a counter to the *scambiar de la punta* is given, which should then be a *contra-contrario*, but again, this figure is denoted as a simple *scolaro*.

[26] It is because of this that many students and some scholars refer to this as the "swords" or "seven swords" drawing.

[27] For example, Achille Marozzo has a similar swords diagram that includes the sword but dispenses with the animal-based symbology.

[28] Especially in escrima, where the attacking angles are identical.

[29] Within the 13th century Aberdeen Bestiary, the writer says that the elephant could not rise if he fell, and that he had no joints at the knee (so he could not actually bend). *Bestiary: MS Bodley 764*, Trans. by Richard Barber, Boydell & Brewer, 1999.

[30] Indeed, one of our first students (now instructor) Mr. Colin Hatcher, has done an immense amount of research and thought on Fiore's *segno*, and his insights are well worth investigating. Colin's Powerpoint presentation is especially well presented and may be seen at some of the larger Western Martial Arts events.

[31] I am again indebted to Mr. Colin Hatcher, who provided this reference.

[32] Richard Barber writes in his introduction to the Aberdeen Bestiary that the tiger was generally unfamiliar to most medieval writers, and was frequently confused with other big cats, such as the panther or cheetah. In this case, given the spots and the lightning speed, I believe a cheetah is what mave been intended. Colin Hatcher has made an interesting case for the tiger, arguing that the leopard was known (and sometimes included in medieval bestiaries), where it was known as the Gattus Pardus, or "spotted cat."

[33] From the *Aberdeen Bestiary*, trans. by Richard Barber, p. 29.

[34] An old version of the modern Italian for *l'occhio*, or eye.

[35] This word is certainly related to the sextant, the device navigators have used for centuries to measure their place on the globe. The tool in the *cervino's* paw is a divider, or compass. Not in the magnetic sense, but in the distance sense. Dividers were commonly used for measure in many crafts; as an armourer, I have used them extensively. The medieval / early Renaissance context for the word sesta and the possible tools is describes would be an interesting avenue for futher research that might lend more insight as to how Fiore intended the *cervino* to be understood.

[36] It is so mentioned in the Aberdeen Bestiary, Richard Barber translation p. 37.

[37] My father Lt. Col. J. R. Price used this skill extensively in more than twenty years as a U.S. Air Force officer, navigating using the stars alone to fix his position even in the middle of the open ocean—I have a special place in my heart for the skill, which against all odds can fix the navigator's positition often more reliably than using modern satellite-based systems, if the navigator has the skill.

[38] I have a friendly debate with Schola instructor Colin Hatcher over which animal is more important in Fiore's schema. I maintain it is the *cervino*, which tempers and governs the other virtues on account of its position at the top of the *segno*, correlating with the compositional rules of High Renaissance art. Mr. Hatcher contends that it is the lion, and there is also evidence of that at least in the PD manuscript, in the form of the final martial poem at the end of the Prologue.

[39] The work of Filippo Vadi is important to advanced students of Fiore or to anyone who is interested in how swordsmanship changed during the course of the 15th century. The Chivalry Bookshelf has published a translation as *Arte Gladiatoria Dimicandi: 15th Century Swordsmanship of Master Filippo Vadi* by Luca Porzio & Gregory Mele, 2002.

[40] From Luca Porzio & Gregory Mele's translation, p. 88.

[41] *In Service of the Duke: The 15th Century Fighting Treatise of Master Paulus Kal*, Trans. by Christian Henry Tobler, a limited edition facsimile edition by the Chivalry Bookshelf, 2007.

CHAPTER FOUR

SWORDS & ARMOUR

t the time that Fiore was teaching, Europe found itself in a period of upheaval; the old social order of the Middle Ages was being largely swept away, replaced by a money-culture as commerce opened new avenues of opportunity. Italy led the way in this new social order, even if it did not command cultural dominance. But the ideas that germinated in Italy gradually spread throughout the continent.

Predictably, this dramatic social change brought conflict. In Fiore's day, intermittent warfare gripped the whole of Europe. Combined with new technology and a powerful commerical base drove advancements in military equipment. The medieval knights began their transition into what would become the officers of Renaissance armies. For the average man-at-arms it was now possible both to acquire well made armour of plate and he could advance based on accomplishment and renown as well as by birth.

For centuries, the man-at-arms and knight had been defended by coats of mail, interlinked flat rings of riveted iron worn over a padded coat or *aketon*. During the 14th century, these defenses were gradually augmented, first by plates for the limbs made of *cuirboille*—hardened leather—later made of iron plate. Plate armour developed rapidly during the third quarter of the 14th century, exactly during the time that Fiore taught. As furnace technology improved, plate became more available even to the rank-and-file man at arms. The average combatant became difficult to wound using the single-handed sword that had long dominated the battlefield.

In response, during the 14th century swords became more tapered so that the point could better penetrate between the plates. The older hexagonal cross-section gradually gave way to a diamond cross-section better suited to thrusting. Similarly, the handle was

extended a few inches so that a second hand could be brought to bear. With two hands on the handle, a strike to the head would at least jar or potentially discomfit the opponent enough to make a final, killing strike.

THE MEDIEVAL LONGSWORD

Many myths surround the medieval sword, many of which have been perpetuated by popular films, some by unskilled swordmakers. Original swords are much lighter than people think. I have had the pleasure of handling a number of medieval originals, and they are usually characterized by a livliness quite unlike the ponderous things people usually associate with medieval sword weapons.

The swords presented in Fiore's treatise appear to be relatively simple, long, elegant tapering swords that seem to be as long as the magistro from his sternum to the ground. The cross is straight, tapering slightly towards the ends, and the pommel is what we now call a "scent-stopper," which allows for its use as part of the handle. Such swords are commonly depicted in Italian iconography of the time, although surviving examples in England, France and Germany often show regional preferences in design. Although tapered, swords from this period are equally useful with the edge and point.

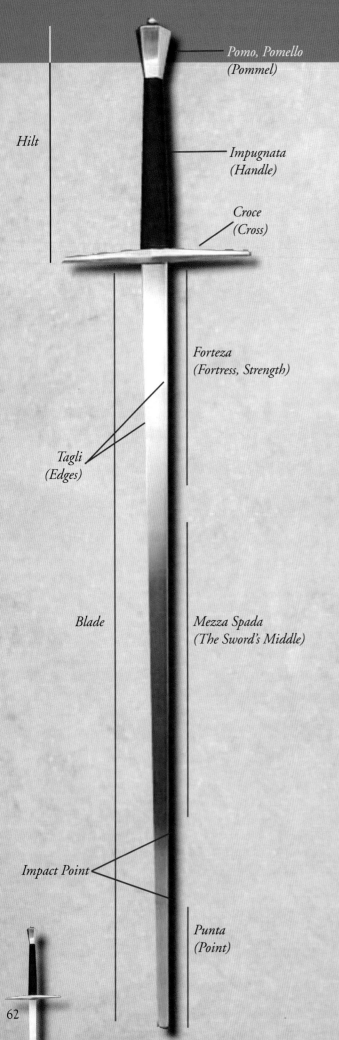

Pomo, Pomello
(Pommel)

Hilt

Impugnata
(Handle)

Croce
(Cross)

Forteza
(Fortress, Strength)

Tagli
(Edges)

Blade

Mezza Spada
(The Sword's Middle)

Impact Point

Punta
(Point)

The best source for history and details on European swords must be Ewart Oakeshott's *Records of the Medieval Sword*. For the first time, Mr. Oakeshott presented a polished typology of medieval swords that has become the gold standard for scholars, curators, conservators, makers of reproductions and students of swordsmanship. Of all his swords, types XVa and XVII most closely depict the swords shown in Fiore's treatises: They are long, elegant, tapering to an acute point, and usually feature straight or slightly curved cross and often have similar pommels. Here are Mr. Oakeshott's introductions for the respective types:

"XV & XVa: The general outline, or silhouette, of this type is very much like that of type XIV, but the section of the blade is totally different, as is the prime function of the sword. The XIV's were made and used when most defensive armour was still mail, with or without metal or leather or quilted reinforcement. The function of a XIV, like all of its predecessors, was to be a slashing and hewing weapon. A XV was meant to be able to deliver a lethal thrust, even though armour was largely of plate. It seems to have ben developed along with the development of plate armour… The illustrations and notes which follow demonstrate the form and general appearance of the type and its long-gripped, hand-and-a-half subtype, which by the 15th century would be called espée bastarde, or Bastard Sword. With this type, unlike some of its predecessors, dating becomes impossible without some kind of firm evidence, preferably external or contextual, for the type was popular from the late 13th century to the late 15th—indeed, the blade-form continued in use to the 19th century."

"With the coming of this sword-type, we have reached the era of complete plate armour. Though, of course, complete and homogeneous armour would not have been worn in its entirety, or even at all by men-at-arms, knights or otherwise. Mail, and occasional reinforcements of plate, or plain leather was often the only defense of the European man-at-arms. All the same, a type of sword had been devised to have some sort of capacity to deal with, at least to dent and hopefully bore holes in, complete plate armour. These swords which I have classified as Type XVII had always a long hand-and-a-half grip, and a very stout blade of hexagonal section, occasionally with a shallow fuller, and often very heavy and always very rigid and stiff…There are many survivors of this type, nearly all of them alike and most not all that handsome. I have shown a few representative examples of a very large class of survivors, those which for some reason seem more interesting (such as those which have a long 'ricasso') than the general run…."

Sadly, Mr. Oakeshott did not record weights in his study, but in the few places where he does talk about the weight, XVII.1 (The "Ely" sword), it was, "surprisingly light and lively in the hand." Contrast this with XVII.2, which weighs in at a monstrous 4lbs, and he says, "this is very heavy, even clumsy" and the Cambridge Sword, which weighs in at just 2 lbs. Swords of this type, if they are lively, will weigh between 2 and 3 pounds, with 2.5-2.75 being closer to the average. In both forms, the blades seem to average from 31-35", excluding the handle. Medieval swords were forged from billets of heterogenous material that included large amounts of slag, worked with hammers into their approximte shape, ground and heat-treated by quenching, followed sometimes with tempering. The ideal final product would be hard on the edges yet soft at the core. The blade would be able to bend (along the flat) considerably and then spring back to shape. They are light, and lively, able to be used all day as a tool of defense.

Not only would swords of the period taper in profile, but they would taper too on edge, in what modern craftsmen call "distill" taper. This lightened the point considerably, so that the balance point was from 2" – 4" from the hilt; this has been true for all of the historical examples that I have had the honor of handling, and in the few examples where the balance point is further up the blade, Oakeshott notes this in his text as feeling "clumsy," a sentiment I heartily agree with. This is really true for any sword that approaches 3 pounds, although it is a question of balance as much as weight.

One long-ignored aspect of the sword is its point of harmonic balance. If struck, the blade will occilate. At a point somewhere between the *punta* and *mezzo*, we find a place where the occilations are neutral; this is usually the "point of percussion" where the sword will strike with the maximum impact and with little jarring to the hand wielding it.

In order to achieve this, many swords have a far heavier pommel that might be supposed. My guess is that the pommel would have been crafted last, forged and ground to make the desired weight before being piened into place. In some cases, in order to get the weight of the blade down, "fullers" or grooves where forged into the blade, removing material (and thus weight). These were most certainly not "blood grooves," despite some high-profile Internet claims to the contrary.

Another common myth is that the blades where necessarily sharpened. While some where, as is recorded in literature, there are many, many illustrations within the fighting treatises that show an ungloved hand gripping the middle of the sword. This would indicate either that the blades were not razor-sharp, as is sometimes believed, or that the combatants used a particular method for gripping that kept the palm and fingers away from the edge, clamping the sword tightly. We'll never know for sure, because surviving swords have been cleaned and "maintained" for generations, and the edges are very easy to alter by design or accident. My personal belief is that both are true, and it is certainly possible to grip a sharp sword securely without being wounded.

The sword of this period is an elegant but workmanlike hewing and thrusting weapon. Indeed, in his text Fiore refers far more often to *colpi*—strikes or blows—than he does to *tagli*, which are cuts. The medieval sword delivers blows, striking at an oblique angle to make its cut. A razor edge is unnecessary for this: For an opponent wearing a quilted cloth defense, the sword will have sufficient energy to cut and/or crush. For an opponent defended by mail, the sword will be more likely to crush through the mail, or puncture using the point. For one defended by iron or steel plate, the blade can dent the armour (especially good at the joints), or momentarily

Surviving German training sword from the 16th century, courtesy of the Metropolitan Museum of Art, New York. Swords like this one feature a narrower blade (but thicker, especially on the edges, hence the term "rebated.") than on blades carried in the field since the object is to train effectively but as realistically as possible. Models like this have provided inspiration for modern swordmakers in their quest for an ideal training weapon.

stun him with a blow to the head. He can be disarmed with blows to the hand. But repeated blows along a sharp edge will leave their mark, no matter how good the steel, forging and heat-treating that follows. The edge does not need to be razor-sharp unless it is deisgned for cutting a softer surface, such as cloth or leather.

All in all, taste in medieval swords is largely individual. Some prefer more weight, some the balance point slightly forward or slightly back. But most people agree when they pick up a truly fine specimen, so I don't think the individual preferences are as solid as many people think, except in terms of overall weight. A fine sword is generally agreed to be a fine sword in terms of performance and feel.

MODERN SWORDS

For the modern student of swordsmanship, the lightness and liveliness of authentic blades stands out, and it is difficult to capture this even for some of the best modern craftsmen. But there are a few who produce authentic blades for use by students, collectors and reenactors. I'll introduce a few of these who I have personally worked with after I discuss the needs of a modern student.

Ideally, the modern student would work with a sword that is as close to the original examples if possible. In a perfect world, we would conjure a "replicator" that would duplicate, in every aspect, an original. But this is a tall order, we don't have a replicator and duplicating the originals is much harder than might be supposed. Arms and armour-makers have long been secretive, and the techniques used to produce medieval blades were closely guarded trade secrets. Today, reproduction artists and production houses strive to duplicate the originals with varying degrees of success.

There are a few makers of modern reproductions whose work strongly invokes the feel of the originals. Given the attention to detail required to get a close match, good swords tend to be on the expensive side. In general, modern craftsmen grind rather than forge their blades, since few are willing to pay the price of a hand-forged weapon. But some of these ground weapons are quite good!

Because working exclusively with duplicates of medieval originals is both expensive and dangerous, modern students of medieval swordsmanship need different kinds of weapons for different circumstances. For forms and individual work, a reproduction is an excellent choice, if the student has the means to acquire one. In class, when drills are done in pairs, sharp weapons don't make sense, and the weapons should ideally be matched to avoid excessive damage to one or the other. When sparring, there are different considerations, depending upon the kind of protective gear to be used. If the students wish to test cut, then a "performance" blade is often the selection of choice.

Reproductions

A reproduction attempts to duplicate an original, or to create an original in the style of the historical models. By and large, reproductions will be expensive, but finely wrought exemplars of medieval swords. They are ideal to use for individual work, for presentations and demonstrations, and to have as collector's items.

When shopping for a reproduction, historical accuracy and quality craftsmanship should be the two main guiding factors, with performance based on these two factors. As much as possible, the reproduction should have a similar feel to the original. It should be dimensionally as exact as possible, as should be weight. The weight distribution is also important: The balance point should be at the same point as the original. Since most of us don't have originals to test, the student is well served to ask the craftsman if this is true in his version. If the information isn't available, then the balance point would ideally be 2" – 4" from the cross.

Under the handle, sword's tang should be wide and thick, made in one piece with the hilt. It is common for mass-market sword manufacturers to use "rat tail" tangs, barstock welded to the blade. This weld itself is at a crucial point in the blade's structure, and these swords will generally break at this point if used at all. For the same reason, the join between the tang itself and the blade should have a radius. If the join is made sharply, then stress cracks can form and the tang will again snap, no matter its width.

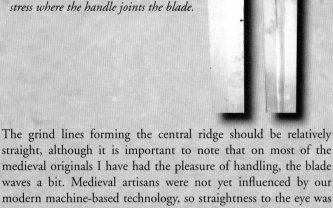

Sword tangs:
These two disassembled swords show different constructions under the handle, called the "tang."
On the left, the common "rat tail" construction used on inexpensive swords, where a piece of bar-stock is welded to the blade. This construction method is insufficient for blades which must withstand contact.
On the right, an "integral" tang, suitably wide. The tang should be as wide as possible in order to support the stress where the handle joints the blade.

The grind lines forming the central ridge should be relatively straight, although it is important to note that on most of the medieval originals I have had the pleasure of handling, the blade waves a bit. Medieval artisans were not yet influenced by our modern machine-based technology, so straightness to the eye was less precise than the absolute straightness of a modern metal ruler.

On a higher quality reproduction, the blade thickness will taper towards the tip. The metal used will be some form of spring steel—not stainless (too brittle)—and it will be able to take some bend and spring back to shape. The blade will have been heat-treated and tempered, a risky phrase of the process because some blades will warp or twist, ruining the swordmaker's work.

The cross should attach without rattling, being set firmly in place. The handle will usually be made of wood, often covered in leather or occasionally cloth. Wire wraps are not common in this period. The pommel should be held in place either with a well-concealed nut or be piened into place, that is, the tang is hammered over to secure the whole handle assembly in place.

ARMS & ARMOR CO.
MINNEAPOLIS, MN

rms & Armor is dedicated to providing the highest quality blades and service. Their method—individually handcrafting reproductions of the highest caliber—allows modern students of the Art to experience of the true feel and majestic look of swords from the past. As Craig Johnson says, "The originals are our pattern book. We strive to replicate the elegant feel as well as the look of the swords and weapons that inspire us."

Working closely with museums, they incorporated as much historical detail as possible into each model, capturing not only the look, but also much of the original performance. Original medieval swords are truly inspirational and eminently functional tools.

Craig's mentor, the late Ewart Oakeshott, provided a great wealth of knowledge to expand their study of the medieval sword. They continue to cooperate with museums and collections around the world, developing research and contributing to exhibitions and interpretation of the Medieval and Renaissance period.

Arms and Armour is the preferred provider to the Schola Saint George for swords in the intermediate or advanced student of the Art, especially for steel trainers. Their spada di zhogo and fechtspiel (shown left) rebated training weapons are, without question, the finest we've had the pleasure of using.

Find them on the web: **www.armor.com**

Above: *Arms and Armor's single-handed rebated training sword, shown with Revival Martial Arts' cuirboille and steel buckler.* Above left: *Arms & Armor Fechtspiel, their trainer based on originals in German fighting treatises.*

Below: *A Hanwei "practical hand and a half" sword— a good beginner's weapon—showing the width of the underlying tang riveted over the end of the pommel. Most medieval swords seem to have been finished this way: in the field, the rivet could be quickly and easily retightened without needing a wrench.*

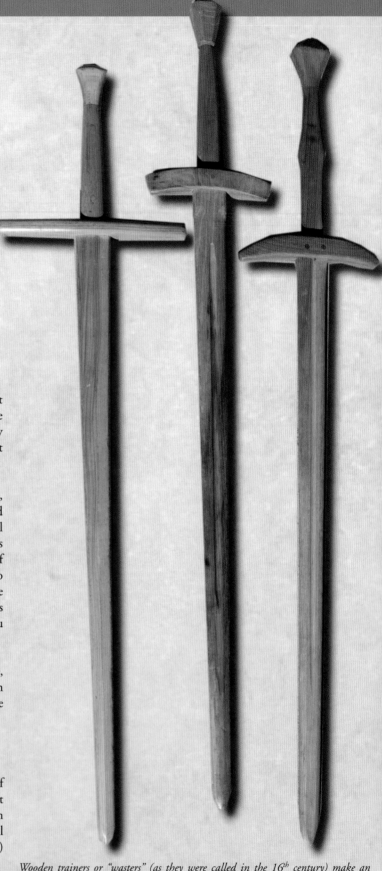

The whole sword should feel as alive in the hand as possible. It should want to dart from place to place. In delivering a blow, the balance point should enable it to quickly change its trajectory without undue strain, and it should be comfortable in the thrust or in the strike.

Such a blade will, at today's pricing, run between $500 and $2000, with the vast majority being closer to $800. For a hand-forged blade done by an expert, figure between $2000 - $3000. Medieval originals on the market typically sell for around $20,000, in today's market, placing them well beyond the reach of most students. If you are in the market for an original, use care, since it is easy to be taken with a forgery, especially at an online auction. My advice would be to start with Peter Finer of London, perhaps the world's most respected dealer in historical arms, and tell them what you want.

Middle quality blades, which lack several of the key features above, can be had for about $300 - $500, and these can be had from such manufacturers as Hanwei, Windlass, and Del Tin (my preference of these three is for the Del Tin).

Performance Swords

Alongside reproductions, there are a very few makers of "performance" swords, very high quality manufactured blades that move beautifully, but which are to modern standards rather than being reproductions of medieval originals. Amongst this very small group, Michael Pearce (aka "Tinker") and Angus Trim (aka "Gus") stand out as amazing craftsmen.

Performance swords are created using modern engineering techniques to scientific specifications. The result is finely made, solid weapons that have perfectly tuned resonance points and

Wooden trainers or "wasters" (as they were called in the 16th century) make an excellent beginning training sword, although more and more study groups within the Schola have begun to go away form wood and over the rebated steel. But they remain an excellent, cost-effective answer to a trainer. The center model is made by Purpleheart Armouries, and they are highly recommended for their quality and high level of customer service.

ANGUS TRIM, SWORDMAKER

High-performance "cutting swords" like this one are beautiful distillations of medieval style, perfect for test-cutting on Tatami mats, as shown in chapter 9. This one is made by Angus Trim.

that feel very lively. They are exellent weapons for form work, or better, for test-cutting (see chapter 9). The blades arrive razor sharp, and for this reason alone they must be handled with great care. You can expect to pay from $450 - $600 for a performance sword.

Within the Schola, we use **Angus Trim** swords almost exclusively for test cutting, because they are a superb choice for the job. While the standard hilts are definitely modern in character, there are a few artisans, such as Christian Fletcher, who have done superb work rehilting the weapons with more reproduction-quality fittings. The addition of fittings can add $400 - $700 to the sword's price, but the final product is a thing of beauty.

For those who want to emphasize test cutting, then I'd strongly recommend the purchase of a Gus Trim weapon to use for both form work and for test cutting.

Trainers

In class, students will execute countless drills and form exercises. In some cases there may be sparring. For this, compatible training swords—trainers—are necessary, and cost-consciousness is important. Rather than using reproduction swords, nearly all instructors recommend some kind of trainer, but there are many different trainers to choose from, including those made from wood, aluminum, rebated steel, and most recently, from high-tech carbon-kevlar composites. What you select will depend on safety, objectives, cost and availability.

Any kind of trainer distorts the historical technique somewhat. "Rebated" steel swords have their edges thickened, resulting in increased weight. Neither they nor aluminum swords are typically very good at yielding on the thrust, but they don't often cut. They do, however, pack a punch with blows because they are typically much heavier than the originals. Wooden weapons are usually cost-effective and serviceable, but are usually also heavier than the originals, plus they can splinter into dangerous shards. Weapons of rattan, popular with the SCA, are usually much heavier than the original weapons and are for use against armoured opponents. Shinair-based weapons have served the Schola for a time, but even these are generally heavier than the medieval originals and combatants have a tendency to want to armour up. Padded weapons, popular amongst LARP groups and some Western martial arts groups for their inclusiveness, are often too light, and they bounce. Most recently, we have developed a carbon-kevlar high tech composite sword that looks promising.

Wood

In Dom Duarte's *Regimen per Aprender Alguas Cousas d'Armas*, he mentions the use of wooden swords for training. This is mirrored in several of the German texts, especially the *dussak*, a 16th century trainer for the steel *messer*. English referneces make note of wooden "wasters," being used for training, and such weapons have for years been the staple of students working in the Western martial arts. A good quality waster, such as those made by **Purpleheart Armories** (www.woodenswords.com), will be of a known hardwood, relatively stout and should be under a hundred dollars. There is ample historical precedent for their use, and they are the most common trainer in use today. I favor hickory or ash, but there are other woods that are sometimes used as well. On the downside, wooden weapons are not good for sparring, since they will shatter under heavy impact. The low-cost imported versions should be avoided for anything but form work, as they are made from indeterminant wood and will often soon break.

"Rebated" steel

We know that, at least by the 16th century, heavier steel training swords were in use because several of them have survived. One of these is in the Metropolitan Museum of Art, NY. These weapons play surprisingly well in the hand, at at least one reproduction artist, Craig Johnson of **Arms & Armor** (www.armor.com) in Minneapolis, have made excellent models that are very good, especially for the advanced student. These weapons play very well in the hand, yield a bit on the thrust, and feature a tapering thickness. These are in the $400 range, and must be considered the best available today for students who have the resources.

Thicker steel weapons were also in use during the 15th century, as we have evidence their proposed use in King Rene's tournaent book, dated to the 3rd quarter of the century. Rene shows a short slashing sword, thickened on the edge, and heavily grooved to reduce its weight. The pommel is over-large and could be heavy, heavy enough perhaps to balance the blade. Dom Duarte also advises in his *Regimento* that students should, "test himself with a heavier weapon, which is something more than those he seeks to carry on the day of combat."

Today, European reenactment societies rely mainly on rebated steel weapons. Many of these weapons are extremely heavy, which some of their proponents prefer, claiming that it slows down the fighting, resulting in safer competition. Whether this is true or not, the weapons are very heavy, and hard to stop once a blow has been begun. They hit with significant force, also.

But because there are so many groups using this style of blade, rebated weapons have begun to be made available by manufacturers such as **Hanwei** (find through their many distributors) and our own **Revival Martial Arts** (www.revival.us). They are cost-effective, retailing for around $100 - $150. They have full tangs and simple, cast steel hilt furniture and because of their durability are frequently used in tournaments featuring steel weapons, in reenactment, and amongst Western martial arts groups.

Steel weapons will quickly develop nicks in the blade, and these must be quickly filed or sanded down, otherwise they can cause stress fractures. Over time, they will become unusuable, or more likely, they will eventually break.

In sparring, the swords are unsuitable except for those moving at very slow speeds or those wearing complete armour. Their extra mass makes them very hard to stop; while a single-handed rebated sword can be reigned in with relative ease, a bastard- or longsword is much harder to stop. While not a problem on padded areas, it can be devastating to a fencing mask or the bones of the hand, elbow, shoulder or knee. Because the weapons are rebated, they have pretty much no flex in the thrust, so combats using them tend to be restricted with respect to thrusts.

Using a steel blade has advantages over other materials. The weapons play much more realistically against one another. They are excellent for demonstrating the art at speed. The only major downsides is the extra weight, and to a lesser degree the cost.

Within the Schola Saint George, this class of rebated weapons is a common first purchase for our students, since they can use them in class, for form work, and eventually for armoured sparring. They are also excellent against a pell.

Aluminum

For many years, stage combatants and Hollywood propmen have used special hard aluminums to make lighter, rebated copies of medieval and medieval-like weapons. Aluminum, being lighter than steel, has the advantage that it can be thicker on edge and weigh less than the steel models, but it has the downside of being a much more expensive material (especially the 7075 series favored for blades).

Propmen, such as David Baker from the **Hollywood Combat Center**, create aluminum weapons for stage and training. These can be had in diverse styles and with a great deal of customization, and I must say that for several years I prefered them for their weight and performance. They were light enough to mimic the moderately weighted originals, and as such, were extremely safe for sparring and light competition, as well as drill. On the downside, because the blades are not made for production, their availability is often a problem. Similarly, they are not usually made for the rough-and-tumble constant use of a school of swordsmanship, so the handles would loosen and eventually fail. Still, I very much like these weapons and still recommend them for sparring.

Some armourers, such as Rob Valentine of **Valentine Armories** and Robert Jenkins, have offered more durable aluminum simulators. These usually use the "messer" method of handle construction—like those used on modern kitchen knives—that never rattles loose. The weapons are pretty much bullet-proof, but lack the refinement of the custom-made and better-balanced aluminum replicas noted above. Some of these weapons, such as those made by Rob Valentine, are made from 3/16" thick aluminum, which gives some in the thrust. Others are ¼" thick, which although durable, hits very hard and is about the same as a rebated steel weapon.

Aluminum weapons have the advantage of lightness, and if durable production models become available, could become the "gold standard" for light sparring. I still recommend them for those advanced students who want to spar with the metal weapons, but the blades should be 3/16", not ¼". Unfortunately, they are still composed from multiple pieces and tend to be more expensive and

Aluminum and steel sword trainers in use by the Schola Saint George:

(outer left) - Rebated steel blade by Paul MacDonald of Scotland, excellent craftsmanship! Weight, 2 lbs. 12 oz.

(inner left) - 3/16" thick aluminum sword by Valentine Armouries. Weight, 2 lbs. 7oz.

(center) - Rebated steel blade by CAS Iberia / Hanwei, a good budget choice. Weight, 2 lbs., 10oz.

(inner right) - Spada di zhogo by Arms & Armor, superb handling and durability. Weight, 3 lbs., 1 oz.

(outer right) - Spada di zhogo, maestro version, by Arms & Armor, the best performing trainer I've handled. Weight, 2 lbs, 13 oz.

less readily available than their rebated steel counterparts, ranging from $120 - $200.

Rattan

The Society for Creative Anachronism (SCA), has long experimented with full-contact combat technique. Their weapons are made from a solid form of bamboo-grass known as rattan, which is durable, relatively cheap, and fairly readily available. But SCA rules require all weapons to be at least 1 ¼" across, which makes bastard swords made from this material for the SCA heavy, but very durable for use against an armoured opponent. SCA weapons pack a punch, but this is part of their art. For students of the art who want to try their skills in North America's largest community of medieval combatants, a rattan weapon will be needed.

Rattan was also and is also used by single-stick players for simulating light, single-handed swords. This rattan is generally 5/8" in diameter, is light and plays well. We are experimenting with the use of this lighter rattan for simulators, but the tests are still in progress. We have found that a 5/8" piece of rattan, surrounded by dense closed-cell foam and sheathed in cloth, makes a very good contact trainer for children, and we will likely continue development along these lines.

With rattan, the downside is that it is hard to shape, since it is a loose, fibrous material. Making it into a blade shape is very hard, and efforts to try to band smaller pieces together have not met with much success. So the subtlety of the edge and flat dynamics fo the blade are unfortunately lost. Also, the rattan bounces on contact, yielding an unrealistic movement.

Overall, rattan is perfectly suited to the combat of the SCA, but because the blade shape is lost, it is less ideal for use as a sparring trainer in the context of historical swordsmanship because of its weight, springiness, and difficulty in shaping. There also no ready supply for weapons—they must generally be made by the student himself.

Shinai

The Japanese art of Kendo has long relied on another kind of bamboo-grass weapon for their combats. These are the *shinai*, relatively common and easy-to-acquire light sword trainers. Shinai are indeed the main weapon used in competitive Ken-do meets, as well as for training. However, pracititioers of Ken-jutisi or other Japanese sword arts frequently complain about the art as practiced for tournament, observing that many techniques evolve to the training tool, stepping ever further from the original art. Western sport fencing has experienced this same distortion as specialized weapons have evolved to take maximum advantage of the sporting rules (such as the pistol-gripped sword). As a whole, shinai as they are are too light and they have the same lack-of-edge that makes rattan problematic.

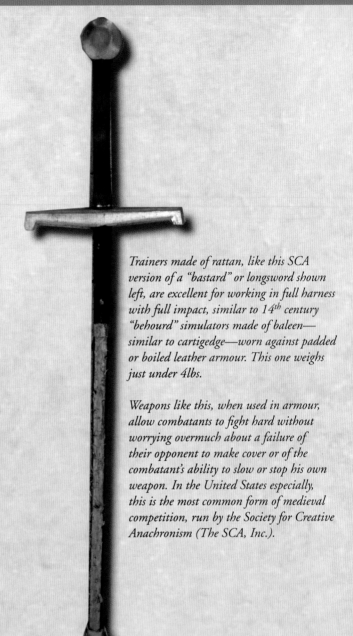

Trainers made of rattan, like this SCA version of a "bastard" or longsword shown left, are excellent for working in full harness with full impact, similar to 14th century "behourd" simulators made of baleen— similar to cartigedge—worn against padded or boiled leather armour. This one weighs just under 4lbs.

Weapons like this, when used in armour, allow combatants to fight hard without worrying overmuch about a failure of their opponent to make cover or of the combatant's ability to slow or stop his own weapon. In the United States especially, this is the most common form of medieval competition, run by the Society for Creative Anachronism (The SCA, Inc.).

Many groups, such as the Chicago Swordplay Guild, have experimented extensively with modified shinai used as sparring trainers. We have done this also in the Schola Saint George, and in both cases, the results are somewhat satisfactory. By adding an edge of self-adhesive window insulation or similar, and covering the whole with tape or cloth, a shinai can be made to take on a more blade-like shape. The shinai can also be fitted with a cross, or even a pommel, and then used against lightly armoured opponents. But the resulting weapons have an irritating tendency to break, and except for our own **Revival Martial Arts** products, there are as yet no commercially available crosses or pommels.

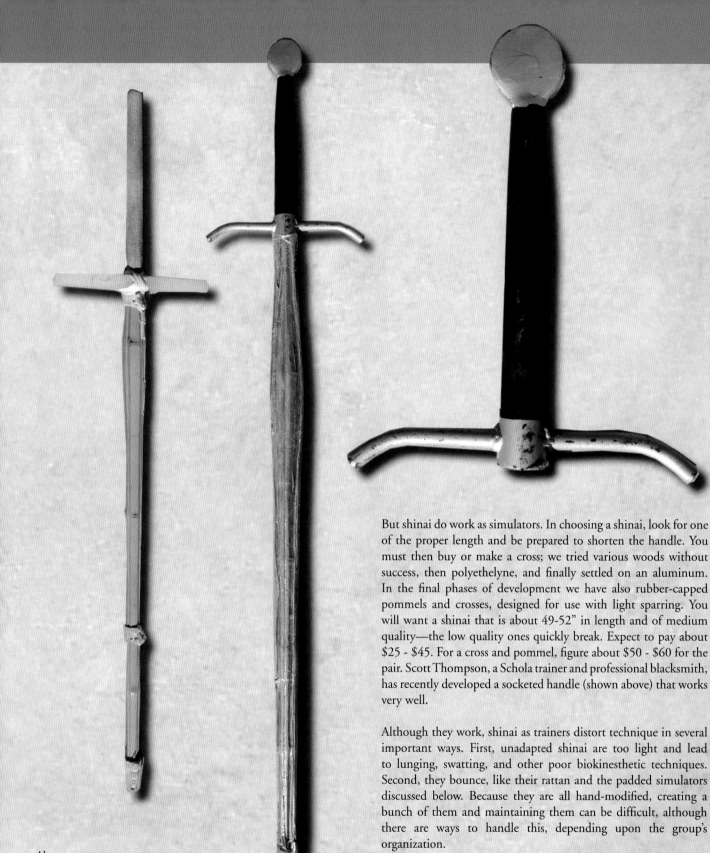

But shinai do work as simulators. In choosing a shinai, look for one of the proper length and be prepared to shorten the handle. You must then buy or make a cross; we tried various woods without success, then polyethelyne, and finally settled on an aluminum. In the final phases of development we have also rubber-capped pommels and crosses, designed for use with light sparring. You will want a shinai that is about 49-52" in length and of medium quality—the low quality ones quickly break. Expect to pay about $25 - $45. For a cross and pommel, figure about $50 - $60 for the pair. Scott Thompson, a Schola trainer and professional blacksmith, has recently developed a socketed handle (shown above) that works very well.

Although they work, shinai as trainers distort technique in several important ways. First, unadapted shinai are too light and lead to lunging, swatting, and other poor biokinesthetic techniques. Second, they bounce, like their rattan and the padded simulators discussed below. Because they are all hand-modified, creating a bunch of them and maintaining them can be difficult, although there are ways to handle this, depending upon the group's organization.

Being aware of the distortions will certainly help you to avoid "fighting to the rules," but it cannot eliminate it, and this becomes increasingly problematic the closer students get to free-sparring or in tournaments.

Above:
Shinai make excellent simulators for unarmoured sparring, although safety equipment must still be worn. Shown above is a bare shinai with a polyethelyne cross held in place with rawhide. On the right is a shinai edged with self-adhesive window insulation (1/2" thick), 1" of foam at the tip, and covered in a silver-colored duct tape. The result is more European blade shape, and the use of a hilt by Scott Thompson makes the trainer quick an economical to make.

Daga, Lanza & Azza trainers

In addition to the sword, Fiore shows his principles with other chivalric weapons of the period, including the dagger (*daga*), spear (*lanza*) and poleaxe (*azza*). Within the Schola, we have developed training tools for each weapon.

Daga

The medieval dagger was really what we might think of as a sturdy ice-pick used almost exclusively for thrusts from above. Students have made good use of wooden *daga* simulators made by Purpleheart Armories. For our purposes, however, we needed a softer trainer that would enable the partner to strike fully without pausing for safety. Most *compagni* would pull their strike in order not to injure their partner meant that either they would delay just prior to impact (exhibiting excellent control), or they would pound their opponet. In response, we developed a rubber training *daga* that allows combatants to use a full strike, yet still work the disarms. Better still, they seem to be perfect for sparring.

Lanza

Although we focus our coursework on the medieval longsword, there is a great deal to be learned through the use of the short spear, what the Italians called the *lanza*. We use the spear to introduce our students to sparring because it is a far simpler weapon. In this context, we use the point only, and the whole body is a target. Combatants learn about controlling distance, timing, exchanging and breaking the thrust, and they gain an appreciation for tactical decision-making.

Our lanzas are rubber tips made by Revival Martial Arts and mounted on 1 1/8" ash poles. They can be used with minimal armour, such as light sparring gloves, a 3-weapon fencing mask, groin and throat protection.

Azza

Another of Fiore's weapons is the poleaxe, or *azza*. This is a consumate weapon of power, a medieval assault weapon designed to wound a man fully armoured in plate. As such, wooden and metal-headed varieties are extremely dangerous to practice with, much less to spar with.

Our *azza* heads are also made by our very own Revival Martial Arts, but they are designed for use in armour. The are solid rubber, and when married with a square or octagonal ash haft and two rubber *lanza* tips, we have a complete trainer for the poleaxe.

Composites

Very recently, I have been developing a high-tech carbon fiber based, single-piece trainer designed to serve as a single tool for form work, pair drills, and light sparring. Composites are on the whole lighter than steel, so the edges can be thicker while simultaneously more closely duplicating the weight of the medieval originals. The material can be made flexible, yielding on the thrust. And composites blended in the right mix can be extremely tough. Finally, once the expensive tooling is paid for, the per unit cost might be quite low. I really feel that this is the future of medieval swordsmanship in the Western martial arts, and the results of our experiments can be found on the Schola Saint George website and through one of our companies, Revival Marial Arts.

ARMOUR AND EQUIPMENT

In order to practice medieval swordsmanship, it is most helpful to acquirc or gradually build up a set of gear appropriate to training. Of course this will include a training weapon of some kind, but other things—such as gloves and appropriate shoes—are very useful even in the early stages. As the student progresses, defensive equipment—armour—will become increasingly valuable. Because each student is different, the level of protection they adopt is an individual choice.

At the most basic level, students need only footwear and gloves, plus a trainer. For their first sparring, which we do with a spear, students usually wear a light helmet or three-weapon fencing mask, gorget, *zuparello* (gambeson, arming coat) or WMA training jacket, knee pads, and groin protection.

For higher level work, and for those who want to continue with their study, an appropriate medieval jacket (*zuparello*), sparring gauntlets, a light helmet and gorget, and *cuirboille* (hardened leather) elbows and knees are recommended.

At this high end, combatants often want to assemble a full harness of transitional or 15th century plate armour in order to participate fully in various feats of arms, the challenge, tournaments we hold to celebrate and showcase hard-won skills alongside the rest of the knightly virtues.

Hand Protection

Swordsmanhip can be practiced with the bare hand, but hundreds or thousands of repetitions will tear the hands, so gloves are useful, also providing some protection against incidental strikes that happen from time to time when working with a partner or in a drill line. Within the Schola, we prefer long-cuffed gloves akin to those worn in RA MS I.33, soft but durable leather that doesn's restrict the hand. Just such a glove will protect the hands against cuts caused by nicks in the blade and cross that will soon develop in any metal practice weapon.

Better, we have made what we call padded "light sparring" gloves, a very similar design but enhanced with several thin layers of a high-density martial arts foam. They reduce the chances for incidental contact to break the small bones of the hand and wrist, and have become very popular in the martial arts community.

Advancing this one step, we have Kevlar-armoured gloves that provide more solid protection to the small bones of the hand and wrist which provide a much better layer of defense against shocking blows from most training weapons. Because they are light, they do little against heavy rebates or weapons of rattan. But for most of the trainers used in the Western martial arts, they offer a relatively strong level of protection without sacrificing finger mobility. Many students have in the past selected ice, roller or street-hockey gloves to fill this role, but these hand defenses rely on soft, thick layers of foam that is less able to protect the hand from a rebated sword blade than they are from a big hockey stick. Still, they are easy to find at online auctions and may be purchased for very little money.

Ultimately, truly serious students assemble one or two pairs of medieval gauntlets. The "mitten" varieties common to the 15th century work well, if they are made in light tempered spring steel. Likewise, light "finger" gauntlets are very useful as they convey more freedom with excellent protection against the light sparring blades we use in the Schola. The mittens serve well for combats with heavy weapons such as the poleaxe or with rattan trainers, while the finger gauntlets are often used for sword and spear.

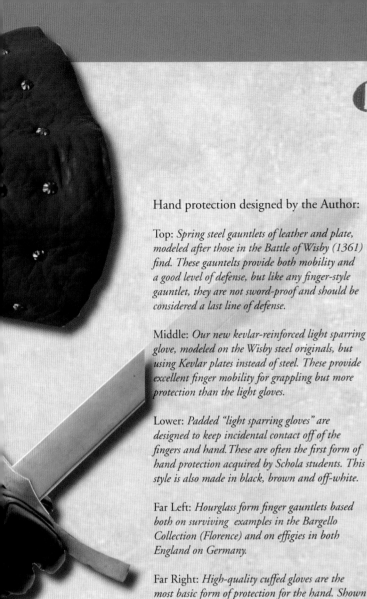

Hand protection designed by the Author:

Top: *Spring steel gauntlets of leather and plate, modeled after those in the Battle of Wisby (1361) find. These gauntlets provide both mobility and a good level of defense, but like any finger-style gauntlet, they are not sword-proof and should be considered a last line of defense.*

Middle: *Our new kevlar-reinforced light sparring glove, modeled on the Wisby steel originals, but using Kevlar plates instead of steel. These provide excellent finger mobility for grappling but more protection than the light gloves.*

Lower: *Padded "light sparring gloves" are designed to keep incidental contact off of the fingers and hand. These are often the first form of hand protection acquired by Schola students. This style is also made in black, brown and off-white.*

Far Left: *Hourglass form finger gauntlets based both on surviving examples in the Bargello Collection (Florence) and on effigies in both England on Germany.*

Far Right: *High-quality cuffed gloves are the most basic form of protection for the hand. Shown here is the Revival.us model embellished with embroidery drawn from the gloves shown in the earliest fighting treatise, Royal Armouries RA MS I.33.*

Defending the body

For the most part, the body should be protected by a padded fighting coat (a gambeson or what Fiore calls a *zuparello*), that provides protection in its own right and serves as the foundation for armour. Gambesons may be made or purchased, but they should always be made from 100% natural fibers, and should be made to medieval specifications, as the arm attachments are specialized and optimized for swordsmanship. While imported gambeson-like garments are available from many online vendors, few of these actually provides the freedom of movement that the originals do, largely because the authentic patterns are complicated and tend to drive tailors or seamstresses mad with frustration. But these inexpensive versions will serve to a degree; expect to pay from $90 - $125 for one in this class.

The better quality gambesons will be made from linen, hemp cloth, or wool. The arms will be set with the "grand assiette" or sleeve, and the garment will come down to the crotch or mid-thigh level. Expect to pay from $300 for an off-the rack or $500 or more for a custom gambeson in this class. Although expensive, quality gambesons are worth every penny! A few sellers, such as **Revival.us**, offer high-quality gambesons of linen, or many Schola students decide to sew or attempt to sew their own. Another good source has been **Matlus**, in Poland, which does custom-made work at a fair price.

We have also worked with a jacket that features a series of protective plates, what we call our "WMA" jacket. This works well as a loaner bit of protection, because it goes on quickly and offers defense over the elbows, shoulders, sternum, ribs, and back. Because they fit a wide variety of persons, and are relatively inexpensive, we can arm many people quickly—useful qualities when teaching large classes of beginners.

Overall, the student will definitely find it advantageous to begin to wear a gambeson as early as possible. The fighting coat helps protect the body and arms when working with a partner, something that within our own Schola begins very soon in the program.

Head and Neck

Defense of the head is to some degree problematic. Many schools, ours included, use 3-weapon fencing masks, which suffice for the basic work, but don't provide much protection for sparring. Ideally, combatants will have light helmets of cuirboille or light spring steel fitted with the appropriate visors.

For pair training, we often rely on good-quality fencing masks because they are readily available. In the past, we have tried escrima helmets, kendo masks, hockey helmets, and even SCA helmets. All work to some degree, but all have weaknesses.

During the time that Fiore taught, the dominant helmet was the bascinet. A sleek, simple and very practrical helmet that could be fitted with an aventail of mail, or sometimes of cloth. Bascinets

Zuparelli, gambesons or arming cottes can be made or purchased in different weights, each type ideal for a particular activity.

The black cotte above is the SSG fighting zuparello, a lightweight cotton garment by www.revival.us based on the grand assiette sleeve inset.

The middle one is a heavy duty padded leather cotte, suitable for added safety needed in intensive "unarmoured" sparring.

The lower one is a medium linen fighting cotte suitable for unarmoured sparring.

varied in weight, ranging from 3lbs to more than 8 lbs, which we know from surviving examples. In the *Flos Duellatorum*, Fiore even shows curious grilled bascinet visors used with the poleaxe. For the major part of the manuscript, the combatants practice with open or visors removed (although not with the poleaxe).

Within the Schola we favor light bascinets, crafted from 16 or 18g. spring steel. We have crafted also a pierced form of visor that mimics the correct hundskul sometimes seen on early bacscinets. The visors are removable, and interchaneable, so that other visors such as a grille, a full medieval visor, or even one of Lexan.® Grilles, for example, are ideal when working with padded or rattan trainers, but do little when used with blades.

When working with trainers, protection for the head and throat is critical. Most trainers have significant mass, and the default fencing mask offers precious little protection. When working with metal trainers, special care must also be taken to protect the throat.

One of the benefits to selecting a bascinet as the head defense is that bascinets were often fitted with mail defenses for the neck called aventails. A correct aventail scoops up alongside the face, which protects the chin and throat from the weapon's edge and point. Good mail will be riveted, with fairly small rings from ¼" to a maximum of 3/8" diameter, and will be a 4-in-1 weave that falls to below the shoulder-point.

Under the mail, there are even more defense options available. We have various forms of gorgets that provide another layer of defense under the aventail, or the fencing mask bib. Although gorgets are not historical prior to the middle of the 15th century, they are in fact a useful addition for defense to the throat in a day where safety consciousness is of paramount importance.

Masks or light helmets should be worn whenever training is conducted in pairs. Masks are sufficient where limited drills are being done, or when using light trainers, but they are insufficient for full-contact work with medieval weapons.

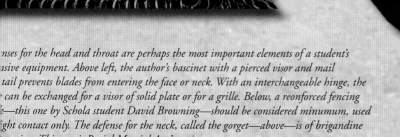

...nses for the head and throat are perhaps the most important elements of a student's ...usive equipment. Above left, the author's bascinet with a pierced visor and mail ...tail prevents blades from entering the face or neck. With an interchangeable hinge, the ... can be exchanged for a visor of solid plate or for a grille. Below, a reonforced fencing ...—this one by Schola student David Browning—should be considered minumum, used ...ght contact only. The defense for the neck, called the gorget—above—is of brigandine ...ruction. This one is Revial Martial Arts' version.

Elbows, Knees & Forearms

Although the gambeson adds a good foundational layer of defense for the body, hips and arms, it is useful to have rigid yet light protection over the knees and elbows. We prefer boiled leather for the task, the medieval equivalent of plastic. Simple elbows and forearm protection may be simply buckled into place and does not appear out of place on the medieval tournament field. Because the base of the art is done unarmoured, we have endeavored not to add large amounts of armour, as this steps the combatant closer to armoured combat, which has a very different dynamic.

Likewise, the knee is relatively delicate. Some of our combatants use medieval riding boots while others wear knee pads or pads with *cuirboille* poleyns (armour for the knee itself) attached.

Last but not Least—Shoes!

When working with medieval swordsmanship, it is extremely helpful to have medieval footwear. There are two reasons for this. First, medieval shoes have a smooth sole and a flat heel. This can prove decisive when working on the *volta*—turns. Second, this ability for the foot to slide around helps to protect the ligaments in the knee, which are easily damaged with sideways movement. As we will discuss in the chapter on stance and footwork, keeping the weight properly placed on the ball and along the inside of the leg keeps the knee joint in alignment and sharply reduces slipping. For both of these reasons, medieval shoes are one of the first things that I recommend for new combatants on their "new equipment to acquire" list.

The practice of the Art does not require as much equipment as skiing or scuba diving, but authentic gear changes how it is practiced.

Below left - *A pattern for an arming coat, a zuparello in the Italian. A zuparello can be purchased or made, although fabric and stuffing choice is important (use natural fabrics such as wool and linen).*
Center left - *The shoe style preferred by most Schola students, the 14th century Low Boot by Revival Leatherworks. The sole can be left smooth or a layer of vibram can be added for traction.*
Center - *Revival Leatherworks' riding boots provide some protection for the knee and calf.*
Right upper - *Another Revival Leatherworks shoe, this one a buckled-boot, also from Fiore's period.*
Right lower - *Author Brian R. Price (right) spars with his opponent. Brian wears a sturdy leather zuparello, hourglass gauntlets, a bscinet with pierced visor and a mail aventail, plus riding boots. His opponent wears a fencing mask, a brigandine gorget, "Wisby" style finger gauntlets made by Brian, and a custom*

WHAT SHOULD I GET FIRST?

Medieval shoes, since they change how the footwork is done. If you're on a very tight budget they can be made, or flat-soled chinese slippers or even old dress shoes will work, but modern tennis shoes with the high, padded heel should be avoided.

Early on a pair of gloves are recommended, as swordwork will create calluses and blisters. For a training weapon, I would advise that the new student purchase a rebated steel trainer, or if they are available, the carbon-kevlar models.

Once the combatant begins to work on the plays, they should acquire padded or armoured gloves, a zuparello (arming coat), helmet or mask and throat protection, along with a shinai- or carbon-kevlar based sparring weapon. Elbow and knee pads will also be needed at this point, along with athletic groin protection.

SSG Scolaro Russell Kinder of the DFW branch in tutta porta di ferro

CHAPTER FIVE

PRINCIPLES IN THE FIOR DI BATTAGLIA

 iore's system is a series of principles taught through the example of plays. Important variants on the principles are presented for each weapon according to its performance differences. What looks on the surface to be a broad collection of techniques are actually bound together by a few simple, potent and effective combat principles that can be adapted to any hand to hand combat environment.

Within the Schola, our intent is to follow and attempt to reconstruct the original material as closely as possible. We charge our students to internalize the principles and to think on their own, since the probable outcome of a fight is based as much on out-thinking the opponent as out-maneuvering him.

With respect to interpreting the original treatises, it is our belief that the virtue of **martial efficiency** is *the* guiding principle: judging by the surviving text and illustrations, Fiore wasted nothing and included nothing that was in any way useless: no extra flourishes, no grandstanding maneuvers designed to capture the gallery's attention. What he offers is a straight-forward approach for fighting *a oltranza* in *sbarra*—within the barriers—or in war, when the combatant's life was on the line.

But Fiore's principles are also easily adapted for combats *à plaisance*, such as for use by members of modern combat societies such as the SCA, on stage, in medieval tournament societies or in reenactments. Or they can be studied as an art in their own right, with no further end other than for the pleasure of experiencing the brutal elegance of it all.

In this chapter we'll take a brief tour of Fiore's core principles. The student may want to return to this section from time to time in order to reinforce aspects mentioned elsewhere in this book or the next.

As the system is taught through example, most of these principles are distilled interpretations rather than being called out in the text. I have carefully observed trends in the text, collated them together and generalized them through both teaching and observation, as well as through discussions with other instructors. But the principles can be understood in many different ways, using many different models, and this is one part of the Schola curriculum which is likely to evolve over time.

SIMPLICITY – *CERVINO*

It is an accepted axiom of combat that simpler is better, as in "KISS: Keep It Simple, Stupid!" Fiore adds nothing which could be considered superfluous, and indeed he states in the prologue that he has endeavored to make the system as easy as possible to understand:

"E questo sintende solamente per che chosi bisogna esser guardie e Magistri in le altre arte e rimedy e contrary some in larte de Abrazare azo che lo libro si possa licera mente intendere. Ben che le rubriche e le figure eli zoghi mostrarano tutta larte si bene che tutta la si pora intendere. Ora atendemo ale figure depinte a alor zoghi et a loro parole le quale ne mostrara la ueveritade [Getty. F.4r]."

"And this means only that there should be guards and masters in the other arts [with the other weapons], and remedies and counters as there are in the *abrazzare*, so that the book will be easily understood, although the verse, figures and the plays show the art well, so that the whole art may be comprehended. Now we attend to the plays and figures depicted, and to their speech, which will show the truth."

We have striven for the simplest explanation as a guide to our interpretation, because simplicity equals efficiency and durability in a combat environment.

Fiore's system is based on a series of core fighting positions which serve as a simple set of anchors. These *poste* or *guardie* simplify the combat calculus that each combatant must perform as he analyzes a fight, creating a model for action, an "if-then" algorithm for solving combat challenges. Another way that simplicity manifests itself as a core principle is that what can be done with one weapon can be done with the others, within the bounds of performance characteristics.

It is for this reason that Fiore does not show all permutations available with each weapon, or with each play—once the core idea is understood, the combatant is free to apply the principles as they see them.

DIRECTNESS – *LIONE*

Directness is *simplicity* applied to *position* and *time*. It is also the *lione's* courage, driving into the fight rather than dancing around its edge. The lion drives to and through the opponent, using oblique movements to find momentary positional advantages. But the directness and passion—the audacity—is characteristic and may even be a paramount combat virtue. It is a principle that underlies all of Fiore's plays, and he believes boldness or directness to be a core value:

> "Armorum actus si de delectate amice
> Noscere tecum habeas totum quod carina monstrant
> Sis audax ui atgam animo nec senix adesto
> Nil menti sit timor ades perficere posses
> Huius in exemplum mulier sit pauida nunquam
> Nudum expectaret gladium formidae capta
> Sic homo formidans ut femina nulla ualebit
> Defrest et totum cordis si audatia deesset
> Audatia et virtus talis consistut in arte [PD c2A]."

> "If the actions of Arms you want to know, friend,
> Have within you all the verse espouses.
> Be audacious in mind, and not old.
> Your mind must have no fear; be brave, make it so.
> Be not the fearful woman,
> She will wait with panic against the naked sword.
> And a frightened man is the same, worth nothing.
> He lacks all if in his heart he possesses no courage.
> Audacity is the virtue that makes the Art."

Within Fiore's system there are only a few elements of footwork to be remembered, advancing steps (*acresare*) and passing steps (*passare*), their retreating and traversing options. Blows are simply transitions between *poste* or guardie made with power, simple and direct changes in position. Nothing is wasted as the sword moves directly from one place to another in as close to a linear fashion as possible, since lines are quicker and more direct than are curves. Covers are made by adopting another *poste*, again in the most direct way possible.

EFFICIENCY – *TIGRO*

Efficiency refers to *simplicity* applied to *energy*. Efficiency expresses martial grace and confers both speed and power. It is always better to have power than to not.

Fiore's art harnesses the body's large muscle groups to find an efficient means to delivering maximum power in the least amount of time. All other things being equal, the combatant must strive to maximize his power or potential energy within the time available so that he may preserve as many combat options as possible.

Within the plays we see a powerful theme of dealing with the opponent's attack in the most efficient way possible, using the least amount of energy in order to achieve a positional or time advantage while preserving freedom by protecting potential energy through coiling and recoiling (as we'll explore in chapter 10).

Always seek to protect your available energy by avoiding expenditure of the body and by recoiling to preserve potential energy. Speed is also a function of energy, because the most direct force vector is also the fastest. But it is not enough to arrive on-target without sufficient energy to cause *offense*—damage—so **the combatant must deliver both speed and power to be effective.**

STABILITY – *ELLEFANTE*

Fiore equates stability with the earth. Like the *ellefante*, he carries his weight low, at his center, and returns to the stability of the earth whenever possible. All of the low *guardie*—those which are near to the ground, he classifies as *stabile* (as we shall see in chapter 7). When completing his *abrazzare*, he seeks to take the opponent to the ground (but not going to the ground himself), returning to the stability of **porta di ferro**.

It is vitally important under a combat environment for a combatant to maintain his stability both in a physical and in a mental sense. He must keep his fighting platform—his *ellefante*—in place as a foundation for all other elements, which precludes gathering the feet, crossing them, stepping too wide, or leaning. Similarly, only very rarely in the longsword play does he cross his hands or arms. He must keep his mental facilities in balance as well, tempering (but not subsuming) emotion with judgment. Maintaining the combatant's *ellefante* and *cervino* is absolutely critical.

SYMMETRY

Within Fiore's system, what can be done on the right can also be done on the left, unless it threatens stability. There are *poste* on the left and right, and they are not always specifically called out. There is a **posta di donna** on the left, and one on the right. There are **poste di finestra** on the left and right as well. There are central *guardie* where either foot can be forward.

But: Right and Left are Not the Same

But the principle of symmetry must not break the more important rule: **neither the hands nor the feet ever cross**, because doing so creates instability. Therefore, we do not find a **posta tutta porta di ferro** on the left side, nor a **posta dente di zenghiaro** on the right. This would cause a forward crossing of the hands, which could be dangerous and ineffiecient. Instead, as we will see in chapter 7, **posta dente di zenghiaro** *is* the manifiestation of **posta tutta porta di ferro** made on the left.

Fiore recognizes that fighting on the left and right are not the same in other ways, too. The *rebattemento* and *redoppiando* are methods of controlling the incoming weapon with power, yet the amount of power will depend upon whether the weapon is attacked in front or behind, on the right or the left. This critical positional distinction is a matter of perception that must be internalized and it is one of the key elements behind our development of the six core plays demonstrated in chatper 11.

Likewise there are strikes (*colpo*) on the right and left, but again, they are not the same, as we shall see in chapter 9.

SAFETY (THROUGH CONTROL)

It may sound oxymoronic to talk of safety in combat, but Fiore seems to strongly eshew the "spray and pray" approach, instead preferring to control the weapon before committing to an attack. If this is not done, there is nothing to stop the opponent from striking the combatant in return, a miserable "double kill" (what we call a *doppio*) which in a combat environment is very, very expensive unless one unit is worth far less than the other. Indeed, Fiore mentions his intention to safeguard his *scolari* through the use of the Art itself and by offering nothing which is not solid and safe:

"Nec quisquis in volumine presenti falssam rem aut errorem non promisctum credit opositum; quoniam ambigua resecando, sollummodo uisa et a ame probata et inuenta describuntur. Incipiamus itaque intencionem nostrum exponere cum omnipotentis auxilio, cuius nomen benedictum et collaudatum in secula. Amen. [PD c.2A]"

"And so that no one thinks this presented work false or in error, I have removed things which are ambiguous, intending to include only those things which have been discovered and tried by me personally. We therefore begin to explore with the Almighty, whose name is Blessed and Praised through the centuries. Amen."

Fiore's **First Masters of Battle**—the *poste*—are designed to find and exploit positional advantages in the opponent's defense, based on comparison of one *posta* against the other.

Our first module attempts to introduce the **First Masters of Battle** and to imprint a feeling for their strengths and weaknesses upon our new students. Fiore's **Second Masters of Battle**—the *remedi*—counter the attempt to make a positional advantage by making cover. This provides security for the opponent who has not struck first, but who needs to respond to an opponent who has.

Once the swords are crossed—*incrosa*—Fiore's tactical sensibilities come into play through the *zhogo largo* (long play) and *zhogo stretto* (close play). Here the more subtle aspects of initiative and response are explored in a simple if-then model discussed in Book II. Pressure on the blade, intention, and exploiting foundational weaknesses are all advanced methods of ensuring of safety before committing to an attack.

Another aspect of this rule is examined in detail in chapter 10, when we look at how and where to attack from the First Masters of Battle or as a follow-on attack. Essentially, each attack should progress and end with the blade in a position to make cover against likely avenues of attack by the opponent. I call this technique "striking to cover," a critically important way to avoid striking but being struck simultaneously in return. Cover can also be made using time or psychology, but these are advanced topics.

In a modern context safety also means seeing to the protection and defense of our companions-in-arms, practicing the art with *concordia* and *amor*—harmony and love—taking care to defend our opponent's safety above our own desire to win.

OTHER PRINCIPLES—THINK!

Fighting is as much about mental work as it is about the physical. Fiore's framework offers a simple model to understand what is happening in the fight, but I firmly believe that he intended his *scolari* to think and to apply the principle rather than to slavishly attempt to follow a specific play in a given circumstance. To do so would create a dangerous predictability.

Fighting is a function of perceiving, analyzing, and then choosing based on the best available information about the relative positions of weapons and combatants while managing resources of power and time. The brain is the most important weapon available.

Even if the student practices just for the sake of the Art itself, the valuable development of his or her mental abilities are what will stay with them forever, rather than specific skills related to the sword in two hands.

CONTROLLING THE CENTER IS CRUCIAL

Fiore is all about *control*. And controlling the center of the fight is a cornerstone objective, akin to controlling the four center squares on a chessboard. Fiore uses several simple mechanisms to achieve this control, depending upon circumstance.

In general, he recognizes that distance is the most fundamental method of control. When the combatant is far away, the upper reaches of the body only can first be reached, because the sword's lever-arm is attached to the shoulder, making a right-angle triangle governed by the Pythagorean Theorem (Our first play presented in chapter 11 applies this principle).

As the distance closes, things become more dangerous. Hence, as the distance narrows from *misura larga*, the chosen *guardia* must also descend, because the lower body becomes more vulnerable. As the distance continues to close, things get even more dangerous, and Fiore's response is to increase control commensurately, usually in the form of a *presa*. In practical terms this means that combatants must make a conscious effort to lower their hilt as they close with their opponent in order to cover more of the exposed body area.

When the distance has closed further, or when the opponent has made cover, when the combatant or the play has expended itself, the combatant would do well to extend his control using a *presa* against the weapon or, when better trained, with the *abrazzare* against his opponent's body.

At all times the combatant should maintain control over the center, yet this center may also be manipulated. In many plays, the front foot steps, "a little out of the way" in one of Fiore's favored oblique movments, the *passo a la traversa*. These oblique movements have the effect of changing the center of the fight, akin to changing which squares are central on the chessboard. This is an integral part of many plays both in this course and in the *zhogo largo* work that follows in Book II.

Another way that this control over the center manifests is clear during a thrusting attack. Fiore consciously manipulates this in his exchanging (*scambiare*) and breaking (*rompere*) of the thrust, and we will appy the lessons in chapter 11, Play #5.

In all cases the combatant must exhibit enough *lione* to **seize** control, rather than expecting it to come on its own. He must make his own destiny, in swordsmanship as in life.

BREAKING FROM ABOVE AND FROM BELOW

Gregory Mele of the Chicago Swordplay Guild has called out an important principle, which he calls, *What Goes up, Must Come Down*. This is a keen insight into how Fiore clears the center of the fight for an attack either against a passive opponent or during an active attack while maintaining maximum efficiency, without cumbersome repositioning.

Using the *poste* in high/low pairs, an incoming attack may be broken from below or from above using a *posta* transition to make an attack against the incoming weapon. If he breaks the incoming attack from above, then he will usually (but not always) follow-on with an immediate attack from below. The same is true in reverse: an attack broken below will usually be followed up with a follow-on attack from above. In the process, the centerline of the fight is opened.

TIME AND DISTANCE ARE TWO PARTS OF THE SAME THING

Fighting is a manipulation of time, distance and power. Time and distance are aspects of the same thing; if an object is further away, then its relative time to reach a given point will be greater. This point of view reflects an internalization of the physical universe described by Aristotle in Books IV-VI of his *Physics*.

From a combatant's point of view, time and distance are manipulated simultaneously. When the sword is further away from the fight's center, it will take longer to arrive and provide cover, or to strike the opponent. As the distance closes, the available time decreases. It is important to bear this in mind as the student strives to develop a tactical sense.

Time

Fiore's sense of time is, if we follow Filippo Vadi, comprised of three types. Most fighting actions take place in the slowest of the three, *duo-tempo*, what we think of as full-tempo "whole note" responses. These actions take place in an action/reaction/reaction/reaction sequence, one after the other in full measure. Together they have a tempo, a rhythm, which can be manipulated. Most fights take place in *duo tempo*, as one combatant acts, and the other reacts, and so on.

But the problem with *duo tempo* is that the opponent gets to respond. He gets a vote. We will see this in most of the first six plays, where the opponent can respond simultaneously as the combatant strives to follow-on with an earned positional advantage.

The solution to this enigma is to play either simultaneously, as the Germans do with their *meisterhau*, in what the Italians term *stesso tempo*, or "simultaneous" time. But this can be dangerous if it breaks the principle of safety, if the opponent's weapon(s) are not first controlled.

"Half" or "middle" time, *mezzo tempo*, seems to be Fiore's preferred solution. In *mezzo tempo*, what I sometimes call "broken" time, the follow-on action happens fractionally **after** the control has been established, but not too long after, or it would be *duo tempo*. This is done usually be redirecting the initial attack using a turning of the sword, what Fiore calls a *volta stabile*.

These complex actions of time manipulation are one of the foundational aspects of the intermediate play, which we cover in the next book on the *zhogo largo*. But the curriculum contains at least one, **Finding the Point**, Play #5, done in chapter 11. Most of the other plays are generally executed at the basic level in *duo tempo*, until the combatant has internalized the other more important principles.

Distance

Just as there are three times, there are three distances. We can say that the combatant is "out" of distance when he is too far away to attack effectively in one unit of time. We say that he is at wide distance—*misura larga*—when he can attack using one passing step. At wide distance there is relative safety, but the time needed to make a powerful opening attack is also greater. As the distance closes, so does the danger, so control must be extended by lowering the hilt and either striking, making cover, or using a *presa*.

At the point when the blades can cross (*incrosa*) between the tip and middle, we say that the combatant is in middle distance. At this distance the *magisto remedio* has usually been made, and very quickly the fight can progress through it to the *contra-remedio* and the *contra-contra remedio magistro*. Things at this point are spinning quickly out of control, so at this distance the *lione* must be brought to bear to seize the initiative before the opponent does. If the fight begins to become sloppy, it is time to either enforce discipline upon it or to retreat. For the most part this is where the *zhogo largo* comes into play, but it is also where four of our six basic plays will take place in chapter 11.

Closer than this is the *misura stretta*, the close distance. This is the range at which prese against the body may be made using the *abrazzare*, the subject of Book III. The German authors call this distance *krieg*, the same word for "war." This is "danger-close" for combatants who are untrained in the grappling arts, and it can be avoided through distance management and positional manipulation.

POWER

Distance also has a similar relationship with power. More distance equals greater potential energy. In the case of Fiore the distance is created by a turning of the body (the *volte*), which harnesses the large muscle groups. Less turning—less distance—equals less power. Too little power to make an effective attack is a state I call *expended*, while striving for too much power can result in too little time. The triumvirate of time, power and distance dominates all aspects of the fight.

The Longer Point

The one with the longer point will offend first," as Fiore says in the Getty, fol. 21v., and in other places. The principle of distance and time is easy to see: the longer point is closer to the opponent, so it can land first.

In this case, it is important to remember that several things can make a "longer" point. The weapon can be longer, certainly. Or their weapon can be closer to you than yours is to them, either by distance or because the opponent has a longer arm. Or, bearing in mind the idea of Aristotle's motion continuum, if the opponent is faster to respond, he has essentially won a time advantage which translates into free distance.

This idea must be balanced against the idea of **expenditure**. If the above rule is taken to its logical conclusion, then the weapon should ideally be resting against the opponent's skin in order to minimize the time necessary for the attack. However, the principle of requisite power must be kept in mind, balancing how much force is necessary with how much time is available. Power requires motion, the turning of the body if not linear travel of the weapon itself. Too little motion equals too little power: the *expenditure* defined in chapter 9. In trying to gain too much power, the combatant may run out of available time. A balance is needed, a careful judgment of available time, so that the available power can be maximized within that time.

This is less of an issue with the sword's point than it is with the edge. The point requires very little power to wound, if applied against a soft target. But the point is both easily set aside or exchanged (*scambiare*), broken (*rompere*), or turned aside by a hard defense, such as armour.

The Schola's approach to the fight focuses on the balance between distance, time and power, striving to set these concepts as guides learned through exemplar plays. In the first module—this book— we do this through six plays drawn from Fiore's descriptions of his **First Masters of Battle**, the *poste*. Later work follows Fiore's drawn plays as presented in the *zhogo largo* and *zhogo stretto* sections, by which time he should have a very powerful set of tools with which to analyze a fight's environment.

INTERMEDIATE/ADVANCED PRINCIPLES: PRESSURE, RESPONSE & TURNS

When the blades are crossed, or when the line is closed even though the blades are not in contact, we have a crossing of the swords, an *incrosa*. there are core principles related to the pressure against the blade. We have introduced this briefly as *sentimento di ferro*, what the Germans call *fühlen*.

Through the **actual** or **potential** *incrosa* the combatant must gauge the pressure and intent of his opponent. If the pressure is light or non-existent, he invokes the *lione/ellefante* and drives through, using the *volta stabile* of the sword by redirecting it to a target in *mezzo tempo*.

But if the pressure is moderate or the line is closed, a different kind of turn may be used, the *mezza volta*, where the sword makes a small loop, is reset for power, and drives back into the target, this time on the other side of the defender's weapon. In this way the *mezza volta* of the sword is the same as the *mezza volta* of the body, where the body changes its side with respect to power, as we will see in chapter 6. The *mezza volta* is *duo tempo*, unfortunately, so the opponent may have a chance to counter if his fighting platform is intact.

If there is strong pressure, then the sword can make a full turn, a *tutta volta*, using gravity (usually assisted with an off-line step to gain a time advantage, as a *tutta volta* takes place in *duo tempo*) to bring the sword all the way around to the other side.

Fiore's tactics in the *zhogo largo* section deal extensively but simply with these concepts, and we cover them in detail in Book II.

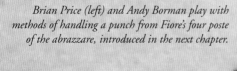

Brian Price (left) and Andy Borman play with methods of handling a punch from Fiore's four poste of the abrazzare, introduced in the next chapter.

PRIMARY VS SECONDARY WEAPONS

It is clear from Fiore's work that he considered the whole sword as a weapon, not just the blade. Not only could the edge and point find their uses, but so too could the pommel and cross. The combatant himself also has other secondaries in his hands, feet and head. He or his opponent may carry a dagger, which can sometimes be acquired. The opponent's sword itself may even be captured and turned against him.

Secondary weapons are generally brought to bear only when the primary weapon—the sword—has been checked or countered in some way and the secondary weapon can attack faster. As the blade becomes expended, for example, it might be expedient to bring the pommel around, to drop the left (or grappling) hand for a *presa* or a strike, use the leg to kick, or even use the head to head-butt the opponent (not in combats *à plaisance*, please). Of course, these secondary weapons are only available as the distance closes, one of the two reasons it becomes more dangerous: your opponent has both more weapons and more targets on you to attack.

The system is also rich in disarms, as one of the key tactics is to extend control by eliminating the opponent's weapon. It can be grasped directly—as with a *presa*—or it can be removed by attacking the arms with the *abbrazare*. But this is also true in reverse. If the opponent's primary weapon is checked, he may quickly resort to a secondary, so the combatant must defend accordingly.

There is an unfortunate tendency amongst new students to abandon their primary weapon and go immediately for a secondary. But it should be remembered that the primary weapon is primary for a reason: it is the most effective weapon at all distances. Don't be too quick to get rid of it.

A SPECIAL NOTE ON FOOTWORK
AND THE INTERPRETATION OF THE PLAYS

There is a broad tendency within today's Western Martial Arts community to strive to recreate, in the minutest detail, every aspect of the plays as shown within the treatises. This is a laudable thing to do from a research perspective, but from a combatant's point of view what is more important is to internalize the principles through the plays, developing the ability to apply the principles to the trillions of combat situations which might arise in the course of a fight. Not all of these are coverd within the 47 leaves of the largest copy of Fiore's book, or even in all of the books that survive.

To this end within the Schola we strive to prepare out students by using the feet in order to move the fighting platform from place to place, rather than to mechanically copy each play. As the plays are executed, if the *ellefante* is intact, and the required positional advantage has been secured, then the feet have done their job. At no point should they be gathered, over-extended, or crossed.

For example, Fiore definitely shows the **posta tutta porta di ferro** with the left foot forward. This makes good sense, as the left-foot lead charges the right hip, providing ample power. Fiore appears to recognize this, as he calls the resulting position *pulsativa*. But it is also possible to make a *passare* or a *tornare* from this position while not moving the sword. This too could be valid, as the sword still ready (although less powerfully charged) low and on the right. I believe this would now be *stabile*, as I have written elsewhere. *Time* has been gained at the expense of *power*.

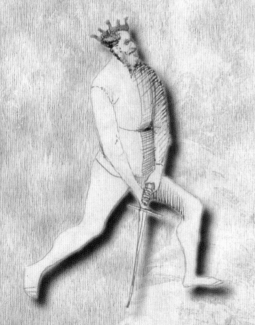 

Fiore's guardia or posta tutta porta di ferro, which he classifies as pulsativa, with the left foot forward. Here Brian makes a variant of the guardia with the right foot forward, which is probably valid within the system, but which is also probably no longer pulsativa (see chapter 7).

CHAPTER SIX

STANCE & FOOTWORK

"Noi disemo che acognossi le guardie ouero poste e liçeria chosa, prima che le guardia ano lor arme in mano luna contra laltra enon si tochano luna cum altra. E stano auisade e ferme una contra laltra per uedere ço lo compagno uol fare. E queste sono chiamade poste ouero guardia primi magistri de la battaglia [Getty F.4r]."

"We say that knowing the *guardia* or the *poste* is an easy thing. First that the guardia have their weapons in [their] hands, not touching, one opposite the other. And they stand ready and firm, one opposite the other to see what the *compagno* will do. And each is called *poste* or *guardia*, the first Masters of Battle."

"Noy semo doi guardie una sì fatta che l'altra, e una è contraria de l'altra. E zaschuna altra guardia in l'arte una simile de l'altra si è contrario salvo le guardie che stano in punta zoé posta lunga e breve e meza porta di ferro che punta per punta la più lunga fa offesa inançi. E zò che pò fare una pò far l'altra. E zaschuna guardia pò fare volta stabile e meza volta. Volta stabile si è che stando fermo po' zugar denunci e di dredo de una parte. Meza volta si è quando uno fa un passo inanzi o indredo e chossì po' zugare de l'altra parte denanzi e di dredo. Tutta volta si è quando uno va intorno uno pe' cum l'altro pe' l'uno staga ferma e l'altro lo circondi. E perzò digo che la spada si ha tre movimenti zoé volta stabile, meza volta, e tutta volta. E queste guardie sono chiamate l'una e l'altra posta di donna. Anchora sono IV cose in l'arte zoé passare, tornare, acressere e discresse(re)."

"We are two guards, one made opposite and countering the other. And likewise each of the other guards in the art has a counter save for the guards that stand in the thrust, such as **poste longa**, **breve** and **meza porta di ferro**, because in thrusting with the tip the longer offends first. And that which makes one can make the other. And each guard can make *volta stabile* and *mezza volta*. *Volta stabile* (stable turns) are those which stand firm, playing the one side and the other as one. *Mezza volta* are those in which one makes a *passo* forward or back, which enables him to play on one side or the other. *Tutta vola* are those in which one makes a turn (*intorno*), one foot in a circle (*circondi*) around the other, which stays still. And therefore the sword has three movements called the *volta stabile*, *mezza volta*, and *tutta volta*. And this guard [from which we play] is called **posta di donna**. Also likewise [there are] four in the art called *passare*, *tornare*, *acresare* and *dicresare*."

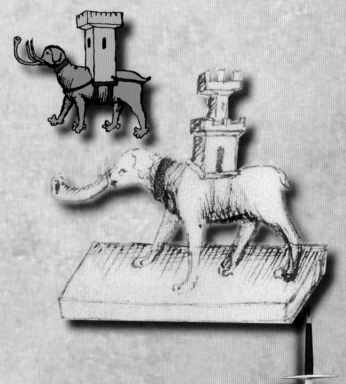

study of Fiore's combat system must begin with the stance and fighting positions, what he termed *poste* or *guardie*. Core guard positions are first presented in the *abrazzare* or unarmed wrestling section of the treatise, then repeated and expanded in the dagger, sword, spear and axe sections. Since the unarmed positions represent the core of the system, we will review each of them in turn.

The reader may recall that at the base of Fiore's *segno* is the Elephant, and upon the Elephant's back rests a tower. This elephant and tower combination is a metaphor for your stance, your body; keep your upper body straight and tall, like the tower upon the Elephant's back, and you must be as secure in your "space" and placement upon the terrain as is the elephant. Before we pick up a sword, it is critical to develop our elephant, our fighting platform, to the point where we feel solidly rooted to the ground, yet mobile enough to move with an easy grace from place to place upon the fighting field.

Fiore presents the core of his fighting positions in the first page of his techniques, and these illustrations remain largely consistent through the three surviving manuscripts. They include **porta di** ferro (the "iron gate"), **posta frontale** ("frontal position" or "front guard"), **poste longa** ("long position" or "long guard"), and **dente di zenghiaro** (boar's tooth). Although within the Schola we delay a detailed study of the *abrazzare* until the **zhogo largo** play has been internalized, it is useful to take a quick look at the four *poste* Fiore presents in this section and to use them in balance and movement exercises designed to create a framework for the use of the longsword. We will see iterations of these same *poste* again with each weapon.

STANCE

The feet control the combatant's position vis à vis his opponent. All of Fiore's *poste* share a common set of stances or positions for the feet, and once learned, the stance can be adopted in any of the *poste* with any weapon.

The feet are placed to yield **maximum stability while preserving the ability to move quickly in any direction.** The feet are shoulder width or just a little wider apart, and the weight is on the ball of the foot, rather than being distributed evenly along the whole foot. The front foot points directly at the opponent, or perhaps as much as 30° off, depending upon the combatant's comfort.

For a right-sided stance, the left leg is forward. This "charges" or "coils" the rear hip with potential energy to allow for an unwinding action that supplies critical power. The knees are slightly bent, and the back leg nearly straight, **but not locked.** The stance should convey ready motion; kinetic potential. Note that there is space between the feet, as if the feet are "on rails." **Do not cross the feet.**

The core position for the stance is symmetrical, that is, it may be adopted on the right or left. For a left-sided stance, the right foot is forward and the **left** hip is now back in the charged and ready position.

If the weight is maintained correctly on the inside of the foot (above left), the knee stays in alignment and the leg can act as a buttress holding the body in position. If the weight shifts to the outside of the knee (above right), then the knee moves sideways, carrying the thigh, hip and eventually the upper body with it.

It is extremely important to **keep the weight on the ball of the foot**. This keeps the knee in alignment and makes it easier to lift the leg. If the weight shifts to the outside of the foot, the knee is also pressed sideways, drawing the hip and eventually the upper body with it. Under the stress of a fight, in order to retain balance the combatant with his weight improperly on the outside of his foot might well have to shift his weight before moving, which costs valuable time. He may also find himself in the *presa* off-balance and forced to step in order to regain his balance. Additionally, moving the weight to the outside of the foot draws the knee out of alignment, which is structurally weak, and pushed further, the hip and entire upper body (the tower) begin to list dangerously.

Left-Sided Stance

This is the left-sided version of the stance, which is slightly less powerful for a right-handed combatant. Because it coils the left hip, blows thrown from the left side are stronger.

Note that the feet are approximately shoulder-width apart and the weight should be held on the inside or ball of the foot.

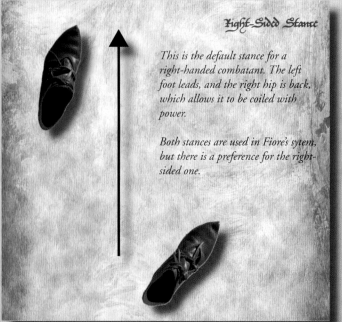

Right-Sided Stance

This is the default stance for a right-handed combatant. The left foot leads, and the right hip is back, which allows it to be coiled with power.

Both stances are used in Fiore's sytem, but there is a preference for the right-sided one.

FOUR COMMON STANCE ERRORS

The combatant's body is his fighting platform, his base from which to make his martial effort. His legs act as buttresses, and the placement of his feet define the stability of his body. Below are the four most common footwork errors that rob combatants of their balance.

Gathered feet - Bad!

The most common error. "Gathered" feet are too close together, and the legs cannot provide a strong enough base of support. The combatant's balance is compromised.

Linear stance - Bad!

A "fencing" style or linear stance also presents weakness for encounters where grips and wrestling may be applied..

Overextended - Bad!

An overextended stance occurs most often when students lunge in an attack. Such an attack is overcommitted, and should it fail, the combatant must rebalance before he can move.

Legs crossed - Bad!

Crossed legs are the worst support for a solid fighting platform. Combatants most often make this mistake when over-thinking where to put the feet.

Unlike a modern fencing stance, the feet are not placed in a line, because movement is often not made directly towards or away from the opponent, but on an oblique angle roughly 30° to the right or left. Such a linear stance is favored in modern fencing because the use of the point is optimized and the legal movement is along a narrow piste. In medieval swordsmanship, however, the primary attacks are incoming on an angle, movement is in the round, and there may well be grappling involved. Having a linear stance provides for a very strong elephant in one direction only.

Similarly, the combatant should avoid gathering their feet together, because this defeats the buttressing and pyramidal stability provided by the legs, strongly reducing their ability to maintain a balanced position in the face of force.

A STRONG STANCE

A nicely-supported right-sided stance with the left foot forward, the weight held to the inside of the feet and enough space between the feet to support a solid buttressing system (see the next page).

A Note About Foot Position

As with most medieval treatises, Fiore presents no "principles" section that conveys to students foundational material shown by example throughout the book. The modern interpreter must thus become familiar with the entire treatise, attempting to reconstruct the core movements and principles of the system from clues in text and images. This is difficult work, fraught with the possibility of error, which is why it is so useful to have talented martial artists, skilled atheletes, linguists and historians all working on the same material, so that the "gaps" may be plugged with the most efficient interpretations, which I believe was probably what the old masters were seeking as well. Most of the material in this footwork section is taken from the few instances in the text where Fiore specifically mentions details of the steps necessary to complete one of his plays and from the paragraph where the steps, turns and blade movements are first mentioned. From this, we have extrapolated and filled in, experimenting copiously in order to find a simple, elegant system of footwork that seems to answer the requirements of the whole text.

Why are your heels on the ground?

Fiore often depicts his combatants with the heels well off the ground. Inasmuch as he emphasizes the combatant's need for grounding, I believe that there may be some degree of artistic license being exercised to remind the student of the paramount importance of having the weight along the ball of the foot, rather than the heel. It is possible that Fiore actually taught combatants to keep their weight so far on the ball or even the toes, but without Jörg Bellinghausen's time machine, we'll never know for sure.

PORTA DI FERRO

Note how the legs form a stable pyramid that supports the upper body, or the elephant's tower and how the legs form a buttress for the body, as on a gothic cathedral.
Getty fol. 6

"In Porta di ferro io ti aspetto senza mossa per guadegnar le prese a tutta mia possa. Lo zogho de abrazzare aquella è mia arte. E di lanza azza Spada e daga ò grande parte. Porte di ferro son di malicie piena. Chi contra mi fa sempre gli dò briga e pena. E a ti che contra mi voy le prese guadagnare, com le forte prese io to farò in terra andare."
[Getty fol. 6R3]

In **porta di ferro** I await you, without movement, to gain the *prese* with all of my strength. The play of grappling is my art, and I have a great place in the *lanza*, *azza*, *spada* and *daga*. The gate is full of malice. [He] who acts against me I will always give trouble and regret. And for he who wishes to gain the *presa* against me, with [my own] strong *presa* will I make him go to the ground.

"Se per inçegno non me uinceray, zò creço Che cum mia forza ti farò male e peço."
[Pissani-Dossi 4A-3]

If you don't defeat me with your cleverness, I believe that with my strength I will injure you, and worse.

One of the first four positions Fiore presents in his text is the unarmed version of **porta di ferro**, the "**iron gate**." I believe **porta di ferro** is the core guard and position within Fiore's work; he includes it for each weapon and speaks of it as being both strong and capable of setting aside even the most determined attacks. In the wrestling components, when making a throw or a counter, usually the correct movement involves finding an efficient *volta* or turn that will take you to **porta di ferro** on the other side. And so, for many of the movements within Fiore's system, **porta di ferro** may well be considered to be *the* key position, the place that students might want as their "home" guard.

There are several things to notice about Fiore's figure. First and foremost, note that the upper body is upright, as is the tower upon the elephant's back. The combatant must hold himself almost aloof, back straight, shoulders square but not tense, the arms and hands limber, but ready for action. The head is erect, the chin held proudly high. The elbows are slightly bent. The stance is set for balance, the upper body is carried balanced between the feet, which are shoulder-width or just a little further apart. The back foot is depicted with the heel raised, hinting that the weight is strongly on the ball of the foot. Note that in the illustration the back hip is strongly charged to power the right hand, whether is comes to the *presa* or directs a weapon. As with all of the *poste*, the *zugadore* wears a crown because he is a *magistro* or Master, a visual definition of an important position.

Notice that Fiore emphasizes in both descriptions that this is a *strong* position, one that is good to wait in. As the *ellefante*

is strongly connected to the earth, so must the combatant have a firm connection to the ground, yet he must not be rooted to that place, for this reduces his movement options, which in turn can be an important vulnerability. Motion is necessary to manipulate both distance and position.

Fiore's zugadori always rely on a powerful triangular arrangement of the legs to support and balance the upper body.

*A zugadore in our interpretation of **porta di ferro**, from the front and side. In the base position, the weight is equally distributed between the balls of each foot, although it can be shifted to the front or back according to need. This is a symmetrical posta in unarmed combat, the left version is shown above left.*

It is imperative that the weight be correctly distributed in the feet. I teach that the weight must be on **the inside ball of the foot**, so that the combatant feels tension along the inside of the leg. In this way, both legs are buttresses—as on a gothic cathedral—that serve to support the combatant's upper body, his "tower." The weight must be mostly on the ball of the foot rather than distributed evenly across it, because otherwise the leg cannot be moved with sufficient speed to avoid direct attacks, and the combatant will often find himself unable to move quickly enough to take advantage of an opportunity.

As with the stance, the **porta di ferro** position is symmetrical and is used on both the left and right. As shown in Fiore's illustration, the combatant is in a right-side **porta di ferro**. If the combatant steps forward with the back foot or backward with the front foot, maintaining the hands ready at the waist, they will transition to **porta di ferro** on the left.

From this position, which Fiore uses to receive all sorts of attacks, the combatant is now ready for action. Practice this *posta* with the aid of a mirror, striving to copy all aspects of the original illustration. The combatant should, over time, refine their comfort with this *posta* in particular, as I believe it to be the foundation underlying Fiore's entire system.

Using this as a base, we turn now to Fiore's other three *poste di abrazzare*. All four work as an integrated set. Out of these four simple guards—and the transitions between them—could be created a modern self-defense system that would share elements

with many modern systems, sharing solutions for strikes, grabs, and throws. By briefly reviewing the other three we'll get a better idea of how Fiore might have expected his students to move and also learn something of his tactical principles.

*Brian shows how **porta di ferro** may be shifted to the front or back.*

POSTA LONGA

THE LONG POSITION

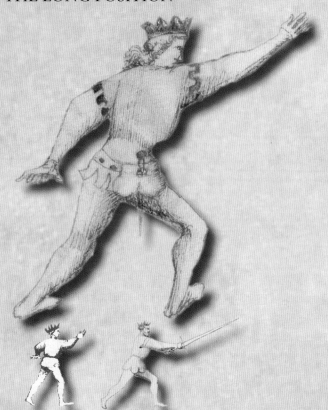

"Io son posta longa e achosì te aspetto. E in la presa che to mi voray fare, lo mio brazo dritto che sa in erto, sotto lo tuo stancho lo letterò per certo. E intrerò in lo primo zogho de abrazzare, e cum tal presa in terra to farò andare. E si aquella presa mi venisse a machare, in le altre prese che seguen vigrinò intrare."
[Getty fol. 6R1]

I am the Posta Longa [Long Position] and I await you like this. And in the *presa* that you wish to make against me, I will position my right arm, remaining upwards, with certainty under your left, and enter into the first play of *abrazzare*. With this *presa* I will force you to the ground. And if to this *presa* you should bring to me from the left, I will enter into the others that follow.

*"Per guadagnar le prese e' son aparichiato,
So non te igano, tu harai bon merchato."*
[Pissani-Dossi 4A-1]

To win the *prese* I am ready,
If I don't deceive, you'll have a good bargain.

Posta longa is the first of Fiore's unarmed *poste* or guards presented in *Fior di Battaglia*, and it is a useful position from which to launch a throw or even a strike. As with its longsword analogue, any punch moves the combatant through **posta longa** as the strike reaches is apex and the potential energy in the hip is transformed into kinetic energy. At the same time, the left hip is now charged, with a potentially powerful attack ready from that side. This half-turn forms what I interpret to be the **mezza volta**, or half-turn that is so critical throughout the system. Like **porta di ferro**, we find **posta longa** executed with all weapons, including the dagger, sword, spear and axe.

Notice first and foremost that the right foot has come forward. Whenever Fiore's figures have struck or made cover, the right leg is forward, suggesting that Fiore usually accompanies an attack with a step. The weight favors the front leg, although the upper body is still in balanced between the feet. The upper body remains upright, the tower upon the Elephant's back, and the front hand is extended in a generic attack; this could be a strike or the seizure of a positional advantage in preparation for a throw or *prese*. In this case the *left* hip is charged, as it is back, powering the *left* hand. The left hand is now back and open, ready to take advantage of whatever needs to be done and the hips on the left side are charged for an attack driven from that side.

Like **porta di ferro**, **posta longa** can be used from either side. Within the manuscript it is shown with the right arm forward, as would be used with an aggressive thrust or a punch. However, with a *mezza volta* shifting the stance to a right-sided stance, the combatant can easily and usefully adopt **posta longa** on the left.

A thrown punch as a variant of posta longa.

"Moreover I deem it very important to know how to wrestle, for it is a great help in the use of all kinds of weapons on foot."

-- Baldassare Castiglione, *Book of the Courtier*, Book I, F. 21, p. 30.

Posta longa on the right and left. It is important to maintain balance between the feet and not to risk over-extension. A thrust to posta longa is not a lunge, where the knee advances further than the ball of the foot.

A fundamental use of the unarmed **posta longa** position is to make a counterbalancing throw over the hip. By stepping into an opponent's stance, the *scolaro* can thrust the arm under the chin or across the face to quickly toss the hapless opponent to the ground.

Alternatively, **posta longa** is used as a counter to an overhand strike, say with the *daga*. In this case the opponent comes with an overhand strike, and the *scolaro* captures the strike using **posta longa**, keeping his other hand free and ready to play. Many *prese* and *ligadure* are available from this position, and it is fundamental to Fiore's defense against daggers, pommel strikes, and overhand blows in general. If **posta longa** is adopted with the opposite hand, a *presa* or cover is most likely; if on the same side as the attack, then a deflection is usually found.

Above - *A thrust to posta longa to catch an overhand dagger strike.*
Left -*Poste longa used as part of a counterbalancing throw.*

THE BOAR'S TOOTH

"In dente di zenghiar contra to io vegno. Do romper la tua presa certo mi tegno. E di questa isirò e in porta di ferro intrerò. E per metterte in terra sarò aparechiado. E si aquello ch'i ò ditto mi falla per tua defesa per altro modo cercherò di farte offesa, çoè cum roture ligadure e dislogature. In quello modo che sono depende le figure." [Getty fol. 6R2]

I counter you with **dente di zenghiaro**. Through it I shall break your *presa*. And after this I will close, adopting **porta di ferro**, so that I will be able to put you to the ground. And if I fail owing to your defense, I will make offense by another method; that is, with *ligadura* and *dislogature*, as is shown in the figures.

"De pugna mutacion cercho de fare
E cum quella in tera ti farò andare."
[Pissani-Dossi 4A-2]

I make a change to the fight,
And with this to the ground I shall throw you.

Dente di zenghiaro is used to break holds; it attacks as a board does, thrusting upwards from below. The transition from **porta di ferro** to **dente di zenghiaro** should be a sharp, quick, almost vicious movement upwards. This motion can be used for the thrust Fiore mentions, to break a hold, to catch the wrist as is done in many of the *daga* plays, or to deflect an incoming attack coming from the opponent's right or strong side. The counter-movements of the hands are also instrumental in making the throws using counterbalancing leverage depicted later in the *abrazzare* section.

Once again Fiore's *Magistro* stands with his legs forming a solid triangle, his left hand open and ready for coming to the *prese*, and the right hand is upward, but bent. The upper body remains upright, and the right leg is forward. By having the back heel so highly lifted, Fiore would seem to intend that the weight is carried more on the front foot that the back, which makes sense if we consider that this is an aggressive, close-in *poste* used to create and break different kinds of *presa*, especially the *ligadura* and *dislogature*. In the picture shown it is the left hip that is back and charged, storing potential energy for the left hand.

In the unarmed play, **dente di zenghiaro** can be adopted on either side, as is true with **porta di ferro** and **posta longa**. To adopt the right-sided version, the *zugadore* simply passes forward with the back foot so that the left foot is forward, executing a *mezza volta*. The right hand is then back and ready to grapple, while the left is forward.

Dente di zenghiaro is used primarily to break holds, although it can also displace strikes. This same action is repeated with the *daga*, as the combatant receives overhand blows, deflecting them to the outside with the forearm. With the longsword, the action is similar; from **dente di zenghiaro**, the *zugadore* strikes upward with a *sotano* against a right-handed or *mandritto fendente*—an overhand strike—deflecting the blade harmlessly to the side. We shall see that this is a fundamental movement within the system, so it is worth practicing
(see chapter 11, play #4).

Boar attack thrusting upwards with their tusks while moving around their opponent. Photo by Roman Kazmin.

Above: *Fiore's dente di zenghiaro from the front and side.*

Below: *The author deflects a punch from the outside using dente di zenghiaro and a traversing step. This kind of deflection is the same as the redoppiando done weith the sword in two hands, which we will see in chapter 11.*

POSTA FRONTALE

THE FRONTAL GUARD

"Posta frontale son per guadagnar le prese, chi in questa posta vegno tu me faray offese. Ma io mi moverò di questa guardia e cum inzegno ti moverò di porta di ferro. Peço ti farò stare staresti in l'inferno. De ligadure e rotture ti farò bon merchanto. E tosto so vederà che avera' guadagnato. E le prese guadagnerò se non sarò smemorato." [Getty fol. 6R4]

[Adopt] **poste frontale** to gain the *prese*, if in this *posta* I give offense. But I will move from this *guardia* with cleverness into **porto di ferro**; from there for you it will be worse than hell. With the *ligadure* and *rotture* I make excellent bargains. And then see what you have won! I will win the *presa* if I act without pause.

"Cum li braci eugno acusì ben destese
Per guadagnar in ogni modo le prese."
[Pissani-Dossi 4A-4]

[I come] with my arms well extended,
To win the *prese* in any way.

Poste frontale is used to gain control over the opponent's weapon, be it an arm, a *daga*, *spada* or his entire body. Unarmed, it can be used to come to grips against an opponent, bringing two hands for superior strength and leverage. The *zugadore* may grasp the collar, soft tissue about the face, neck or head, a wrist or a weapon. The essence of the *posta* is **an aggressive forward attack**, a theme that we can find executed as Fiore makes cover with the *daga* and longsword. With the longsword, an incoming strike is engaged aggressively with **posta frontale**, accompanied by a step forward, collecting the blade at the *tutta spada*, the junction between the blade and cross where leverage and control are maximized.

In the Getty illustration above, we can see that the right foot is now forward, indicating that the *zugadore* has taken a *passare* step to bring him forward. This theme is repeated in the PD version as well. The weight is slightly forward, perhaps as much as 70/30 between the front and back foot. As in all the *poste*, the upper body remains straight, balanced between the legs, which creates the now-familiar pyramid buttressing support. Both hands are extended and the fingers are shown open, ready to grasp as will be needed in the *prese* to come. Although both hands are forward, it is the left hip which is charged when the right foot is forward, giving a power advantage to the left hand. If the *Magistro* would have come forward with his left food instead, the right hip would be been the source of more power.

Fiore seems to indicate in the Getty text that **posta frontale** is used unarmed to draw an opponent out of **porta di ferro**, for as the hands come forward, he must respond. But he also seems to hint that from this position, perhaps having achieved the *prese*, he will move explosively back to **porta di ferro**, making a bind—the *ligadura*, *dislogitura* or *rotura*—then completing the action with something like a *mezza* or *tutta volta* back to **porta di ferro**. It is very efficient, and potentially very brutal.

With the longsword the movements are very similar. The *zugadore* transitions with power into **posta frontale**, capturing the blade an enabling him to continue with a *punta* or thrust if there is enough space, and if not, then the combatant comes in range for any number of *zhogi stretti* or close plays. Note that the hand position is almost identical for both the unarmed and longsword version.

Right: *Posta frontale is used to make an aggressive attack against the opponent's weapon to seize control, as is done here against a daga...*
...or against a fendente mandritto, an overhand strike. In each case, the principle is the same—the zugadore attacks into the weapon rather than waiting for it, gaining his cover or defense early and reducing the chances that the opponent will be able to change his attack vector.

Above: P*osta frontale* from the front and side.

PHYSICAL BALANCE

To test the stability of your *ellefante* as expressed in **porta di ferro**, we have developed some balance exercises. Many others could be devised, but we use these as games in an effort to introduce the all-important concept of initiative and to teach the combatants to lower their center of gravity and to practice setting the weight on the correct portion of the foot. If you look like Fiore's illustration and you can hold your balance with ease and grace in the games and exercises that follow, then your *ellefante* is set and you should be ready to work on movement.

DRILL
THE UNARMED POSTE FRONTALE

Objective: Helps students to refine the explosiveness of movement needed for effective use of the **posta frontale** and for similar actions with the sword in two hands.

Instructor: Form a drill line, the *zugadore* in hand-to-hand fighting distance and in porta di ferro on the right.

On the count, *scolari* step forward explosively with two hands, seeking to grasp the *compagno's zuparello* or his throat with both hands. On "return," scolari return to **porta di ferro**. Repeats five or six times per round.

In the next round, the *compagni* counter the *prese* by transitioning quickly into **dente di zenghiaro** and sweeping both hands as they transition from **porta di ferro** to **posta frontale**.

The *compagni* are now armed with a *daga*. This time, the *compagni* strike *fendenti mandritto*, trying to hit the *scolari* in the upper chest (a rubber *daga* is recommended). The *scolari* step forward and into **posta frontale**, attempting to catch the strike in both hands.

Crossing the Stance

We maintain the stance as shown in the earlier section because most of the force vectors in a medieval fight are coming not from straight-on, but are given and received along oblique lines. An opponent can be defeated by "making the cross," and I have applied this observation to an attack made against the *compagni's* stance, another kind of cross. This is a core element of unarmed *abrazzare*, and it works by directly attacking the opponent's *ellefante*.

For medieval forms, and with Fiore in particular, there seems to be a strong preference for the *colpo*, a strike or blow, over the *punta* or thrust. With a strike, the natural vector is on an oblique angle from the right or the left, the same natural angle that an untrained man

uses with two hands on a stick. It is the most powerful, and would be most useful in having a chance to cause at least some harm to a man in armour or even an arming coat.

Given this oblique angle, a linear stance places the defending combatant at a disadvantage, because a linear stance is extremely strong from front to back, but grows increasingly weak as the vector approaches the perpendicular.

In a classical fencing stance, reflected even in the work of Filippo Vadi just fifty or so years after Fiore's *Flos Duellatorum*, the swordsman emphasizes the use of the point with the linear thrust. Increasingly, force was applied to reduce necessary time using a line instead of an arc toward the target. A linear stance maximizes the distance available for the thrust and the strength for front-to-back movement while sacrificing strength side to side.

A stance for power-based medieval weapons, by contrast, must maximize flexibility of response as the attack might come in from a variety of angles, but should optimize around the most likely avenues of attack. Usually, this would be incoming attacks on roughly a 30° vector. And we can see, in the illustration below, how our medieval stance is strongest along exactly that angle of attack.

A modern fencing stance is strong front to back, but is weak side to side.

Our interpretation of the medieval stance, which is strong on the oblique, better against both force-based attacks and against the prese.

Above: *Two stances compared. First, a generic version of the classical and modern fencing stance, with the characteristic "L" shape to the feet oriented in a precise line. This stance is very strong from front to back, but is weak from side to side. In my interpretation of the medieval stance, which requires the absorption and generation of a great deal more power, the feet are moved to help generate and receive that power along likely attack vectors.*

Below: *The stance we use as a baseline for medieval weapons, shown with two opponent's facing off. Notice how the most likely avenues of attack—coming from the right shoulder—is the line most strongly opposed and reinforced by the stance.*

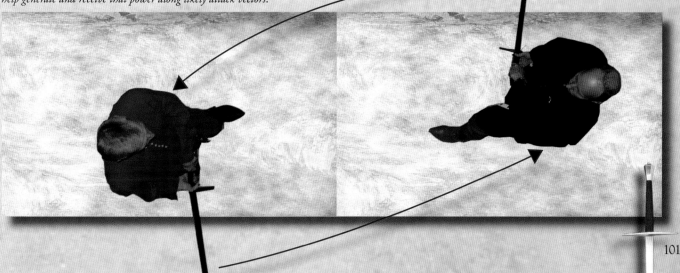

Making the Cross: *The black-shoed combatant makes a passing step forward in order to "cross the T" of his opponent, pressing or attacking perpendicular to the compagno's line of strength.*

line of strength

Any stance is weakest along a vector perpendicular to the angle of the feet. Therefore, one way to attack any opponent is to attack their balance by seeking a position that enables a perpendicular attack. There are several interesting ways to do this.

In the simplest case, the combatant might simply step to a place to realign their strength across their opponent's weakness. We call this "making the cross."

Another method of attacking across this line by movement alone is to close to the *zhogo stretto*, close play, and simply extend the arm into one of Fiore's four unarmed *poste*, the **posta longa**. Using the principle of counterbalancing leverage, the attack vector is made perpendicular to the *compagni's* cross, and they find themselves thrown.

"Attack your opponent's *ellefante* by *Making the Cross*"

GAME
PALM TO PALM

Objective: Teaches students to rely on their legs as butresses and to keep their center of balance low.

Instructor: Pair off the students, spreading them around the practice space. If possible, conduct the exercise in a small circle, such as in the center of a basketball court. Alternatively, the space for the contest can be made with a rope, or even with several sword trainers laid into the shape of a box.

Zugadori adopt **porta di ferro on the right**, their left hands meeting palm to palm at or below chest height. On the signal, the *zugadori* attempt, without removing their palm, to press their *compagno* off balance while preserving their own. If a *zugador* steps beyond the boundaries, that player loses the game and the two should either reset or be paired with another student.

Variants: Try using the right and left hands. I have found it useful to work this drill with pairs of students matched by size, although it is interesting to conduct a "hold the field" kind of game in the center of the fighting space. Other interesting variants include a version where neither student is allowed to move their feet, or when they are blindfolded.

Seen from the top, an attack against the Cross *puts the opponent at a disadvantage, striking directly for his balance platform. Without a platform—his* ellefante*—he cannot easily fight.*

GAME
CROSSING THE STANCE

Objective: Teaches students to to be aware of the relative strengths and weaknesses of their stance's orientation, vis à vis their opponent's.

Instructor: Pair off the students, spreading them around the practice space.

Zugadori adopt **porta di ferro on the right**, or if they are advanced, in any *posta* of their choosing. At the instructor's command, each tries to step to a position of advantage with respect to their *compagno's* cross. If achieved, they may press with light force to the mid-section or shoulder to demonstrate that they have successfully attained a positional advantage. No one should be thrown to the ground.

Generally this drill is run for three to four minutes, sometimes having the *zugadore* rotate to work with a new partner. The game is very aerobic, a lot of fun, and can be useful in teaching the students to watch for the vulnerability of the cross in both themselves nd in their opponent.

DRILL
BALANCE WITH THE SINGLE STAFF

Objective: Allows the students to work on balance and to observe and attack their *compagno's* cross, while also exercising perception and initiative.

Instructor: Pair off the students, spreading them around the practice space. Each pair should receive a staff from 3' - 6' long. A wooden waster will also work, but a staff is a more neutral and variable-free tool.

The *scolaro* adopts the unarmed **posta di ferro** position on the left or right, taking the staff up with two hands. The *compagno* takes the same position directly before him, and also takes up the staff so that both *zugadori* have hands alternating on the staff.

In the first series, upon the instructor's command, without removing their hands from the staff, the *scolari* attacks the *compagno's* balance by pressing and pulling with the staff (it should not be raised above the chest). The *compagno* strives to fluidly respond to the *scolaro's* efforts, maintaining his balance. The exercise continues for 1-3 minutes, at which point the exercised is halted and the roles reversed, and repeated. When both *scolari* and *compagni* have had a chance to lead, the exercise may be repeated again, this time wtih no defined leader.

Combatants may discover that sometimes it is effective to counter their opponent by quickly pressing upwards into **poste frontale**, which if done quickly may cause the *compagno's* weight to shift to his heels, after which they may be easily thrown (but should not be, without mats or soft ground). This move parallels Fiore's own use of the unarmed **posta frontale** as a method of breaking **porta di ferro**.

I often do this exercise as a warm-up, after stretching, to hone balance and get the student's cardio-vascular system going. The exercise seems effective at teaching grounding, especially when accompanied with frequent admonitions for the students to keep their weight low.

Variants: For students who perpetually move back out of a fight, the exercise can be done in a circle from 6' - 10' in diameter, the object being to press the opponent out of the circle.

104

DRILL
BALANCE WITH TWO STAVES

Objective: Allows the students to work on balance and to observe and attack their compagno's cross, while also exercising the perception of intitiative.

Instructor: Pair off the students, spreading them around the practice space. Each pair should receive two staves from 4' - 6' long.

Both *zugadori* take up a position opposing one another with a staff in each hand, such that by a push one *zugadore* creates a pull in the other, and visa versa. In the first series, at the instructor's command, the *scolari* attempt to attack the *compagni's ellefante* by pushing and pulling. This time, the hands may go as high as the head.

The exercise continues for 2-4 minutes, at which point it is stopped, the roles reversed, and then repeated. When all *zugadori* have had a chance to lead, the exercise may be repeated again, this time with no defined leader.

Both of the staff drills make an excellent combatative exercise with which to end a practice session.

Varaints: Like the single-staff exercise, this one can be done in a closed circle from 6' - 10' in diameter, the object being to press the *compagno* from the circle. Other variants for both staff drills include working blindfolded and on different surfaces, such as sand, wet grass, etc.

I was introduced to the *Balance with Two Staves* drill by Bob Charron in 2002, as we traded drills at the Kalamazoo Congress of Medieval Studies. In exchange I showed him the *Balance with One Staff* drill on the previous page.

FOOTWORK

The idea behind "footwork" is to move you as a fighting platform smoothly from place to place, committing as little as possible and preserving as much freedom as possible for as long as possible. Fiore says just a little about this:

"…Also likewise [there are] four [steps] in the art called *passare, tornare, acresare* and *dicresare*."

There is nothing yet found in the surviving treatises that spells out precisely how steps are done in either the German or the Italian medieval/early Renaissance texts. Although Fiore was kind enough to name his steps, they are not defined. From clues in the text, however, we can surmise what he might have intended, and combining this with practical use, we've come up with an interpretation that I feel is robust, efficient, and answers the various instructions found throught the treatise.

There are two forms of steps in the text, small, compact *acresare* used to make small adjustments to position (also called by some "advancing" steps) and *passare*, larger "passing" steps used to make larger changes to your place. Each of the steps has a reverse, the *dicresare* for what some call a "retreating" step, and a *tornare*, which means literally "to return," a step that is essentially a passing step to the rear. The *acresare/dicresare* are generally used to small manipulations of distance, while the *passare/tornare* as used for gross movements.

As we will see later in the chapter, these simple steps are generally accompanied by a turning of the body, the *volte*. The *volte* serve both as a method of channeling power and of changing the body's orientation.

Much of the work is also done using traversing or oblique steps rather than working in a line towards and away from the opponent, as we will examine once the steps have been briefly covered.

Because footwork is the basis upon which the fighting platform is moved from place to place, I *strongly* recommend consistent practice and continual development of the student's smoothness and efficiency with respect to the footwork. Ideally, each practice would begin with some aspects of footwork done by the whole class, even as students progress from intermediate to advanced skill levels. The fundamentals are never completely mastered; there is always room for improvement, improvement that can yield important advantages in a martial encounter.

The footwork presented is simple, efficient, and seems to answer all of the text's requirements. In general, I have found no instances where the feet are crossed, gathered, or over-extended. Use the feet to create and maintain your *ellefante*, moving as necessary from place to place without losing the *ellefante*.

ACRESARE (TO "INCREASE")

In every *posta*, the *magistri* are shown with one foot or the other forward. With a right-sided stance, the left foot is forward, charging the right hip with power. To advance, the combatant merely steps forward a small amount with the front foot, and then moves the back foot forward to reestablish the stance.

Fiore calls this step *acresare*, defined literally as "increasing," or "growing larger." Indeed, as you move closer to your opponent, he does appear to grow just a little bit larger. *Acresare* are generally used to find the right range or distance for an action you'd like to accomplish. Although we encourage the use of strong *passare* accompanying a *mezza volta* for strikes, a few attacks are accompanied with an *acresare*, which are faster but less powerful than a *passare*.

Acresare are the small steps that are used to make minor adjustments to your distance or position. To execute *acresare*, pressure is brought from the back leg, causing a brief tension, then the front foot moves first, not widening the stance too much, the weight still on the ball of the foot (ideally, the step is one half of the combatant's foot in length or less—many are only an inch or two). This draws the body smoothly forward. Finally, the back foot is moved forward and the stance is regained. It is important, when stepping, to place the foot down properly on the ball of the foot, rather than the heel. Failure to do so will cause the combatant to be rooted to that spot for a moment in time and that anchor point can be exploited by an alert opponent.

ACRESARE
ADVANCING STEP

*A combatant makes an **acresare** to advance on his opponent. The **front** foot moves first, but not too far, to avoid over-extending the stance.*

An acresare is an advancing step where the front foot moves forward first, followed by the back foot. It is used for making small adjustments in distance rather than for covering ground.

Use of the *acresare* is very conservative in terms of both time and distance. It takes little time, and can be used only to adjust distance in small increments. Try to avoid moving the foot too far forward—more than a foot's breadth—because this dangerously widens the stance, exposing more of the cross and destabilizing the pyramid. A combatant who finds himself with a stance that is too wide must correct it quickly. The combatant should learn to do this immediately, without distributing the flow of the fight, training himself also to take smaller steps with the *acresare*, rather than larger ones.

When bringing the back foot forward to regain the stance, the combatant must maintain the same comfortable, stable width. There is a tendency to gather the feet too much, as was shown earlier, making the support pyramid too narrow and thus casting balance to the winds of luck and the opponent's perception. Remember that the back foot should land and maintain its weight on the inside ball of the foot, rather than on the heel or outside.

DECRESARE
(TO "DIMINISH" OR "GROW SMALLER")

A *decresare* is the reverse, a small adjustment step made to the rear. It is important not to discard our balance pyramid, so the feet should not be allowed to gather or narrow. To maintain a stable platform, the *back* foot moves a bit to the rear, then the front foot follows. It is important to try to keep the same measure for the *acresare* and the *decresare*, since the combatant who is trying to manage distance front to back should be able to rely on a predictable distance from step to step.

DICRESARE
RETREATING STEP

In the dicresare, it is the back foot that moves first in order to avoid gathering the stance.

Again, these are small adjusting steps.

Fiore calls this step the *decresare*, meaning literally "to diminish" or "grow smaller." Like the opposite *cresare*, the importance of moving with smoothness, *sprezzaturra*, cannot be over-emphasized.

There is a tendency with the *decresare* to move the front foot first or to plant the weight on the back heel. Avoid both errors at all costs—they are very common and create an extremely unbalanced, gathered position that is easy for an opponent to manipulate.

An important skill is to be able to match your opponent's changes in distance precisely. If he moves forward slightly with *acresare*, you should move with a similar *decresare* so that the distance between you remains where you want it to be, rather than where he wants it to be. Practice this skill using the partner exercise below, striving for fluid motion without jerky redirections or over-commitments.

EXERCISE
Keepiong Distance

Objective: To develop smooth footwork, integrating the steps with visual cues provided by the tactical situation.

Instructor: Pair off the *zugadori*, using a two-line arrangement of *scolari* and *compagni* (see chapter 12).

The students all adopt posta longa on the right, or if they are advanced, any other valid *posta*, reaching out to just barely touch with the forward hand.

On command, *scolari* begin to move towards and away from the compagni using acresare and dicresare steps. The idea is for the compagni to move reactively and in harmony with the *scolari*, so that the two as much as possible move as one in a clean, elegant and efficient unit. Later, the exercise can be repeated using all of the steps.

Variations of the drill use sticks suspended between the hands, or for a more difficult test, between each combatant's abdomen.

PASSO
(FROM *PASSARE*, "TO STEP")

To cover more ground, or to generate significant power, execute a passing step. This is done just like regular walking, except that the "rails" between the feet must be maintained and the "new" back foot must pivot to roughly 45° in order to restore the stance, this time on the other side.

Fiore seems refer to this movement as *passare*. In a *passo* the back foot moves forward and takes the strong position in front, while the back foot remains in place but pivots smoothly on the ball of the foot to reset the stance on the opposite side.

*A **passo** is a simple step where one foot passes the other. As the front foot moves the back foot pivots so that when the step is complete, the combatant is now once again in the stance, but on the other side.*

Passare are bold, aggressive steps that make a dramatic change to distance or position. Within the Schola, we avoid making wide, circular "compass" steps that are suggested in many later treatises. The reason is that we like to keep the combatant relatively grounded and ready to fight, without exposing the cross of their stance. Instead, the foot moves directly to its intended position, without any additional arc. I believe this is faster and less risky than the compass step.

The passo *without an accompanying* volta *of the body*

The effect of the *passo* on the upper body and hips depends on the intention of the combatant; the combatant has the choice of keeping the charged hip in position, as would be the case entering a fight, say, in **posta di donna**, per the example below. Note that in this case as the combatant steps forward the right hip does not accompany the step, but remains charged, supplying potential energy to *colpi* or *punte* from the **posta di donna**.

The passo *with an accompanying* mezza volta

In this counter-example, the combatant elects instead to change the side upon which he fights, in which case we interpret this to be a *mezza volta*, a "half-turn" of the body that accompanies the step. In this case, he uses the movement to make a smooth transition from **posta di donna** to **posta di donna sinestra**.

The combatant should practice and master both kinds of step/turn combinations shown above. With the first choice, the combatant covers ground quickly and boldly while maintaining his charge on one side of the body. With the second he changes sides of the fight, transitioning from one *poste* or *guradia* to another and potentially unlocking the potential energy stored in the body. The goal of this practice should be to able to make both variants smoothly and naturally while properly storing or unleashing power.

Above: *A passo accompanied with a mezza volta of the hips: notice how the sword moves from the right to the left.*
Right: *A simple passo without accompaniement of the hips: notice how the sword stays on the right side, even though the left foot is now forward. He will have less power, as the hips are not in agreement with the forward foot, but he will have gained distance by stepping this way and the sword will remain on his right side instead of shifting to the left, as in the illustration above.*

As with the *acresare* and *descresare*, the combatant must strive to maintain the balance pyramid in order to keep the elephant balanced and strong upon his ground. Step to the ball of the foot, resetting the front leg to form the powerful buttress. Avoid the tendency to step across the rails. Many new students have a tendency when making a *passare* to bring the feet into a linear stance, or even cross their feet, which makes for a very weak elephant. He must also guard against over-extending caused by an overly large step as he strives to over-extend towards the opponent (especially during a thrust, as there is no lunge in our interpretation of Fiore's system). The combatant should strive to make the step as natural as possible, as smooth as when he is walking down the street.

TORNARE (RETURNING STEP)

To go backwards, the front foot passes backwards, *landing at a 45° angle* (there is no time to shift it). Watch especially for gathering or linear foot placement.

Fiore refers to the reverse step as *tornare*, which defined as turn or returning. It is possible that Fiore meant a more tangential, compass-like step with the choice of this word, but for the present we interpret the tornare in the sense of returning, the opposite of the *passare* (which moves forward).

Acresare/passare a la traversa / traversare / traversando

For the most part, steps are made not directly at the opponent, but on an oblique angle of up to 30° as discussed earlier. This movement is a form of crossing, and Fiore gives frequent directions for crosses to be made (*passa a la traversa* to "step across." *Traversare* is the verb expressed as an infinitive).

Within the Schola, to make a *passo a la traversa* or an *acresare a la traversa* is to make an oblique step at approximately 30° to the right or left. Interestingly, these are the same angles the *segno* illustrates if the swords are envisioned as a stepping diagram from the top.

We consider it an error to cross the feet in the manner of some later rapier texts. The balance pyramid is always maintained, even in cases where there is a desire to step in a direction where one feet must first be moved to maintain the pyramid (see the section and sidebar below on **fora di la strada**).

In many cases, they are made not forward, but on an oblique "offline" vector. Such "oblique" *passare* are used to move the combatant out of the line of attack and secure a positional advantage by moving in front of or behind the incoming attack.

(RI)TORNARE
RETURNING STEP

*A **tornare** is a passing step made in reverse. The front foot moves first. As it does, the back foot pivots so that the stance is now the same, but on the other side. We think of this step as returning rather than retreating.*

As with the *passare*, the *tornare* can, but might not, be accompanied with the hip turn that creates a half turn or *mezza volta*. The *zugadore* has the choice of whether or not he wishes to stay charged on this side he begins in or whether he wishes to change sides with the *mezza volta*.

Using these steps , you can adjust your distance to your opponent with care. NOTE: It takes more time to execute a *passare* than a *cresare*, so you want to keep your opponent at a distance where they must *passare* to attack, giving you a time advantage because you only have to *cresare* to respond.

Usually, but not always, such steps are made to the side of the back foot, because otherwise the feet are likely to be crossed.

FORA DI LA STRADA / "OUT OF THE WAY"

Recall that the combatant may be situated with either the right or the left foot forward. In either configuration, he may need, in a given tactical circumstance, to pass obliquely either to the right or to the left. We'll consider how both of these movements are made from each of the right- and left- foot forward configurations, starting with the "right-sided" stance with the left foot forward.

If the right hip is charged, and the left foot is forward, we say that we are *fighting on the right side*, for reasons explained in the next chapter. To pass *a la traversa* to the right presents no difficulty; the back foot simpy passes on the oblique as the action is made, followed by a stabilizing movement of the left foot, which moves to orient the combatant and to reduce the risk of the opponent's making the cross against the stance.

Moving to the left is a bit harder. If we try the same motion, our legs would cross, violating one of our cardinal rules with respect to maintaining the *ellefante*. Instead, Fiore gives a very precise and yet flexible instruction: *"E cum lo dritto passa a la traversa fora di strada…."*

Supposing that the left foot remained forward, how could this pass be made without crossing the feet? The anwer is, I believe, that the front foot makes a small adjusting *acresare*, taking it's new position where it will become the new back foot. This is a very small step, as is correct for an *acresare*, and the pass is now a simple pass, the

TRAVERSARE
TRAVERSING (RIGHT)

From a right-sided stance, **traversing right** *is easy.*

The back foot simply moves forward on an angle. Once placed , the back foot is slid into place.

TRAVERSARE
TRAVERSING (LEFT)

Traversing left is more difficult from a right-sided stance, because the leading left foot is "in the way" of the desired direction of travel.

The solution is to move it just a bit "out of the way," *fora de la strada*, before the traversing pass is made.

Once the passing step is complete, both feet pivot in place.

right foot traversing across. Under the stress of a fight, the first *acresare* movement is often, but not always, accompanied with blade contact as an *incrosa* is sought.

This is the same from the left. If the desired movement is oblique to the left, then a simple pass is made and there is no reason to move the front foot, which then becomes the back. A small adjusting step is often made after the weapon or attack connects, just in case it fails. Going to the right is now tougher, but the right foot repositions itself to its new home with a small acresare, the the pass with the left foot can take place normally.

By using the small adjusting step only when traversing in the direction of the front foot, to avoid crossing into a state of imbalance the front foot must move, "a little out of the way," at which point the traversing pass can take place normally. The movement is small and quick, but only required when going in the oblique direction of the forward foot. Moving to the side of the back foot, the movement is eliminated to avoid cueing the opponent and because it is not necessary.

TRAVERSARE
TRAVERSING (LEFT)

Traversing left from the left is simple.

The back foot moves forward on an angle. Once placed, the book foot pivots into place.

TRAVERSARE
TRAVERSING (RIGHT)

Traversing right is more difficult from a left-sided stance, because the leading left foot is "in the way" of the desired direction of travel.

The solution is to move it just a bit "out of the way," *fora de la strada,* before the traversing pass is made.

In an ideal case, like this one, the first foot to move is already in its final resting place and need not be moved again.

In order to make a strong traverse on the oblique in the direction of the forward foot—in this case the left—the front foot is first moved a little out of the way, fora de la strada, then the other foot passes aggressively. The result is to cross the opponent's stance, useful both in grappling and with the sword.

EXERCISE
SIEZING GROUND

Objective: Reinforce importance of audacity and boldness in the seizing and possession of ground.

Instructor: Create a drill line (see chapter 12), with students at about 12 - 15' between the *compagni* and *scolari*. If available, a mat is useful.

The *compagni* may adopt any unarmed *posta*, but should begin with **porta di ferro** (on either side). They will attempt to hold their ground under assault from the *scolari*.

On command, the *scolari* advance audaciously across the floor or mat. They will attempt to move directly to and through the *compagni's* piece of ground, moving them with pressure. They may push on the body or shoulders, but may not strike, tackle or trip. They must make the *compagno's* space their own.

Once the *scolari* attempted to take the ground the *compagni* immediately walk to the *scolari* side of the mat and prepare for their own assault. Meanwhile, the *scolari* turn and take their posta to make a stand against the same kind of attack. The students should move boldy—as lions—aiming to drive the defender from his place and take it for his own. If he steps to the cross, as discussed earlier in the chapter, he will have more success.

A LA TRAVERSA

Within the Getty text, some form of *traversare* or *la traversa* appears in the description of **posta di donna destraza**, *...dredo passa ala traversa...* (23v-b); in the **posta di donna la sinestra**, *e intra in lo zogho stretto per lo suo saver traversare* (23v-d); in the *zhogo largo* play #4, the **colpo di villano**, *E cum lo dritto passa a la traversa fora di strada...* (26-a); in *zhogo largo* play #7, the **scambiar di punta** (exchange of the thrust), *una punta subito acresse lo tuo pe' che denanci fora de strada ecu lautro pe' passa a la traversa anchora la sua spada cum...* (26v-a); in the play of the **punta falsa** (false thrust), *...salvo io che passo a la traversa per trovar lo compagno più discoverto...* (27v-a); and in the three companions attacking vs **dente di zenghiaro**, *...e cum passo a la traversa del arm che me incontre...* (31a-b).

Within Florio, the 16th century Italian dictionary that has proven indispensable to students of Fiore's works, we have the following definition: "*Traversa*: to cross, to thwart, crossly, thwartly."

This is a very interesting and important definition, since in the descriptions of the sword in two hands plays where it appears, the "crossing" step has both meanings: to **cross** and to **thwart**. In *crossing*, I do not believe tht Fiore meant that the feet should in any way cross such that the combatant's balance—his *ellefante*—is at risk. The feet should stay at their shoulder-width orientation. What is crossed (thrwarted) is the opponent's *ellefante*—by stepping obliquely and without losing or even risking the combatant's balance, the opponent's stance may be crossed to his detriment, as discussed above.

TURNING THE BODY

Fiore uses the *acresare*, *decresare*, *passare* and *tornare* to describe the motions of the feet. But the feet can move independently from the body, as we notice above in the comparison of the *passare* and *mezza volta*. Fiore powers his actions by a turning of the body, centered on the hips, called simply a turn or *volta*. We find three such turns in the text, a *volta stabile* (which turns the hips without an accompanying step), a *mezza volta* or half turn (which accompanies the hip turn with a *passare*), and a complete turn or *tutta volta* (which uses a *tornare* or *passare* step pivoting around the forward or back foot). In each of the three cases, the most important thing is not what the feet are doing, but the hips' rotation, which coordinates the large-muscle groups of the body to store and generate the power needed for both attacks and strong defenses.

Volta, in the Italian expressed by Florio, can mean "to turn," or it can mean "a time." Certainly most uses of the term within Fiore's treatise relate to some kind of turn, either of the combatant's body or of the sword. These are subtly woven into the text, but they are core to an understanding of how the system works.

But it is important to maintain both senses of the term *volta* when it is described in the text, since we cannot know precisely how Fiore might have intended the word to be used in each instance. Even when the text discusses what is clearly a *volta* in terms of physical movement—of feet or sword—the movement must happen with something like simultaneity to work correctly. Think of the term as meaning perhaps, "a turn done at once," or something similar.

VOLTA STABILE ("STABLE TURN")

The *volta stabile* is Fiore's method of unwinding the hips without having to commit to a change of distance using a step. It is a stable turn of the body because there is no risky step accompanying it. The hips are uncoiled and a *posta* transition made without a step, extremely useful when executing a *colpi* or making cover when the range is already well set or when there is no time to accompany the movement of body and sword.

This is the root of Fiore's power generation, and it allows the combatant to fight in multiple directions. To execute a *volta stabile*, the combatant must simply turn the upper body, allowing the feet to pivot in place.

The essence of the *volta stabile* is a powerful uncoiling of the hips that draws the feet into their natural pivots, which are made on the ball of the foot. Interestingly, using a *volta stabile* allows the combatant to change which side is charged with a stable turn of the hips.

This kind of *volta stabile* allows the combatant to turn through approximately 110°-135°, which is in turn useful for meeting and combating multiple threats, and it explains why in some of Fiore's illustrations the figures appear to have a "backward" kind of stance, where the heels are forward. In most cases, the *magistro* probably achieved this position through a *volta stabile*.

Since there is no step, the turn is made on the ball of the foot. This should happen as a natural consequence of turning the hips, although it can be a useful learning tool to set the hip motion into the *zugadore's* mind.

The combatant should use *volta stabile* when attacking and making cover when they don't want to step, or when making some *posta* transitions.

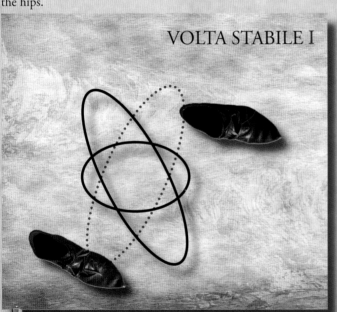

VOLTA STABILE I

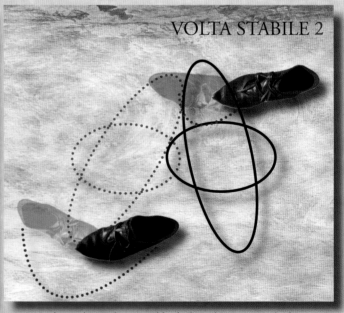

VOLTA STABILE 2

*At right we have presented two versions of the volta stabile. In the first version, the combatant has turned his body without moving the feet. This is the simple interpretation (see chapter 9). In the second version, the combatant changes direction of at least his lower body by pivoting approximately 120 degrees on the balls of his feet. This version accounts for the "heels first" version of some poste, such as **posta di donna soprana**.*

MEZZA VOLTA ("HALF TURN")

Like the *volta stabile,* the *mezza volta* unleashes the potential energy stored in the hips, but is adds the power of an agreeing step.

For the most part, the *mezza volta* is simply a *passare* step accompanied by a turning of the hips. This powerful unwinding of the hips can be used to make cover, to propel the sword forward into a *colpo* or *punta*, or just to change the side the combatant draws his power from.

It is easy to see the *mezza volta* when changing *poste* from right to left. For example, if the combatant begins in a right-sided **posta longa**, they can easily transition to the other side using a *passare* step and a *mezza volta* with the hips. When the action is complete, instead of a right-sided stance with the right hip charged, they are now in a left-sided stance, with the left hip charged.

The *mezza volta* is a fundamental building block of the system, as most attacks and even most defenses are made using an accompanying step and harnessing the power of the hips in a *mezza volta* or half-turn.

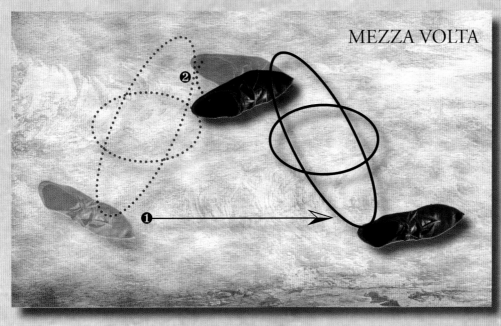

MEZZA VOLTA

A mezza volta of the body is a half-turn. When the combatant begins the motion, their right hip is charged. The body makes a half turn as the combatant takes a passo step. Contrast this with the action in B, where the hip stays charged and the body does not turn in conjunction with the passo. When using a passare when engaged with an opponent, the body will usually turn to accompany it with the mezza volta.

PASSARE

A passo step without the accompanied movements of the body. This kind of step is usually done when advancing to a fight out of distance. The upper body is "frozen" and the potential energy remains with the rearmost hip rather than slewing forward and changing sides as it does with the mezza volta.

Tutta Volta in the Abrazzare

One of hte places where the tutta volta is most effective is in the unarmed grappling, Fiore's prese / abrazzare. In this case, we see an aggressive attack (above left) countered with Dente di Zenghiaro (upper right). As the arm shoots forward under the chin, Brian makes a simultaneous mezza volta with a passare step, stepping so that his knee is behind his opponents'. Brian's right foot is now the pivot (lower left) for a tutta volta, which simultaneously throws his opponent to the ground as Brian simply seeks the stability of porta di ferro on the other side. Rather than memorizing complicated footwork, many throws within the system may be made in this natural way, simplying by stepping towards the goal of "porta di ferro on the other side."

TUTTA VOLTA ("COMPLETE" TURN)

The *tutte volte* are used not only to unleash the power in the hips, but also to change direction by as much as 270°. Because it involves a *tornare* or turning of the foot along a curved line, it is the slowest of the three turns, but also the most versatile.

To execute a *tutta volta*, the combatant focuses on changing direction while pivoting on the front or back foot. To maintain the position of the front foot, he pivots upon it and moves the back one in an orbit around it to change his orientation. This is usually how it is done when the combatant wishes to *advance* and turn.

Another way is to use the back foot as the anchor, pivoting around it instead of the front one. This is useful when the combatant wishes to *retreat* and turn.

Tutte volte are usually done when executing a dramatic change in the fight. As such, they are less common than the *mezza volta* or *volta stabile*, but they should be practiced, as they are very important in the *abrazzare* and dagger work.

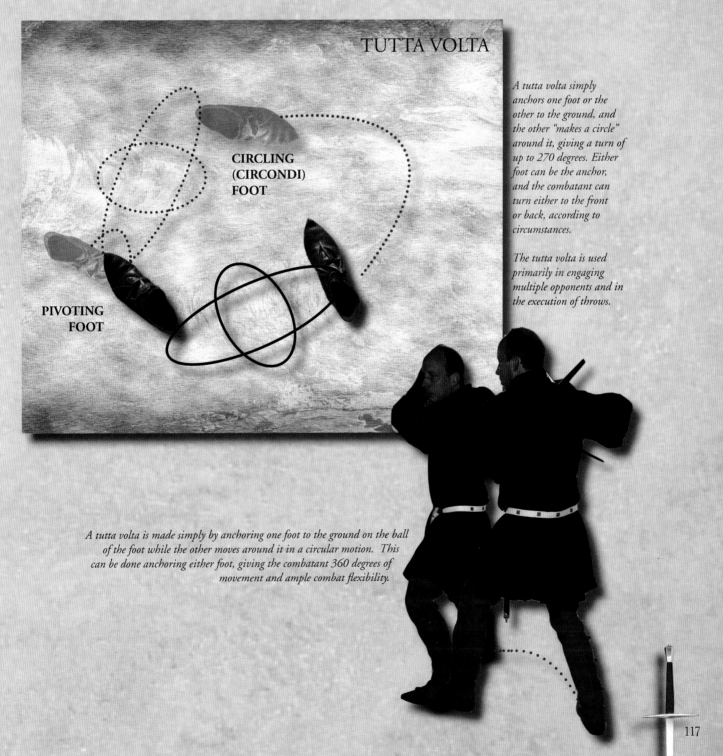

TUTTA VOLTA

CIRCLING (CIRCONDI) FOOT

PIVOTING FOOT

A tutta volta simply anchors one foot or the other to the ground, and the other "makes a circle" around it, giving a turn of up to 270 degrees. Either foot can be the anchor, and the combatant can turn either to the front or back, according to circumstances.

The tutta volta is used primarily in engaging multiple opponents and in the execution of throws.

A tutta volta is made simply by anchoring one foot to the ground on the ball of the foot while the other moves around it in a circular motion. This can be done anchoring either foot, giving the combatant 360 degrees of movement and ample combat flexibility.

FORWARD MOVEMENT

In general, Fiore's text seems to evince a strong preference for forward movements. The combatant moves with judgment, when the time is right, with the heart of the lion seizing control of the situation and turning it to his advantage rather than dancing at range with an opponent. In many cases this will result in an *incrosa*—a crossing of the swords—from which he can immediately (*celeritas*) judge (*prudentia*) how to best seize the initiative with courage (*audatia*). The tactical framework that governs what to do in the *incrosa* is presented in Book II, which are really, I believe, Fiore's tactics. But you will gain some tools in the six core plays we use at the Elephant level, enough to begin to spar.

Within the Schola, the preference is thus for moving forward with the lion rather than hanging back. If you simply retreat, you offer your opponent information about your movements and responses free of charge, and nothing in the fight has changed, except that the situation is reset with neither party having any advantage. The trick is to counter this tendency to back off continually, yet not to rush forward with abandon. Move forward purposefully, with personal control and seek to control your opponent's weapon(s), quickly assessing his weakness and taking immediate advantage of them.

STANCE PROBLEMS

Beginning combatants frequently make gross errors of stance. Often this occurs when they are either trying to move aggressively forward, (as with the combatant to the right), when they wait nervously (as with the red-shirted combatant below), or when they advance and check their movement en route, (as with the combatant lower right).

Any of these errors jettison the balance, the ellefante, and represent a structural weakness which can be exploited by the opponent.

USING FOOTWORK AND THE TURNS

In stepping during swordplay the purpose of the footwork is to move the fighting platform—the *ellefante*—from place to place, ideally to a position that yields an advantage in terms of position, leverage, or time/power. The feet manage distance between the combatants, and they should be placed to preserve maximum number of options. As long as you don't break one of the rules, you can move straight ahead, obliquely right and left, forward and back according to the situation.

There are places in Fiore's text where he states explicitly how to step in a given circumstance, but there are far more instances where footwork is unspecified. Within the Schola, we tend to focus on creating an open framework so that combatants can maximize their flexibility and achieve maximum transference to combat situations. In keeping with this idea, we have generated a series of rules of what *not* to do when moving:

1. **Do not cross the feet**—this causes immediate instability by inverting the balance pyramid.
2. **Do not gather the feet**—feet close together create a less stable pyramid.
3. **Do not step too widely (a lunge)**—An overly wide stance also creates a less stable pyramid.
4. **Do not plant on the heel**—keep the weight on the ball of the foot.
5. **Do not give the opponent a cross against your stance.**

In each play, Fiore may demonstrate his optimum foot placement. However, it is important to keep in mind that the plays are exemplary illustrations of principle, rather than being merely a collection of techniques. In each case, you want to place your feet such that you achieve the underlying principle, have the most solid *ellefante* possible, and maximize your tactical options while restricting those available to your opponent.

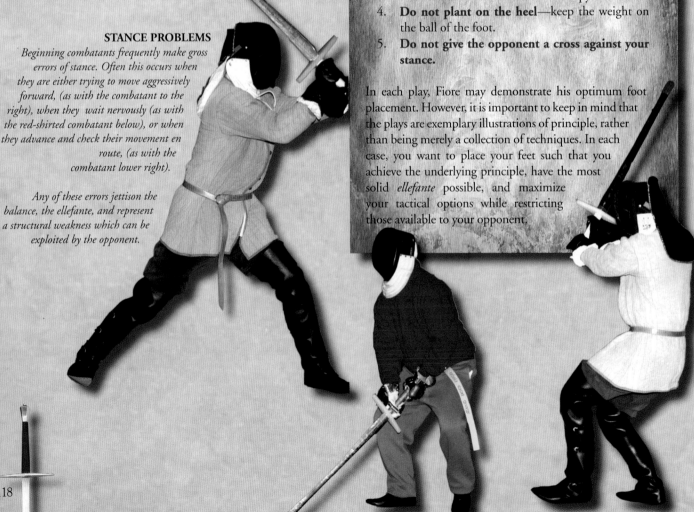

TAKING UP THE SWORD—THE GRIP

Once the combatant has a sense of how the movement works, it is time to take up the sword in two hands. For right-handed opponents, this is done by placing the right hand at the cross and keeping it there. The left hand rides behind, acting as a support, guide or lever, depending upon circumstance.

The forefinger and thumb do the majority of the work when the blade is gathered near to the body, but when it extends control passes instead to the last to fingers, which are inherently less stable. In this case the support of the left hand is important.

The sword is never depicted as being held in the left hand, nor is the right hand depicted as leaving the sword to make *prese*. The right hand should be able to wield the sword tolerably by itself, as the bastard-sword is meant to be wielded in one hand or with two. If this is uncomfortable, then the sword is likely over-heavy for the wielder.

The left hand is the auxiliary or grappling hand; it can act as a potent secondary weapon for *prese* or strikes, it can reinforce the weapon by gripping it in the middle (swords were likely not sharpened at the *mezza spada*). In the thrust it directs the strike. With the sword ready and loosely but firmly gripped, it is time to examine the longsword *guardie* or *poste*.

Normal Grip: *The right hand is at the cross, the sword supported mostly by the first two fingers and thumb on the each hand.*

Extended Grip: *When the sword is extended, as in posta longa, the support in the fingers shifts to the last two on each hand.*

In general, the right hand will guide the weapon while the left supports it. There are *guardie*, however, where the left hand seems to be primary, and the right guides the weapon. We shall explore each of these cases in turn in the next chapter. For some poste, such as the **dente di zenghiaro** or Boar's Tooth, the left hand may play very, very loosely near the pommel, just enough to provide minimal support but close enough to support and power the thrust that is likely to follow.

It is important that the sword be carried lightly in the hand, flexibly, until just before impact, when sufficient pressure is made to secure control. More pressure is *not* better, it simply reduces mobility and wastes energy; many combatants make this mistake, just as they sometimes carry extra tension in the shoulders, neck or arms. All of this excess tension must be avoided.

LOOSENING THE SWORD

Each combatant takes a comfortable stance. Before the sword is taken up, each focuses and takes a very deep breath—to a full count of four—holding the breath to another count of four, then slowly letting it out, concentrating the whole time on relaxation. Taking up the sword, they should strive to clear the mind entirely.

We generally offer a salute at this point, just after the sword is taken up. Then the combatant makes lazy circles on one side of his body and then the other, not as a way of trying to intimidate anyone (à la a bad martial arts movie), but as a method of keeping the motion as fluid as possible, keeping the shoulders, arms, neck and hands loose. The motion should be done on both sides, both forward and backward, until the motions are smooth, the breathing is regular, and the combatants are relaxed.

LONGSWORD GUARDS

GUARDIE PULSATIVA

TUTTA PORTA DI FERRO   POSTA DI DONNA   POSTA DI DONNA SINESTRA   POSTA DI DONNA SOPRANA

GUARDIE STABILE

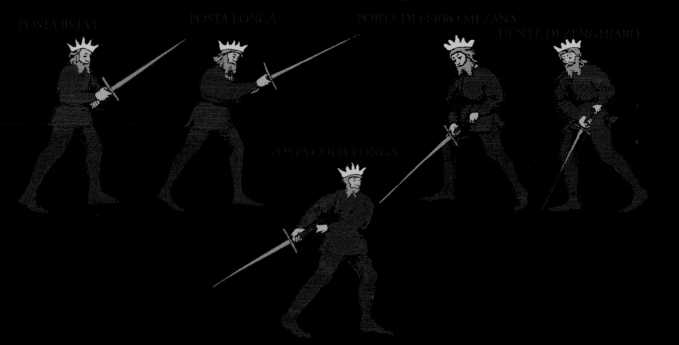

POSTA BREVE   POSTA LONGA   PORTA DI FERRO MEZANA   DENTE DI ZENGHIARO

POSTA CODA LONGA

GUARDIE INSTABILE

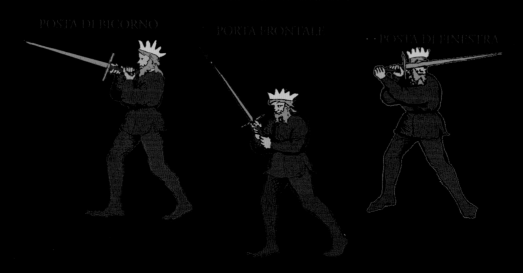

POSTA DI BICORNO   PORTA FRONTALE   POSTA DI FINESTRA

120

CHAPTER SEVEN

FIORE'S LONGSWORD GUARDS
THE FIRST MASTERS OF BATTLE

"Noi disemo che acognossi le guardie ouero poste e liçera chose, prima che le guardie ano lor arme in mano luna contra laltra enon si tochano luna cum laltra. E stano auisade e ferme una contra laltra per uedere ço che lo compagno uol fare. E queste sono chiamade poste ouero guardie owera primi Magistri de la Batagla.

"E questi portano corona intesta perche sono poste in logo e per modo di fare grande defesa cum esso tale aspetare. E sono principio di quallarte çoe di quellarte delarma cum la quale li ditti magistri stano in guardia. E tanto e adire posta che guardia. E guardie e tanto adire che lomo se guarda, e se defende cum quella, de la feride del suo inimigo. E tanto e adire posta che modo de apostar lo inimigo suo per offenderlo sença periculo di se instesso. [Getty F.4r]"

"We say that to know the guards or poste is an easy thing. First, that the guards have their arms in hand, without touching, one against the other. And that they stay watchful and firm, one against the other, to see what the compagno wants to do. And that these are called poste or guardie or the First Masters of Battle.

"And these [Masters] wear a crown on their heads because they are positioned to make as great a defense as they could hope for. And they are the Principals of the Art, called the Art of Arms, with which the said Masters stand in guard. And it is as much to say poste as it is to say guardie. And guardie is as much to say that the man guards himself, defends himself from the wounds (feride) of his enemy. And it is as much to say that posta is a way of positioning his enemy to make offense without danger of the same."

"Poste e guardie chiamare per nome si façemo	We are called post and guards by name
E una simille cum l'altra contrarie noy semo;	And we are one contrary to the other;
E segondo che noy staxemo e semo poste,	And depending on how we stand or are positioned
De far l'una contra l'altra façemo le mostre."	We'll show how one stands against the other

"Poy uederiti xij magistri incoronadi uno dredo l'altro li quali magistri stano in le guardie de la spada."
"Shown after, twelve crowned masters, one right, the other opposing who also stands in the guards of the sword." [PD 18r]

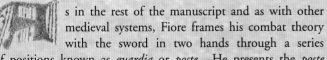

s in the rest of the manuscript and as with other medieval systems, Fiore frames his combat theory with the sword in two hands through a series of positions known as *guardia* or *poste*. He presents the *poste* through a series of illustrations following the *segno*, where each *posta* is illustrated by a crowned master. These are the core fighting positions of the system, Fiore's **First Masters of Battle**, and through them combatants seek positional advantages from which to attack. Each masters has strengths and weaknesses. By internalizing these relative strengths and vulnerabilities, the combatant develops a powerful and simple positional model that he uses to quickly analyze a fight to his advantage.

Fundamentally, any movement of the sword takes place beginning from and moving to a *guardia*. By learning these *poste* and comparing his current position to that of his opponent, a combatant can quickly assess tactical possibilities because the *poste* greatly simplify his assessment, resulting in more speed and clearer communication.

"Here begins the guards of the sword in two hands;
there are twelve guards."

Fiore presents twelve guards in each manuscript as he says, "Here begins the guards of the sword in two hands, and there are twelve guards." But there are actually thirteen, as the twelve presented in the three editions are not exactly the same. For the student of medieval swordsmanship, this is both a convenience and an annoyance. Although there are twelve *core* positions, they may be conveniently remembered as categorized by Fiore and/or according to what lines they follow in relation to the body (i.e., lowline, centerline, right, left, etc.). We will look at other methods of classification as well as Fiore's presentation order later in the chapter.

Fiore follows sound military practice, preserving his combat options while simultaneously reducing those of his opponent(s). In terms of the *poste*, this means that the system is mostly symmetrical, as discussed in our chapter on stance and footwork. Therefore, what can be done on the right can also be done on the left, so long as the arms or feet are not crossed.

From the point of view of a modern teacher, the *poste* provide a dynamic, well framed foundation. In our school, we teach the original Italian terms, to better connect the students with the rest of the Western martial arts community and, ideally, to maintain as much continuity as possible with the original material.

It is perhaps interesting to note that all the *posta* classified as *instabile* are in fact high positions that seek to bring the point to bear, while the low lines are all either *stabile* or *pulsativa*. The closer to the ground is the blade, the more stable it becomes.

Note again as I emphasize that Fiore did *not* define these terms, nor do they appear in the Morgan or PD manuscripts. Although it is useful to know how Fiore's classified them—at least in one edition of his work—in many ways we find it more useful to think of the *poste* according to the blade's position.

FIORE'S CATEGORIZATION

In the Getty edition alone, Fiore adds a note following each *posta's* name, classifying it. *Poste* can be either *pulsativa*, *stabile*, or *instabile*. Fiore does not discuss the definitions for these terms in his surviving work, but in working with them I am comfortable with the definitions offered below:

Pulsativa *poste* are those that are full-powered. The hips are well-wound, the body's potential energy fully behind a blow (*colpo*) or cover (*coverta*) with the sword. The name presumably comes from the Italian verb *pulsare*, to strike. These are *striking* guards. They are: **tutta porta di ferro, posta di donna, posta di donna sinestra, posta di donna soprana.**

Stabile (stable) *poste* are those that are lesser powered, but which are suitable for waiting. I think of these as *half*-powered, usually very good along a more limited spectrum of attacking angles, but also fairly difficult to break by pressure or position. These are, **posta breve, posta coda longa, mezana porta di ferro, dente di zenghiaro,** and **dente di zenghiaro mezana.**

Instabile (unstable) *poste* are those that are for the most part transitory, rather than positions as suitable for waiting. The reason is that their inherent instability conveys particular advantages—usually bringing the point or *punta* to bear as the primary threat. Interestingly, the older interpretation of the term *instabile* is more akin to "mutable" or "fickle," rather than "unstable." This mutability or fickleness, like the sword itself, can cut two ways—it can make a "fool" (*ignana, nesum*) of the opponent, luring him by its apparent instability, or the instability can be used against the combatant himself, rendering *him* foolish! Thus these are best used as transitional positions, often taken from the *incrosa*, rather than in opposition to another *poste*. As such, the combatant should not usually wait in this position, but should instead proceed immediately with a *punta, colpo* or *volta* with the sword, depending upon circumstance. Waiting here can very quickly get you killed! Instabile *guardia* are **posta longa, posta frontale, posta di finestra,** and **posta di bicorno.**

STABILITY IS FOUND IN THE EARTH

One of the interesting aspects of Fiore's poste is that they seem to recognize the principle that things closer to the ground are inherently more stable than are those higher up. As such, the preference for keeping the hands near the waist discussed in the last chapter is extended to the sword; for the most part, there seems to be a distinct preference for seeking the stability of the ground and of the body's center of gravity.

Contrast this to the German system, where the favored guards—Ochs and vom Tag—are held high, and much of the blade work is at or above the shoulder line, rather than at or near the hips, as it is in Fiore.

This is one of the aspects about the art that drew me to Fiore in the first place; I tend to favor the low lines, and I have always seemed to gravitate towards systems and sports that do the same.

FULL IRON GATE

Pulsativa

Getty 23V, upper left; Morgan 12r, upper left; Novati 18a, upper left

"Qui cominzano le guardie di spada a doy man e sono XII guardie. La prima si è tutta porta di ferro che sta in grande fortezza e si è bona di 'spetar ogn'arma manuale longa e curta e pur ch'el habia bona spada non una di troppa longheza. Ella passa cum coverta e va ale strette. Ela scambia le punte e le soy ella mette. Anchora rebatte le punte a terra e sempre va cum passo e de ogni colpo ella fa coverta. E chi in quella gli dà briga grande deffese fa senza fadiga"

"Here begin the guards of the sword in two hands, and there are twelve guards. The first is **tutta porta di ferro**, which lies with great strength. It is good to wait against every hand-weapon long or short. And yet it doesn't matter if his sword isn't very long. It passes with a cover and comes to the close. It exchanges the thrust and places her own. Also, it rebates the point to the ground, going always with a *passo* and [from] every *colpo* she covers. And in which she brings great defense without fatigue." [Getty 23v, upper left]

"Tuta porta di fero so la piana terena
Che tagli e punta sempre si refrena."

"Tutta porta di ferro finds the ground
His cuts and thrusts are always resisted."
[PD 18r, upper left]

I believe that **porta di ferro** is the core *guardia* in Fiore's system. It represents the greatest level of consistency throughout the treatise and is a fine "home base" which, as Fiore says, stands in great strength, doesn't care about sword length or even different weapons, can exchange the thrust, and easily makes powerful covers. It is here that he presents the important idea of *rebattemento* (beating the sword aside).

To find **tutta porta di ferro**, stand first in the unarmed version we explored earlier to set the stance. Now, take up the sword with the hands in essentially the same position they were in for the unarmed **porta di ferro**.

The sword point should be 90 degrees off to the right, or very slightly canted backwards. This is critically important; if the tip is too far back, the combatant will find it very hard to make cover in **posta breve** or **frontale**. The further back the tip goes, the more like **posta coda longa** it becomes, and the slower responses will be because it will take longer to get back to the centerline. Hence, the further back you carry the point, the more distance you will need to keep in order to make cover.

Note that the weight is slightly forward. I often teach that this can be true, but it is also possible to have the weight equally distributed, so long as the weight is to the inside of the foot and not on the heel. This is particularly useful because when speaking of the core movement a few pages earlier in the text, where Fiore says that the front foot must move "a little out of the way," which means it cannot be extensively front-weighted, otherwise the foot

cannot be quickly moved. Therefore, I must prefer a neutral weight distribution in **tutta porta di ferro**.

It is important that the *true* edge be facing forward, rather than the flat. In order to make this comfortable with the hands, they must be fairly loose on the handle. For kinesthetic stability, I prefer the left arm to be straight and in-line with the sword. This creates an unbroken moment arm powered by the right hip.

Above:
It is important to have a loose grip in porta di ferro in order to keep the true edge (la dritta taglia) forward.

I believe that **porta di ferro** is the core *guardia* in Fiore's system. It represents the greatest level of consistency throughout the treatise and is a fine "home base" which, as Fiore says, stands in great strength, doesn't care about sword length or even different weapons, can exchange the thrust, and easily makes powerful covers. It is here that he presents the important idea of *rebattemento* (beating the sword aside).

To find **tutta porta di ferro**, stand first in the unarmed version we explored earlier to set the stance. Now, take up the sword with the hands in essentially the same position they were in for the unarmed **porta di ferro**.

The sword point should be 90 degrees off to the right, or very slightly canted backwards. This is critically important; if the tip is too far back, the combatant will find it very hard to make cover in **posta breve** or **frontale**. The further back the tip goes, the more like **posta coda longa** it becomes, and the slower responses will be because it will take longer to get back to the centerline. Hence, the further back you carry the point, the more distance you will need to keep in order to make cover.

Note that the weight is slightly forward. I often teach that this can be true, but it is also equally possible to have the weight equally distributed, so long as the weight is to the inside of the foot and not on the heel. This is particularly useful because when speaking of the core movement a few pages earlier in the text, Fiore says that the front foot must move "a little out of the way," which means it cannot be extensively front-weighted, otherwise the foot cannot be quickly moved. Therefore, I prefer a neutral weight distribution in **tutta porta di ferro**.

It is important that the *true* edge be facing forward, rather than the flat. In order to make this comfortable with the hands, they must be fairly loose on the handle. For kinesthetic stability, I prefer the left arm to be straight and in-line with the sword. This creates an unbroken moment arm that is powered by the right hip.

Tutta porta di ferro is perhaps the most effective place to lie in wait for an opponent, should you wish to. Many combatants find it comfortable, and as the system becomes more internalized, it seems even more natural. Because it doesn't rely on a thrust, it doesn't "care" who has the longer sword (or arm). By extension, it accounts well for an opponent who is faster, because it is relatively easy to make a safe cover and follow-on with an effective thrust (via *exchange of the thrust*) or strike after safely dealing with their attack. As he says, it will defend well for anyone who seeks to "make contention." An opponent who tries to thrust will find his attack easily broken.

Tutta porta di ferro is a power position, underscoring Fiore's emphasis on gathering potential energy and power which is then tempered by judgment. In the Getty manuscript he classifies it as *pulsativa*, associating it with the Italian verb *pulsare*, "to strike." In order to power the guard, the hips should be coiled, the right hand resting near the right hip. It is sometimes helpful to picture a physical connection between the right hand and the hip in order to envision the relationship between the body and hand.

The core movement from **tutta porta di ferro** Fiore talks about both in its descriptive passage and in an earlier section where he talks about the single-handed sword,

"Voy seti cativi e di quest'arte savete pocho. Fate gli che parole non ano loco. Vegna a uno a uno chi sa fare e po' che se voi fossi cento tutti vi guasterò per questa guardia ch'è chossì bona e forte. Io acresco lo pe' ch'è denanci un pocho fora de strada e cum lo stancho io passo ala traversa. E in quello passare incroso rebattementole spade ve trovo discoverti e de ferire vi farò certi. E si lanza o spada me ven alanzada, tutte le rebatto chome t'ò ditto passando fuora di strada, segondo che vedreti li miei zochi qui dreto, de guardagli che v'in prego. E pur cum spada a una mano farò mia arte como n'è dereto in queste carte."

"You are brutish and know little of this art. Do what you will; words have no place here. Come one by one, he who knows the art, even if you were a hundred, I would ruin you with this guard I have chosen as it is good and strong. I *acresse* (advance) the forward foot a little out of the way and with the back (or weak) I make a *passo ala traversa*, and, making the cross, rebating your swords, which will then find you uncovered for sure. And if a *lanza* (spear) or sword is cast at me I will always beat it aside with said *passo* out of the way. And so you will see in the plays that follow. And thus with the sword in one hand I make the art as you will find in these pages." [Getty 20v lower left]

Here Fiore is not necessarily speaking of taking on all the combatants at once, as he says, "come one by one." He says that they know that they are doing, "…he who knows the art," but, that he will "ruin all of you with this guard, which is so good and strong." This is the single-handed version of the **tutta porta di ferro**, and movements are very similar.

He then discusses how to set aside the opponent's attack using a *rebattemento*, one of the most important movements in the system, when he says, "I advance the front foot a little out of the way and with the left I perform a *passo ala traversa*. And in that pass I cover myself by beating aside your swords and I find you uncovered. Now I will make certain to strike you." Combining this with the text under the *guardia* for **tutta porta di ferro**, we have also, "And it passes with a cover and goes to the close…always going with a pass, it beats aside the thrust to the ground, and from every blow it makes a cover." In the PD, we have another, more compact statement, "His cuts and thrusts are always resisted (*refrena*)."

The essential movement is thus a tiny adjusting *cressare*—if needed—followed by an oblique *passare* and a cover that opens the opponent's center, leaving him "uncovered." This is done throughout the manuscript, with the dagger, sword in one hand, with the spear and poleaxe. Change the line by stepping on the oblique with an aggressive *passare*, make simultaneous cover, and follow by striking something that is open.

Tutta porta di ferro can be used to wait comfortably against a sword, long or short, or any other kind of weapon. Its inherent stability is due to its closeness to the ground, and I always implore students to keep the tip near to the ground, as it increases available power and denies the *incrosa* to the opponent—by keeping the blade down, it is further away from the opponent and he will find it more difficult to control. It breaks thrusts and strikes alike with the passing offline-cover-strike intention and sits in a very stable, uncrossable, relaxed position ready for anything the opponent might do.

The single-handed version of tutta porta di ferro from Getty fol. 20. The magistro will take the figures one by one, countering a thrust, missle or a blow with the same technique.

CODA LONGA DISTEZA

GUARD OF THE LONG TAIL
Stabile
Getty 24v, upper right; Morgan 13r; PD 19a

"Questa si è posta di coda longa ch'è destesa in terra di dredo, ella pò metter punta e denanci pò covrir e ferire. E se ello passa inanci e tra' del fendente, in lo zogo stretto entra senza fallimento chè tal guardia è bona per aspettare che de quella in altre tosto pò intrare"

"This is the **posta di coda longa** (the long tail) that extends along the ground in back. It can put aside the thrust; in front it can cover and strike. And it passes forward and gives a *fendente*, entering into the *zhogo stretto* without fail. This particular guard is good for waiting because it can quickly enter into the others." [Getty 24v, upper right]

"Posta di coda lunga son in terra destesa;
Denançi e dredredo sempre io faço offesa:
E se passo innançi e entro in lo fendent,
E' uegno al streto zhogo sença faliment."

"[In this] *posta* the long tail extends along the ground;
In front and in back I always make offense:
And passing forward I enter into a *fendente*,
And come to the *zhogo stretto* without fail."

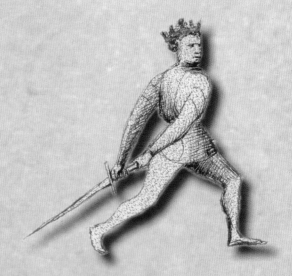

Posta di choda longa Stabile

Coda longa is the guard of the "long tail," where the tail is "extended" (*destesa*) along the ground. It is easy to find from **tutta porta di ferro**; simply rotate the tip from the side to the back, and let the arms trail, so that the tip still rests near to the ground. The hips should be well-wound, with great potential energy, so that the sword may be brought swiftly forward to strike *fendente* or to make cover.

The first thing that should be apparent about this guard is that the sword is very far from the center of the fight, which has major implications for the distance at which it should be adopted. It should be made at a relatively wide distance; if adopted at close range, the combatant will find it difficult to make cover or to set aside the opponent's sword.

In all three texts, Fiore is explicit that the tail is near the to the ground, "posta longa extends along the ground." (PD) and "... **posta coda longa** (the long tail) that extends along the ground in back" (Getty). Keeping the point near to the ground charges the weapon with potential energy.

From this extended position, the guard plays very well in multiple attacking directions, as is mentioned in the PD text, "In front and in back I will always make offense," and it is

in this context that the guard finds its supreme usefulness. With a simple *volta stabile* of the feet, the opponent can turn and find himself in **mezana porta di ferro**, and the same can be done with more freedom (albeit a bit slower) with a *tutta volta*.

But facing the opponent in front, the guard still has uses, even if it is very far from the centerline of the fight. As Fiore mentions, "in front it can cover and strike...it passes forward with a *fendente* and enters without fail into the *zhogo stretto*." Thus, he will either make offense by opening with a powerful *fendente*, continuing his

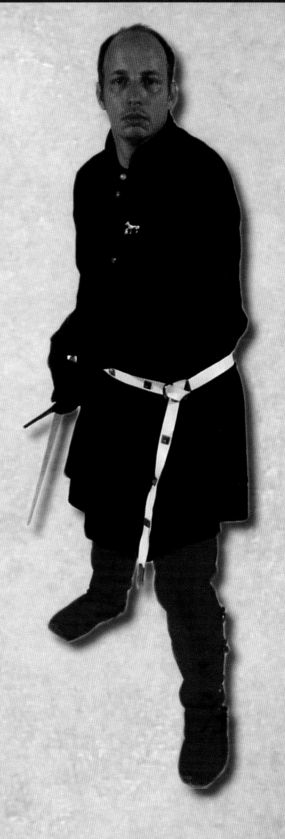

forward motion, coming to the *zhogo stretto* should the opponent make cover (if he doesn't make cover, then he has probably been struck). In the unlikely event of a void, the sword will pass through **posta longa** and end in the comfortable and hard-to-break **mezana porta di ferro**. This demonstrates some of the elegant efficiency that is the hallmark of Fiore's system—a flowing set of movements that yield a smooth algorithm of "if-then" trees from one basic maneuver. If the opponent fired first, then cover is made the same way, with a *fendente* to **posta breve** or **posta frontale**, which will close all available lines, and the combatant may again continue to press forward into the *zhogo stretto*.

There is a curious point about the **posta longa**, however, and that it that Fiore classifies it as *stabile*. In all other respects it is like **posta di donna**; but it is *stabile* rather than *pulsativa*, as are the **poste di donna**. I believe this is because the guard is more stable than it is powerful; being close to the ground, it would be stable. With the arms extended, or expended, there is less available power.

The guard is useful for one thing in particular against an opponent to the front: The blade can be hidden behind the combatant, yielding uncertainty for the opponent.

All in all, we little emphasize the use of this guard in the core Schola curriculum, because **Posta di donna** can handle most of her tasks and is easier to handle. But it is an integral part of the system, and some combatants are both comfortable with and intrigued by it.

MEZANA PORTA DI FERRO

Stabile

Getty 24r, upper right; Morgan 12r, lower right; PD 18A, lower right

"Questa è mezzana porta di ferro perché sta in mezzo è una forte guardia ma ella vole longa spada. Ella butta forte punte e rebatte per forza le spade in erto e torna cum lo fendente per la testa o per gli brazzi e pur torna in sua guardia. Però ven chiamata porta perché la è forte ed è forte guardia che male se pò rompere senza periculo e venire ale strette." [Getty 24r, upper right]

"This is the **mezana porta di ferro** since it stands in the middle and strongly guards me, but she desires a long sword. She throws strong thrusts and rebates the sword upwards with force, and returns (*torna*) with a *fendente* to the head or to his arms, returning then to her guard. And thus it is called *porta* (gate) because of its strength and because it is a strong guard that is hard to break (*rompere*) without danger and it can close to the *stretto*."

"Meçana porta di fero 'son la forte
Per dare cum punta e fendenti la morte:
E per lungeça' de spada che io me sento
Del streto çogho sempre me deffendo."

"I am the strong **mezana porta di ferro**
For it offers the thrust and mortal fendente (blows):
And because of the sword's length I feel
From the *zhogo stretto* I am defended."

Porta di ferro mezana / Stabile

Mezana porta di ferro is probably one of the most useful of Fiore's core guards favored by modern students. The blade rests easily already near the fight's centerline, threatening with the point or with a quick *sotano* against incoming *fendente* attacks. It is the landing place for most *fendente*, and is the natural endpoint even when the combatant's attack is forced aside with a *rebattemento*, as we'll see.

To find **mezana porta di ferro** from our starting position of **tutta porta di ferro**, simply move the tip of the sword along the ground to the body's centerline facing the opponent. The tip should remain near the ground, otherwise the opponent may seek his own *incrosa* to control it. The hands rest at the hips, as they do with **porta di ferro** with the sword or dagger.

As Fiore mentions, "It is called *porta* (gate) because of its strength and because it is a strong guard that is hard to break (*rompere*) without danger." It is indeed hard to break, although there are good methods to use which we'll explore in chapter 8. This is because the sword is already near the fight's centerline, and Fiore writes, "this is the middle iron gate since it stands in the middle and strongly guards me." The threat to make offense with the point is not an idle one, as this guard is supremely good at thrusts.

Being in the "middle," as Fiore says, presents another useful strength. As with all guards in this "centerline" position, either foot can be forward, which means the *poste* can be easily found from a wide variety of positions, without forcing a foot movement, as might be the case with **tutta porta di ferro** or **dente di zenghiaro**. This freedom to have either foot forward is true

with all "centerline" guards, including **mezana porta di ferro**, **posta breve**, **posta longa**, **posta di bicorno**, and **posta frontale**.

It does make a difference which foot is forward, however: Since the primary attack will be with a thrust, the ideal ending point for a thrusting attack will have the right foot forward as well as the right hand. This yields an advantage of range that can be as much as 2-4", a very long way given the *guardia's* sensitivity to the sword length, as he says, "…she desires a long sword." Thus, if the left foot is forward in **mezana porta di ferro**, the thrust can be made

with the more powerful *passare*, rather than with a *volta stabile* or *acresare* that is available if the right foot is forward.

Fiore does mention that, "she desires a long sword." By this he means that the main attack is a thrust, and that the combatant must be wary of opponent's armed with a longer weapon, or who have longer arms, or who are very fast. Because a fast opponent can make up for his lack of length with speed, giving himself more time to make offense. The fact that the sword threatens with the point—held near the ground and thus hard to control—yields the "strong defense," against wrestling that Fiore mentions in the PD.

As with most of the *posta*, Fiore also gives an important example of how the *posta* can be best used. In this case, perhaps the most fluid and deadly technique is what we call a *redoppiando*. Fiore says, "she...**rebates** the sword upwards with force, and returns (*torna*) with a *fendente* to the head or to his arms, returning then to her guard." This is really a deflection, where the sword is redirected, possibly upwards and off the line, which opens the opponent's entire body for a strike, "returning with a *fendente* to the head or arms, and returning then to her guard." This is our 5th play in our core curriculum, treated more fully in chapter 11.

Once the weapon has been knocked aside, passing in the process towards **posta di donna**, it is then immediately brought downwards, "and returns with a *fendente* to the arms or head...." This quick pairing of a break from below made with a powerful *sotano* and returning with an immediate *fendente* is another key fundamental element of the system, a quick "1-2" the moves along the jaw/knee line we'll discuss in more detail in chapter 9.

Using **mezana porta di ferro** is easy, and most novice combatants quickly develop a fondness for it. Because it resides near the fight's center-line, it is quick to make cover and rebate incoming attacks, yielding for a pretty strong defense. And because the sword is already close to the all-important centerline for defense, the combatant can even be late with their response and still have a chance to make cover, if not *rebattemento*.

As this *guardia* is in the middle, with the hands in the middle of the body rather than resting near the rear hip, it has much less power than does its cousin the full iron gate, **tutta porta di ferro**. We can think of *mezana* not only in the sense of "middle," but also in the sense of "half." Therefore, **mezana porta di ferro** has perhaps *half* the power of **tutte porta di ferro**. But in the practical world this is fine, because the targets she selects are generally those that don't require as much power: The delicate bones of the opponent's hands—which don't take much force to break or "discomfit"—or the *redoppiando*, which beats the incoming strike from behind in order to redirect it, rather than meeting and opposing its force directly.

One very effective method of responding to an opponent's *fendente* is to make an oblique step, behind the blade or to the back, catching his hands or arms with the rising *rebattemento* Fiore mentions. This is our 2nd play in our core material, because it teaches the combatant to measure distance carefully and to take advantage of the closest target—which is almost always the hands or arms. In tournament systems where hand strikes are illegal, the blow is easily moved to the arms instead. And even if the combatant steps back too far, he can still attack the blade with a *redoppiando*, deflecting it, as we'll discuss later.

THE BOAR'S TOOTH
Stabile

Getty 24r, lower right; Morgan 12v, lower right; PD 18B, lower right

"Questa si è dente di zengiaro però che dello zengiaro prende lo modo di ferire. Ello tra' grandi punte per sotto man in fin al volto e no si move di passo e torna cum lo fendente zò per gli brazzi. E alchuna volta tra' la ponta al volto e va cum la punta erta, e in quello zitar di punta ello acresse lo pe' ch'è dinanzi subito e torna cum lo fendente per la testa e per gli brazzi e torna in sua guardia e subito zitta un'altra punta cum acresser di pe' e ben se defende delo zogo stretto."

"This is the **dente di zenghiaro** because it takes its manner of upward wounding (*ferire*) from the boar. And she makes great, dangerous thrusts (*punte*) to the face from the hand below. And without a *passo* (step), returning with a *fendente* to his arms, or sometimes with a return to the face, with the point raised. And in which she throws the point she *acresses* the foot in front at once and returns with a *fendente* for the head or for his arms, returning again to guard, and at once throws another thrust with an *acresare*. And she defends well from the *zhogo stretto*." [Getty 24r, lower right]

"Io son la forte posta de dent de zenchiar.
Cum tute le guardie me son uso de prouar."

"I am the strong *posta* of the boar's tooth.
With all the guards I am fashioned from proof"

The boar's tooth, **dente di zenghiaro**, is another favorite amongst our students, because the sword is well-controlled—being held close to the body—is stable, and threatens with both thrusts and dangerous rising blows, the *sotani*. Just as the unarmed version of **dente di zenghiaro** is used to break grips, so too this one can be used not only to break them, but to discourage them as well.

There are two good ways to find **dente di zenghiaro**. First, from **mezana porta di ferro**, with the right foot forward (remember that either foot can be forward in centerline *guardia*), simply draw the left hand back to the left hip, so that the hands are essentially in the same position as they would be for the unarmed *porta di ferro* on the left side. It will often take some work and a fairly loose grip on the sword to find a comfortable position with the hands; many students have far too much tension involved in the way they grip the sword, and for this guard, it can be a dangerous mistake.

The second way answers a fundamental question: "If the system is by and large symmetrical, why is there no **porta di ferro sinestra**, or iron gate on the left side?" The answer is that there is, but unlike the German guards *shrankhut* or *nebenhut*, Fiore adopts the position without crossing his hands. Begin first in the unarmed **porta di ferro** position on the right side. Step *passare* with a *mezza volta*, transitioning smoothly to **porta di ferro**, but on the left. The left hand should now be near the left hip, as if ready to "quick draw" a firearm, and the right should play a bit out front. Now, simply pick up the sword, keeping the hands in this same position. If the point is directed towards the opponent and the grip is relatively loose, as the hands are in the unarmed **porta di ferro**, you are essentially in what would be **porta di ferro sinestra**, or on the left side. But you have not crossed your hands, and are thus in a much stronger position. This is the **dente di zenghiaro** for the sword in two hands.

Because this *posta* emphasizes the use and deterrent value of the sword's point, it is important **not** to have what I call "flying" or "wandering" boar's tooth. If the point is not snugged up and pointed straight at the opponent, then it is a weak deterrent. This deterrant value is mentioned in the very last sentence of the Getty and Morgan, "And she defends well from the *zhogo stretto*."

Another common error is to have the point too far forward, closer to what would be correct for **mezana porta di ferro**. In this case, the point is now closer to the opponent, and since this guard may be adopted and is effective even when the opponent is quite close, the tip becomes very vulnerable this far out. It can be rebated aside, covered, or even stepped on without much difficulty. In Fiore's illustrations the point is close to the foot, within a couple of inches in the PD and even behind the heel in the Getty.

Dente di zenghiaro is, as I mentioned, a very potent *guardia* against all other *poste*, and it is very hard to break. As Fiore says in the PD, "With all guards I am fashioned from proof." From this I believe Fiore meant that **dente di zenghiaro** is well-proven against all the other guards, and this is something that has been validated over and over again in our work with the system. It's hard to break and intimidating if done properly.

Indeed, in the section before, Fiore has a curious illustration with a *magistro* facing what appear to be three different *zugadore*, each wielding a weapon in a different way. He writes:

> "Questi sono tre compagni che voleno alcider questo magistro che aspetta cum la spada a doy mane. Lo primo di questi tre vole lanzare la sua spada contra lo magistro. Lo segondo vole ferire lo detto magistro d'taglio o de punta. Lo terzo vole lanzare doy lanze ch'ello à aparechiado come qui depento.

> "Io 'spetto questi tre in tal posta, zoè in dente di zengiaro e in altre guardie poria 'spettare, zoè in posta de donna la senestra, anchora in posta di finestra sinestra, cum quello modo, e deffesa che farò in dente di zenghiaro. Tal modo è tal deffesa le ditte guardie debian fare. Senza paura io 'spetto uno a

uno, e non posso fallire nè taglio nè punta nè arma manuale che mi sia lanzada, lo pe' dricto ch'i ò denançi acresco fora de strada, e cum lo pe' stancho passo ala traversa del arma che me incontra rebatendola in parte riversa. E per questo modo fazo mia deffesa, fatta la coverta subito farò l'offesa." [Getty 31r, upper figures, see next page.]

"Here are three *compagni* who wish to attack this master, who expects them with the sword in two hands. The first of these three wants to throw his sword at the master. The second wants to wound the said master with a cut of his sword. The third wishes to throw his spear that he has prepared, as is depicted.

"I wait for these three in such a *poste*, called **dente de zenghiaro** or in other guards good for waiting, called **posta de donna senestra**, also in **poste di finestra sinestra**, using a similar method as the defense made in **dente di zenhgiaro**. Such methods and defenses this guard can make. Without fear of edges, points or thrown hand-weapons. I wait [for them] one by one, the right foot, which is in front, *acresses* out of the way, and with the left (or weak) *passo ala traversa* with the weapon before me beaten from the back (*rebattemento…riversa*). And in this way I make my defense, making the cover (*coverta*) and at once offend him."

The guard is shown against diverse opponents, and it is said directly that it is, "good for waiting (or expecting)." It is "without fear of the edge, point or thrown hand weapons." Again, Fiore discusses the same method of clearing the attack with a small *acresare*, followed by a larger oblique *passare*, simultaneously striking the weapon from the back (what we call a *redoppiando*). Immediately, of course, the combatant should "offend" him, meaning that he will follow-on with a *fendente* to the arms or head, depending upon what is safe and open. This reiterates or fortells what the parallel text accompanying **dente di zenghiaro** in the *xij guardia* section.

Fiore also mentions that the guard takes its name from the way a boar wounds (*feriri*), with great sweeping attacks from below. Usually these are thrusts, but they can be *rebattemento riverso*, as it describes in the passage above, always returning immediately with a *colpo* to the head or arms.

All in all **dente di zenghiaro** is a potent anchor in Fiore's system, one of the major places where it is safe both to wait—she is, after all, *stabile*—and one that carries a solid way of both making cover and powering an attack.

One *posta* is offered only in the Getty manuscript, and it is **dente di zenghiaro mezana**, or the middle boar's tooth.

> "Questo si è dente di cengiaro lo mezano e perçò che sono doy denti di zengiaro l'uno tutto, l'altro si è mezo però è ditto mezo, perzò ch'ello sta in mezo de la persona e zò che pò fare lo ditto dente pò fare lo mezo dente. E per modo che fieri lo zengiaro a la traversa per tal modo se fa cum la spada che sempre fieri cum la spada ala traversa de la spada del compagno. E sempre butta punte e discrova lu compagno e sempre guastagli le mane e talvolta la testa e gli brazzi. –posta di dente de zenchiaro mezana stabile."

"This is the **dente di zenchiaro mezano**, because there are two teeth of the boar, one whole, the other in the middle (or half), because she is found in the middle of the body. And she can make everything the complete one can. As the boar wounds by traversing, in the same way you wound with the sword, traversing from that of the *compagno*, because casting the point like this uncovers the opponent and it is possible to ruin his hands and at certain times his head or arms." [Getty 24v, lower right]

Fiore says that there are, "two teeth of the boar, one whole, the other in the middle." Just why this poste is not mentioned in the other versions, or what is unique about it is not mentioned at all.

But the position is a little different. The *magistro* of this *guardia* still has his right foot forward, but amost the whole of his weight is on the back leg, as opposed to the whole **dente di zenghiaro**, where it is even or perhaps weighted a bit forward. But the feet have made a *volta stabile*, with the left heel pointing forward while the right one is in a more toe-forward orientation. The hands are unstressed and widely placed on the handle, and it is clear that there is great potential strength; the *magistro* carries his body as if he was going to lift a great weight upwards. It appears that the false edge is upward, and crucially, the point should be, as the text says, in the middle of the body.

In the text Fiore gives another version of the method of a boar's tooth attack, that is, a break from below on an oblique angle, accompanied with an aggressive step. In all other ways, this guard appears to be just a variant of the regular **dente di zenghiaro**, so no more will be said about it here.

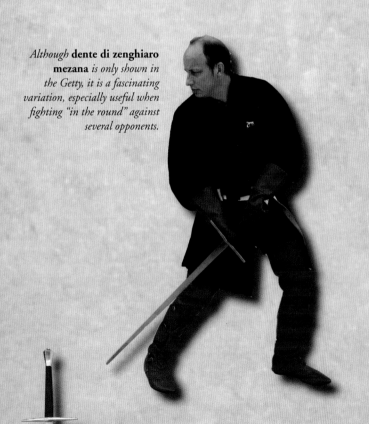

Although **dente di zenghiaro mezana** *is only shown in the Getty, it is a fascinating variation, especially useful when fighting "in the round" against several opponents.*

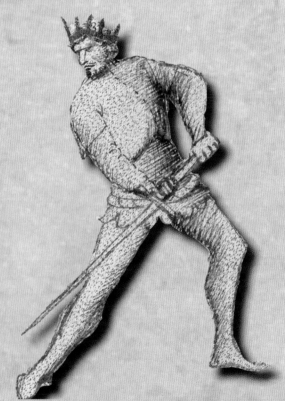

The
POSTA DI DONNA
Family

Posta di Donna (PD); Posta di Donna Soprana (Getty, Morgan); Posta di Donna Senestra (Getty, Morgan, PD – Vera Posta di Finestra)

"Guardia e posta di donna son chiamata perché cum queste altre prese de spada 'e son divisada, che una non è tal presa che l'altra, ben che questa che m'è contra mi pare la mia guardia se non fosse forma d'azza che la spada s'i intrada."

"The *guardia* and **posta di donna** are so-called because with each, the other *prese* (grips) of the sword are divided into whether or not certain *prese* (grips) are good, which I take with my guard if it is not in the form of an *azza* or the *spada* as the [opposing one] that I enter [against]."

[Getty 22v, lower left]

"Questa spada si è spada e azza. E gli grandi pesi gli lizieri forte impaza. Questa anchora posta de donna la soprana, che cum le soi malicie le altre guardie spesso ingana, perché tu crederai che traga de colpo io trarò di punta. Io non ho altro a fare che levar gli brazzi sopra la testa. E posso buttar una punta che io l'ò presta."

"This sword is a sword and an axe. And owing to its great power, guarding [against it] is very difficult. This is also **posta di donna la soprana**, whose malice makes fools of the other guards, because you believe [I will] hurl a *colpo* but [instead] I fling the *punta*. I don't have to do a thing except move the arm from over my head and I can quickly [and] powerfully cast the point."

[Getty 22v, lower right]

There is a great deal written about **posta di donna** and all her variants as they appear in the different manuscripts. While there is only one version of **porta di ferro** and I believe that it is *the* core guard, there is no question that the **poste di donna** are extremely important fighting positions familiar to combatants in many different traditions.

Posta di donna translates neatly as "Woman's Guard," or "Guard of the Woman." I have heard some intriguing theories as to why this is called the woman's guard; that it is an invitation, that it has a "come hither" invitation that suggestively highlights openings in order to lure the opponent inward and that the guard is the natural position for swinging a sword for someone with less upper body strength, as a woman would have. It might be interesting also to note that in the earlier German treatise, RA MS I.33, which includes the only woman pictured in a European fighting treatise—the enigmantic Walpurgis—who is pictured in a guard that shares the essence of a well-wound, powered position held near the shoulder, something like **posta di donna**.

This well-wound, shoulder-anchored position is the essence of all the **poste di donna** variants. They are different in terms of foot placement, and in the exact placement of the blade, but all share the powerful potential energy presented by the twisting of the body, the working together of the large muscle groups connected at the hip (this will be discussed in more detail in the chapter 9 on developing power).

Because the sword is behind the body, it is relatively far from the crucial centerline that protects the body. As such, combatants should be careful about the distance, because they need to trade distance for time in order to be able to make an effective cover. Thus, in general this is a guard for long distance—the closer one gets to the opponent, the less time there is to make cover.

Fiore discusses these *poste* not only in the descriptive passages accompanying the individual *guardia*, but also in some of the preliminary sections, where he throws in a bunch of important concepts: the system's footwork, the three *volta* of the feet and of the sword. He says also that the *poste* can be adopted on either side, which we can also corroborate in the *poste's* illustrations (the key paragraph has already been translated and discussed in chapter 6).

POSTA DI DONNA DESTRA

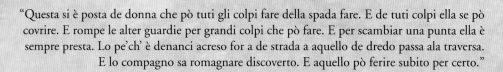

Morgan Carta 12v;
Getty Fol. 22v
Novati Carta 18r

"Questa si è posta de donna che pò tuti gli colpi fare della spada fare. E de tuti colpi ella se pò covrire. E rompe le alter guardie per grandi colpi che pò fare. E per scambiar una punta ella è sempre presta. Lo pe'ch' è denanci acreso for a de strada a aquello de dredo passa ala traversa. E lo compagno sa romagnare discoverto. E aquello pò ferire subito per certo."

"This is the **posta di donna** that can make covers from all *colpi* and can make all seven *colpi* of the sword. And [it can] break the other guards with the great blows she can make. And she can quickly exchange the thrust. The front foot acresses out of the way and the back [foot] passes *ala traversa*. She will discover the *compagno* uncovered, so she will immediately wound him for certain."

"Guardia e posta di donna son chiamata perché cum queste altre prese de spada 'e son divisada, che una non è tal presa che l'altra, ben che questa che m'è contra mi pare la mia guardia se non fosse forma d'azza che la spada s'i intrada." [Getty 22v]

"[The] guard [is] called **posta di donna** because the grip of the sword is different from other certain grips, which can counter my guard if not in the manner of an axe which the sword can also enter."

This is an interesting guard, presented in the Getty treatise in opposition to **tutta porta di ferro** (although in the Pissani Dossi it opposes **dente di zenghiaro** instead). This guard is also *pulsativa*—powerful—and Fiore says that it can "break all other guards with the great blows she can make."

To find **posta di donna**, the sword is brought to the right shoulder, the hilt near to the head, the right hand near to the right shoulder. The hips are well-wound, and the weight appears to be evenly distributed or perhaps favoring the back leg, which makes sense if "the foot in front advances a little out of the way (*for a de strada*)" as the "back one passes *ala traversa*."

In practice, this means that we usually execute this guard with about 85% of the weight on the back foot, 15% on the front, so that it can be quickly placed "a little in front," which sets the direction of travel. Next, the back foot makes a traversing *passa* as the blow is made.

It is important not to flare the elbows outward in this or in any other guard, as they will be an attractive target.

Because the sword is so well wound behind the combatant, this is a guard that is generally taken, in its "perfect" form, from a very wide distance. This makes sense, because it takes longer to get to the target from "way back here," as I like to say. The further back the sword is, the longer it will take to come to the all-important center of the fight.

As we will see in the next chapter, this is one of the guards where the essence of the guard is important, because in an engagement the combatant will not always have the time

to achieve the "perfect" version, so it will become important to recognize that the essence is the sword high, strongly connected to a well-wound body full of potential energy.

Fiore says that the guard can make and defend against all seven blows. This can be tricky; because a rising strike from the left side seems impossible, although I have seen some impressive gymnastics as combatants attempt to demonstrate it. It is my belief that Fiore may have been referring here to both **poste di donna**, the *destra* (right) and *sinestra* (left) versions, in which case the passage makes much more sense. Alternatively, he may be referring to use of the *posta* from different directions.

But she certainly can defend strongly; she simply comes forward with a *colpo* (blow) and drives directly into the oncoming attack, passing through **posta longa** if there is some distance or **posta breve** for better cover when there is too little distance. Additionally, the combatant defends with the most fundamental aspect of protection, the perception and manipulation of distance itself. When taking **posta di donna**—or any of her variants—the combatant must be very aware of the precise range between the combatants.

WOMAN'S GUARD (HIGH)
Pulsativa

Getty Carta 25V (page 23v) Upper Right; Morgan 12v; PD Carta 18r Upper Right

"Questa si è posta di donna che pò fare tutti gli setti colpi fare de la spada fare. E de tutti colpi ella so pò croverire. E rompe le altra guardie per grandi colpi che pò fare. E per scambiar una punta è sempre presta. Lo pe'ch' è denanci acresse fora de strada e quello di dredo passa ala traversa. E lo compagno a romagner discoperto e quello pò ferire subito per certo." (Getty)

"This is the **posta di donna** that makes all seven *colpi* of the sword. And she makes all her covers. [She] breaks (*rompe*) the other guards with the great *colpi* she can make. And she quickly makes the exchange (*scambiar*) of the thrust. The left foot acresses out of the way and the right passes *a la traversa*. And the *compagno* is uncovered so she can surely and certainly strike."

"Io son la posta de dona soprana e altera
Per far deffesa in zaschaduna mainera;
E chi contra de mi uole contrastrare
Più longa spada de mi conuen trouare." (PD)

"I find the upper or changed **posta di donna**
That makes true defense in each play;
And he who wants to come against me
It behooves him to find a longer sword!"

Posta de donna destraza / pulsatua .

Fiore shows this guard with some interesting variants, but first we'll deal with the essence of the position. Fundamentally the same as the other **poste di donna**, the hips well wound and the sword chambered for great power, as Fiore says when he classifies it as *pulsativa* and writes, "she breaks the other guards with the great *colpi* she can make."

Fiore also says that she makes all her covers, which means that she can transition easily to the other covering *poste*, possibly in all directions. This is echoed in the PD text, which says that this *posta* "makes true defense in each play." This is true so long as the combtant maintains the proper distance; as with the last play, the sword is far from the fight's centerline (when facing opponents to the front), so range must be carefully measured.

Fiore also says that from this *posta* the combatant can make the *exchange of the thrust*, one of the key methods Fiore's combatants use to deflect an incoming thrust and threaten with their own point. We'll cover this in much more detail in chapter 11.

In the last sentence, Fiore tells the combatant how to make a small step with the left foot (which is shown as being in front), "out of the way," so that the back (the right) foot can "change" or pass forward. This is done both to change the line that opens the opponent to an easy attack. In this case Fiore says *ferire* (wound), rather than specifying *colpo*, which I take to mean either a *punta* or *colpo*, according to what looks best.

Finally, Fiore offers one way to counter this guard—maybe with a thrust! In the PD he says, "And for he who wants to come against me, it behooves him to find a longer sword!" This is especially useful in a thrust, where the longer weapon/arm combination has an advantage, but is also true in a *colpo*—so the opponent is advised of the danger this *posta* offers and is counseled not to attack unless he has a longer sword (which can just mean a longer *poste*, remember). There is another possibility, that is, that Fiore intends rather that the opponent should mind his distance carefully, essentially lengthening the sword.

POSTA DI DONNA SINESTRA

WOMAN'S GUARD (LEFT)

Pulsativa

Getty Carta 25V (page 23v) Lower Right
Morgan 13r, (TBD)
PD Carta 19v, Upper Right

"Questa si è posta di donna la senestra che di coverte e de feriri ella è sempre presta. Ella fa grandi colpi e rompe le punte e sbattere a terra. E intra in lo zogho stretto per lo suo saver traversare. Questi zogi tal guardia sa ben fare." (Getty)

"This is the **posta di donna la senestra** that makes her cover and is always quick to wound. She makes great *colpi*, breaks the thrust, drives it to the ground, and enters into the *zhogo stretto* by skillfully to setting upon him. This *guardia* knows well how to make these plays."

"Io son la stancha posta de uera finestra;
Cussi de la drita como de questa son presta." (PD)

"I find the left posta de vera finestra (posta of the true window);
That cuts from the right with quickness."

posta di donna la finestra pulsatiua

Fiore shows this guard with some interesting variants, but first we'll deal with the essence of the position. Fundamentally, this guard is simply the left-sided version of **posta di donna**, with the hilt held high, this time on the left side, with the blade well back, powerfully coiled, and ready to strike.

To find **posta di donna senestra**, from **posta di donna destra**, simply make a *mezza volta*, preferably accompanied with a *passare* step. As the *mezza volta* is made, simply raise the sword slightly and drop it efficiently over the head, from one side to the other. When the *mezza volta* is complete, you will be in a simplified version of the **posta di donna senestra**. You should now feel very powerful, and it should be clear that the most obvious line of attack is from left to right, "that comes to the right with quickness," as Fiore says.

I consider this the most basic, simplified version of the guard because in the Getty, the figure is illustrated with the feet turned in a *volta stabile*, with the heels towards the opponent. It is the same in the PD illustration shown above. In both cases the sword could well be interpreted to be pointed directly at the opponent, which would accord with the odd name that Fiore calls the guard in the PD, the "true guard of the window," rather than the "woman's guard, left," as it is titled in the Getty and Morgan.

With a *volta stabile*, as we will see, the combatant can quickly pivot (or turn) both feet without stepping to generate significant power.

It is perhaps an odd thing that the guard's name changes between the manuscripts, and that it differs so much in the PD from the **vera posta di finestra** (which, as we'll see, is on the right side). This outlines the potential for a close and perhaps surprising relationship between the **poste di donna** and the **poste di finestra**, especially considering that all three **posta di donna** are considered *pulsativa*, the **poste di finestra** is indeed *instabile*. Another interesting difficulty is that, facing forward, it is awkward to transition between the **poste di donna** and the **poste di finestra**, but there is an interesting way out of the dilemma; by executing a *volta stabile* or a *tutta volta* with the feet and changing directions to face an opponent to the rear, the transition suddenly becomes very easy.

In the Getty and the Morgan, Fiore says that the guard "makes her cover and is quick to wound." The means that the transition to a position in front must be very fast, especially since the sword is again back, in a well-powered but relatively far away position.

From this position, as with the **posta di donna** and the **posta di donna soprana**, the combatant can "step with the front foot a little off the line," and *passare* on the oblique the strike or to strike down incoming attacks. This is especially effective against a thrust, as Fiore notes, "it breaks the thrust and beats it to the ground." This will be the essence of the *rebettare*.

It is also important, as mentioned earlier in the chapter, to know which side of the body the sword is on. Since this posta strikes "to the right" with great force, if an opponent strikes from the right, as is most common (usually with a *fendente*), a *rebattemento* will place your weapon behind theirs, which is both more efficient and more powerful. This play is examined in detail in the chapter 10 on fundamental tactics.

As with the other **poste di donna**, this guard should be adopted at a wider distance than guards that have the blade closer to the center, because it will take some time to retrieve the sword and make cover. If the combatant is caught here at a closer distance, the available time may as usual be increased by stepping *tornare* (passing back) as the sword is brought forward.

In a fight, the **posta di donna senestra** has proven very useful in countering the other two **posta di donna**, and like them, she breaks all other *poste* through her powerful strikes. For the most part I have trained our novice and intermediate students to treat it more like a left-shoulder version of **posta di donna** than to have them struggle

with generating power through the *volta stabile*, although future study may eventually change this preference.

POSTA DI FINESTRA

GUARD OF THE WINDOW

Instabile

Getty Carta 23V lower left
Morgan 12r, lower left
PD Carta 18a, lower left

"Questa si è posta di finestra che di malizie e ingani sempre la è presta. E de covrir e de ferire ella è magistra. E cum tutte guardie ella fa questione e cum le soprane e cum le terrene. E d'una guardia a l'altra ella va spesso per inganar lo compagno. E a metter grande punte e saver romper e scambiare quelli zoghi ella pò ben fare."

"This is the **posta di finestra**, which quick, deceitful and ever full of malice. And at making cover and wounding she is a master. And she tests all the *guardie*, those above and those near the ground. And from one *guardia* to another she goes, deceiving the *compagno*. And the can make great thrusts, which she knows how to break and exchange, plays she does very well." [Getty 23v]

"Io son la posta di vera finestra
E do in tuta l'arte sempre io son presta."

"I am the *posta* of the True Window,
And the whole art I can quickly do." [PD 18v]

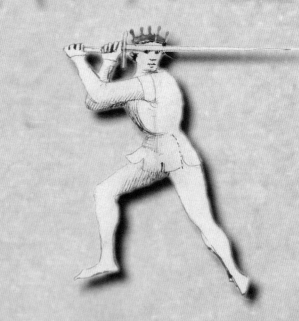

The **poste di finestra** present the student of medieval Italian swordsmanship with several conundra. Remembering that Fiore's system is by and large symmetrical, this *posta* is done on both the right and the left, although it is shown in all three manuscripts made on the right.

To find **posta di finestra** from **posta breve**, simply roll the hand back towards the right shoulder. The grip does not change, and, uniquely, this is one time when the hands are crossed in the *posta*. The blade should be straight, the combatant's eyes looking along the blade, directly at the opponent.

In **posta di finestra**, the point is "shortened" as it will be with the next group of *posta*, in **posta breve** and **posta bicorno**. With this shortened point, the combatant may maintain an *incrosa* with his opponent's sword and find an open thrust. We discussed this briefly in chapter 5, but we'll see it again in more detail in chapter 10.

Posta di finestra is indeed, as Fiore calls it in the Getty, *instabile*. Even very slight pressure against the blade will deflect the shortened point, so this is not the best place to wait. **Posta di finestra** invites strong contact. Using malice—*malicosa*—the combatant may also deny the contact and thus effectively make the incrosa with the sword via a false.

Like **posta longa**, the swordsman will briefly "test" the opponent's defense to see if there is an open thrust. AS SOON as it is found, the *punta* will be cast forward, driven

from the shoulder. Posta di finestra is one option for finding the thrust, although posta breve and posta di bicorne can also be used, depending upon the relative positions. The combatant would do well to select posta di finestra when the opponent's sword is relatively high, as opposed to when it is realtvly low (in this case, **posta breve** or **posta di bicorno** would make more sense).

This is the most common use for posta di finestra, to "test" the opponent's *guardia* while the swords are crossed. From **posta breve**, the combatant may decide to test the opponent's *posta* by

maintaining contact with their sword and essentially exchanging the thrust by rolling to the side that the sword is on. It is vitally important to adopt **posta di finestra** on the same side as the opponent's blade, otherwise the combatant will be open to wounding via thrust or strike.

In Fiore's text, he seems to advocate the use of **posta di finestra** as a momentary place to threaten, and he notes that she is especially good in the thrust, both in exchanging and breaking.

The combatant must use care, however, not to wait in a *guardia* that is *instabile*. **Posta di finestra** is easily broken with a strike, something to bear in mind if your opponent adopts it.

POSTÁ BREVE

SHORT GUARD
Stabile
Getty 24r, lower left
Morgan 13r, upper left
Novati 19v, upper left

"Questa si è posta breve che vole longa spada et è maliciosa guarda che non à stabilità. Anche sempre si move e vede se pò entrar cum punta e cum passo contra lo compagno. E più è apropiada tal guardia in arme che senz'arme."

"This is the **posta breve** (short guard), who wants a long sword. And it is a malicious guard without much steadfastness. Also it moves quickly and looks to see if she can gain entry with a thrust with a step against the compagno. She is more appropriate with guardia in armour than [she is] out of it." [Getty 24r]

"Io son posta breue e ò de spada lungeça; Spesso meto punta e in lei torno in freça."

"I am **posta breve** and with the sword I extend; Spending her thrust and darting back."

Posta breve, the short guard, should look familiar to practitioners of almost any other two-handed sword art. This position, with the hands at the waist, allows the combatant to very quickly make cover, but it offers very limited offensive potential, because it lacks sufficent power for powerful strikes. Like its longer cousin, **posta longa**, it is "malicious" (*maliciosa*), in that it can "taste" the guard to find an opening for the thrust. Fiore offers only a little about this guard, but it turns out to be a cornerstone position through which the sword will end, transit through, and from which many covers will be made.

To find **posta breve** from **mezana porta di ferro**, simply keep the pommel in place and raise the point to the opponent's face or throat. Like other centerline *poste*, either leg can be forward. The hands are held very low at or even below the waist, but not awkwardly so. For the most part, the hands and sword are in the center of the body. In this conservative form of **posta breve**, the avenues of attack are evenly distributed between the right and left, and the point retains it effective threat, "I am posta breve, and with the sword I extend, spending her thrust and darting back" (*Io son posta breue e ò de spada lungeça; Spesso meto punta e in lei torno in freça*), as he says in the PD.

To make a *punta*—a thrust—Fiore says to simply to extend the sword, which is another way of saying to transition with force towards **posta longa**, where the thrust ends. Simply extending the hands to the point where the elbows are just short of fully extended, with the hilt at a level below the point.

As we will see with **posta frontale**, while the point remains centered and directed to the opponent's face, the hilt can be set anywhere between the hips, or even slightly beyond them, in some instances. This is evident from one of Fiore's later plays in the *zhogo largo*, the **Exchange of the Thrust**, where an incoming thrust is edged to the side while the combatant's point remains a threat.

With the point directed to the opponent's face, the feet a stable width apart, the position feels comfortable and stable—and it is. And yet, Fiore adds that, "…it is a malicious guard without much steadfastness" (…*è maliciosa guarda che non à stabilità*). This seems

to fly in face of the Getty's categorization of it as stabile. I believe the difficulty here has to do with the relative vulnerability of the *posta* in a defensive sense, because the very next section of the treatise, the *zhogo largo*, he discusses what to do from the crossed-swords position, the *incrosa*. The weakness of **posta breve** is that it passively offers the *incrosa* to the opponent and has ready only the thrust. In essence, it offers the sword to the opponent and returns very little. Therefore, as a starting position, **posta breve** is perhaps not the strongest choice.

But as an ending point, **posta breve** has much to recommend it and we have found it exceedingly useful. When striking at the opponent at your midrange or longer, attacks pass through **posta longa**. But when striking close, the movements instead transit through or end in **posta breve**, in order to strike with the optimal point on the sword and to avoid bringing the hands closer to the opponent, where they would present a grappling target. If far away, strike through/to **posta longa**. If close, strike through/to **posta breve**. Long, long guard; Short, short guard.

Another interesting use for **posta breve** is that, if used as an alternate landing point for a broken attack, it provides strong cover while simultaneously offering the point for "malicious" thrusts. If you don't like what's happening during your attack, one good response is to abort the attack and draw the sword in, conservatively, to **posta breve**. This leverages the sword's length to make cover for most of the body while keeping the point forward as a threat. But because it passively offers the *incrosa* to the opponent, it is not an ideal waiting place. Such a transition will in fact counter most of

the plays we present in the book, as well as the rest of the **zhogo largo** plays that Fiore shows in his treatises.

Fiore mentions another thing, that the guard is "better in armour than without" (*e più è apropiada tal guardia in arme che senz'arme*). Looking ahead to where Fiore discusses armoured combat, it is clear that from **posta breve** the combatant is ready to take up the sword at the *mezza spada*, the middle, and use it as a short, nasty spear or poleaxe, an idea strongly paralleled in the German tradition, with the idea of the *halbschwert*, or "halfsword."

As we will see, **posta breve** also has a key symbiotic relationship with two other *poste*, **di bicorno** and **di finestra**. All three threaten with a shortened point, unwinding explosively into an immediate thrust. Of the three, *posta breve* is the most stable (it is, after all, the lowest to the ground), and is anchored at the hips, whereas **posta di finestra** is anchored at the shoulder and **posta di bicorno** at the chest. In experimenting, I have found that following the *incrosa*, the combatant can, while maintaining contact with the blade, find any of these three *guardia* (although in any given instance, one of the three will be the best option), placing the point as a threat while simultaneously maintaining cover. The ability to **find the point**, as I call it, following the *incrosa* is a core skill that will become increasingly emphasized as fencing changes through the ages.

POSTA LONGA

THE LONG GUARD
Instabile
Getty 24r, upper Left
Morgan 12v, upper left
PD 18r, upper left

"Posta longa si è questa piena di falsità. Ella va tastando le guardie se lo compagno pò ingannare. Se ella pò ferir de punta la lo sa ben far e gli colpi la schiva e po' fieri s'ela lo pò fare più che le altre guardie le falsità sa usare."

"This is **posta longa** (long guard), full of falseness. She will taste the compagno's guards [to see] if she can make fools [of them]. She knows well how to wound with the sword, avoiding his *colpi* (blows) and wounding with her own if she can. She uses falsing (or falseness) more than the other guards." [Getty 24r, upper left]

"Io son posta longa cum mia spada curta
Che cum inçegno la golla spesso furta."

"I am the **posta longa**, with my shortened sword
With an inclination to spend myself stealing the throat." [PD 18r, upper left]

Posta longa is another cornerstone guard within the system, as it is the primarily place through which attacks will transit or end. By itself, it may be used to break all other guards through deception, indeed the guard relies on deception since it is inherently *instabile*.

To find **posta longa** from **posta breve**, simply extend the arms forward such that the hilt remains below the point and the arms are just short of fully extended, "with an inclination to spend myself stealing the throat" (*che cum inçegno la golla spesso furta*) as Fiore says in the PD. Do not lock the elbows or force the joints in any way. Holding the point directly at the opponent's eyes has a further jarring effect, since he cannot quite tell exactly how far away it is.

As a *guardia*, Fiore calls it *instabile*, which makes sense owing to its extended position. Out here the sword begs for the opponent to initiate contact with it, probably brushing it aside en route to a more devastating attack. At first glance this might seem to make it look weak, but, as Fiore mentions, she is "full of falseness" (*piena di falsità*) and "makes use of falsness more than the other guards" (*s'ela lo pò fare più che le altre guardie le falsità sa usare*).

To see what Fiore means here, it is useful to look ahead a bit to the work of Filippo Vadi, where in Chapter XII he discusses principles of sword feints:

> "And I advise you again to be mindful of what I say:
> When you have closed to the mezza spada,
> You can act well from each side,
> Following the Art with good feints (*offulsa*)
> Feints mean confusion,
> Which bewilder the other's defense
> So that he can't understand
> What you want to do on [either] side."

Although this section discusses in specific handling the sword *mezza spada*, it applies equally in this instance and it clearly indicates the use of "false" movements to midirect the opponent's weapon. The indecision is, in effect, a form of crossing swords, because it conveys momentary control, effectively pinning his sword in place or causing it to take an uncertain direction. A good swordsman can use this "virtual cross" as if it were physical and then strike to something advantageous. But the combatant should not allow

blade contact, because it will likely be at a disadvantage, since the arms are extended and the guardia thus *instabile*.

From **posta longa**, what this means is that the combatant offers the sword, inviting contact and threatening with the point itself. If he fails to act, the point can "make a taste" of his guard in order to see if an avenue is open for a thrust. If so, he may immediately strike. The point and should move about a bit, "tasting" various places, but the point must remain firmly pointed at the opponent, or the threat fails.

If the opponent does react, it will likely be to move the point out of the way. In this sense, the combatant may easily deny the *incrosa*, making small corrections so that the strike misses while still keeping the point as a threat. In this sense the guard is a powerful invitation that is very hard to resist, even for experienced swordsmen. The movements in this instance share much with later rapier work, save that there are two hands involved and the movemens are consequently a bit larger. But by using a bit of "falseness," the combatant tricks the opponent into making an opening that is immediately exploited.

In addition to posta longa's use as starting point that is "full of falseness," it is a key transit and ending-point for attacks (both thrust and blows) made at medium or long distance, where much of the fight happens (As mentioned in the discussion on posta

breve, long, long guard; short, short guard.) Indeed, in making a transition between any of the high **poste di donna** positions and any of the lower *guardia*, such as **porta di ferro mezano**, the blade will pass through **posta longa**. Indeed, if the combatant strikes at his opponent and the opponent responds by stepping back, the combatant's blade may be halted at **posta longa**, dramatically changing the momentary equation, since the point is now a direct threat.

POSTA DI BICORNO

"Questa è posta di bicorno che stà cossì serada che sempre sta cum la punta per mezo de la strada. E quello che pò fare posta longa pò fare questa. E similemente dico de posta di fenestra e di posta frontale."

"This is the posta di bicorno, which stands *cossi serada*, that is, it stands with the point in the middle of the line. And that which the **posta longa** can do, this can do. And similarly therefore as **posta di finestra** and **posta frontale**.

"Posta di bicornio io me faço chiamar
So io ho falsitade asay non men domandar."

"Position of the Two Horns I am called,
I have sufficient falseness; don't ask more of me."

The "two horned" guard, **posta di bicorno**, is perhaps one of the most misunderstood of Fiore's guards. Obviously unstable, it has led many to wonder about its possible utility. But taken together with the text in the Getty or Morgan versions of Fiore's book, it becomes a little less difficult, as he specifically links it with the **posta di finestra** (which also has a shortened point) and the **posta frontale** (which makes cover).

To find **posta di bicorno** from **posta longa**, simply draw the hands directly back to the center of the chest, as the point should stand *cossì serada*, that is, in the center of the body, directly at the opponent. Fiore shows two different hand positions for this posta. In the Getty, the hand is turned awkwardly, while in the PD, the hand is shown in a more relaxed position. I adopt it with the pommel loosely secured by the palm of the left hand, which moves the point while the right hand acts as the fulcrum. Because this is a centerline guard, either foot can be forward.

Fiore doesn't talk much about what is unique about this posta, except, "that which posta longa can do, this can do (*e quello che pò fare posta longa pò fare questa*). In this sense it would be considered good for falsing, which is confirmed in the PD, "I have sufficient falseness; don't ask more of me" (*so io ho falsitade asay non men domandar*). I find this last part especially interesting, since it suggests that a feint is really all the *guardia* might have going for it!

But in practice, the guard is actually quite useful. Whenever you'd adopt **posta longa** to threaten with the point, but there is insufficient room, you can generally wedge into the **posta di bicorno**. More expressly, from the *incrosa*, if you look to

find the point, you can often use the **posta di bicorno** much as you would the **posta di finestra**, as the text says, "And similarly therefore as **posta di finestra**…" (*e similemente dico de posta di fenestra*…). Taken together with **posta breve** and **posta di finestra**, there are interesting triangular anchor points through which a thrust might be found.

Posta bicorno is an effective way to change the leverage point on the sword, which can enable a quick thrust even against an opponent who has made cover in something like posta breve.

POSTA FRONTALE

FRONTAL POSITION
Instabile
Getty 24v, lower left
Morgan 12v, upper right
PD 18v, upper right

"Questa si è posta frontale chiamada d'alchun magistro posta di corona che per incrosar ella è bona e per le punte ell'è ancora bona che se la punta glie ven tratta erta ella la incrosa passando fuora di strada. E se la punta è tratta bassa anchora passa fuor di strada rebatendo la punta a terra. Anchora pò far altramente, che in lo trar de la punta torna cum lo pe' indredo e vegna da fendente per la testa e per gli brazzi e vada in dente di cengiaro e subito butti una punta o doe cum acresser di pe' e torna di fendente in quella propria guardia."

"This is the **posta frontale**, called by some masters **posta di corona** (crown position). And from the cross [she] is good as she is with the point. Which if his point comes pulling up, she passes from the *incrosa* (cross) out of the way. And if the point pulls down, [she] also passes out of the way, rebating (beating) the point to the ground. Also [she is] able to do something else; with the flick of the point she returns with the foot in back, and makes a *fendente* for the head or for his arms, and returns ending in **dente di zenghiaro**, at once throwing the point (thrusting) or giving a *fendente* with an *acresare* of the foot, returning to his guard." [Getty 24v, lower left]

"Poste frontale, é son chiamata corona
De tagli e de punte a nesum non perdona."

"Frontal Position is called Crown
The edge and point it is foolish to forget." [PD 18v]

Posta frontale ditta corona Instabile

Posta frontale is an excellent place to make cover from a *fendente*, or more likely, a position to adopt from the *incrosa*. It is intruiging that "other masters" call this guard the posta di corona, since within the Liechtenauer school it seems very close to the leger *kron*, or simply "crown," almost the same as the Italian *corona*.

To find **posta frontale**, the best place to start is **posta breve**, and as it is a centerline guard, either foot can be forward. Imagine the swords crossed at the *mezza spada*, and in response to an imagined thrust, the hands are simply raised until the cross is above the eyes, sitting as an imagined coronet at the brow. In this position, the tip canted slightly outward, the head is safe. This position can also be adopted from any other posta, where it would make excellent cover against an incoming fendente. From here, the combatant may enter into the zhogo stretto, as they have "collected" or "captured" the opponent's sword at the tutta spada, the joint of cross and blade, its strongest point. The blade has passed "out of the way" (*passando fuora di strada*) and there are now many options available.

Like **posta breve**, the ideal for the position is in the center, but the hilt can float from side to side where it will make covers for *fendente mandritto* and *manriverso*. It is important that the point remain in the center if the hilt does traverse from side to side, or the head become exposed. "Windshield-wipering" must be avoided at all costs, because it exposes the head.

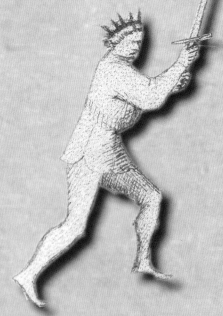

We use this *posta* in two ways. The first, as outlined above, is usually made from a very momentary *incrosa*, seizing or capturing the blade firmly in preparation for *zhogo stretto* or, as Fiore seems to describe in the Getty text, returning with a *tornaro* and a sweeping downward *fendente* for the head or arms, potentially ending

in **dente di zenghiaro**. Another follow-on, also mentioned in the Getty text, is to drive a thrust to the ground, where it essentially "breaks" the thrust and is then followed-on in the usual way.

The second way relates to **posta breve**, the short guard. One can lower the point downwards, or over into the other shortened thrusting *guardia* (**di bicorno** or **di finestra**), to **find the point**. At one end of the spectrum, one can execute the plays in the paragraph above, capturing for *zhogo stretto* or setting aside and breaking a thrust. Or, one can instead attempt to **find the point**, working between **posta breve**, **posta di bicorno** and **posta di frontale**.

POSTA FRONTALE

Posta frontale is the gateway to most of the zhogo stretto plays. These "close" plays rely on extension of control through prese or "grips." It also extends control over the opponent's blade by capturing it.

Typically one comes to posta frontale after the swords have been crossed, stepping aggressively forward to make the capture.

The most successful attacks with continue to move forward, taking immediate advantage of the capture (see play #6, chapter 11).

OTHER FORMS OF CATEGORIZATION

POSITION

One way that I've often taught the *poste* is according to which side of the body they are on, or whether they are high or low. This has proven effective at seminars, where the material must be taught within a very limited spectrum of time.

In this context, I generally present the low-line guards first: **posta coda longa disteza**, **tutta porta di ferro**, **mezana porta di ferro**, and **denti di zenghiale**. From the centerline, one can begin down in **mezana porta di ferro** and efficiently find **posta breve**, **poste frontale**, and **posta di bicorno**. I then look at the positions used in *finding the point*: **posta breve**, **posta di bicorno**, **posta di finestra**. Finally, the **poste di donna**: **posta di donna**, **posta di donna sinestra**, and **posta di donna soprana**.

Alternatively, one can explore the *guardia* according to their right/center/left positions:

Right	Center	Left
Tutta Porta di Ferro	Mezana porta di ferro	Dente di Zenghiale
Posta di Donna	Posta breve	Poste di Finestra (Sinestra)
Posta Coda Longa	Poste Longa	Poste di Donna Sinestra
Posta di Finestra (destra)	Poste di Bicorno	
Posta di Donna Soprana	Poste Frontale ditta Corona	

Lowline	Middle Line	High Line
Tutta Porta di Ferro	Posta breve	Posta di Donna / Poste di Finestra
Posta Coda Longa		Posta di Donna / Finestra Sinestra
Mezana porta di ferro		
Denti di Zenghiale		

It is important, when using the *poste* as the anchor for a fighting framework, to realize what side of the body the sword is on. I have found in teaching the *poste* that it is much easier for students to grasp the *poste* when they are either presented by their positions (chiefly along the low- and center-lines).

BEGIN – END

Another effective way to teach or practice the poste, as we'll see in the next chapter, is as beginning and endpoints for common movements. I will often defer to this presentation when there is less time; combining the introduction of the *poste* themselves with the simple exercises in *posta* transition we do in the following chapter.

Using this presentation, the students can quickly grasp the relationship between the guards, rather than focusing merely on their academic relationship. I have had very good results teaching the poste through these transitions, and they make very good practice drills in their own right.

As the poste are extendable to any hand weapons, positions like Fiore's **posta di donna destra** *with a single handed sword are certainly valid, and are shown in many iconographical references of medieval combat.*

A QUESTION OF ORDER?

The order that Fiore presented the poste in the treatise may also have some significance. In addition, Fiore states in his text that:

> "We are called poste and guardia by name, and we are one contrary to the other; and depending on how we stand or are positioned. We'll show how one stands against the other."

What he is saying is that the guardia are presented in matched pairs; as they appear on the page, one faces the other.

As mentioned above, Fiore's manuscripts are not precisely the same in terms of the guards. Although each has twelve, the Getty includes one that the PD and Morgan do not, and visa versa. Additionally, the guards are presented with different oppositions, that is, they are presented in a different order.

It may be read that the guards are presented already in opposition, that is, that the counter to each guard is presented opposite it. I believe this to be true, and we will discuss this aspect further in the next chapter.

In order, Fiore presents the poste in this way (in the Getty mss.):

tutta porta di ferro	posta di donna
posta finestra (destra)	posta di donna sinestra
posta longa	mezana porta di ferro
posta breve	denti de zenghiale
posta coda longa	posta di bicorno
posta frontale	dente di zenghiale mezana

In the PD, the order is slightly different:

tutta porta di ferro	posta di donna soprana
posta finestra (destra)	mezana porta di ferro
posta longa	posta frontale
posta di donna	denti de zenghiale
posta breve	posta di donna sinestra
posta coda longa	posta di bicorno

It may well be that Fiore intended for the progression to have some mnemonic meaning, but it is curious then that the two progressions are so very different. I suspect that it was a memory exercise of some kind, and that perhaps it changed over the years. We'll discuss the order and countering of each at great depth in the following chapter.

LEFT-HANDERS

One thing that very few medieval swordmasters address is the question of left-handedness. Some believe that combatants were simply taught right-handed, but there is little evidence one way or the other.

As a modern teacher, however, we are faced with left-handed students who are used to working with their left hand instead of training with their right. Whether this is historical or not, it remains an important issue.

This means that the student must grasp the sword in their left hand, rather than their right. The *posta* will all work in this way, but of course the lines will be very different if they are facing a right-handed opponent. We will discuss left-handers more in the next chapter, but for now simply they should simply work through the *poste*. The **posta di donna sinestra** will actually be their strong side; **posta di donna soprana** must for them be done on the left, to maintain consistency.

EUREKA!

In 2000, Robert Holland and I were working through the Fiore material, assembling the content for our very first Fiore-based medieval class. It was a brisk Bay Area night, clear and clear, and we were working outside at Mission College. We had only a very rudimentary partial translation available to us, but Fiore's material beckoned with the siren-like seductiveness; there was obviously much locked in the pages, and there was a tangible air of expectation that clung to the evening. At that time, the idea of the *poste* as framing movements in a fight was known to a very few, but unadvertised. It had not been mentioned at the first seminar that we'd attended on Fiore, but there was something about the *poste*....

We were looking at the individual *posta*, one by one, working through what was possible from each. Then, while looking at the facsimile of the PD reprinted from the 1902 Novati, it magically gelled. In particular, I was looking at **posta di donna** and mezana porta di ferro. I began in **posta di donna**, then stepped forward to adopt **mezana porta di ferro**, because Robert said something about a point on that *guardia* (sadly, I don't remember what it was). As I made the transition, the insight arrived with shocking clarity: *A* colpo—*blow or strike—was merely a posta transition from one to the other*—and more, it passed through **posta longa**!

It was the first of many "Eureka!" moments, and this is a special reward for those working to rekindle interest in the Western martial arts. There is much more to be discovered, and it is very likely that we have only just scratched the surface.

SSG Scolaro Andrew Borman "strikes short" from posta di donna destra to posta breve, showing how transitions between the poste form the movement framework for the system.

CHAPTER EIGHT

POSTE TRANSITIONS & BREAKING THE POSTE

This chapter will explore transitions between the *poste* in terms of transitions used to reposition a combatant for better advantage and to deliver cuts and thrusts. We will then compare the *poste*, one against the other, to see how such a comparison suggests open avenues for attack, primarily using our **Breaking the Poste** drill. By the end of the chapter students should feel even more comfortable with the *poste*, have a better idea of moving between them, and begin to refine their sense of how they compare in their offensive and defensive properties.

Recall that the techniques recorded in medieval treatises appear to take place between certain *poste*, *wards*, *guardia* or *leger*. These *poste* may be thought of as anchor positions through which a fight will progress. By studying the *poste*, the combatant builds a simplified analytical model which makes it easier to quickly figure combat calculus because variables are grouped by properties and studied together. Combined, the *poste* provide a shorthand for the millions of possible positions that allow combatants and instructors to communicate in common and to share their ideas.

The *poste* are thus the starting point for understanding movement within the system. Transitions within the sytem form the boundaries through which the sword will move, while transitions made using the body's full power are the mechanism through which blows and thrusts are made. When combined with footwork, the combatant will have the full spectrum of movements that frame the system.

TRANSITIONS

There are two forms of *posta* transition. The first is a simple move from one *poste* to another, a repositioning. The second is a transition accompanied by a turn of the body, one that harnesses the body's power. This chapter will largely deal with the first kind, while the next will deal with generating power in the *colpi* and *punte*.

Repositioning Transitions

In a *posta repositioning*, the idea is to change the combatant's position in order to gain a *positional advantage*, to set up a particular approach, or to alleviate a positional weakness.

Rarely during a fight will combatants simply rest in a *posta*, as this gives their opponent ample time to consider how and where they are carrying their weapon and what their intentions might be. Instead, most medieval systems seem to advocate smooth but relatively rapid changes between posititions that complicate the opponent's combat calculus.

Good fighting is graceful yet powerful. Fiore's lion, tiger, lynx and elephant all exemplified these qualities. Indeed, the easy grace that predators have in common is a function of efficiency (think of a shark, for example). For the combatant, working through complex physical motions to make them smooth means gaining crucially valuable fragments of time, fragments that build to create substantial improvements in performance.

It pays to work through thousands of *posta* transitions. Begin first in one *poste*, and work transitions to every other one. Then work in the "most common" transitions discussed below, executing literally thousands of repetitions. Add aerobic *poste* transitions to your workout to achieve improvements in aerobic and anaerobic performance, efficiency and strength.

Within the Schola, we begin students on simple repositioning transitions. First, we begin along the low line, working from **tutta porta di ferro** as the base-point. We then work between the common cutting angles.

REPOSITIONING POSTE TRANSITIONS ALONG THE LOW LINE

For each of the transitions, it is useful for the combatant to read through the paragraphs with a sword in hand, stepping through the transitions slowly, developing a feel for what changes as the repositioning is made. Practice slowly, rather than at speed, striving for perfect position. When the position and transition is as efficient as it can be, speed is a natural by-product.

Tutta porta di ferro → Coda longa disteza

When executing a *posta* transition along the low line, the key is to maintain potential energy coiled within the body. From **tutta porta di ferro**, the combatant can move further back, towards **posta coda longa disteza**. It is easy to see how extra power can be generated, but as the sword is also moving further away from the centerline, it will take longer to make a cover, and thus more distance is usually required. This transition has the benefit of concealing the sword somewhat from the opponent, but it also reduces the available attacking avenues. Smooth movement back towards **tutta porta di ferro** is simply a matter of bringing the hands forward again until the blade is angled approximately 90° from the body's direction of attack.

moving back to **tutta porta di ferro**, the combatant should avoid the tendency to bring the point of the blade back too far, which will make it very difficult to find cover should the opponent attack.

Another simple positional shift from tutta porta di ferro is made by simply drawing the hands to the center of the body and swinging the blade efficiently forward to find porta di ferro mezana.

In this transition from tutta porta di ferro to posta coda longa disteza, nothing moves except the hips, arms and hands.

Tutta porta di ferro → Mezana porta di ferro

From **tutta porta di ferro**, it is a very easy thing to find **mezana porta di ferro** by simply moving the blade forward and re-establishing the hilt in the center of the body. No step is required, but as the *guardia* is in the center, either foot could be forward, so a step is certainly possible. One important element is to maintain as much stored energy in the hips as possible when making the transition—often students will unknowingly **expend** their weapon's charged energy during the transition, creating a dangerous opportunity for the opponent. In a fight, this transition is often made when the combatant judges that they lack sufficient information about the opponent's intention and wish to get closer to the centerline without yielding most of the combatant's offensive freedom. It also offers a fine platform from which to attempt the *redoppiando*—a *rebattemento* behind—but that will be covered in chapter 11. In

Mezana porta di ferro → Dente di zenghiaro

From **mezana porta di ferro** it is very easy to move right towards **tutta porta di ferro** or left towards **dente di zenghiaro**. When moving towards the boar's tooth, I have found it useful to reset the stance in a more linear fashion in order to "make room" for the hands. Thus, the back foot may end up in more of a line as the hands draw back, or, alternatively, the combatant may simply offer a more linear stance from **mezana porta di ferro**, which then requires only bringing the pommel back to anchor on the left hip as the point draws back. This is exceptionally useful in a fight where the opponent signals their intention to close, since it withdraws the blade from his ability to control it. As a result, the intention to come aggressively forward will likely be abandoned. In this way the **dente di zenghiaro** is used to break grips just as the unarmed version does—but in this case the grip is broken before it is begun, rather than after.

More fundamentally, a transition from **mezana porta di ferro** to **dente di zenghiaro** moves the combatant to the left from the center, while a transition from **mezana porta di ferro** to **tutta porta di ferro** puts him on the right side of the centerline. A very important and useful distinction.

If the right foot is forward, the transition from porta di ferro mezana and denti di zenhgiaro is very simple--the blade is simply snugged back so that the pommel rests against the left hip.

Tutta porta di ferro → *Dente di zenghiaro*

Sometimes it will be useful to reposition from the left side to the right side, and visa versa, without spending time in **mezana porta di ferro**. In this case, a step will usually accompany the transition.

Beginning in **tutta porta di ferro**, the combatant steps *passare* and simultaneously moves the sword smoothly to the other side. With another step forward or back, the sides are reversed. The objective is to move as smoothly as possible, without any extraneous movement and without errors in balance.

To make the big transition from tutta porta di ferro all the way to denti di zenghiaro, step with a passo while bringing the hands into position.

REPOSITIONING POSTA TRANSITIONS ALONG THE CENTERLINE

Since control of the centerline is of paramount importance, *posta* transitions along the centerline are fundamental. In this case, we begin in **mezana porta di ferro**, in the center on the low-line, and transition to the other centerline *poste*.

Mezana porta di ferro → *Posta breve*

Beginning in **mezana porta di ferro**, with either foot forward, the combatant need only raise the sword's tip and orient it towards the opponent's face to find **posta breve**, the *short* position. **Posta breve** is also the place where most covers are made, either by design or because it represents the point where the blades will naturally intersect. Throughough the entire transition, which should be very smooth, the *punta* should remain a threat before, during and after. The transition may be accompanied with with an *acresare* or *passare* step, or it can be done without one.

A useful way to practice a variant of this *posta* is to begin from **mezana porta di ferro**, imagining the opponent before you in **posta breve** (or better, with an actual *compagno* standing in place), his point menacing your face. Stepping with a *passo a la traversa* to the right or left while you make the transition, you will end up in **posta breve** with the point menacing his face and having changed the center of the fight to your advantage. This should be practiced to both sides using the rules discussed in the footwork chapter.

Mezana porta di ferro → *Posta longa*

This transition can be thrown either to reposition or as part of an offensive transition. As a repositioning, it is a useful way to "taste" the opponent's *guardia*, to sense their intention.

To make the transition, with or without a step, the sword's *punta* or tip is simply brought upwards as the hands extend slightly outward. **The hilt should remain below the tip.** Remember that **posta longa** is *instabile*, so this is a dangerous position to rest for long. Ideally, the left foot will be forward, so that if the combatant wishes to continue the attack with an aggressive *punta*, he can enjoy agreement of hand and foot (see chapter 9) in his attack. If the opponent fails to react, an immediate thrust can be made. If they attempt to make contact with the sword, it can either be withdrawn slightly or it can change sides using a *mezza* or *tutta volta*, which will be covered at greater length in Book II (although the concept is introduced in chapter 5).

The offensive transition between **mezana porta di ferro** and **posta longa** will be discussed below.

Centerline transitions are elegant because either foot can be forward in any of the poste, allowing the combatant great freedom of position.

Here, the transition from mezana porta di ferro is powered with a passo transitioning to posta longa—the core movement in a powered thrust.

SPREZZATURRA

Writing not too long after Fiore, Baldasarre Castiglione discussed this quality in the 1494 *Book of the Courtier*. He termed it *sprezzaturra*, or "the making of making the complex look simple." Fighting is an immensely complex ballet of movements, all choreographed in response to and in order to direct the opponent. By training and practice, we can make actions we initially execute with clumsy, gross actions into sleek, efficient movements. In the process it is attain martial grace.

LOW-LINE POSTE DRILL

We use this drill to help develop efficiency and comfort with the poste transitions. It runs through the poste in a logical manner along the low-line.

 *Begin in* **tutta porta di ferro**

 *Draw the hands back into* **dente di zenghiaro**

 Move the sword back to **posta coda longa disteza**

 *Advance with an oblique passare step and transition to* **mezana porta di ferro**

 *Return to* **tutta porta di ferro**

 *Transition to* **tutta porta di ferro**

 *Transition to* **mezana porta di ferro** *(no step)*

 *Step forward, remaining in* **mezana porta di ferro**

DEFENSIVE OR COVERING TRANSITIONS

Transitions to and from Posta Breve and Posta Frontale

It is very important to be able to transition from any *posta* quickly into both **posta breve** and **posta frontale**. This will be necessary in order to find or make cover—the essential defensive maneuver that re-establishes control through contact. Practice transitions from every *poste* to both **posta breve** and **posta frontale**, working out the footwork needed to move with smoothness and grace in each instance. This is an often overlooked set of transitions, but it is the foundation needed to establish a quick response to a threat. Be sure to emphasize forward movement with the footwork, but also practice returning steps.

Tutta porta di ferro → *Posta breve e frontale*

This is a common and useful method of making cover and gaining contact (control) of the opponent's sword as it strikes. The transition should be smooth and without chop, executed with a traversing step. The hands move very little; the body should really rotate around the center of gravity, the hands moving only slightly forward while the tip carries the sword blade across the body, ending at a point where it threatens the opponent. It is crucial that the hands remain low, as near to the hips as possible, or even lower.

If the opponent had struck for the combatant's left side (the most usual attack), the combatant's hands should be moved a little left of center towards the left hip, which draws his blade a little futher across the body. In the ideal, the sword would then be captured at the *mezza spada* while the *punta* would simultaneously threaten his face. The centerline is thus opened, and the quickest offensive weapon available with the point. All in all, a satisfying development.

To transition to **posta frontale** from **tutta porta di ferro**, the *passo a la traversa* is still important, as it moves the body under the sword. The hands now move up towards the correct **frontale** position as the body moves, both ending their motion at the same time. Had the opponent thrown a *fendente*, it could be caught between the *mezza spada* and the *forteza*, and slid down the blade towards the *forteza* as the step lands. This is very aggressive and extremely effective.

It is important to be able to transition smoothly and efficiently between all poste and posta breve, the short guard, because this is how cover is made and how the opponent's sword is contacted in the incrosa. Practice going from every posta to posta breve, figuring out smooth footwork to accompany each transition.

Mezana porta di ferro → *Posta breve*

Starting from the centerline, it is relatively easy to adopt **posta breve** as discussed above. This should also be practiced imagining an incoming strike from the right or left.

If the attack comes from the **left**, the combatant steps *passo a la traversa* to the **left** and brings the sword up to make cover in **posta breve** with the hands near the left hip.

If the attack comes from the **right**, the combatant steps *passo a la traversa* to the **right** and brings the sword up to make cover in **posta breve** with the hands near the right hip.

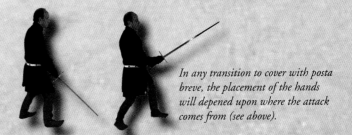

In any transition to cover with posta breve, the placement of the hands will depened upon where the attack comes from (see above).

Posta di donna destra e sinestra → *Posta breve*

Because the **poste di donna** are adopted at a wide distance, in an encounter a *passare* step will often accompany any need to make cover. Therefore, this transition is best practiced with a forward *passo a la traversa*, keeping in mind the intent to capture and dominate the centerline in response to an opponent's attack. Thus, it must be done crisply and using **posta di donna's** massive reserve of power. It should be a definitive action and should leave little if any room for the opponent to own the center. It can be done and should be practiced from any of the **poste di donna** variant positions.

From **posta di donna destra**, with the left foot forward, the combatant steps *passo a la traversa* to the right while simultaneously bringing the sword down and across the body. The pommel and left hand will anchor on or near the left hip while the point should remain in the centerline, ending at the opponent's face. From here, it will be an easy matter to make a thrust or respond to pressure against the sword.

The powerful transition between posta di donna and posta breve, a very common entry into a fight.

REPOSITIONING FOR A THRUST

Once a threat has been dealt with by making cover, the combatant will need to immediately reassert his desire to control the fight with an appropriate follow-on. To develop the movements in advance of the tactical considerations (the movements are the *what* and *how* of the action, the tactics are the *when* and to some degree the *why*), transitions from **posta breve** to key attacking *posta* are important.

Posta breve → Posta di finestra

This transition charges the sword either for a high-line thrust or for a strike. Typically, we teach that it is used after the opponent's weapon is already in contact, so it is controlled (see chapter 11, "Finding the Point").

From **posta breve**, the point is held at the opponent's face and the hilt is rolled (or wound) upwards towards **posta di finestra**.[1] Remembering that there is a **posta di finestra** on each side, it is important to **roll the sword to the same side as the opponent's weapon**, striving to maintain contact. For the transition drill, simply imagine which side of your weapon his blade is on, and roll to that side.

The transition should never take the point away from the opponent's face, and at any point during the transition the combatant should be able to abort the transition and step forward, striking. Indeed, when executing this transition as part of our **Finding the Point** play, an advancing *passare* step is made simultaneously so that the whole movement is compressed into a very small time. Once in the **finestra** position, a thrust should be made immediately or, if the opponent presses strongly, a *volta* of the sword made to strike in response.

The transition from posta breve to posta di bicrono is easy to find: the hilt is merely raised slightly and the left hand changes position, which in turn changes the pivot point, allowing the combatant to place a thrust against a closed line.

Some students have difficulty with the transition from posta breve to posta di finestra. Sometimes it helps to begin in posta di finestra and roll back to posta breve, to get a feel for the movement.

Posta breve → Posta di bicorno

From **posta breve**, it is easy to find the **posta di bircorno**—simply maintain the point on-target and raise the hilt towards the chest, taking care to keep the hilt below the point. As the transition is made, the left hand will release it's grip on the hilt, and either adopt the "palm-forward" or "reverse" grips that characterize this interesting *posta* (see details in the last chapter).

Posta di bicorno is used—as we discussed in chapter 7 and as will be explored further in chapter 11—to make a thrust from a compressed space or when the opponent has closed the line. From **posta di bicorno**, the combatant should practice quickly and explosively transitioning immediately to **posta longa**, preferably in conjunction with a *passare*.

FINDING AN ENTRY
Precontact Transitions

When opponents first meet, each adopts a guard; a Fiore student would adopt one of the **First Masters of Battle** or a variant. During the first phase of a fight, the opponents "taste" one another's defense, using *posta* transitions in order to strive for a positional advantage sufficient to give them a safe avenue of attack, or at least one with a low level of risk. Both combatants sense this and change from *posta* to *posta*, hoping for advantage. When one or the other sees or thinks he sees an opening, he closes with an attack which either succeeds or fails. At this point the opponent may have made cover—adopting a **Second Master of Battle**—and the first to apply the tactics for the *incrosa* should win. It is this "shadow fighting" that takes place before the entry into the contact phase of a fight where a *poste* can be broken to advantage.

OFFENSIVE POSTE TRANSITIONS—THE PUNTE

The third form of *poste* transitions are the offensive ones, transitions that, when accompanied with a turn of the body (the *volte*) harness the body's large muscle groups, forming the foundations for attacking movements. These movements include *punte* (thrusts) and *colpi* (strikes), with the sword, the hand or any other hand-weapon. The biomechanics of attacking movement will be discussed in the next chapter, but for now the combatant should strive to focus on making the essentials of each key transition smooth and efficient.

Posta breve → *Posta longa*

The most offensive transition is from **posta breve** directly to **posta longa**. This transition, accompanied with a *mezza volta* of the body, is the essential core of the *punta* or thrust. It is the fastest method of striking an opponent whose sword has crossed with your own, because the combatant has sufficient energy to do damage with the point even though a strike with the sword would be underpowered unless it was retrieved and recoiled prior to the strike.

To make the transition, the ideal is to use a *passo a la traversa* while simultaneously extending the sword to **posta longa** with a *mezza volta* of the body. The thrust is now well-coiled and sufficiently powered to do real damage. This is an *offensive* transition, rather than a *repositioning*, and it represents the quickest way to land a definitive blow against the opponent in a single step.

It is possible to execute this with an *acresare* instead of a *passare*, but this will result in a much lower-powered attempt that lacks the penetrative capability. It is faster because the *acresare* requires less gross movement than does the *passare*. The lack of penetrative capability might not be an issue if the target is an exposed face or neck, but in many case the strike is likely to be discomfiting rather than definitive, and our ideal within the Schola is for strikes to have the capacity for finishing the fight whenever possible. Hence, our preference in most cases is for the use of the *passare* step.

Transitioning from mezana porta di ferro forms the basis both for an efficient thrust and for a redoppiando, or rebbettamento behind.

To extend the exercise, a *compagno* stands opposite the *scolaro* in **posta breve**, the point menacing the *scolaro's* face at middle distance. In response, the *scolaro* steps to the side his sword is on, raising and thrusting at the same time. Practice from the left and right.

A transition from posta breve to posta longa is the movement frame for a thrust.

Mezana porta di ferro → *Posta longa*

Another way to make an offensive thrust is to explosively transition from **mezana porta di ferro** to **posta longa** while simultaneously stepping an *passo a la traversa*.

To do the transition, the sword point is raised and extended towards the opponent as the step is being made behind the opponent's blade. This should be practiced from the right and left, using the *passo a la traversa*.

THE IMPORTANCE OF POSTA TRANSITIONS

Most students make the novice mistake of glossing over the foundational material in favor of the sexier intermediate and advanced work, which is a gross mistake. These techniques are fundamental, but they are not basic; a lifetime of refinement and practice could be spent on them alone. In my experience, the strongest combatants all have their core biokinesthetics—what some call mechanics—as tuned as possible, and they spend a surprising amount of time tweaking very small variables in order to squeeze every bit of efficiency out of each movement. Focus your time on this material and learn it well before moving on and your skill will increase much faster.

OFFENSIVE POSTE TRANSITIONS—STRIKING THE "V," "X," "W" AND "N"

For the strikes—the *colpi*—more of the *poste* are brought to bear. There are many possibilities, but for tactical reasons the bulk of the strikes are made along acute angles along the body's centerline. As we will see in the next chapter, pairs of such attacks characterize the system, and to practice them, we will step through the underlying *posta* transitions, organizing them into common combinations that, when seen from the front, take on the movement pathways of the letters capital V, capital X and small n.

One particularly useful element about using the letters as a memory device for the offensive transitions is that they are comprised primarily of straight lines—and the object is the make the movement of hands and blade as much like a line as possible, striving for the efficiency of a line instead of the lost energy of a curve. A line is more efficient than a curve because it is the most direct route between two points.

Striking the "V"

The most fundamental strikes are descending attacks from the right and left that will progress from the variants of **posta di donna**, through **posta longa**, ending at variants of **porta di ferro mezana**. When accompanied with the appropriate footwork and *mezzi volte* turns of the body directed by the arms, they are the most powerful, and the most common form of attack.

Posta di donna destra → *Poste longa* → *Porta di ferro mezana* (and back)

Recall that **posta di donna destra** is a *posta pulsativa*, meaning that it is a *guardia* used for or that threatens striking. The most common and powerful strike, a *fendente* that begins on the right side and progresses across the body as combatant turns with a *mezza volta* and steps with a *passare*, arms directing the strike and hands manging the sword itself.

To make the transition, simply begin in **posta di donna destra**, stepping forward and, keeping the hilt relatively close to your body, letting the strike move to **posta longa**. For the interim, halt the strike at this point, keeping the *punta* directed at the opponent's face, making sure that the hilt is lower than the point. This is an intermediate step, but it is important to be able to be able to halt at this point, since during a fight there may be an opportunity to give a *punta*. Practice the transition from **posta di donna destra** to **posta longa** until it becomes smooth and automatic. An intermediate form of the drill has two parts; the first ending at **posta longa**, the second extending with a second *passare* step and a powerful thrust.

To complete the transition, begin as before in **posta di donna destra**, stepping forward, but this time moving *through* **posta longa**, letting gravity take the sword and moving it downward to a left-sided variant of **porta di ferro mezana**.[2] When the transition ends, the body should be comfortably resting in **porta di ferro mezana**. Ideally, the body carried itself through a *mezza volta* as the step was made so that it has recoiled and the left hip is now charged and ready. This movement from **posta di donna destra** through **posta longa**[3] and towards **porta di ferro mezana** is one arm of the "V," the essence of Fiore's *fendente*, a descending blow "too the teeth" that we'll discuss in more detail later. The sword can efficiently be returned along back along the same line, in what Fiore calls a *sotano*. Practice single aspects

of the arm, working with different steps and working back and forth, striving for smoothness between the *posta* and occasionally halting in **posta longa**.

To explore the other arm of the "V," begin in **posta di donna sinestra** (on the left). The right foot should be forward, the grip unchanged with the right hand nearest the cross. A step is once again made, the hands driving downward, relatively near to the body, again to **posta longa**. Be able to stop here, threatening with the point, as with the same on the right side. After practicing this, next allow the sword to progress all the way to the ground in what will be a right-sided variant of **porta di ferro mezana**. Of course, it can return by the same path, forming the other arm of the "V."

These transitions work equally well even moving through crossed strikes that form the *manroversi*. Beginning in **posta di donna destra**, for example, the combatant can move the sword downwards from the left side, the hilt staying in front of the head (not over it), the blade striking obliquely along the other arm of the "V", and ending more towards the middle of the "V" in **porta di ferro mezana**. This can be done from both **posta di donna destra** and **sinestra**.

One of the fantastic things about the centerline *poste* is that the combatant is not yet committed to the left or right. This freedom is made at the expense of power, but in a given tactical situation, it is possible to return to either side. We like to integrate this into a combatant's repertoire by running a "v/V" drills below:

"V" DRILL

Begin in **posta di donna destra**
Step *passare* and transition to **posta longa**
Step *passare* and transition back to **posta di donna sinestra**
Step *passare* and transition to **posta longa**
Step *passare* and return to **posta di donna destra**

Repeat 3 times

From **posta di donna destra**
Step *passare* and transition using a *manroverso* to **posta longa**
Step *passare* and transition back to **posta di donna sinestra**
Step *passare* and transition using *manroverso* to **posta longa**
Step *passare* and return to **posta di donna destra**

Repeat 3 times

Begin in **posta di donna destra**
Step *passare* and transition to **porta di ferro mezana**
Step *passare* and transition back to **posta di donna sinestra**
Step *passare* and transition to **porta di ferro mezana**
Step *passare* and return to **posta di donna destra**

Repeat 3 times

From **posta di donna destra**
Step *passare* and transition using a *manroverso* to
     porta di ferro mezana
Step *passare* and transition back to **posta di donna sinestra**
Step *passare* and transition using *manroverso* to
     porta di ferro mezana
Step *passare* and return to **posta di donna destra**

Repeat 3 times

Both of the above drills can be done with different steps, but the combatants should practice working between these posta many times, running each drill over and over until the movemens are second nature. The speed can be increased as the transitions become smoother.

Striking the "X"

In the "V" drills, we looked at usage of attacks made from the **poste di donna** and **porta di ferro mezana** that extended through **posta longa**. In the "X" drills, we'll look at essentially the same transitions, but this time progressing not through **posta longa**, but through **posta breve**. This will be what would be used for more close-in work, or when you want to abort and attack and make cover, for which **posta breve** is ideally suited.

For offensive transitions to or through **posta breve**, the powerful turning of the body—the *mezza volta*—and the holding of the hands very close to the body are critical. The hands should anchor on the back hip; the tip should menace the opponent's face.

For the most part, these transitions do not end in **porta di ferro mezana**, but rather if they finish commiting further to the side, ending in **dente di zenghiaro** or **tutta porta di ferro**, depending upon the vector of the transition. Achieving these close-in *poste* along the lower line is tougher; the transition from **posta di donna sinestra** to **tutta porta di ferro** is particularly challenging for new students.

As with the "V" transitions, these can be used with straight or crossing striking motions, demonstrating the a strike can begin on either side and progress along either arm of the

"X," although there is a preference for working on the strong (non-crossed) side.[4] We have already worked the strikes to **posta breve**, several sections above, so the drill that follows completes the "X".

Posta di donna destra → Posta breve → Dente di zenghiaro (and back)

Beginning again in **posta di donna destra**, the combatant will step *passare*, striking into **posta breve** as before. The point should be menacing the opponent, the pommel anchored between the left hip and the body's centerline, and hilt low, at or below hip level.

To continue the transition, this time the combatant once again begins in **posta di donna destra**, but as he steps, he continues through **posta breve**, the pommel now firmly anchoring on the left hip, the point snugged in as far as possible to deny the control of it to the opponent. In this case it is helpful to adopt a more linear stance in order to "clear" the back hip for the left hand. The transition from **posta di donna destra** through **posta breve** and to **dente di zenghiaro** should be compact and efficient, leaving the opponent well attached of his *ellefante* and threatening with is point.

Of course, it is relatively easy to return. In this case, the back edge (the *falso*) of the blade will be drawn upward through something like **posta breve** and ending back in **posta di donna destra**. This transition between **posta di donna destra** and **dente di zenghiaro** is one arm of the "X," and we'll explore the other arm in the next section.

An alternate is to begin instead from **posta di finestra**, transitioning downwards using as powerful a *mezza volta* as possible. In order to make his work, the sword must turn (a *volta*). Within the Schola this is usually done as a strike in response to pressure against a **posta di finestra**, as we'll explore more briefly in chapter 11 and in more detail in Book II.

Tutta porta di ferro → Posta breve → Posta di donna sinestra (and back)

The most difficult of the offensive transitions is the one between **tutta porta di ferro** and **posta di donna sinestra**. Fiore states specifically that strikes thrown *dritta*—from the right—are to use the true or front edge. In order to make this transition smooth, it is necessary for the grip to begin relatively loose in **tutta porta di ferro**, the true edge forward.[5]

To make the transition, begin in **tutta porta di ferro**. Make a *passare* step, transitioning the blade towards **posta breve**, the left hand or pommel near the left hip, the point menacing the opponent's face, the left hip charged and ready to power a *punta* or thrust. Realistically this transition is made in order to make cover into **posta breve**, although it can be an attempt to gain the center in order to finishe with a *punta*. Practice this transition and it's return.

Next, begin again from **tutta porta di ferro**. Make the same *passare* step—*a la traversa* will be helpful—this time following through the movement all the way to **posta di donna sinestra**.

While this is not too difficult, returning is harder. This time, begin the action in **posta di donna sinestra** (until the movements are efficient and smooth). Remember that the right foot will be forward. Step *passare* forward, simultaneously striking through **posta breve**. Once the sword has reached **posta breve**, stop and look at your hands. They should *not* be crossed. Because the true edge should be forward, the thumb of the right hand should be up (radial side up), the pommel near the right hip. Practice this until it is smooth.

To complete the movement, starting from the **posta breve** position above, the sword now pivots, the *left* hand being the fulcrum. This is perhaps counter-intuitive, but it is an accurate description of how the most efficient transition from a right-sided **posta breve** to **tutta porta di ferro** works. This little turning or *volta* of the sword is crucial to making the transition work. Once it works from **posta breve**, begin again all the way up at **posta di donna sinestra**, stepping forward all the way through to **tutta porta di ferro**. This is the second arm of the "X."

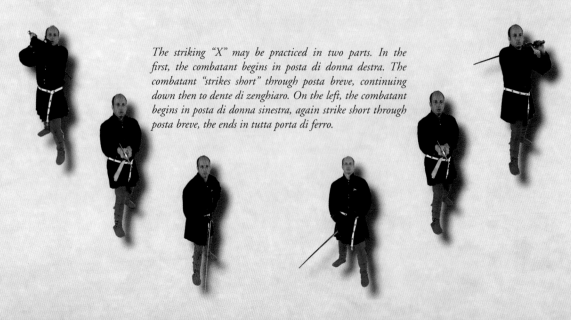

The striking "X" may be practiced in two parts. In the first, the combatant begins in posta di donna destra. The combatant "strikes short" through posta breve, continuing down then to dente di zenghiaro. On the left, the combatant begins in posta di donna sinestra, again strike short through posta breve, the ends in tutta porta di ferro.

"X" DRILL

Begin in **posta di donna destra**
Step *passare* and transition to **posta breve**
Step *passare* and transition back to **posta di donna sinestra**
Step *passare* and transition to **posta breve**
Step *passare* and return to **posta di donna destra**

Repeat

From **posta di donna destra**
Step *passare* and transition using a *manroverso* to **posta breve**
Step *passare* and transition back to **posta di donna sinestra**
Step *passare* and transition using *manroverso* to **posta breve**
Step *passare* and return to **posta di donna destra**

Repeat

Begin in **tutta porta di ferro**
Step *passare* and transition to **posta di donna sinestra**
Step *passare* and transition back to **tutta porta di ferro**
Step *passare* and transition to **posta di donna sinestra**
Step *passare* and return to **tutta porta di ferro**

Repeat

From **poste de donna destra**
Step *passare* and transition to **dente di zenghiaro**
Step *passare* and transition to **poste de donna destra**
Step *passare* and transition to **dente di zenghiaro**
Step *passare* and return to **posta di donna destra**

In working the "X" drill, combatants begin on the right, come to posta breve, then return on the left, and visa versa. By working both sides, combatants develop a sense of returning to either side, according to where they have the best advantage.

"W" DRILL

Another drill we use to teach offensive posta transitions is the "W" drill; it builds comfort with the different ending points, while also helping to do repetitions designed to build effiency.

Begin in **posta di donna destra**
Step *passare* and transition to **posta breve**
Step *passare* and transition back to **posta di donna sinestra**
Step *passare* and transition manroverso to **porta di ferro mezana**
Step *passare* and transition to **posta di donna sinestra**

Repeat

From **posta di donna sinestra**
Step *passare* and transition to **posta breve**
Step *passare* and transition to **posta di donna destra**
Step *passare* and transition using *manroverso* to **porta di ferro mezana**
Step *passare* and return to **posta di donna destra**
Striking the "n"—Setting Aside

In working the "W," combatants practice coming to cover in posta breve, seizing the center of the fight, and completing the motion all the way down to porta di ferro mezana. It is important to remember that porta di ferro mezana may be found anwyere between a 60 degree arc in front of the combatant—it need not be ridigly in the center.

The last important offensive transition takes place between **tutta porta di ferro** and **porta di ferro mezana**. This is really the core "setting aside" motion that Fiore uses to seize the center of the fight using the sword, dagger, spear, poleaxe, or in an unarmed setting. With the sword in two hands it is perhaps a bit more difficult to master, but its importance is hard to overstate, so central is it to Fiore's method of controlling the opponent's options.

Tutta porta di ferro → Posta breve → Porta di ferro mezana →

In this transition, the combatant begins in **tutta porta di ferro**. Stepping *passare a la traversa*, he simultaneously pivots the sword—again around the left hand—sweeping the blade across the center of his body, seizing the centerline of the fight with his sword, and if necessary, continuing beyond the centerline and potentially driving the opponent's weapon to the ground. This is the essential play in Fiore's **Breaking of the Thrust** and in his *azza* play, where in both cases the opponent's weapon is cast to the ground with a powerful hammering motion. It is indeed helpful to picture this as a hammering motion, encountering an opponent's blade and hammering it into the ground. The pivoting motion of the "n" is the round motion the blade makes, and the stem the discomfiting strike that will be available once the opponent's weapon is expended on the ground.

It is of **paramount** important that the hands **not** rise as the *setting aside* is being done. Doing so expends the weapons' energy along a tangential line. It **must** pivot from the left hand, which should move as little as possible.

The combatant should be able to stop the action in the middle—at or near **posta breve**—in order to take advantage of a thrusting opportunity or a need to make cover.

The all-important "setting aside" motion is a key movement of Fiore's system, found repeated in the wrestling, daga, spada in one and two hands. We practice it in the form of a small "n" because once the combatant is in porta di ferro mezana, the next movement is a rising strike or sotano (to be discussed in the next chapter). The combatant should picture making contact with the opponent's blade near posta breve, then forcing it to the ground towards portta di ferro mezana. He would thus be on top of the opponent's weapon and have successfully "cleared" the centerline enough for a strike.

BREAKING THE POSTE

We say that a *posta* is "broken" when the man holding it feels that it has become untenable. There is a nearly irresistible pull to move, a sense of danger caused by the overlaying of one *guardia* against the other. When a *posta* is broken it is time to move because a tangible vulnerability has been uncovered, and things are about to change for the worse. Finding a match in the combatant's favor from which he can strike with safety is the essence of the First Masters of Battle, the ideal case in which the defender never has a chance to make cover. Of course, this is a game of probabilities rather than of certainties, but it is better to win by striking a single blow; if the opponent makes cover—finding the **Second Master of Battle**[6]—more advanced rules are then brought to bear and the fight continues to resolution. But as it goes down into successive layers of action/response, it becomes riskier, as Fiore notes in the Prologue.

Strive to break the opponent's *poste* and then harness the *lione* to drive in for an attack with a high probability of success. If he covers, then the fight will continue at a higher level of danger and complexity.

One goal of training is for the combatant to learn when a *posta* is *about* to be broken, rather than when it has *already* been broken. This anticipation requires keen judgment and experience, learning about how the **First Masters of Battle** match up one against another. But if the relative strengths and weaknesses of each *posta* are strongly internalized, the combatant will enjoy a significant advantage in time because he will have preprocessed mental programming with likely success routes when the *guardia* are matched one against the other.

But because elements of time and distance are subjective according to the individual combatants and their particular weapons, there is no hard and fast rule to be held that one poste necessarily breaks another. What is broken at one distance might not feel broken at another, or if the center of the fight is moved with a *passare a la traversa*, this too can change the impression of being broken or making a break against the opponent.

In order to exercise this perceptive ability, we have a drill called Breaking the Poste, which is really a kind of fighting that is done without contact, exercising the precontact phase of the fight. Learning to break the opponent's poste is the first key to using the First Masters of Battle effectively, and the *primi magistri* are superior because end the fight with the least resistance thus with the greatest safety.

BREAKING THE POSTE

1. The combatants face one another, one denoted as *scolaro* and the other as *compagno* at *misura larga*. The **compagno** will adopt one of the **First Masters of Battle** (excepting *posta breve*, and *longa* which make cover), and stand ready to make his defense. The *compagno* will not move until he feels sufficiently threatened that if he does not, he feels that he will be struck. The *scolaro* will begin at *misura larga*, wide distance. He will adopt a beginning *poste* also.

2. The *scolaro* will make repositioning transitions from *posta* to *posta*, testing the feeling of his *posta* versus that of his opponent, looking for a match in his favor. The **compagno** will also carefully feel each position, alert for danger, but without moving. The transitions should be smooth and relatively slow—nothing is to be gained by hurrying.

3. When the *compagno* feels that it his *poste* is broken, he states as much and chooses another *posta* where he doesn't feel at risk. Note that having a *posta* broken is **not** losing—it is a point of learning for both students.

4. The exercise continues for a specified length of time—not to the number of breaks (it is not a contest, this drill must be practiced with *concordia*—then the combatants switch roles.

- If the *compagno* never feels that they are broken, the distance can be reduced.
- Note that some defenders have their ego in play and are too insecure to feel that their position is broken. This signals a potential lack of martial humility and should be addressed early in the training, or it can fester into great problems later.
- An advanced version of the drill allows for the *compagno's* use of **posta breve** and **posta longa**, but in response the *scolaro* may strike the blade to knock it out of the way and open the fight's centerline.
- Another advanced version keeps the *scolaro* in the same poste, but allows him to change his distance and position, finding where each *posta* breaks each of the others.

Essentially, the **Breaking the Poste** drill is practicing a fight without actually engaging beyond the precontact point, without the entry into contact. It is beneficial to repeat this drill from time to time; within the larger Schola groups I like to bring the intermediate and advanced students into the beginner classes when we're doing **Breaking the Poste** so that they can both mix with and continue to learn from the exercise.

FINDING MISURA LARGA

The combatants stand facing one another. The *scolaro* will have his right foot forward and the sword extended in a strike, his balance centered, his feet neither gathered nor over-extended. The sword is placed to the opponent's body, at about chest level, at the nexus between the *mezza spada* and the *punta*, his optimal striking point. The right foot is forward because when an attack is made, the right foot will be accompanying the strike. Now a tornare or returning pass is made back into a comfortable poste. This is the misura larga, the distance from which with a single, comfortable passing step an attack can be made.

-Notes-

[1] In this contact the system strongly resembles the German *winden*. Fiore gives little instruction for what to do from the finestra or how to take it, and this seems to be the most efficient and safest way to adopt it.

[2] Recall from the last chapter that the core position for **porta di ferro mezana** is aligned with the body's centerline facing the opponent, but that valid variants exist across the base of the "x" formed by the *segno's* illustration. In this case, because the strike is being made from right to left, the blade will end up on the left side of the "x," but will still be a valid "shadow" form of **porta di ferro mezana**.

[3] Or **posta breve**, if the distance is short. See chapter 9.

[4] In other words, there seems to be a preference for striking *mandritto* (from the right) on a right-sided *posta* such as **posta di donna destra**, and from the left on a left-sided *posta* such as **posta di donna sinestra**.

[5] We discussed this at length in the last chapter in the section on **tutta porto di ferro**, but it worth repeating here, since this orientation of the blade is both important and as of today, unique to the Schola. Most schools interpret Fiore's illustration of **tutta porta di ferro** to have he flat of the blade forward, resting naturally in the right hand. Within the Schola we interpret the illustration literally, the true edge forward, the grip loose. As strikes are made from **tutta porta di ferro**, we have found it more efficient to strike directly without having to turn the sword in the hand and keeping the wrist straight rather than having to twist the sword in mid-flight and deal with an awkwardly bent wrist.

[6] These are the two *magistri* of the *incrosare* depicted in the *zhogo largo* section, the gateway to all of the plays that follow.

CHAPTER NINE

GENERATING POWER
COLPI & PUNTE

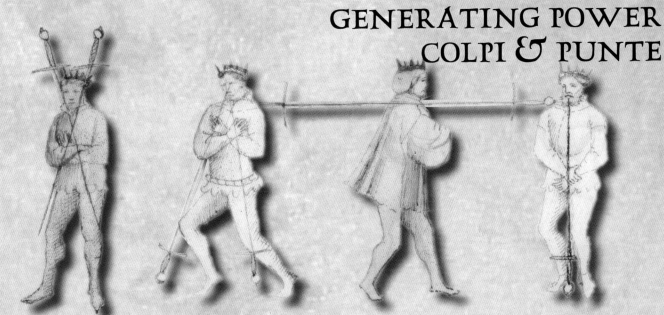

talian medieval swordsmanship features three mains ways of attacking; with a *colpo* (a strike or blow); a *punta* (essentially a thrust); or with a *presa* (a grip). In all cases, the system strives to maximimize efficiency, which in turns leads to elegance and power. The bio-kinesthetics necessary to develop power harness the body's large muscle groups, rather than being "thrown" from the arms, much as in any modern ball, stick or combat sport.

It is often said that power originates in the hips. In reality this is a shorthand way of focusing the combatant's attention on the point where the majority of the large muscle groups come together—and this happens at the hip. It is also comfortably close to the body's center of mass, what the Asian martial arts refer to as the *hara*. In order to generate power, the body rotates around its central axis much as a coiled watch spring would operate: the combatant's muscles tense on one side or the other, creating *potential* energy. They may then explosively uncoil, releasing *kinetic* energy. Then, as the hips recoil again on the other side of the body, the coil is tightened again, resulting in a ready state on the other side. This is the essence of *posta* transitions, since they move from one side to the other harnessing this "watch-spring" energy through turns or *volte*.

This energy development, storage, and expenditure is core to the system's movement framework. By turning the body, there is energy—full power—available on the left and the right. The *poste* which are *pulsativa*—including **posta di donna**, **posta di donna sinestra**, and **tutta porta di ferro**—are full-powered and are completely coiled and ready to strike, maximizing potential energy either on the left or right.

Fiore seems to have understood this and integrated it into his art, although he discusses it only in a single paragraph, the one discussed previously in the section on footwork:

"Noy semo doi guardie una sì fatta che l'altra, e una è contraria de l'altra. E zaschuna altra guardia in l'arte una simile de l'altra si è contrario salvo le guardie che stano in punta zoé posta lunga e breve e meza porta di ferro che punta per punta la più lunga fa offesa inançi. E zò che pò fare una pò far l'altra. E zaschuna guardia pò fare volta stabile e meza volta. Volta stabile si è che stando fermo po' zugar denunci e di dredo de una parte. Meza volta si è quando uno fa un passo inanzi o indredo e chossì po' zugare de l'altra parte denanzi e di dredo. Tutta volta si è quando uno va intorno uno pe' cum l'altro pe' l'uno staga ferma e l'altro lo circondi. E perzò digo che la spada si ha tre movimenti zoé volta stabile, meza volta, e tutta volta. E queste guardie sono chiamate l'una e l'altra posta di donna. Anchora sono IV cose in l'arte zoé passare, tornare, acressere e discresse(re)."

"We see two guards, one made opposite and countering the other. And likewise each of the other guards in the art has a counter save for the guards that stand in the thrust, such as **poste longa**, **breve** and **meza porta di ferro**, because in thrusting with the tip the longer offends first. And that which makes one can make the other. And each guard can make *volta stabile* and *mezza volta*. *Volta stabile* (stable turns) are those which stand firm playing the one side and the other as one. *Mezza volta* are those in which one makes a *passo* forward or back, which enables him to play on one side or the other. *Tutta volta* are those in which one makes a turn (*intorno*), one foot in a circle (*circondi*) around the other, which stays still. And therefore the sword has three movements called the *volta stabile*, *mezza volta*, and *tutta volta*. And each guard [from which we play is called **posta di donna**. Also likewise [there are] four in the art called *passare, tornare, acresare* and *dicresare*."

This paragraph has been variously interpreted by various students of Fiore's art, but we have found that our interpretation seems to fit both the letter of the description and the images as presented through the manuscript. The movements "of the sword" and "of the feet" create several different body motions that power the sword in flight. Evidence for this may also be seen in the text, as we will see below, but it may also be inferred from the **Masters of the Crossed Swords** (the *zhogo largo* section), Getty fol. 25 and 25v.

VOLTA: *A TURN*

The Italian term *volta* means "to turn," but it also has connotations of time. Fiore uses the term to describe the motions of the feet and the sword blade, but it can also be used to describe the movement of the body in its development and expenditure of power.

There are three main ways that the *volta* is made: a "stable" turn—*volta stabile*; a "half" turn—*mezza volta*; and a "complete" turn—*tutta volta*. Using these three combinations of foot and body motions, the turning potential of the body is harnessed and the body's fighting platform may be moved to a more advantageous position. I'll start with the *mezza volta* or "half turn," because it is the most essential and basic turn in the system, the one we emphasize the most in our novice and intermediate classes.

Mezza Volta: *Half Turn*

> "Meza volta si è quando uno fa un passo inanzi o indredo e chossì po' zugare de l'altra parte denanzi e di dredo."

> "[A] *mezza volta* is that which one makes a *passo* forward or back, which enables him to play on one side or the other."

A *mezza volta* is used to change sides. It is a mechanism used to change the body's coiled state from one side to the other. We glimpsed the *mezza volta* in the footwork section when we examined the *passare*. Recall that during those lessons, we separated the movements of the foot (the *passare* or *passo*) from those of the

body. In the case where the sword remained coiled and ready to strike, we termed this a *passare* (or *tornare*, when returning). In the case where we changed sides, we were in fact executing a *mezza volta*.

In the *mezza volta*, the large muscle groups power the body in a turn about the central axis discussed above. It begins as potential energy on the right or the left. In a normal movement, the combatant will turn the body around the axis, expending the potential energy and transforming it through force from the body's gross muscles (*not* the relatively fine musculature of the arms, which are used to *direct* the blow). This is the kind of movement executed in throwing a *colpo*. Indeed, the fully-powered *poste*—**tutta porta di ferro** and all of the **poste di donna** variants—have the strongest potential for strength and power. **Tutta porta di ferro** is thus ideal for setting blows aside, while the **poste di donna** are capable "of all seven *colpi*" of the sword, especially since there are right-side and left-sided variants.

It is the harnessing of the body's large muscle groups that generate the power for blows. For maximum power, the body should be held upright, as if a post were running through it, and a coiled watch spring was in the hip.

*A mezza volta is used to change sides. Here, the combatant has stepped forward, using a repositioning transition to move from **posta di donna destra** (on the right) to **poste di donna sinestra** (on the left). Although he can deliver blows still from either side, his power is based on the left and the more powerful strikes will be on the left. We say in this case that he is fighting on the left side*

In another repositioning posta transition, the combatant begins in tutta porta di ferro and steps forward into dente di zenghiaro. In the process he has changed which hip serves as the anchor for his power—it began as the right with tutta porta di ferro and changes sides to the left with dente di zenghiaro.

A colpo—a strike or blow—is merely a posta transition delivered with power. A mezza volta is used to deliver this power as the body's rotating motion drives the blade. In this case Andrew Borman has begun in the **posta di donna sinestra** and stepped forward, driving the blade downward (in a fendente mandritto) towards **mezana porta di ferro**. The body has made its turn and the left hip should now be charged and ready to power the next motion. He is then well situated to immediately return using a sotano (a rising blow), transitioning with a mezza volta back up to **posta di donna**.

Colpi—strikes or blows—are thrown using this method. To deliver a fully-powered colpo, the combatant turns his body, starting from a fully-coiled or chambered posta, unwinding or expending the energy and transferring it to the target, and finally continuing the winding action in order to recoil the hips, usually on the opposite side. Thus, the body has "changed sides," with a half turn, and the energy should once again be recharged on the opposite side. Usually, but not always, the motion is accompanied by a passare or passo a la traversa step (see illustration above).

Returning our attention to the hips, the *rearmost* hip is the anchor point for a most strikes. If the combatant has his left leg forward, as is usual in **tutta porta di ferro**, for example, then his *right* hip is the powered one. We say then that he is *powered on the right side*. If he had the right foot forward, as is usually the case in **dente di zenghiale** or **posta di donna sinestra**, then the *left* hip is rearmost, so we say that he is powered on the *left* side. In the unarmed **porta di ferro**, the rear hand maximizes its powerful potential by resting on or near this point.

For the generation of power, it is the rear hip that anchors the blow. When the sword is on the right, it is the right hip that is the anchor and which will drive forward. When the sword is on the left side, as in dente di zenghiaro, it is the left hip that is the anchor and which will drive forward.

The rearmost hand anchors near the hip to maximize power. We can see this in Fiore's two illustrations of **porta di ferro**. Note that the rearmost hand floats near to the rearmost hip.

As we will see later, it is always possible to make a *colpo* across the powered side, but with reduced power. In this case, power is traded for deception and position. This is certainly possible, but in most cases Fiore seems to have preferred maximizing his potential for power and energy, hence no emphasis on falsing, feints, or on "trick" blows.

EXPENDITURE AND RECOILING

One important characteristic of the *mezza volta* is the "point of expenditure." In every strike, or more obviously in a thrust, all of the energy in the blow has been expended and the sword lies "spent." With a sword, unlike a staff weapon, this time represents a time of vulnerability that must be minimalized. Thus, a combatant fighting in Fiore's system moves between the *poste*, using a *mezza volta* to change sides and recoils to be ready again on the other side rather than expending himself and remaining over-extended. This *mezza volta* powers his blows. He can use this to attack his opponent, his opponent's weapon, or simply to change sides during the fight. The *colpo* is thus simply a *posta* transition made with the body's power (from his *ellefante*) and directed by the arms (the *lione* and *tigro*).

Being "expended" refers to resting or passing through a state where there is insufficient potential energy available to power the sword with a meaningful strike. It lies "spent." It is important to avoid or severely curtail the amount of time during which a combatant's sword is expended, and this is best done by recoiling on one side or the other.

If the combatant's transition is blocked, he must, using this principle, seek to immediately return to a state of coiled potential energy. Usually this is done by continuing the rotation of the hips, even if the sword's path of travel is impeded (by the opponent's blade, or a new intention by the combatant himself). Sometimes he can quickly return the hips (and his weapon) to the same side, although this generally takes a bit longer than it does to continue the hips traveling in the same direction).

By practicing recoiling the hips and steadily reducing the time of expenditure, a combatant preserves his freedom of action by maximizing the time his sword is powered and ready to strike. It is an important, and often overlooked, point of kinesthetics that intermediate combatants in particular would do well to focus on as part of their development (see photo series opposite).

EXERCISE
Driving through Expenditure

Objective: Begin to instill the idea of conservatism with respect to energy preservation—available energy equals power and speed.

The zugadore, armed with a longsword, will take **posta di donna destra**. On command, they will step forward and strike *fendente* (downward) towards **posta longa**. As the sword is expended, they should strive to recoil the hips so that they can again drive forward with another step using a thrust. This exercise can be repeated using any strike, striving to ensure that the hips are ready for an immediate follow-on attack once the first action has been completed. Over time, the objective is to blend the actions together into a smooth whole.

There is more evidence for this kind of turn in the illustrations that accompany the text. In the two *magistro* of the crossed swords that introduce the *zhogo largo* (or "long play"), each combatant has a leg forward. The one on the right, depicted as a *magistro* in the PD (but not the Getty, interestingly), has his right leg forward, as if it accompanied the strike. This is a classic *mezza volta*, and the student can see clearly how the hips have recoiled or expended.

TUTTA VOLTA: COMPLETE TURN

Just as the body can make a half-turn as it changes sides, so too can it make a full-turn. This is the *tutta volta*, or "complete turn," used most often in the context of multiple opponents. Fiore offers some clear directions for making the *tutta volta*:

> "Tutta volta si è quando uno va intorno uno pe' cum l'altro pe' l'uno staga ferma e l'altro lo circondi."

> "[A] *Tutta volta* is one which makes a turn (*intorno*), one foot in a circle (*circondi*) around the other, which stays still."

In this case, Fiore seems to be discussing specifically how the feet move, but there are no clearly identifiable instances in the text other than this sentence. While we have discussed the footwork underlying the *tutta volta* in Chapter 6, in all cases the hips will accompany the turning so that the energy follows the same coiled-expended-recoiled model.

Two different responses to an opponent who has broken (rompere) a combatant's cover and driven it to the ground. In both cases, the opponent in black attacked with a fendente (a downward blow). In the first case, the combatant has allowed himself to be expended while the opponent's hips are charged. In the second case, both combatants have their hips coiled, giving each a number of options and both could be in a position to seize the initiative.

In terms of the body, a *tutta volta* results in a "complete turn" of the body. This can be done storing energy—i.e., without a strike or movement of the sword—or it can accompany the *tutta volta* of the feet, in which case the turn can be made while uncoiling and recoiling in a strike.

One way to see the principle and to illustrate the need of maintaining the coil/recoil state of potential energy is through the cutting at targets in multiple directions. While the exercise of test-cutting is discussed later in the chapter, we can see here how potential energy is absolutely necessary in order to cut multiple targets with efficiency. This multiple opponent test is something like one might find in battle. In the illustrations, notice how the combatant's body is always recoiled at the end of a strike, and how the hips accompany each strike. Ideally, the combatant will always be ready to strike or respond with power sufficient to cut the mats.

We have found that although the *tutta volta* is mentioned in the text, it is not emphasized, possibly because it is most useful in a multiple opponent engagement. Therefore, in terms of our teaching progression, we work on it at the middle levels of develoment, saving it for presentation just before the combatants begin their work on multiple opponent engagements.

VOLTA STABILE: *STABLE TURN*

"Volta stabile si è che stando fermo po' zugar denunci e di dredo de una parte."

"*Volta stabile* (stable turns) are those which stand firm playing the one side and the other as one."

Another variant of the turn is offered in the same paragraph, the "stable turn" or "volta stabile." The *volta stabile* may in fact have several interesting aspects, and it answers questions about the curious "heels first" stance shown in some of Fiore's figures. But it may have other meanings, too.

The most basic meaning in terms of body movement would be a turning of the body unaccompanied by a step. In this sense Fiore's words are preserved, "those which stand firm playing one side and the other as one." "Side" in this context may well means from left to right. This might be the case when combatants are coiling or turning about their axis but not stepping.

Another interpretation is the turning on a front-back axis, and this is interesting in the case of multiple opponents. Using the *volta stabile* footwork discussed in chapter 6, the combatant can changes directions "in front and in back," giving him a 360° field of movement.

Looking at Fiore's *poste* in both the Getty and PD versions, there are some curious positions where the combatant has a stance with his *heels* face the opponent, rather than his toes. This is particularly true in the **posta di donna soprana** (PD, shown in the Getty as **posta di donna destreza**), **posta di donna sinestra** (or **posta di vera finestra**, PD), the **dente di zenghiale mezana** (Getty).

The volta stabile is one method of explaining the curious heels-first orientation of some poste. By pivoting on the balls of the feet, the combatant can orient himself one way or the other with great speed.

In each of these cases, the combatant is well-wound, the body showing obvious potential energy and readiness. From each position, there are two different kinds of attacks possible—some use a full step to approach a target in the direction that the combatant is looking (a *mezza volta*, since the body changes sides), while others may simply pivot on the balls of both feet, maintaining connection with the ground.

We discussed this movement in chapter 6, but it can be married to the turning of the body in order to yield a new—and for some alien—kinesthetic very different from the *mezza volta* discussed above. Using this technique, one can begin in a heels-forward *posta*, such as **posta di donna soprana**, and make a *colpo*, turning on the balls of the feet rather than taking a step.

In these figures drawn from the PD, the figure begins in posta di donna soprana, his heels facing the target. In order to strike, he pivots all the way around on the balls of his feet as the sword comes around in a strike to posta longa.

But remember that all Fiore says about the turn is that the feet "stand firm, playing on one side and the other as one." If the distance and position are already ideal, a step accompanying an attack is unnecessary. In this case, a *volta stabile* would likely be a simple twisting or coiling and recoiling of the body during an attack. I believe that both interpretations answer the text and are important parts of the system, but students working at the lower levels can focus on the simple version, essentially a *mezza volta* without an accompaning step.

In order to coordinate the muscle groups and to change the position of the attacker to seize a more favorable line of attack (and to complicate the defensive calculus necessary for his opponent to process), the combatant in Fiore's system will generally accompany his attack with a step.

In this series Andy Borman (in red) sfinds his attack thwarted by an incrosa, and having the right distance, he turns his body with what Fiore might have called a volta stabile.

Importantly, the sword itself makes a mezza volta— because it changes sides

SWORD ACTIONS

As mentioned above, attacks with the sword can involve strikes or blows (the *colpi*), strikes with the point (mostly thrusts, the *punte*), and wrestling (the *prese*). In all cases, the weapon is powered by the body as it turns. Remember that in Fiore's prologue, he emphasizes his intent that there is nothing within the system that will cause risk, whether in or out of armour, on foot or on horseback.

Power is thus at the heart of Fiore's system, and it is useful to quickly review the *poste* in terms of their power potential:

Pulstativa	Stabile	Instabile
full powered	*half powered*	*mutable, fickle*
Tutta porta di ferro	Mezana porta di ferro	Posta di finestra
Posta di donna destra (soprana)	Posta breve	Posta longa
Posta di donna sinestra (vera finestra)	Dente di zenghiale	Posta di bicorno
	Coda longa desteza	
	Dente di zenghiale mezana	Posta frontale

Recall also that these *poste* represent "Platonic" ideals of end or transit points through which a combatant will move during the course of a fight. There are an infinate number of (valid) points between these *poste*, but as the position moves from one *posta* towards another, it loses aspects of the starting position and gradually takes on more characteristics of the destination *posta*. Thus, in the practical world of a fight there are an infinite number of positions, but the *poste* offer the combatant a method of analyzing and planning strategy, of breaking down the fight into comprehendable units that can be learned and committed to memory.

Poste that are *pulsativa* are those which carry the most power in both the *colpo* and the *punta*. The body is wound as far as possible, emphasizing maximum power, but often at the expense of time. A combatant can wait in this positions, but must use care when the blade is far from the centerline of the fight, as with the **poste di donna**. These are the most effective points from which to throw a *colpo* against an armoured opponent, as they have sufficient power to do damage, even through harness.

Poste that are *stabile* are more stable, are often suitable for waiting, trading time for power. While the *colpi* can be thrown from these *poste*, they are more suitable to deflecting or making cover, or perhaps for striking small-boned areas such as the hand or forearm. Making cover is particularly easy, since the blade is often (except in the case of **coda longa disteza**) close to the fight's centerline. These positions are also fairly good at making thrusts, as Fiore mentions in his descriptions of **dente di zenghiaro**, **mezana porta di ferro**, and **posta breve**. They essentially trade power for time.

Posta that are *instabile* can be thought of as **mutable** or **fickle**. In this sense they *are* unstable, both for the combatant and for his opponent. They possess little power, and the point is generally forward (except in the case of **posta fontale**), making them well-suited to a quick thrust. They may be *malicoso*, full of deception, both for the attacker and defender. They are most often (but not always) used in transition and to "find the point," which we'll study in more detail in chapter 11.

It is useful to develop an innate sense for how much power is available from each *posta*. In the course of a fight the combatant will need to constantly balance available power and time, striving to maximize the available power without spending more time than he has in a given circumstance. As we look at the specific types of attacks below, keep the potentials from each *posta* in mind.

COLPI : *STRIKES OR BLOWS*

The most fundamental, and strongly emphasized, attack in the medieval art. A *colpo* is harder to deflect than is a thrust, and it is versatile and easy to change or redirect along different attacking lanes. After Fiore—even with Filippo Vadi, who followed just fifty or so years later—the point is much more strongly emphasized.

Colpo are thrown with the entire body, as we've discussed, and directed to the target with the hands and arms. As in the German system, a step usually (but does not always) accompanies.

Using the sword for blows

The farthest point of resonance for a sword represents an optimal point of striking. For any blow, the combatant should avoid striking to the *forteza* or the *mezza spada*, since force is lost when the strike is made in these regions. Strikes with the *punta* or tip are a different case, and are dealt with separately below. The farthest point of resonance is usually found at the juncture of the *punta* (tip) and *mezza spada*.

Because of this, the combatant will want to manage his fighting distance to keep an optimized strike possible. In unarmoured combat, this will often mean advancing boldly with the first step, since the fight begins at a wider distance than does a similar armoured encounter. As the distance closes, however, it is sometimes harder to maintain the optimal distance. During a *colpo*, the combatant can adjust to keep the distance using his feet or his hands, or both in combination.

To use his feet, the distance is managed using the steps discussed in chapter 6; the *acresare* and *passare* to move forward, the *discresare* and *tornare* to move back.

To use his hands, the position of the hilt is manipulated. This is a more subtle and sophisticated response; instead of striking directly towards the target with the hands, the hands instead move across the target towards the opposite hip, towards or through **posta breve** (towards on a downwards blow, a *fendente*; through on a *sotano*, or rising blow). By anchoring on the opposite hip, the sword simultaneously provides physical cover, allows the use of the farthest point of resonance, and may be

> *The optimal striking point on the sword is the nexus between the mezza spada and punta.*

able to get the point "on-line" as an immediate threat. This is also a very good method to break an opponent's incoming attack, or to break his response to your strike. As the sword reaches the opposite hip, the hips will continue to coil, as we'll see below in the third *colpo* from **posta di donna**.

Colpo (mandritto) from posta di donna

The most fundamental *colpo* is thrown from **posta di donna**. In this first strike, the combatant's hips should have significant potential energy as reflected in the position of the hips. The right hip is back, so the combatant is said to be *powered on the right*. Thus, blows from the right will be easier (this will be a *mandritto*, a blow thrown from the right). To strike, the combatant steps forward using a *passare* step, usually just a bit off the line with respect to himself and his opponent. The step helps to turn the hips, much as the raised heel in a golf swing helps to transfer

the golfer's weight from back to front. Simultaneously, the hands guide the sword to a position near to **posta longa**. The timing of the step is crucial; the foot should land at the same time that the sword would encounter resistance to maximize stability and the body's turning action. George Silver, writing in the 16th century, termed this "agreement of hand and foot." This action should be practiced many, many times, as it is both fundamental and benefits from continual refinement.

Having struck to **posta longa**, the combatant is now in an *instabile posta*, and in this case he is also **expended**; a doubly dangerous combination. His quickest response might be to "find the point," as we'll see in the next chapter, or he can retrieve his sword, either retracting it or collecting under it as he steps forward.

Another alternative, if the blow is finished without encountering any resistance (because the opponent moved, or the tactical situation changed), the blade will naturally progress downwards towards **mezana porta di ferro**. The combatant has the choice of allowing the blade to progress down to this more stable resting point, or stopping it with the point "on line" in **posta longa**. We call this striking to the middle a *mezana*. Thus we can clearly see the *posta* transition powered by the hips leading from one *posta* to another using a *mezza volta*.

Another way to strike a *mezana* is to strike to **posta breve** rather than to **posta longa**. This is done either when the combatant wants to make cover and seize the fight's centerline—often in response to the opponent's move—or when the available distance is too close to land a *colpo* with the best impact area of the sword. In this case, instead of striking to **posta longa**, the hands are instead kept on an inside line, closer to the body, and driven towards the opposite hip. If done decisively, this has the effect of closing the centerline, even when the combatants are dangerously close—and potentially lining up the tip for a *punta*.

Below: Compagno Dan Sepham demonstrates a fendente mandritto.

Three ways to finish the colpo mandritto.
*The combatant can finish in **posta breve** or **posta longa** (both mezani), into **mezana porta di ferro** (a fendente).*

Colpo or rebattimento from *tutta porta di ferro*

Another commonplace strike is made from **tutta porta di ferro**. In this case, the overhand (*fendente*) is a bit harder to coordinate, but it is a fundamental action within the system. Again, the combatant begins from a well-wound position with the left foot forward and the right hip back. Therefore, he is fully-powered on the right. To make the *colpo* from here, he once again steps forward, simultaneously driving with the right hand towards *poste longa* or *breve*, or somewhere in between. The student should beware, as there are two common mistakes that rob the strike of power:

- **Raising or "bobbing" the right hand:** In this case, the sword hilt "bobs" upwards before dropping towards the opponent. The combatant should strive to reduce the circular motion of the hand as much as possible, striving for a nearly straight line of travel for the right hand.

- **Mistiming the footwork:** Frequently the step is made too early or too late. In both cases, the body's effort to move the sword fails, and the arms take over, resulting in a far weaker strike.

The strike from **tutta porta di ferro** need not be made just for the opponent. Incoming blows are also set aside using the exact same motion. The combatant will be likely to be striking in this case not to **posta longa**, which has little stability, but rather to **posta breve**, keeping the hilt near to his body for stability and strength; also to make better cover. This is a fundamental movement in the system, a primary method of taking command of the fight's centerline and the opponent's weapon simultaneously. Sometimes the image of the incoming blow being "hammered" to the ground is useful. This is the *rebattemento*, the repelling action we'll see over and over again and which is presented in several sections of Fiore's original text.

175

A fendente mandritto from **tutta porta di ferro** *completed this time against an incoming strike, a* **rebattemento**. *The same motion is used whether the attack is made against the opponent or his weapon, simply a posta transition made with power. In this case the result is a powered attack against the opponent's weapon that expends it, opens the centerline, and yields time for two follow-on attacks, a discomfiting sotano to the head followed by a stronger fendente, also to the head.*

Colpi from *posta di donna sinestra*

With the sword over the left shoulder, in **posta di donna sinestra**, the combatant is in a *posta pulsativa*, but because the *right* foot is forward and the *left* hip is back, he is now *powered on the left side*. In the first case, we'll execute a blow from the simpler "toes forward" version of the *guardia*, then progress to the harder "heels forward" version.

With the toes forward, the combatant simply steps forward with the left foot, striking this time from the left. This is still a *riversa* or "reverse" blow, since all blows from the right are termed *mandritto*, while those from the left are *manriverso*. Because it is a downward blow towards the head, neck or shoulders, it is termed *fendente*. The strike is thrown along the line of maximum strength, from left to right, a *passare* step accompanying the *mezza volta* turning of the body. In this context it is simply the reverse of the first blow we demonstrated. This is the method of throwing blows taught within the Schola at the first two levels.

In the original text, the combatant is in the heels-forward stance unique to Fiore's swordsmanship (but he does not always use it). We'll now look at a different kinesthetic that can be studied as an option, and which seems to have characterized some of Fiore's movements in a unique way. In this case, the combatant stands heels facing his opponent, rather than toes facing. This can be found by simply doing a *volta stabile* with the feet from the usual toes-forward stance.

Now, with the sword over the left shoulder, the feet and body both make their *volta stabile*, never leaving the ground, turning the hips. The arms still simply guide the sword; the work is done by the body's turning. Often, the strike would be made to **posta breve** rather than to **posta longa**, because the combatant will likely be closer to his opponent in this case (otherwise he'd need a step to come into fighting distance).

*A fendente mandritto from **posta di donna** thrown with a mezza volta, followed by a fendente roverso, thrown with a volta stabile (the foot "does not lose contact with the ground."*

This is a more difficult method of generating power, and it generates less than does the *mezza volta*, but it has the advantage of turning the combatant on a front-back orientation, rather than on a left-right one. Making skilled used of the *volta stabile* keeps the combatant capable in multiple directions, reducing the chances of losing track of multiple opponents. But it also provides less power than the *mezza volta*, and is harder to do fluidly.

A more common method of generating throwing *colpi* from these *poste* is done with the other form of *volta stabile*, where the *colpi* are thrown still accompanied with the body's rotational movement, but without the accompanying step. This can be done on the left or right, is quite powerful.

In General

The example cases above show different blows made from the strong- or powered-side on both the right and left from a *guardia pulsativa*. Of course it is also to throw blows "in reverse" of this line, and to throw blows from *stabile* or even *instabile poste*. These will be dealt with in turn after a few other concepts are introduced.

Most blows in the Italian medieval style seem to originate from the hip area, as opposed to the chest or shoulders as is more common in the German system. The hip area is closer to the center of balance for a human being, what the Asian martial arts often term *hara*.

Most attacks in the system are made using an oblique *passare* step that accompanies the *mezza volta*. More rarely, this can be done in reverse, using a *tornare* step to clear distance, increase the available time, and to manage the fighting distance. In both cases, it is critical that George Silver's "agreement of hand and foot" be observed; that is, that the blow should land as the foot does.

Sometimes, it may be desireable to advance along the side of the forward foot, or to just advance with more speed than is available with a *passare* step. In this case, an *acresare* or *discresare* makes sense.

Silver's rule of Agremeent should still be observed, but the whole operation is less stable and less powerful than is a comparable *passare / tornare* step. It is, however, faster.

Colpo may also be thrown without any steps, as in our interpretation of the simple version of the *volta stabile*. There is a limited application for this in unarmoured combat, but it has more potential when fully armoured. The problem with this approach is that it leaves the combatant's fighting platform rooted for several beats of fighting time, which gives the opponent more time to react and respond, taking advantage of what he sees. By moving, his combat calculus is complicated and the combatant has the chance to change the centerline of the fight in his favor (see chapter 6).

Just as there are three turns of the body—the volta stabile, the mezza volta, and the tutta volta—so we will see later than there are also three turns of the sword. Volte (turns) of the body are used to provide power, while volte of the sword change its position relative to your opponent's weapon.

MANDRITTO / MANRIVERSO

Colpi may be thrown from the right or from the left. For a right-hander, a "right-handed" blow thrown from the right side would be known as a *mandritto*, literally "right hand." This is the "strong" side, and a *mandritto* will be the strongest attack possible.

For a left-hander, the situation is much more difficult. I am aware of no guide from the period that discusses the case of a left-handed combatant, but for the purposes of the Schola, a *mandritto* is thrown from the right side. Thus for a left-hander, a *mandritto* would be thrown from the *right*.

Blows thrown from the weak side are termed *manriverso*. Since there is no documentation for dealing with a swordsman who wishes to fight "left-handed," the meaning of the word in Italian swordsmanship would generally mean a blow that comes from the left. For a right-hander, a *manriverso* blow is more difficult and has less power than does a *mandritto*, since the right hand must be propelled by the muscles focused on the left side of the body.

The "seven swords" from the Getty, fol. 32r. There are some important differences between this illustration and the one from the PD below (carta 17a).

First, the overall nexus point for all of the swords is lower in the Getty, reflecting an overall interest in getting the combatant to lower his center of mass.

Second, notice that the highest swords intersect the combatant at his elbows, rather than through the shoulder point as in the case of the PD.

Third, the sotani lines—those coming from below—are aligned near the lower hip, not along the thigh as on the PD.

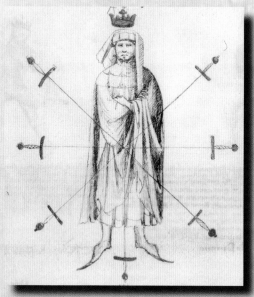

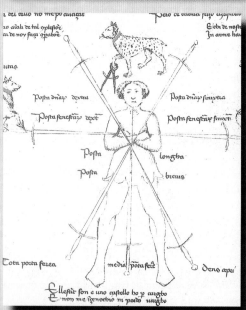

178

Colpi fendenti

"Noy semo fendente e in l'arte façemo questione de fender gli denti e 'rivar alo zinochio cum rasone. E ogni guardia che si fa terrana, d'una guardia in l'aultra andamo senza pena. E rompemo le guardie cum inzegno, e cum colpi fazemo de sangue segno. Noi fendente dillo ferir non avemo tardo, e tornamo in guardia di vargo in vargo." (Getty 23R-1)

"We are called _fendenti_, and in the art make argument by cleaving his teeth and travelling to the knee with intent (_rasone_).' And each guard made near the ground, we go from one to the other without effort. I'll show you how to break them, and with blows we draw blood. We _fendente_, which wound, don't wait; but return defending from guard to guard."

"Noy semo fendenti e façemo questione
De fender gli denti cum drita raxone:
Noy del ferir non auemo tardo
E tornamo in guardia de uargo in uargo." (PD 12B-1)

"We are called _fendenti_ and make argument
By cleaving his teeth with right intent:
We who wound don't wait,
And in turn defend from guard to guard."

According to the _segno_ and to the text, a _fendente_ is a downward blow that _travels_ from jaw to the opposite knee. This is stated in the Getty on Fol. 23r, and in the Novati on Carta 12b. In both cases, he says that the _fendente_ is made to the teeth (_dente_ = "teeth"). The blow is made with "intent" (_rasone_), so it needs force to drive it sufficiently all the way down to the knee. On the _segno_, we see this illustrated in the lines that travel from the combatant's shoulder to his knee.

Fiore does not seem to clarify whether or not the _fendenti_ are employed at any other target than the head. My interpretation of the _segno_ illustration is that a _fendente_ can be thrown anywhere between the shoulder points along a downward trajectory that will carry it powerfully to the ground. Blows below the shoulder point, are, in our interpretation, really _mezani_, and are discussed later in the chapter.

As mentioned above, the combatant will generally want to step with the strike for maximum effectiveness. Ideally, this will be a _mezza volta_, accompanied with the _passare_ or _passare a la traversa_ step.

Fendenti may be thrown from any high _poste_, especially the **poste di donna** but also from **posta frontale** (albiet a weak one). They may also be powerfully generated from **tutta porta di ferro**.

Fendente mandritto from **posta di donna destra**
In order to throw an effective _fendente_, we have combatants at the first level focus on maximizing their efficiency from the _poste_ that are _pulsativa_, especially **posta di donna destra**. To throw a _fendente mandritto_ from **posta di donna destra**, the combatant begins in a well-charged position at the widest possible fighting distance.

When he is ready, assuming that the front foot is already "out of the way" (_fora de la strada_), the _colpo_ begins with slight pressure made on the back leg, which begins the motion with the large muscle groups. The hips begin to turn, releasing the potential energy in the stored spring-state of the large mucle groups. Importantly, the arms stay close to the body until the last possible moment. As the body unwinds, the hands finally direct the blade away from the shoulder, guiding the sword towards the opponent's jaw. The combatant will pass through something like **posta longa**, and, if his blade encounters nothing, will end in **mezana porta di ferro**.

There are two ways he could end in **mezana porta di ferro**. One way would "expend" him, and he would thus have no potential energy stored in his large muscle groups. Neither hip is charged. Had the sword indeed encountered nothing, this would be an exceptionally risky point with which to end the _fendente_!

Instead, the combatant should reset or _recoil_ his hip on the opposite site. In most cases, when a blow is struck with any of the _colpi_, the combatant should, after the point of potential impact, (ie, when the sword would have encountered something, either the target or the opponent's weapon), the hips on the opposite side should begin to coil in the other direction, setting up an immediate and powerful _mezza volta_. The combatant would thus now be powered on the left—as much as possible—

and his overall *poste* would again be **mezana porta di ferro**. But this time, he has the potential energy necessary to make the immediate *sotano* Fiore refers to in both texts (more on that in a moment). Always reset the hips when you strike in order to minimize the exposure of being "expended."

Fendente Mandritto
Poste di Donna

Fendente mandritto from **posta di donna sinestra**

It is the same from the opposite side. Beginning in **posta di donna sinestra**, the combatant's right foot will be forward, and his left hip back, powering him on the left side. The grip does not change, the right hand remaining near the cross.

The combatant now once again steps forward with the left foot, assuming that the right is not in the way (if it is, he moves it first "a little out of the way." As the back foot pushes off, the hips again turn, and eventually the hands reluctantly follow, merely guiding the sword to the target. This is now a *fendente mandritto*, even though it comes from the *left* side for a right-handed combatant. It is as powerful as it can be, although it is slightly less powerful than the *fendente mandritto* that begins with the right side charged, because the charged hip is not in complete agreement with the dominant hand (there is some crossing and a less efficient use of the large muscle groups). But it is enough—and if the timing is right and there is Agreement of hand and foot, then the blow should land with devastating force.

Fendente manriverso from **posta di donna destra**

At the most basic level, students should first perfect blows thrown with agreement rather than trying to strive for "trickiness" using less pure crossing strikes. I call a strike "crossed" when it is thrown in the opposite direction as the powered hip. Therefore, if the combatant is powered on the right, in, say, **posta di donna destra**, and he elects to throw a *manriverso* from the left side rather than a *mandritto* from the right, he is making a *colpo* that is crossed. This may achieve some tactical surprise, but it also costs power and makes the timing and resulting footwork more difficult. The combatant ends crossed as well, his left hip potentially charged and the sword and the right.

In a *mandritto*, the combatant's hands would move downward, towards the opposite hip or the center of the body at hip or waist level. This is an exceptionally balanced position, and leads naturally to a follow-on *sotano* that rises immediately from **mezana porta di ferro**, as Fiore mentions in the text, returning the combatant comfortably and powerfully to **posta di donna destra**.

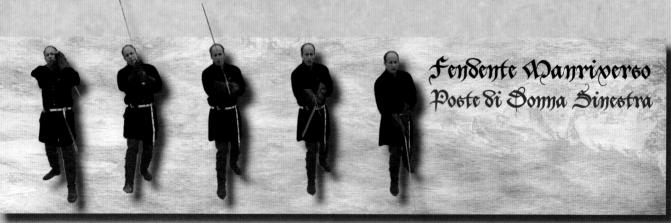

Fendente Manriverso
Poste di Donna Sinestra

In a *manriverso*, the combatant's hands still move downward, but this time they must anchor on the right hip, or even a little further out from the body. The sword must clear the head from the back (which is certainly possible and not particularly difficult, but it takes a little time), and will eventually move on a trajectory towards something like **tutta porta di ferro**, although the little curling turn will have to be made. All in all, the timing is tougher and leaves the sword on the right side while the left hip is probably charged. Not a disaster, but not as clean as is the *mandritto*.

hips with a hammer-like motion that results in a sharp downward blow for the opponent's head, arms, or his weapon—whatever is in the way.

The timing on this key movement is a bit difficult, and there are several very common mistakes. Often, combatants will raise their hands almost to the shoulder level before striking. Instead, he should strive to minimize the upward movement of the hands,

**Fendente Mandritto
Tutta Porta di Ferro**

Fendente mandritto from **tutta porta di ferro**

One of the core strikes expected of advancing novice students are powerful strikes from **tutta porta di ferro**. These are necessary both to execute various *rebattimenti*, but they are also extremely effective *colpi* in their own right.

Despite its being a *posta pulsativa*, **tutta porta di ferro** is as comfortable a position to wait in as are any of the poste classified as *stabile*. Many students do, in fact, have a hard time remembering that the full iron gate is *pulsativa*—a common mistake in the early days is the remember it as *stabile*.

Waiting comfortably, the combatant has powerful options for attacks both against the combatant or against his weapon using the exact same movement. This strike from **tutta porta di ferro** is perhaps the most difficult of the fundamental *colpi* presented in this section, but it is also in many respects the most useful.

In **tutta porta di ferro**, the combtant's right hip is exceptionally well charged and the true edge (*tagli dritta*) is forward, as in Fiore's illustration. He will make the *fendenti mandritto* by stepping forward with an oblique *passare*, simultaneously driving from the

since this is wasted movement and contributes nothing to the *colpo's* power. Second, there is often a difficulty remembering to step on an oblique line, or in timing the step with the strike. Remember, the two must land with near-simultaneity, or the power will be lost.

This movement should be continually practiced as it is the main way that Fiore deals with opponents and incoming attacks—he *sets them aside*. This is a key tactical concept as well as a physical technique, so it is worth spending a lot of time repeating the motion until it is extremely well ingrained.

What about **posta breve?**

Many two-handed sword arts from around the world focus on a position akin to **posta breve**. While we can, as we'll see later in the chapter, deliver a fine thrust from **posta breve**, little power can be generated from this position because the sword is so far in front of the body that the body is very hard to get behind the strike. While a certain amount of force can be delivered by a pivoting blow thrown with the arms alone pivoting on the right hand levered with the left. It has been observed that in order to deliver force from the body from **posta breve**, the sword must in fact progress through another *posta* first.

**Fendente Manriverso
Tutta Porta di Ferro**

SOTANO

Colpi Sottani

"Gli colpi sottani semo noi, e cominzamo a lo zinochio, e andamo per meza la fronte per lo camino che fano gli fendente. E per tal modo che noi intramo (?) per quello camino noy retornamo, overo che noi remanemo in posta longa." (Getty 23R-2)

"We are called the colpi sotani, and we begin at the knee, travelling in the middle of the forehead along the way made by the *fendente*. And the same way we enter we return, or else we remain in **posta longa**."

"Noy semo colpi chiamadi li sotani
Che sempre may cerchamo de ferir le mani;
E dal zenochio in su façemo questione
E tornando cum fendente fazemo lexione." (PD 12B-2)

"We are the blows called the *sotani*,
Which always seek to wound the hands;
An from the knee we make argument,
An turn with the fendenti from guard to guard."

Sotani are thrown just as are *fendenti*, but in reverse. The *sotano* is literally "from below." Usually made from the low guards, especially **mezana porta di ferro** or **dente di zenghiaro**. Generally these strikes are less sharply powered than are their downward cousins, in part because they act in oppisition to gravity, and in part because they begin from *posta* which are generally *stabile* rather than *pulsativa*, which means they harness the body's large muscle groups less efficiently. This is not a particular problem, however, since as Fiore states in his paragraphs the *sotani* "always seek to wound the hands," easily damaging the relatively small bones therein. And if the hands are not in range, then the opponent's downward-vectored sword almost always is, resulting in a very smooth and efficient deflection, what we in the Schola refer to as a *redoppiando*. Alternatively, the *sotano* is frequently employed following control of the opponent's blade in a discomfiting strike, which causes the opponent to "reboot," enabling a much more powerful finishing strike (see chapter 11 for how this is done in conjunction with control over the opponent's blade).

Although Fiore is not specific, the proper edge differs according to whether the blade comes from the right or left. On the right side (for a right-handed combatant), the true (*dritta*) edge is employed. From the left, a *sotano* will use the *taglio falso*, "false edge."

Sotano from **mezana porta di ferro** *or* **dente di zenghiaro**

The combatant begins first in **dente di zenghiaro** or **mezana porta di ferro**. If in **dente di zenghairo**, he will have more power because the left hand should be anchored on the left hip. If in **mezana porta di ferro**, he must be careful to have his hips charged rather than expended, as mentioned above. In this case he will find it advantageous to use a bit of leverage to assist the body's power in causing the sword blade to rise—the right hand will be the fulcrum and the left hand will provide a bit of power. This action, done in conjunction with the turning of the hips, provides more than enough energy for the *colpo's* mission of deflection or causing injury (*ferir*) to the hands.

Sotano Mandritto
Mezana Porta di Ferro

Sotano Mandritto
Sente di Zenghiaro

Sotano Manriperso
Tutta Porta di Ferro

The combatant will once again step forward with his *colpo*, coordinating the lever-action of the hands with the turning of the hips and the step. The result should be a strong rising blow from below that travels upward with great speed and directness towards either of the primary **poste di donna** (**destra** or **sinestra**). In practice, this is often used to control and then attack the opponent.

The *sotani* clearly work in conjunction with the *fendenti*, resulting in the characteristic up-down pair of *colpi* that marks Fiore's approach to control of the opponent's weapon. But this up-down pairing has a more definitive function, as Gregory Mele has well articulated: "What goes up must come down, and visa versa." If the sword clears and controls the weapon on the way down, it immediately returns to strike from below. If it clears from below, it will immediately return from above to end the fight with a powerful *colpo*. This must be done immediately, or the initiative is quickly lost. Another benefit is that, moving along these planes, the sword frequently covers the combatant, allowing him to strike with safety, the subject of chapter 10.

Paired fendente-sotano

In order to internalize this extremely important pairing, I strongly encourage the combatants to practice using them in pairs.

Starting from **posta di donna destra**, the combatant should step forward with a textbook *fendente mandritto*, driving downwards through **posta longa** to arrive already recoiled on the left side in **mezana porta di ferro**. More or less immediately, he should step forward again, this time with a *sotano* which will in turn pass through **posta longa**, but which can easily be returned either to **posta di donna destra** or **sinestra**. Of course this can be done in reverse as well, starting from **mezana porta di ferro** and striking upwards to one of the **poste di donna**.

Doing it this way, the combatant will begin to appreciate some of the elgance and utility of a fight executed between known *poste*. As he strikes downward, the blade naturally comes to a rest in another *posta*, one that will be well-known to the combatant and one which has some very interesting advantages for those who know how to use it. Each strike should lead the combatant to another *posta*, and the adoption of a new *posta* is much like the dawning of a new day, filled with possibility (or danger, depeneding upon your outlook).

This pairing is one of the key motions within the system, so I strongly recommend that the combatant work hard to smooth the progression so that it becomes second-nature; make the difficult look natural and easy, similar to the Italian term introduced by Baldassare Castiglione in the 15th century, *sprezzaturra*.

MEZÁNI

Colpi mezani

"Colpi mezani semo chiamadi perché noy andamo per mezi gli colpi soprani e sottani. E andamo cum lo dritto taglio de la parte dritta, e de la parte riversa andamo cum lo falso taglio. E lo nostro camino si è dello zinochio ala testa." (Getty 23R-3)

"*Colpi mezani* we are called because we travel between the *colpi* above and below. And [we] travel with the true (*dritto*) edge (*taglio*) with the right side; with the *riversa* we travel with the false edge. And our way is found between the head and the knee."

"Noy colpi meçani andamo trauersando;
Dal zenochio in su andamo guastando;
E rebatemo le punte fora de strada
E redopiando lo colpo de ferir è derada;
E si noy del meçano colpo intramo in fendent,
Asay cum tali colpi guastamo zent." (PD 13A-1)

"We, the *colpi mezani*, go traversely;
From the knee I travel to destroy;
And repel the thrust out of the way
And a redoubling (*redopiando*) the *colpo*
    that wounds is the bargain
And if we of the middle *colpo* enter into a blow,
Many with such cuts have been destroyed."

The *mezani* are an intruiging puzzle. Fiore says they *andamo trauersando*—"go traversely"—that they are between the *colpi* "above and below." The *mezani* means literally *"middle,"* blows to (or from) the middle. While *mezani* are not nearly so strong as are their rising and descending kindred, they are useful for "entering into" an opponent's attack, "destroying" them, as Fiore says in the PD. Essentially *mezani* make cover by striking to posta breve and in so doing take command of the fight's center.

A *mezani* essentially strikes short, where a *fendente* strikes long. The *mezani* strikes to **posta breve**, while the *fendente* strikes to or through **posta longa**.

In striking to **posta breve**, the combatant should anchor the pommel somewhere between the center of the body and the opposite hip. The point should be directed at the opponent's face as much as possible, and the sword should dominate the center of the fight. This sets up a powerful follow-on attack, probably a *punta*, a thrust.

From this position it will be difficult to make a well-powered *colpo* for anything except the hands or arms, but the point can be used to great effect. In this case a follow-on attack is made with a thrust, which we'll see later.

Mezana from **tutta porta di ferro**

The other kind of motion can be best seen from **tutta porta di ferro**. In this case, we imagine an opponent's thrust. Stepping and harnessing the body as with the previous play done from **tutta porta di ferro**, instead of breaking the thrust all the way to the ground, we instead strike with a *mezana* towards **posta breve** on the opposite side, effectively controlling our opponent's sword and keeping our own point on-line in what Fiore calls an **Exchange of the Thrust** (see chapter 10). Since this doesn't leave the combatant in an easily reciprocial position as he would be in the *fendente/sotano* combination, he must instead rely on the thrust, which he easily does.

close distance, which makes finding the optimal point on the sword quite difficult (and which is why so much technique shown at this distance involves the *prese* or wrestling.

Managing distance is a difficult art. The combatant must assess not only the physical distance separating himself and his opponent(s), but also the relative lengths of their arms and weapons, and their relative speed of movement. The nature of the ground must also be taken into account. For most combatants, this process happens as experience is gained and is subconscious (fortunately!). But it is an artform in its own right, an important aspect of fighting control that must eventually be mastered.

Mezana
Tutta Porta di Ferro

Striking point on the sword and managing distance

As discussed earlier in the chapter, the main point on the sword optimized for striking is usually between the *punta* and the *mezza spada*. It is at this point where the maximum impact may be found, so the combatant should manage his strikes to land at this point no matter what the physical distance separating them. As long as they are in fighting distance, this part of the sword should be strongly preferred if it is possible to achieve it.

For the longsword, the optimal distance is one where the target will be struck with the optimal striking point for that particular sword when the arms are *just short* of being locked (the arms and knee joints, as mentioned earlier, should *never* lock, as this represents a threat to the ligaments and tendons, it takes time to unlock the joints, and the joint is then vulnerable for kicking or striking). At this distance, the combatant's power is optimized against the target and the sword itself has sufficient room to work. Interestingly, for two combatants with disparate heights, arm- or sword-lengths, the optimal range can well be different for the combatant and his opponent. Ideally, you want to work in your ideal range while denying your opponent the chance to work in his.

Combatants can and will fight at many different ranges during an encounter. When far away, as we'll observe in Book II, the fight begins as the combatants "taste" one another's *posta*. If there is an open line, then a thrust or casting of the point is made at this time, quickly, as the serpent strikes with plenty of *tigre* (tiger). As they close the distance, the swords can easily become crossed as one opponent strives to make his cover against an incoming strike. Finally, the combatants may by intention or accident enter into

One way to manage the distance in terms of striking is to use the feet to move the combatant's fighting platform around the field smoothly. The feet can manipulate the distance effectively, and should be considered to the combatant's primary method of managing distance. However, the feet are by their very nature slower than the movements of the hand itself, and cannot be relied on as steadily when the combatants close to middle or close distance. The hands themselves are the other way to manage distance, and in this we've discovered a key use for two of the centerline *poste*, **posta longa** and **posta breve**.

Zugadore make their two lines, *scolari* on one side, *compagni* on the other. The *scolari* check to find their striking point from wide distance, then reset in **tutta porta di ferro**. The *compagni* present striking batons or swords to use as targets.

On command, the *scolari* step forward with a *fendente* against the striking baton, freezing the blow in contact. A few seconds are allotted to check and correct the weapon's placement, then the return command is given and the exercise repeated as necessary. Once the *scolari* appear to be striking effectively, they should alter their distance and strike from both closer and further away, striving always to keep the body upright and coiled using their hands and feet effectively to manage distance. An advanced vesion of the drill has the *compagni* moving at the same time, complicating the judgments necessary by the *scolari*.

Striking Short vs Striking Long

Since we know that all *colpi* are simply *posta* transitions thrown with power, the *fendente* will begin in a *posta* and end in one. To manage distance for a *colpo*, the combatant may strike either to **posta longa** or to **posta breve**, depending upon circumstance and distance.

A combatant who begins at wide distance will strike at his opponent, the sword passing through or to **posta longa** with the hilt ending slightly lower than the point. The further away his opponent, the higher his sword hilt can be; conversely, the closer his opponent, the lower his hilt must be, or he exposes his belly and exposes his hands and arms.

A combatant who begins at middle distance can adjust his steps to make his *colpo* land at the right point on the sword and he can adjust the final position of his hands to find the perfect range. He moves his hands across his body in order to find the right place, eventually developing a good feel for where he needs to be.

A combatant who begins at middle distance and who closes aggressively (or his opponent could also do the closing) or who begins at close distance does not strike to **posta longa**, or he would hit with the *forteza*, or at best, the *mezza spada*. Instead of striking to **posta longa**, he strikes to **posta breve**.

Far = long (*longa*), near = short (*breve*). It is a simple rule, but it turns out to be exceedingly important. As the combatant closes on his opponent, he must lower his hilt in order to protect his body. Having the hilt high, with portions of the blade over his head, does little for his defense and opens both his belly and arms to attack. Also, the sword becomes expended far easier along the high line, and there is a tendency to anchor on the shoulder rather than the hip, which often draws combatants to keep their weight too high for good balance. *The closer you get, the lower your hilt should be.* Remember, in the Getty edition, Fiore's rendition of **posta breve**, the cross is actually *below* crotch-level, as low as the combatant can possibly go without exaggerated motion.

Tagli : Cuts

Unlike in the Asian sword arts focused on the katana or other curved swords, in the medieval arts there really is no concept of a draw-cut, where the edge is drawn lengthwise across the opponent's skin in order to wound. This is due in part, I believe, to weapon design; it is far less efficient with a straight weapon than a curved one, but a straight weapon generates more impact when it hits than does a curved one. In general, curved weapons are employed against more lightly armoured opponents, and correspondingly we see them in the Middle- and Far-East. There are a couple of places in the treatise where the opponent is actually "wounded with the edge," as in the *zhogo stretto* play on Getty fol. 28 and 28v (from the master of the crossed swords at the mezza spada, a double pommel strike to the face followed by a stepping behind and holding the opponent at the neck with the sword, also see in PD carta 22a(4) and 22b(1). But in general, attacks are made with a *punta* or a *colpo*, rather than a "cut with the edge."

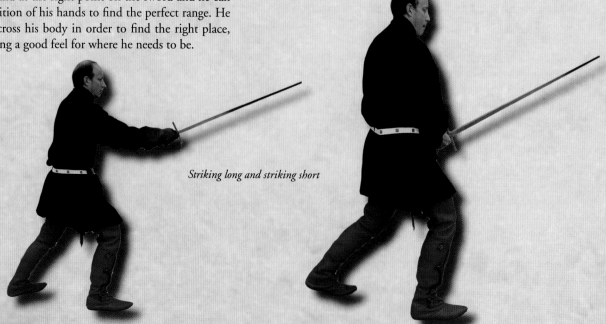

Striking long and striking short

Le punte

"Noy semo le punte crudele e mortale. E lo nostro camino si è per mezo lo corpo cominzando a lo petenichio infin a la fronte. E semo punte d'V rasone, zoè doy soprane una d'una parte l'altra de l'altra. E doy de sotta similemente un d'una parte e l'altra de l'altra, e una di mezo che esse di meza porta di ferro overo di posta lunga e breve." (Getty 23R-4)

"We are the *punte*, cruel and mortal. And our way is in the middle of the body beginning at the pubic area to the forehead. And we thrusts are of five types; we say from above, from one side and the other. And similarly from below, from one side and the other, and one in the middle, we say from **mezana porta di ferro** or **posta longa** and [**posta**] **breve**."

"Ponte semo de grandissima offensione
E a tuti colpi façemo questione;
Venenose semo più che serpente
E più cje tuti colpi alczidemo zente;
E noy ponte a li colpi si disemo:
Tanto no taiaret che noy cusiremo." (PD 13A-2)

"Thrusts are extremely offensive
Questioning each colpi they face;
More venomous than the snake,
And we kill more than all the *colpi*."

The *punte* are deadly, "more venomous than the snake" (*venenose semo più che serpente*), and, according to Fiore, they kill more often than do the *colpi*. However, this does not necessarily mean that they are employed more often; men have a decided hesitation when it comes to thrusting a hand-to-hand weapon into their opponent as has been recently documented. Instead, I find that a majority of the attacks made in Fiore's system are in fact *colpi*, although a fight may be and often is terminated with a powerful *punta* once the opponent has been discomfited with a *colpi*.

Fiore seems to make thrusts to the face, neck, and body above the groin, "in the middle of the body beginning at the pubic area to the forehead" (*E lo nostro camino si è per mezo lo corpo cominzando a lo petenichio infin a la fronte*).

Importantly, Fiore states plainly, "in thrusting with the tip the longer offends first" (*che punta per punta la più lunga fa offesa inançi*). So the man with the longer sword will "offend" (*offesa*) first. In the most fundamental way, this refers to physical sword length. But looking deeper, the "longer sword" equals much more: relative length of the arms, which foot will be forward when the *punta* strikes, and even the relative speed between the combatants. All of these are critical aspects of what constitutes a "longer sword," discussed in Book II.

A thrust uses the same biomechanics as the *colpo*. Most thrusts are made using a *mezza volta* accompanied with a *passare* step, although many students have a tendency to advance with an *acresare* rather than the *passare*, which robs their thrust of much of its power. In general, advance with an *acresare* when the lead foot is on the same side you want to traverse to or when you are very close on time and must trade power for the small increment you gain by selecting an *acresare* over a *passare*. In all other cases, I believe the combatant is better served with a *passare*. Again, the hips turn and the body's large muscle groups power the tip, leaving the arms free to place the point (hopefully with precision).

Fiore mentions in his text that there are "five types" of *punta*. Two from the high line, presumably from **posta di finestra** on each side. "And similarly from below," which he names in the Getty as **mezana porta di ferro**, **posta longa**, and **posta breve**. Interestingly, he does not mention in this paragraph thrusting from **dente di zenghiaro**, although it works extremely well. To this we would also want to add **posta di bicorno**, which is clearly meant for thrusting.

Fiore's Thrusting Poste

Posta di Finestra

Posta Longa

Dente di Zenghiaro

Posta Breve

Posta Frontale

Mezana Porta di Ferro

Although the *punte* are powered with the whole body, not as much force is needed to get the point to penetrate against light armour (although plate armour would be proof agianst most thrusts) or flesh. Hence, we find that in the case of thrusts, *time* is more important than *power*, so the *guardia* that thrust are correspondingly more forward. **Mezana porta di ferro**, **posta breve** and **posta longa** are primary examples of forward thrusting guards.

Working from high to low, each of the *punta* has particular characteristics. On the highline, we have the twin **posta di finestra**, one from each side. Note that like **posta di bicorno**, they are *instabile* and thus "malicious," that is, dangerous places to be caught but equally devious to the opponent. As the sword gets closer to the ground, it becomes less *instabile* and more stable: **posta breve**, **mezana porta di ferro** and **dente di zenghiaro** are all *stabile*. **Posta longa**, owing to its extended nature, is *instabile*.

Thrusts or punte are "more venomous than the snake," and must be made just as fast.

Punta from **mezana porta di ferro**

Perhaps the easiest *punta* to make is from **mezana porta di ferro**. In this case, either foot may be forward and either hip charged. However, the combatant will have more distance if the left foot begins forward and the right foot advances with the thrust. This is because the right hip will then be forward, as will the right shoulder, resulting in maximum distance. If the left hip would be forward, the body would be a bit crossed, and while there would be plenty of power, there is slightly less range available.

To make the thrust, simply step forward, usually *a traversa*, and push the hands forward, thrusting the point directly at the opponent. The target can be anything from the groin to the forhead, even the hands and arms. When the thrust ends, the arms should be just short of locked, *the hilt always lower than the tip*. The thrust will end in **posta longa**, the energy briefly expended. This is a time of great danger, which is why thrusts are generally not made until the opponent's sword is controlled. It is easy for the opponent to deflect a thrust, and if this is done, the expended state of the combatant's fighting platform puts him at a time and positional disadvantage.

If the *passare* step is used during the thrust, as mentioned earlier, maximum power will be available. If an *acresare* is used, the blow will be a bit *weaker* but *faster*, and there will be less available range. This is particularly problematic if the opponent steps back as you thrust, a natural human reaction to an incoming point. If you've moved forward with an *acresare*, you may well run out of range. If you have made a *passare*, however, then you will likely catch him even if he steps quickly and boldly back.

Punta
Mezana
Porta di Ferro

Punta
Dente di
Zenghiaro

The same *punta* can be made from **dente di zenghiaro** or **posta breve**. However, thrusts made from **posta breve** are usually made "in opposition,"—as classical fencers term it—that is, with contact against the opponent's sword for the purposes of control. We'll see this in action later in Chapter 11 while *Finding the Point*. The combatant should practice his thrusts from all three of these *poste*, working for superior point control, trying to be able to hit a precise spot at will using both kinds of steps in both directions.

Punta from **posta longa**

From **posta longa**, the case is a bit more difficult. Because the sword is already extended, developing energy is far more difficult. The timing of the hips must be far more precise, and a *passare* step must be used. Such thrusts can also be made while in contact with the opponent's sword.

The extra distance can be so very important in thrusting guards, as "she wants a long sword." The combatant should strive to maximize the distance advantage in a thrusting situation. In this case, I strongly recommend that when using **posta longa** in a *malicoso* way—when trying to break the opponent's *posta* by invitation and intimidation—that the left foot be forward. This way when the thrusting attack is made, it is done with a *passare* and *mezza volta* led by the right foot, which will then give the maximum distance advantage as the combatant finishes the step: the right foot, hip, shoulder and arm are all extended forward. Again, the arm should be just short of locked, for the reasons previously mentioned.

This is the main attack available from **posta longa**, and a combatant who favors the use of **posta longa** to break his opponent's guard should spend a great deal of time practising and perfecting his thrust from **posta longa**.

Punta
Tutta Porta di Ferro

Punta
Posta di Finestra

Punta from **posta di finestra**

While we will see the thrust from **posta di finestra** used in more detail in the next chapter (when **Finding the Point**), the mechanics of the thrust itself are useful to look at however briefly.

From **posta di finestra** on either side, the thrust anchors from the shoulder, rather than from the hip as is done in the thrusts from the low-line. Because the shoulder is well above the body's center of mass, it is less stable and this thrust must be executed quickly, or the unstable nature of the *guardia* can quickly turn on the combatant and result in a great positional liability.

On either side, the combatant will traverse forward on an oblique, again with preference for a *passare* step. As he does so, the body unwinds and the hands drop a little, so that he ends the thrust in **posta longa.**

We have found that, like **posta breve** and **posta di bicorno**, this thrust is best made "in opposition" once the swords are in contact, the state Fiore calls *incrosare*. This is explained more fully in the next chapter under **Finding the Point**.

Opening with a thrust

It is rare that combatants will be able to launch an opening *punta* and find it successful. Thrusts are too easy to deflect, in most cases, and the longsword is not a tuck, rapier or smallsword; it has more weight, and this weight makes the thrusts a bit slower. Slow enough, in fact, to make an opening thrust a low-probability choice. Added to this is the ease with which a thrust is "set aside" using an exchanging action, or broken (driven to the ground). Instead, the combatant is usually better served reserving the majority of his thrusts for the time after the *incrosare* has been achieved, after which he "finds the point." Opening with a thrust *does* work from **posta longa**, and occasionally from **tutta porta di ferro**, **mezana porta di ferro**, or **dente di zenghiaro**, but from these positions the combatant is vulnerable to effective counters using the exchanging or breaking of the thrust.

Butta la punta : Casting the Point

One interesting technique which has been, I believe, often misinterpreted as a pure thurst is what I call *casting the point, butta la punta,* which is presented by Fiore in several of the *posta* description for **dente di zenghiaro mezana**, but which works exceedingly well on the first two plays of the *zhogo largo* as well, which we'll cover in the next book.

A combatant casts the point when he is too far away to ensure a strike with the optimal part of the blade for a *colpo*. Instead, he will wound with the point. This can be made as a *fendente*, as when "tasting" the guard in *zhogo largo* play number one, or it can be made from a *sotano*, as described in the text on **dente di zenghiaro mezana**. In this case, the tip is thrown or "cast" towards the opponent. If the tip strikes, it will drag and eventually line up the point, and is dangerously fast, causing the opponent to "uncover himself" (*discrova lu compagno*). From the **dente di zenghiaro**, the attacks are generally made to the hands or forearms. From an *incrosare* at the *punta* (per zhogo largo play #1), it can also be made for the hands, or thrown for the arm.

The point digs in if it strikes the body, enabling a final, killing thrust, if this is desireable. If the point strikes a bit short, the combatant need only arrest the movement and stop the point while it is on-line, at which point he may strike in either *mezzo-* or *duo* tempo.

One drill that is excellent for both longsword and lanza is the "targeting ball," a well-reinforced tetherball hung from at least 7' or so of heavy cord. Springing towards the ball provides a moving target, but the combatants should focus above all on maintaining their ellefante during the exercise.

A No-No: The Punta Must Stay Above the Forteza

In all of Fiore's illustrations, the *punta* of the sword (the tip) is always above the *forteza* or the hilt. This is because this is the only way to maintain stability in the thrust, and it avoids a very easy and sexy disarm, shown below. But the disarm works because the *punta*-down orientation creates a substantial positional weakness which is very easy to take advantage of. Study the photographs provided to see the kinesthetic difference in orientation, and compare these with Fiore's illustrations.

Fiore's illustrations always depict the point above the hilt, unlike in the German system, there the point-down orientation is common. The top and bottom row are from the Getty, while the middle figures are from the PD. The top two roses show how a combatant thrusts with the point-up confirguration from posta di finestra. The same "point up" position is common to all Fiore thrusts.

If the forteza does not support the punta during a thrust, one possibility is to seize the blade with a fast disarm.

Incorrect thrust made with the punta unsupported by the forteza: In Fiore, the forteza is always below the punta.

CUTTING TATAMI MATS

One of the most potentially satisfying, and sometimes challenging, tests we use within the Schola Saint George involves the cutting of *tatami* mats. This is an adoption of a Japanese tradition called *Tameshigiri*, but it is one that we have found exceptionally useful for insuring the combatants are harnessing their body properly and have their timing sequence.

A *tatami* mat is a floor covering commonly used in Japanese houses. Because it is made of grass, it is thought to simulate the cutting of a blade through flesh. Whether or not this is true, cutting tatami is a very good way to check the student's mechanics and provides an exceptionally satisfying validation when done properly. They are rolled, soaked, and fixed to a wooden post, and then stand ready as targets for test-cutting.

CUTTING SWORDS

We have found a strong preference for "performance" swords made by Angus Trim in our cutting experience. There are a few others, such as Tinker and Arms & Armor, whose weapons we have tested, but the ordinary sword purchased from commercial vendors will probably not do as well as the performance cutters we tend to favor. Cutting swords need to be razor-sharp, quite unlike how most medieval swords were usually kept.

PREPARING THE MATS

Tatami omote are via the Internet from the Mugan-Daichi company and prerolled through the Keen Mirror company. I advise purchasing them in 10-50 mat sets—enough for the whole group—several weeks in advance. Newer foam targets are also coming onto the market.

The most arduous step is rolling the mats. Each mat must be tightly rolled. Ideally, this is a two-person operation. When finished, sisal string is used to tie the mat in five places. The ties should be tight so that the mats stay tight.

Once bound, they must be soaked from 12 hours to 4 days. They should be completely immersed, as the ones on top will dry out. We have used large plastic garbage cans for this purpose, and we have used the 43" under-bed storage containers as well. I tend to prefer the under-bed containers, as they are lighter and smaller. Once the mat is soaked, it can be withdrawn and set aside for a couple of hours. I prefer to drain the water out of the bins and let them drain with the lid on, so that the air doesn't dry them too much. Nor do I like water running all over the performance blades, so this draining step can be important.

The mats must then be placed onto a sturdy cutting stand, with about 8" of spike extending up into the mat. The stand should bring the top of the tatami to head-height and must be solid, so that the stand and mat do not move.

CUTTING

Safety is of paramount importance for cutting demonstrations and exercises. While this is an excellent activity for spectators, they must be kept relatively far away, as the sharp sword can slip from the combatant's hands. Students must also use great care, since the sword is much sharper than they are used to, and especially in the follow-through, the can cut their shoulders, neck or thigh if they aren't careful. I strongly recommend wearing a gambeson, tall riding boots (if available), and using gloves to help keep the hands from slipping.

Novice students strike simple cuts from *poste* which are *pulsativa*. This includes first **posta di donna destra**, which is where most right-handed students begin, followed by **posta di donna sinestra**. If these cuts are successful, the student generally progresses to try the more difficult strike from **tutta porta di ferro**. Finally, the *sotani* from **tutta porta di ferro** might be attempted. If successful, it is a tradition of ours that the first cut a student successfully makes is kept and often signed with a Sharpie® by the presiding instructor.

To make the cut, calmness and a lack of tension are important. The student should begin by taking a very deep breath, and slowly exhaling. Next, he should find his distance by stepping forward and touching the mat with the power-potion of the sword. Stepping back, he should reset in a powerfully coiled *posta*, and once again breathing deeply and exhaling. He may want to close his eyes and focus at this point: self-doubt is the largest factor in failure, because it causes tension.

The *colpo* is made stepping forward and striving to make perfect agreement between the step and the arms as the strike is made. The edge must be perfectly aligned and the hands must be firm during the strike (yet not tense before impact). Importantly, the combatant must strike *through* the target, not to it. There must be follow through! If all is well, the combatant starting in **posta di donna** will end in **mezana porta di ferro** and the mat will have sliced with no apparent resistance.

Each cut is made 6-8" down from the last one, which should yield between four and six cuts per mat. If each mat costs about $6, this equals about $1 - $1.25 per cut, about the same as two rounds from a pistol.

For intermediate combatants who are experienced at cutting and with Fiore's mechanics, we begin again with the strong cuts from *poste pulsativi*, but then progress to use the more difficult crossing strikes (ie, a *manriverso* from **posta di donna destra**). Compound strikes, where a *mandritto* is followed immediately with a *manriverso*, are also good, as are the much more difficult *fententel sotano* combinations. Advanced students will attempt four or more cuts in a single series, or cuts in different directions using multiple mats in order to coordinate the *volta* with the strikes.

PREPARING TATAME OMATE FOR CUTTING

1) Lay the mat out flat, removing any staples or hard pebbles, etc. 2) Be sure to have jute or hemp twine.
3) Begin by folding 12" or so of the mat, then 4) start rolling around a dowel that matches the diameter of the spike on your cutting stand. 5) When 20" or so from the end, fold the second end over before completing the roll. Hold the tight bundle in place with strong rubber bands, then tie securely with the hemp or jute twine. Remove the dowel. 7) Soak the mats for 24-30 hours (don't go longer), draining for 3-8 hours before cutting. Set the prepared mat firmly onto a solid cutting stand.

193

A well-cut section is smooth and straight, without straggling strands or wave. The straighter the cut, the better.

Problems

There are many things that can go wrong with a cut. Some of the most common are:

- **Tension**: If the combatant is too tense, his muscles do not properly transmit the energy and the result is often an incomplete cut that fails to completely sever the mat.

- **Timing**: The most common flaw is timing between the feet, body and arms. Too often, the feet are late or early, and the resulting blow is made entirely with the arms. The instructor should carefully observe students as they cut and should watch for this easy mistake.

- **Targeting**: Oftentimes, combatants will try too hard, and the resulting tension will in fact severely denigrate their ability to target. This is usually due to excess tension in the arms, which direct the blow. Combatants will sometimes miss the target entirely, which is embarrassing, but also dangerous. If the error persists, then the cutting should be aborted and more drills done to better prepare for the potential danger of cutting.

- **Pushing**: Another symptom of "trying too hard" come in the form of a push. A push will bend the mat, and means that the energy has not been transferred using the preferred snapping motion. Instead, the combatant uses the weight to push the mat, rather than to propel the sword. This is usually a timing error.

- **Confidence**: The psychological state of confidence or angst will cause the mistakes above and provide additional barriers that make execution of the task difficult. One of the reasons to practice cutting is to help build confidence in technique. If a combatant is having difficulty, he must keep at it until he meets with at least some success. Walking away with a failure will plant a fast-germinating seed that is difficult to stamp out once it sprouts (as in "getting back on the horse").

- **Power**: Smaller combatants often have insufficient power generation. Very often this is due to the timing problem above, but for lighter combatants, it is possible that they cannot generate sufficient force without greater efficiency.

- **Dry or loose mat**: If the mats are inadquately rolled or soaked, they will prove very hard to cut.

- **Dull sword**: The swords must be razor sharp in order to get them to cut the mat. We've never had a problem with an Angus Trim sword, however.

- **Instability**: If the cutting stand is insufficiently anchored, the mat will also be harder to cut.

For many of these problems, confidence is the main opponent. Because this is a highly personal art where it is hard to keep much hidden, problems of confidence cause tension and timing issues, sometimes resulting in a spiral that is hard to break. The instructor should watch carefully and stand ready to assist the combatant, offering some but not too much assistance and making sure that safety is observed at all times. In difficult cases, it may be necessary to substitute a "half mat" which will cut more easily and give the needed confidence needed to go on. I keep several in reserve when our class first cuts at just six weeks experience.

Reading the Cut: Cutting Forensics
Once the mat has been cut, a great deal about the blow mechanics by the physical effect of the cut on the mat. Ideally the cut should be straight, and the mat should fall without inertia to the ground near to the post. But there are common errors:

- **Mistargeting:** Results when the combatant misses the target or his intended point of landing. See above.

- **Pushing:** If the mat bends but does not cut, either there is a problem with the sword, the mat, or more likely, the timing is off and the combatant is trying to force the strike, rather than to cut. Often this is found in conjunction with errors of tension.

- **Slapping:** Slapping can occur either when the feet have not found proper purchase, or when the combatant uses his arms alone, rather than his body. This is generally related to problems of timing, or the feet are wrong, usually in terms of placement or weight distribution.

- **Incomplete penetration:** If the cut has not penetrated, the problem is one of power transmission. This is usually a blend of problems with timing, but it can also be related to the mat, the equipment, or the strength of the student.

All of the above, when they occur, can yield or reveal the confidence problems discussed above. Students should be strongly encouraged to "fight through" their confidence issues until they get a satisfactory cut (unless safety is at risk); sometimes the use of a "half mat" is a good starting point for confidence recovery as noted above.

If the cut is made, there are several interesting things that can be read from the cut, what I think of as "cut forensics:"

- **Straight, clean cut, mat drops to the floor:** This is the way it's supposed to be!

- **Straight, ragged cut:** This is often due to trailing the sword or attempting to draw it during the strike.

- **Curving cut:** The hands are insufficiently braced at the impact point, or, in most cases, the timing of the hand and feet is not yet perfect.

Within the Schola, we introduce the idea of cutting at an early phase so that combatants can be saved repeating their mistakes for many months. If they are successful, it is usually a good validation for the kinesthetics developed thus far. If it fails, then it gives immediate feedback on what needs to improve. Over time, the difficulty is increased with crossing and compound cuts and cuts against multiple mats in multiple directions.

The most common problem is shown at left, an incomplete cut. A ragged or curved cut, both symptoms shown below, suggest instability

CHAPTER TEN

STRIKING THE OPPONENT

The name of the game in swordplay is to strike your opponent *without being struck in return*. The combatant following this book now has several tools at his disposal: he should have a powerful set of *colpi*—*mandritto* and *manroverso*—from all three directions: *fendenti*, *mezani*, and *sotani* and can deliver a potentially deadly *punta*.

But how are these skills put to use? Medieval swordsmanship as recorded in the fighting treatises eschews the tendency to simply "strike and pray," aiming a blow at an open target and hoping that the opponent will not reply in kind.[1] Since the idea is *not* to be struck and potentially maimed or killed, *during training any double-strike should be viewed as a double-fail*. This is an important tenet of Schola training, designed both after the principles we find in the fighting treatises and in keeping with our experience in the training hall and within the lists.

Like any military encounter, establishment of control is the key issue. Seizure and maintenance of the initiative is of paramount importance. But initiative is *not* just another way of saying "offense." As we will see, seizing the initiative can be done with offensive or defensive actions, but it should always include opportunity for a successful attack. The trick is to make this attack in such a way as to reduce the chances that the opponent will be able to strike in return. No "strike and pray."

ONE WAY TO SEIZE THE INITIATIVE: *STRIKING FIRST*
THE FIRST MASTERS OF BATTLE

This concept is not clearly articulated in Fiore's text, but he does in several places suggest that "he who offends first" will be in a commanding position.[2] When fighting from the *poste*, whether the opponent is using Italian *guardie* or not, the relative positions of the combatants will yield certain openings and advantages. Once these advantages are sensed or created, the combatant may move immediately (with a great deal of Tiger or *celeritas*) to strike in such a way that the opponent is immediately attacked at his most vulnerable point. This comparison of one *posta* against the other is the essence of Fiore's fundamental techniques in his **First Masters of Battle**.

It does little good to make an attack against a place that your opponent has covered with his weapon, unless your intent is to control the weapon by contact in order to make an effective follow-on attack.

In every *posta*, there are some places that are well covered with the opponent's weapon, and others that are open. These openings[3] are present often for only a fraction of a second. A skillful combatant will begin to anticipate the development of an opening *before* it happens, although it takes time to accrue the necessary experience needed to fuel combat judgment. The first step is to see and recognize openings in a stationary opponent. Later training is focused on developing the linkage between position and time, and the judgment necessary to see and anticipate.

We have already seen, in Chapter 8, how the *poste* create opportunities and how they can simplify tactical analysis. When a guard is "broken," as we say in the Schola, the combatant feels an almost inexorable need to change his position; he is aware that a successful attack might be imminent and he responds by changing his position. An attack made at this moment, just prior to his movement, may well be successful.

Each *posta* has fundamental strengths and weaknesses. Although the advanced calculus of what and when to attack is beyond the scope of a book for novices, we have provided some shorthand notes on how the various *poste* might be successfully attacked. For the most part, this form of attacking strives to achieve a dual advantage of time and distance sufficient to ensure that the attacker's blade will land before the defender's attack can fully develop. I call this a *positional advantage.*

Note that when finding a positional advantage to exploit, your opponent often has exploitable openings of his own, so *it is vitally important to **strike immediately** once you perceive the advantage!* Use of the Lion is absolutely critical to exploit positional advantage, since it will only last for a moment.

Recall from our earlier discussion that the *poste* may be arranged in part according to their position: whether they are high, low or in the middle; and whether they are on the right, left or in the center. Attacking from as far as the blade as possible is a viable strategy. We call this *striking to the openings*, or striking where the sword is *not*. This is the simplest technique, akin to simple, *duo tempo* time management.[4]

For example, an opponent in **tutta porta di ferro** may find it difficult to counter an attack made to his upper left side, because it will take him a relatively long time to move across his whole body and from low to high, although he can increase his available time by increasing the distance by stepping back. But this strategy has some risk for the attacker: your blade is also far from his most likely attacking lanes, so one response he might attempt is to strike you in return—resulting in a double-strike, a double-fail.

STRIKING TO COVER (ATTACKING IN OPPOSITION)

To avoid a "double," your strike should be made in such a way that the opponent's likely attacks are checked by the presence of your own sword in a position of potential cover. We call this *striking to cover*, and a combatant who internalizes the principle will find himself much more confident and successful when making attacks because he is rarely uncovered. You will find good use for both *mandritti* and *manroversi* attacks, because the side you are attacking on matters.

In order to strike to cover against a stationary opponent, the combatant will find the most success (and safety) in *striking such that his hilt ends up on the same side as his opponent's.* The idea is to strike such that your sword will provide a defense against his likely avenues of attack. You make cover—or potential cover—as you attack. In some cases you may be making

contact or be at a point close to contact when you strike, a classical fencing state known as being "in opposition."[5] You cover as you attack.

If, for example, the opponent was in **tutta porta di ferro**, as above, and you are in **posta di donna destra**, you might make a conventional *fendente mandritto* to the left side of his head, but you would take care to ensure that your hilt ended up relatively low (because his guard is low), and on the opponent's right side (where his hilt is), or at the very least in the center of your body. In this way, his most likely avenues of attack are met with solid cover—or the potential for easy cover, with a minimal change in the attacking vector (see illustration page opposite, left).

Taking the same case, let's say you decided to use a *manroverso* and struck instead to the right side of his head. Your hilt could very easily end up on his left, and there would be nothing to make cover with, unless you took a radical action that did not involve the use of any recognized *poste*. You would be exposed to a double-strike. At the very least, you should make your attack such that hilt stays near the center of your body, in order to have a chance of covering a potential counter-attack (see illustration page opposite, right).

Now let's say that your opponent is in **dente di zenghiaro**, and you remain in **poste di donna destra**. Making powerful *colpo fendente mandritto* to the head, your hilt will proabably end up on your opponent's right side, far from his likely avenues of attack. You would once more be exposed.

*There are vulnerabilities in every guardia. In **tutta porta di ferro**, for example, it might well take a long time to make cover against a high attack on the left side.*

But if you made that attack *manroverso*, the hilt would naturally travel towards his, on your right side. If he attacks, you have cover. Or potential cover (see illustration below).

Let's look at another example. If your opponent is in **dente di zenghiaro**, you might find it smart to strike towards **posta breve** with a *fendente riverso*, your hilt moving towards your right hip. You can do this from either side by using crossing strikes.

Whenever you are being more conservative and striking towards **posta breve**, be sure to avoid the common temptation of exaggerating the hilt position too far from the hip. Fiore's **posta breve** seems to be different than the German guard **pflug**, in that it anchors in the center of the body (unlike **pflug**, which anchors on one side or the other). Although the German system works well, in the Italian the more central position maintains a greater flexibility.[6]

In the course of a fight, you must anticipate where an opponent's weapon will be at the moment your strike impacts and make the decision about where you'd like your sword to end up accordingly. In general, you will want to "follow" the opponent's sword, having your sword end up on the same side in case they react quickly and strike.

Striking to Cover

One of the most important unspoken principles in the First Masters of Battle material is striking under cover to avoid a "doppio" or double-kill.

In this example, Brian attacks with a fendente mandritto ❶*, hoping to strike* ❷*...*

...but it is likely that Andy will either make cover or, as in the bottom photo, strike simultaneously.

❸*Because Brian struck from the right side, he has a natural cover simply by redirecting his colpo from an intended posta longa to a covering posta breve.*

Had he struck manriverso instead ❹*, Andy would have been able to easily strike him in return because redirecting to cover would have been very difficult indeed.*

199

CONTROLLING THE CENTER

The second principle governing this section concerns keeping control of the crucial *center* of the fight. All of the central guards—**mezana porta di ferro**, **posta breve**, **posta longa**, **posta di bicorno** and even **posta frontale**—do a good job of controlling the center, but they do so at the expense of power, as there is a direct relationship between time and power.

There is a powerful advantage—maybe even a determinant one—in controlling the center, as crucial as control of the chess board's four central squares.

It is vitally important to control the center of the fight, akin to the four center squares on a chessboard.

Most simply, you control the center by having your sword dominate the area, keeping an "open line" between you and your opponent. When you strike short, intentionally or to make cover, you are trying to win or retrieve control of the fight's center. **Posta breve** is stabile, strong, and if you win the center you can attack with the *punta* in relative safety.

If your opponent's sword already dominates the center, you still need an open avenue of attack. You can create one by by stepping off the line (which is why there is very little plain forward-back footwork, and everything is done using traversing foot movements) and by positioning your sword in such a way that the center is covered. This cover has both right-left and high-low components.

HIGH-LOW

For attacks made at wide distance, the hilt could be relatively high, and it may need to be in order to reach your opponent.[7] This position is, however, extremely unstable and leaves the lower body exposed.

As distance closes, the risks increase. Fiore seems to recognize this, as his *poste* which are high are usually unstable (or *pulsativa*), while those closer to the ground are stable. In practical terms, the sword hilt must be kept low, until at the middle distance it is at the groin (or even below, per the Getty mss.)[8] This dramatically increases the stability and makes use of the whole blade to provide cover for much more of the body.

Many combatants make the fundamental error of raising their hilt when striking, thrusting or making cover at middle- or close-distance. You must work to keep your blade down!

If your opponent's blade is high, you can go under it for a successful attack. But in order to do so you must still be covered or have him

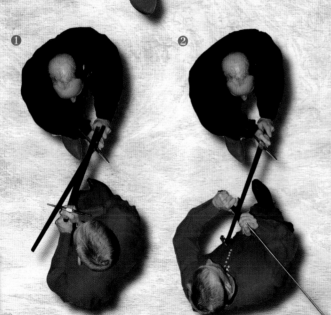

① ② ③

Changing the Center

When a sword commands the center of the fight ①, there are two main choices: to go through it, or around it, as Andy does here ②, using a mezza volta of the sword to change sides on Brian's cover in poste breve, striking him in the head and simultaneously finding his own cover ③.

"expended" in some way (which we'll discuss below). If you do not, he can simply drop his blade onto your head.

Take the example of an opponent in **posta frontale**. This *poste* is often used to make a capture against your blade following contact at the *mezza spada*, but many beginning and intermediate combatants make the mistake of failing to step forward and to complete the capture, leaving the blade only slightly crossed at the *punta*. It is impossible to capture the *punta*, as we will see in the next chapter.

Because his sword is high, the combatant may simply draw his own blade back a little and thrust underneath it. While this does "attack where the sword is not," it provides no cover to the combatant, and the opponent may well recover and strike downwards. Unless he has been fixed or expended in this position through the use of attacks against his **lynx** (psychology, falsing), his **elephant** (pushing or finding him off-balance), his **tiger** (you are just that much faster than he is), or his **lion** (he is unable to respond because he is wary), you may well find yourself the victim of a double-strike. Or you could get lucky. My own impulse in this instance would be to counter this vulnerability by extending my control using perhaps a secondary weapon—such as a hand—or to step out of *colpo* range as my thrust lands, using distance to find a superior position.

Similarly, your opponent may let his point drift too low. This often happens during a *punta*. As we mentioned in the last chapter, the *punta* should never be below the *forteza* during an attack. If it is, the blade is already expended (as we shall soon see), and it would be safe to simply fly above it with a *colpo* or *punta* of your own. Or, the weakness of the hand may be exploited to execute a fine disarm.

This happens also in **posta longa**, if the point is too low. A counter-thrust above the blade, made with opposition or contact, may prove succesful, as is done in many rapier treatises.

This principle is what underlies the idea of striking to **posta longa** if you're far away, but closer to **posta breve** as the distance narrows. When you're far away, the lower lines cannot be reached, so the hilt can rise in order to gain distance. But as distance closes, the combatant *must* lower his hilt, or the lower body becomes exposed. Keep your hilt low!

LEFT-RIGHT – STEPPING PASSO A LA TRAVERSA

For attacks at any distance, as your blade moves from side to side away from the middle of your body, one side becomes more open and the other one less so. This orientation is more easily understood by most beginners, as those without training will strike from side to side in an effort to get around a strongly controlled center.

As a defender, the most common method of controlling the center is simply to make cover with posta breve. While effective at controlling center via management of line, a combatant trained in the system knows how to manipulate both line and pressure to easily defeat such a defense. He can either step *a la traversa*—"step a little out of the way (fora de la strada, see chapter 6)—or he can make contact

with the sword to control it. Manipulation of contact is the essence of Fiore's *zhogo largo* plays, covered in the next book.

Against a defender in **posta breve** (or any center guard), the most effective attack is to use geometry against him. As an attacker, you can effectively strike parallel to his blade, easily striking the arm, hand, body or head. Keep the cross and the *forteza* in the center, using the power-portion of the blade to strike. Your castle defends you while the *punta* attacks (*forteza* means "castle"). By attacking parallel, you make it more difficult for the defender to make his cover, which relies on a crossing of the swords—by definition *not* parallel. This principle holds whenever the weapon is forward and the blade's committed angle is presented. It works also when fighting with a secondary weapon, such as a shield, a polearm or anything else. Attacking parallel to the blocking device will often yield success.

As a bonus, **posta breve** is only half-powered or may even be adopted expended (see below), dramatically reducing the opponent's available attacks. This further increases your potential for success if you maximize your own options while reducing your opponent's.

Another way to attack a strongly held center is to step off the line with the attack. Depending upon which foot is forward and which way you want to attack, you can use an *acresare* or a *passare* step, both on the oblique, to change where the center of the fight is for you and for your opponent, which has the effect of creating a new center—hopefully one open to your attack.

A stance will have one foot or the other forward. If the side you want to attack is on the same side as your forward foot, you would use an *acresare* to move the front foot "a little out of the way" (*fora de la strada*). As the step is made, the blade finds its target. This is quite fast, but not very powerful. We use it mainly as a "discomfiting" strike—explained below—followed with a powerful finish accompanied with a *passare*.[9]

If the side you want to attack is on the back foot's side, the movement is much easier, more elegant and faster. You simply accompany your strike with an oblique *passare*, as the little step with the front foot is unnecessary. Because there is only one step, it is overall quicker, but the *passare* is slower than the *acresare*, so initial contact is made slightly later. But it can be done in *stesso tempo* or single time, rather than in the *duo tempo* required for the previous attempt.

In either case, you can step obliquely to either side in order to change the center of the fight. What you have effectively done is to change the center of the fight, a very powerful initiative control mechanism. This is a fundamental skill that should be practiced exhaustively.

Against **poste longa** or any other *instabile* (thrusting) *posta*, control via powerful contact is better—simply strike the blade (and more importantly, the point) out of the way and strike. We'll use this more extensively in the *zhogo largo*, but for now it is a fine response to an opponent caught napping in **posta longa**, **posta di finestra**, or **posta di bicorno**.

EXERCISE
Exchange of the Thrust with Spears

One of the best ways to see "side to side" openings is using a lanza, or short spear.

Within the Schola we use the *lanza* as the first sparring weapon. We restrict its use to the point only--(intermediate students may use the shaft and may also slash). We introduce the lanza early in a student's training, because we believe it is as important to expose the combatant, as early as possible, to "mental" side of the fight. I believe this can only be done in a fight.

The *lanza* is a short spear, approximately 6' - 7' in length. We use our Revival Martial Arts spear tip, which allows combatants to compete using minumal equipment. A soft gorget, mask, and padded gloves are all that is required. We use an ash spear shaft 1 1/8" in diameter.

Use of the *lanza* teaches awareness and management of distance, introduces the idea of controlling the opponent's weapon before making an attack, and is a fun and relatively soft method of getting combatants used to striking an opponent and being struck in return. In a Schola context we also qualify new students with the lanza so that they have a weapon with which they can participate in tournaments, which adds a whole new level of competition to their base of experience.

To use the *lanza*, students are first shown the most common spear guardia, **breve la serpentina** (the "short serpent's" guard). Fiore illustrates this in the section where he presents fighting with one hand on the *mezza spada*, Getty. fol. 22v, although he provides the name in the armoured sword section, fol. 32v. **Posta breve la serpentina** can be adopted on the right or left, and it offers both leverage and strength.

To make a thrust from this position, the back foot is advanced with an explosive *passo* as the spear is catapulted forward towards **posta longa**. Students first practice transitioning from one side to the other, then making the *punta*, before working against an opponent.

Fiore's main technique for defeating a thrust is known as the **scambiar de la punta**, or the "exchange of the thrust." This technique is presented with the sword in two hands (Getty fol. 26v), but it also the technique through which he defeats all incoming thrusts with the lanza (Getty fols. 39r - 40r).

Students work to internalize this principle by arraying themselves in pairs, both in **posta breve la serpentina**. The **compagno** thrusts, aiming at an open target and trying to strike it. The **scolaro** attempts to deflect the thrust with his spear-shaft, then immediately (ideally in one motion) follows-on with an attach of his own along the now open line of attack. The idea is to seize control of the incoming weapon with an *incrosa*, a "crossing," moving the opponent's point off-line.

Once the combatants are comfortable with the exercise, it is profitably tested in an open sparring environment. Using just the *scambiar de la punta*, a combatant has enough technical ability to be able to compete in a tournament at a rudimentary level. Advanced work adds **rompere de la punta**, "breaking" the thrust, working from Fiore's other *guardia*, especially **dente di zenghiaro**, **tutta porta di ferro**, **mezana porta di ferro**, **posta di donna**, and **posta di finestra**.

Getty fol. 22v, posta breve la serpentina, an excellent guardia for the lanza

*Fiore's main technique for answering a thrust is to "exchange" it, which he calls **scambiar de la punta**. In the plate above, Getty 39v, the scolaro has deflected the incoming punta with his shaft, making an incrosa, simultaneously thrusting along the now-open line in the center. Working with the lanza is a very good way for students to see and begin to use this concept.*

Posta di finestra

Breve serpentina

Frank Petrino

Barry Eisenberg

Dan Sepham

The lanza or short spear is an ideal first sparring weapon, as students can vigorously compete early in their training with less safety equipment, learning about the key principles of distance and time, as well as exercising both mind and body in a competitive environment.

Students of Guy Windsor at Brian's Helsinki spear seminar

203

COILING-EXPENDING-RECOILING

One major aspect of the opponent's state that mut be observed is not only position, as we have been exploring, but also his power state. This determines much of his flexibility, as well-powered *poste* (those which are *pulsativa*) are the most flexible, while those which are *stabile* have fewer, and those which are *instabile* fewer still. If you can observe and take advantage of your opponent's power state by reading his body through the hips, you can make better choices in the selection of an effective attack.

A combatant in a *guardia pulsativa*—**tutta porta di ferro** or the **posta di donna**—should have his body coiled with potential energy and can deliver attacks along many avenues. These *poste* are highly flexible and must be treated with respect.

But if the combatant has not set the hips, he robs the *poste* of their power. The more power is removed, the lower the threat. In terms of blows, it is important to remember that the blades need a certain amount of power to be effective, as they are primarily weapons that wound by crushing along a concentrated edge, rather than by cutting along a thinner one. As such, power is required. No power, no threat.

In this state, the only remaining threat is from the point (which needs little power), or a secondary weapon, such as the pommel or the hands, feet, or maybe the head). This is a moment of opportunity for the attacker, since you can safely strike and not worry as much about the *colpi*, which reduces the need to strike to cover, though you must watch for a serpentine *punta* or an attack with a secondary weapon.

When a combatant strikes, he begins with potential energy stored in the body. As the blow or thrust unwinds, the muscles expend their energy, tranforming it in to kinetic energy and speed. The process is a spectrum, which begins as completely wound and ends when the combatant's power is expended, at which point he must recoil in order to recover the potential energy.[10] There is a moment, when the blow or thrust ends, when the potential energy has been expended. It is a time of great weakness, a weakness often compounded when the elephant is lost as well, which can happen when combatants over-commit to an attack or when he attacks from emotion (exuberance, frustration, anger). The attacking combatant must reduce his exposure at this time by recoiling as soon as possible to recover himself to a more coiled state—the *reposta*—while the defender may seek to exploit his weakness by watching for it. If your attack fails, it is critical that you immediately *reposta* (recoil) to recover your power potential and thus preserve maximum combat options.

Note that the *guardia instabile*—such as **poste longa**, **posta di bicorno**, and **poste di finestra**—are often expended and are only lightly powered at the best of times. It is crucial when in this *poste* to maintain the base of power needed to strike, and the combatant should closely observe his opponent and attack immediately if the opponent rests in an expended state.

THE UNREADY OPPONENT: BALANCE

Another opportunity to strike presents itself if your opponent loses track of his elephant and finds himself off-balance. This often happens when a foot is misplaced during movement, or when he over-commits to an attack against you that is thwarted, when he has little training or body-sense, or when he fights from emotion, as mentioned above.

An opponent who has lost his Elephant must reset it before he can effectively strike with power. He will find it hard to recover his power until he has first reestablished his balance, which extends the time necessary for a recovery. Take advantage of this and move quickly to strike if your opponent is essentially expended because he has lost his Elephant.

Should you lose your balance, it is smart to recover your elephant while concentrating on making blade contact in order to achieve cover.

Although it takes some experience to select the right attack in order to make an attack using simultaneous cover, the rewards are well worth the effort.

UNCOILING WITH A TUTTA VOLTA

*There is an interesting case for **posta di finestra** that illustrates a principle discussed in play #4 of the zhogo largo, the **colpo di villano**. If **posta di finestra** is struck, she can easily make a colpo by turning the blade with a tutta volta—making a complete circle—and striking to **posta breve**. The result is a devastating strike that also lines up the point for a finishing thrust.*

DISCOMFITS & FOLLOW-ONS

There are many blows which, although wounding, will not be sufficient to kill or incapacitate the opponent. I call these blows *discomfiting*, since they can "reboot" or force a "refresh" of the opponent's mental tools, which in turn allows for a more definitive finishing attack.[11]

Such discomfits often happen when time is short and an attack has either been insufficiently charged or is interrupted before it can fully develop. Discomfits often occur from stabile *poste*, such as **mezana porta di ferro**, **dente di zenghiaro**, or **posta breve**. Although *coplo* from these *poste* are effective because they are fast, this speed is achieved at the expense of power. Conversely, a fully-powered *poste* that is *pulsativa*—such as **poste di donna**—trades power for time.

The main benefit to a discomfiting strike is that it gives the combatant more time to recoil and deliver a definitive attack. When time is short, a quick reposition and discomfit can recapture the initiative and set the stage for dominance.

Because of this, discomfiting strikes are often made using an *acresare* step. Why? Because an *acresare* step is quicker than a *passare*, and the reason to make a discomfit rather than a regular *colpo* is because time is short. As with all strikes, a step is beneficial because it complicates the opponent's combat calculus and changes the center of the fight. Once the discomfit is complete, the follow-on is usually made with a passing step in order to fully power it.

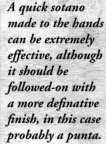

Snipe to the Hands

A quick sotano made to the hands can be extremely effective, although it should be followed-on with a more definative finish, in this case probably a punta.

SNIPING

While these wounding strikes do rack up points in a tournament, they are largely ineffective in a combat sense unless they are followed up with a follow-on attack. Within the Schola we refer to failure to follow-up as *sniping*, which is shorthand for an incomplete attack.

Many attacks may be used to follow on. *Colpi*, *punte*, *tagli*, *prese* (grips), and blows with the hands or even throws are all available. As are strikes with secondary weapons, such as kicks, pommel-strikes, etc.

But the most effective follow-on attack is one that takes advantage of the temporary "reset" in the opponent using the closest effective attack. This means one done with power that takes advantage of the available time, and requires the smallest adjustment to work. Following blade contact, it will often be a thrust, since only a small adjustment is needed to "find the point," as we will see in Play #5, explored in the next chapter.

For example, a discomfiting strike might be made to the hands from **mezana porta di ferro** (see photos below left). While this sharp blow might cause some discomfort or even break some of the small bones in the hand, it is likely that the opponent will quickly recover—and now he might be less than pleased. Instead of allowing him the opportunity, take advantage of the orientation of the blade and make the fastest effective follow-on attack, in this case perhaps a *punta* to the belly (since his arm actually braces the thrusting blade for you!).

For another example, suppose that a well-armoured opponent was struck in the bascinet (his helmet) with our longsword. While the longsword could not possibly penetrate even a poorly made helmet[12]—it does have the effect of causing that temporary "refresh," which gives time for a more powerful blow, or perhaps a thrust delivered under the bascinet, to the vulnerable throat.

Discomfiting attacks might also be thrown as an underpowered main effort when there is insufficient time to properly power the blow or thrust. In this case, the relatively light contact is used as a distraction while a more telling blow is made. In a mortal encounter, this would be effective, although I would not recommend it in tournaments.[13]

As an example, a combatant attempts to capture his opponent's sword by stepping forward from an *incrosa* at the *mezza spada* to **posta frontale** (see play #6 in the next chapter). But his opponent is wise to the maneuver, and steps back, so that the capture not only fails but he clears his point for a *punta* of his own. Because the sword is but poorly charged in **posta frontale** (it being used to extend control and usually to come to the *prese* or *zhogo stretto*), and worried about the thrust, the combatant throws a light *colpo* to the head. It lands without much force, and he should immediately follow it up with a telling and powered blow. But it may well distract the opponent enough to forestall his effort to follow-on. Again, this would not be recommended in a modern tournament, but it would work as a response of last resort in a combat situation.

Essentially, discomfiting attacks should **always** be followed with powerful strikes, or with the ability to make a powerful strike tempered by judgment. Remember to accompany your follow-on attack with a *passare* step in order to maximize power.

COMMON ATTACKING PROBLEMS

The most common problems in attacking our opponent—other than his responsive defense—are incomplete power generation, mistimed attacks, or attacking into the weapon.

Incomplete power generation

By far, a lack of power is the most common reason for an attack to fail, and there are many possible reasons. The most common are:

- **Elephant not set:** If you try to attack without your Elephant, odds are your attack will fail. The best solution is continual work on always having a stable fighting platform so that your Elephant is always available to support the attack or to receive one. Do not fight from emotion, as this predisposes you to miscalculate distance.

- **Attacking while expended (or failing to recoil):** A very common mistake for novices and some intermediates is failing to recoil or attacking while expended. For a finishing attack to be effective, it must be powered. If you don't have sufficient power, then consider the strike discomfiting and follow it up with a more powerful finish.

- **Sword disconnected from body:** Students often strike using the arms alone, which generates little power and makes recoiling very difficult. The arms tire quickly, and their blows are rarely effective.

- **Timing between body and sword:** Often the body and feet will be mistimed. If the feet are early or late, then the hands land late and the arms are forced to provide the power and the benefits of using the entire body to power the attack are lost. They must go together.

Attacks made early or late

The next most common mistake seems to be making a late attack. The usual culprit is conscious thought: you are thinking with the forebrain during the fight, and it is too slow. By the time you have the throught about an opening, it is gone.

By extension, early attacks are usually caused by the same thing, but in this case you plan your attack in the forebrain. Students often become fixated on a technique, trying to force it into a situation where it does not belong because they are focused upon it. Attacks must be executed immediately when it is timed—if they are planned, they are often telegraphed and easily countered.

In either case, training and sparring will develop helmet time and will help to reduce the intrusion of conscious thought, because the confidence and neural "preplans" will reduce the reliance on cumbersome analysis. This analysis and planning should be done beforehand, so that under the stress of combat the fighting platform may simply preform.

Telegraphing

Telegraphing is the modern term applied to the action of an opponent who signals his intention before he makes it. This is the origin of the term "tel" in poker, where almost imperceptible signals of posture, gesture, facial expression offer the opponent clues to your intent. In the extreme, they act as subversive counter-intelligence agents; your opponent even know before you do what you intend! Not a recipe for success.

For example, you might always begin your *fendente* thrown to the right from **posta di donna destra** (which makes sense). But what if you occasionally threw one from **posta di donna sinestra**, as a *manroverso*? The use of both *mandritti* and *manroversi* in seemingly random order will make your tels and patterns harder to read.

Or you might always flick your elbow upwards, or step, or cock your head, or something before you strike. It's hard to become conscious of these small movements, but they are important to eliminate. You must reduce your tels. Watch recorded versions of your fights, and observe for patterns. Have your training partners point them out. Better in the training hall than on the tournament field, or worse, on the hypothetical battlefield! You may be astounded by what you do before you attack.

Patterning uses conscious tels in order to lead your opponent's belief. This is an intermediate technique covered in the next book, but it is good to know it exists.

Attacking into the weapon

Another curious mistake students make is to attack directly into the weapon. If this is done with the skill to control the weapon and to pin it into place, then it is a good tactic. But often it happens that the combatant strikes from side to side, right into the teeth of the defense, without *enough* thought, essentially flailing.

In some instances the intent might be to overwhelm—as Johannes Liechtenuaer advised—but more often it seems that the hope is to "strike and pray" for an opening. Usually, attacks made parallel to the defensive tool or with an offline step will be much more effective.

Attacking out of distance

This error is very common to beginners, but seems to become less common as students gain experience and a sense of combat distance. It is very common in drills. When making this mistake, the attack is made or signalled early, while the combatant is still out of range. Indeed, the attack may be complete while out of range! Learn your distance and do not attack until you have it.

EXERCISE
Striking to Cover

Objective: Build perception concerning the safest side to strike to against different poste.

This exercise will involve each *zugadore* working through various *poste*, discussing between the combatants whether the *scolaro* should strike *mandritto* or *manroverso*.

Compagni begin in tutta porta di ferro, scolari in posta di donna destra. Each scolaro decides whether he should strike mandritto or manroverso, executing then a slow iteration of the attack. The compagno must not counter.

Once the scolaro has completed his attack, the two combatants discuss openings remaining to the compagno that could have been struck during the scolaro's attack. In the case of the first attack, the correct response is a mandritto the strikes to the center, with the hilt perhaps a bit on the scolaro's left (the compagno's right), so that the scolaro's sword is in a position to cover should the compagno strike. *The scolaro's hilt should end up in the center or on the same side as the opponent's hilt.*

Once the first set is complete, the compagni then choose a new *posta*, as do the *scolari*, repeating the exercise about which side to attack. Note that when the compagni begin in a center poste, such as mezana porta di ferro, posta breve or posta longa, the scolaro is best service to change the center of the fight with a traversing step.

This idea of "striking to cover" is critical to success. In parallel, combatants should point out if either becomes expended, striving to avoid expenditure by recoiling the hips as or just after the attack lands.

ATTACKING THE POSTE

Below are tricks I've found personally useful in working with and against Fiore's poste. These are personal observations only, added here for additional information.

POSTA DI DONNA DESTRA (& SINESTRA)

Because the sword is drawn far back—away from the center of the fight—**Posta di donna** is often best countered with distance. If you can work yourself in close enough, it will be hard for the opponent to bring poste di donn'a potent attack strength to bear.

Attacks that move the combatant to the opponent's left during the strike will have the highest probability of success. The left arm or hands are also frequently exposed, and might be in range with careful pre-attack subtle manipulations of distance using small *acresare* and *dicresare* steps. The overwhelming threat is from a *fendente*, delivered either *mandritto* or *manroverso*. A *punta* might also be attempted, especially low on the left side.

Remember that the combatant in this or a similar position wants to step forward boldly and attack with power, and that this action will, if allowed to develop, break any attack you might have in progress. If this happens, you will have to abort your attack and make cover with stability, usually in something like **posta breve**. He can also make more distance for himself, waiting for a moment when your sword is far away (such as on a low-line) before closing once more.

Against a **posta di donna destra**, I personally favor *fendente mandritto*, because the arms are frequently forward, and my sword moves along a line that I can redirect to make cover in **posta breve** without much adjustment. If my opponent steps back during the attack, I keep the point on-line and may finish with a strong *punta* to the face or chest. Alternatively, I sometimes allow the sword to fall naturally to **mezana porta di ferro**, making an immediate *sotano* if the combatant steps forward to exploit the apparent advantage from above (I can step back if I need to in order to strike the arms or hands, or set his blade aside with the Schola play #4, discussed in the next chapter).

For **posta di donna sinestra**, all of the above is true, except that there will be a more pronounced advantage on your left side, especially down low. For the same reasons cited above, I similarly prefer *fendente manroverso*, attacking the guard in a way that will be likely to provide cover should I fail.

TUTTA PORTA DI FERRO

Tutta porta di ferro is also *pulsativa* (and very stable), **tutta porta di ferro** represents a double threat. From this guard it is easy to set aside most attacks and can initiate them just as easily. It is sometimes difficult to defend from other low attacks on the same side (ie, from an opposing **dente di zenghiaro**) using either a thrust or *sotano roverso*. Coversely, attacks from the upper quarter, from the *fendente mandritto*, can be effective if the range is managed properly. Also, the left arm is sometimes exposed.

Personally, I find **tutta porta di ferro** one of the most difficult *poste* to attack. An *incrosa* cannot be made without the opponent moving, so my favorite strategy is to demand the incrosa by striking to **posta longa**, which I quickly redirect into **posta breve**, and the *zhogo largo* can then follow Fiore's tactical prescriptions, which we'll discuss in the next book. But on a basic level, my preference would be to strike as far behind the *poste's* power as possible, using a *sotano roverso*, hoping to disarm the *guardia's* power and resultant strength in setting aside by reducing its available time.

Alternatively, I sometimes try to match power with speed. I will select **mezana porta di ferro** or, less ideally, **posta longa**, attempting to find an open avenue for a thrust. My opponent either reacts or is open for an immediate thrust.

Mezana porta di ferro

Being low and in the center, **mezana porta di ferro** is most vulnerable from above. Either a *mandritto* or *manroverso* thrown along the *fendente* line has some chance of success. Stepping obliquely will help. A thrust is also sometimes effective.

My preference is to adopt one of the *guardia* along a high line, attempting to draw the opponent out into **posta breve** or **poste longa**. From there, as mentioned above, any of the *zhogo largo* plays are possible. But if the opponent does not move, then the *fendente* can be thrown immediately, combined with an oblique *passare*.

Another option is the break the *posta* with **posta longa**. If the combatant reacts, the swords are comfortably crossed (guarding against a *sotano* to the hands or forearms). If not, a *punta* may be immediately delivered.

DENTE DI ZENGHIARO

The Boar's Tooth is relatively easier to break than is **mezana porta di ferro**, because the combatant is committed on the left side. Thus, a *fendente manroverso* will have a very powerful chance at success, although a *mandritto* may also work. Similarly, a *sotano manroverso* will also be difficult to counter, as will a low thrust. Another main vulnerability is the right arm, which is often out front.

I generally break **dente di zenghiaro** using **posta di donna sinestra** or **posta di donna destra**. In either case, I will assess the combatant to see whether I think he adjusts his distance or not. If I can step to the left, so much the better. I have found that a very quick *fendente mandritto* is particularly effective.

POSTA BREVE

Since variants of **posta breve** are used both in nearly all Eastern and Western sword arts, it is useful to know how to attack it. As long as the guard is in the middle, *fendente* can be thrown on a mostly vertical line, striking to the head, neck, shoulder or arm. In addition, the hands are out front, and are vulnerable to rising *sotani*. Most critically, the sword is forward, and available for easy control (although this is the subject of our second module, the *zhogo largo*).

Personally, I will attack straight into **posta breve**, seizing control of the sword with contact and then using that contact to decide where to make the final blow or thrust. However, it is very effective to adopt a low *guardia*, such as **mezana porta di ferro** or **dente di zenghiaro** and attack the arms or hands, since they are forward and are an easy target. From the **poste di donna**, I like to make an aggressive, fast step forward to strike vertically, parallel to the opponent's sword.

Although we don't recommend Schola students make great use of **posta breve** as a starting place, it will become extremely useful once the blade on blade work (*incrosa*) study begins. Posta breve is a common endpoint, however, so combatants fighting in the style will frequently find themselves in it.

POSTE LONGA

Since **posta longa** uses *malicoso* to break all other *poste*, it must be immediately addressed. Although it threatens with an effective *punta*, the blade is inherently unstable, so it can be attacked. But assuming that the combatant is trying to strike for contact with the opponent in this case rather than to his sword, the hands and arms should be considered vulnerable from above or below. From below, the arms, hands, and belly are all attractive targets. From above, the hands and arms, shoulders, head and neck are most interesting.

If you have a longer sword, a thrust looks even more promising, since the opponent has little leverage with which to set it aside. And, as Fiore states, "he who has the longer sword will offend first." If the sword is relatively high, thrust low. If the guard is low, one can in general thrust high.

Although I prefer to break **posta longa** with a direct attack against the blade, I really like attacking it from below with a *sotano* to the hands or arms. This attack is followed up with an immediate thrust in an effort to end the fight, since a blow to the arms will generally not be fatal, but will instead be discomfiting (as we'll discuss below).

POSTA FRONTALE, POSTA DI FINESTRA, POSTA DI BICORNO

These *poste* are generally adopted when the swords are in contact, so different methods will be needed to attack them, as we'll see in the next book.

-Notes-

[1] This does not particularly apply to the SCA's sword and shield combat, since the presence of the relatively large and indestructable shield gives the combatant both offense and simultaneous defense without having to worry about maintaining contact with his sword. But it does apply to the SCA's and other combat society's general use of polearms and two-handed weapons (or even single-handed sword), where too little training is the norm. In sport fencing, this problem is the reason for "right of way," which presupposes that a fencer must first counter his opponent's attack before commencing with his own. Personally, I find the artifice of "right of way" cumbersome, since it removes perhaps the most critical aspect of historical swordsmanship and the use of the sword or any weapon in a self-defense situation. It works for the sport, but to me it creates dangerous weakness in the students of the art that takes considerable personal skill to overcome.

[2] Particularly when discussing the *incrosa* in the *zhogo largo*.

[3] In traditional fencing terminology, the openings are known as "lines," potentially an artifact of the fascination with geometry that began to capture the attention of fencing masters from the time of Filippo Vadi in the mid-15th century.

[4] Other techniques, such as striking into the weapon or parallel to it, are more akin to *stessi tempi* or *mezzi tempi* attacks, covered in the next book. *Due tempi* means "two times" or "double time." It is the most simple and the most common method of responding to an attack, even amongst very experienced combatants.

[5] In fencing discussions, this concept is well-treated, but it appears to have been unarticulated by the medieval masters. Even so, I believe it was known, because the principle is well demonstrated in the tactics and principles illustrated in both the Italian and German systems. For a more in-depth treatment of attacks in "opposition," see Stephen Hand's fine article in *SPADA: An Anthology of Swordsmanship in Memory of Ewart Oakeshott*, "Counterattacks with Opposition: Influence of Weapons Forms," pp. 48-54.

[6] I do not intend that the German system is in some way inferior to the Italian. In this instance what is gained is hardly free, since the speed and cover gained from the central position is made at the expense of power.

[7] As in the case of many Renaissance and later sword treatises, where the focus is on the thrust, which has a longer effective range than does the cut or strike.

[8] Getty mss. fol. 24r (**mezana porta di ferro**, **posta breve**), fol. 32v (armoured **mezana porta di ferro**).

[9] The *acresare* must, in this case, be placed where the back foot would be once the *passare* is done. This requires a good sense of combat movement—judgment—and a great deal of practice. Otherwise, there are extra little adjustment steps necessary, which decreases the efficiency and thus the effectiveness of the pass.

[10] For this reason I teach this as "recoiling" rather than as "rechambering," since there is an on-off connotation with chambering (as on a gun) that inaccurately describes power in the human body.

[11] I take this language from the 15th century treatise *Jeu de la Hache*, the poleaxe treatise which I have translated from the French.

[12] I am a reasonably accomplished armourer, and having made many helmets in the style of the 14th and 15th centuries I can say without hesitation that there is no way a man on foot will penetrate a helmet of iron or steel with a sword, unless he finds a major flaw (such as an incomplete weld) in the helmet. Armour works—but there is always a way. Usually, a strike to the head will discomfit the combatant sufficiently that a second, more deadly strike may be brough to bear. It is this assumption, presumably, that drives the rules in combat societies and in historical feats of arms that recognize head blows against a helmeted combatant.

[13] I don't recommend it because these "light" blows are often thought of as assaults on the opponent's attempts to call out blows that lands upon him, the usual standard in medieval feats of arms as conducted in the modern day. Because he is now thinking about the quality of the blow, there is chivalric pressure upon him to give your blow the benefit of the doubt, otherwise there may be questions about his honor. Taking advantage of this reality is considered to be unchivalrous at worst or poor technique at best.

CHAPTER ELEVEN

DEFENDING WITH THE FIRST MASTERS OF BATTLE

n the previous chapter, we looked at how to seize the iniative by striking first. But sometimes the opponent will strike first, and it is critically important to recover the initiative as soon as possible, responding to an attack with an immediate remedy that can set up an attack of your own. If you allow the opponent to retain the initiative, simply blocking successive strikes or backing up, then you stand a very good chance of facing defeat.

As in any combat situation, extending your control is a good way to increase the chances of success. As the fight closes distance, your control must commensurately be extended also, or your risk rises dramatically. Within the medieval systems great care is taken to recover control in the event that the initiative has been lost to your opponent, and as we will see, there are three main ways this control manifests within the system.

DEFENDING YOURSELF

In order to strike your opponent, you must remain active, alive and able to fight. This generally means not being struck by your opponent's sword. With the medieval longsword, you have one weapon with which to strike and defend.

With the sword there are three main methods of avoiding an opponent's strike: using distance, by making cover, and by attacking the opponent's sword using a **rebattemento**. Other techniques are to extend your control with *prese* (grips) against the opponent's weapon or his body (the *abrazzare*), but we reserve most of these techniques for more advanced students.

Within the Schola, we teach these principles in the same manner found in the original treatises, using "plays" to highlight broader principles. It is important to bear in mind that the plays are simply **expositions of principles**, not merely, "If *a* happens, do *b*." A skillful combatant will strive to internalize key combat principles and then react according to training and judgment, often applying a principle through his own expression of it to solve a knotty tactical problem.

Our **First Masters of Battle** students work through our six plays, striving to internalize the principles underlying defending with distance, with cover, and through the *rebattemento*. The plays we've selected are drawn either from Fiore's explanations that accompany the *poste*, or from the next section of the treatise, the *zhogo largo*. In a very real sense, they are a shorthand way of referring to complex solutions to combat problems.

TRAINING WITH THE PLAYS

Within the Schola, plays are first done using demonstration by the instructor and a senior student. Questions are taken, and the demonstration and its underlying principle explored until the students appear to understand the principle(s) at work. Next, the students array themselves into two lines, one side always taking the *compagni* part, the others the *scolari*. The *compagni* always set up the play, while the *scolari* execute it. In the main school, *compagni* and *scolari* are always on the same side of the hall to reduce confusion.

Training is usually done in light helmets, gorgets, light gloves, gambesons or fighting jackets (if available), and metal trainers.

Students always begin with each new partner with a heartfelt salute. The instructor will call out cadence for the exercise, and students execute it on the count. This allows the instructor to observe more students at once. Cadences are called, "Salute… ready….1…reset…ready….2…reset…etc." Repetitions are made to 5, 7 or 10, and then the line rotates. Each student then rotates one place to the left, while those at the ends switch sides of the line. If there is an extra person, they rotate out and may take a quick water break. Once the line has progressed all the way through, each student has made between 50 and 100 repetitions against many different opponents and has had the opportunity to see different variations.

When there are a lot of students or when time is short, we may "switch roles," before rotating, which means it is uncessary to work through the whole line before rotating.

If students are then ready, they might progress to working with sparring trainers, either the carbon-kevlar or shinai/rattan based ones. This allows for greater speed, and prepares the students for full sparring later.

Advanced students are encouraged to work on variations of the play, and the *compagni* are generally encouraged to think about—but not to execute—counters. Active dialogue between the combatants is a useful tool for training their eye and their combat judgment, but it must be kept efficient or it will interfere with the number of repetitions, hence the structured count.

DEFENDING WITH DISTANCE

At the most basic level, the combatant uses *distance* as a primary method of defense. In defending with distance, the feet (and the head) are the most important tools. In an extreme case, a combatant can distance himself from the fight, as is usually expected in an encounter on the street unless the threat is imminent. In a fight with swords, distance is broken down in to four main measures:

1. **Out of Distance:** Further than the combatant can strike with a single step. I strongly recommend not adopting any offensive demeanor or *poste* at this distance, as it conveys information to the opponent and may provoke an encounter. Alternatively, one can appear strong and ready, securing a key psychological advantage (attacking his Lynx and his Lion).

2. **Wide Distance (*misura larga*):** Essentially the distance at which either of you can attack by taking a single *passare* step. Strikes at this distance are often made along a high line, since the upper body is closer, but if the opponent also steps forward with his defense—as is usual—you may find yourself unexpectedly in *middle distance*, discussed below. In this case, your hilt must be lowered, or your lower body will be uncovered. The head, arms and hands are the primary targets at this range.

3. **Middle Distance:** This is the more dangerous range at which the swords will cross—finding the *incrosa*—simply by having them naturally in front somewhere between **posta breve** and **posta longa**. At this distance, the body, arms, neck, head and upper legs are all in distance. This is the distance for Fiore's first and second **Masters of the Crossed Swords**, the place from whence most of the *zhogo largo* plays he presents occur.

4. **Close Distance (*misura stretta*):** As Guy Windsor skillfully relates, this is the distance at which the opponent's arms are within range of a *prese*. This is wrestling distance, the most dangerous distance because your whole body is exposed to potential attacks by the sword and your limbs are available for *abrazzare*.

As the distance shortens, the danger increases because a larger variety of attacking options are present. This is why it is imperative: *as you close distance, you must commensurately increase your control over your opponent's weapon* and/or your potential to make cover.

This book focuses primarily upon the wide and middle distances. Being out of distance relates to tactical choices and control of psychology, which will also be discussed in the next book, while the close distance relates to the *zhogo stretto*, a topic for our third book in the series.

Schola combatants demonstrate the different distances. The first zugadori are out of distance, too far to engage one another in a single unit of time. Therefore, they need not be in a poste. The second pair is in misura larga, where with a single step either may engage. The third pair have already engaged, and have met with an incrosa. The fourth pair are close enough to engage with the abrazzare, and so may be said to be in misura stretta.

DISTANCE AND TIME

Distance and time have a proportional relationship. If your weapon has more time to travel, then you have the ability to supply more power. This is why the well-wound *poste*—**tutta porta di ferro** and the **poste di donna**—are held fairly far back. The whole body has time to wind and the resulting power is at a maximum.

But this works at the expense of available time. It will take longer for the **poste di donna** to strike than it will for **tutta porta di ferro**, but they are the most powerful strikes. Hence, you need a wider combat distance to use the pure forms of **poste di donna** effectively because it will take longer for the sword to arrive on target, whether in the attack or in making cover. You need a little less for **tutta porta di ferro**, so you can be closer to the opponent. By extension, you need still less for *poste* that are closer to the center of the fight, such as **porta di ferro mezana**. But what this *posta* gains in *time* it loses in terms of *available power*.

At wide distance, must of your defense is made with *measured judgement of distance*. Novice combatants often seek to stay at or just out of wide distance, fearful of being struck or unsure of what do to in order to find security at one of the closer distances. This is normal, and must be countered with training, drill and/or experience.

Under the stress of an attack it does very little good to simply back out. First, it is for the most part easier to move forward rather than back, so a determined attacker might easily outpace your retreat, overtaking you. Second, if he docs not follow, then you havc simply givcn up information about how you move and respond, information he can use against you in successive attacks. Third, you cannot easily see behind you, and there may well be obstacles present that can interrupt your planned escape in a less than elegant fashion. Finally, just backing up fails to retrieve the intiative, so your opponent retains the advantage.

Instead of backing up, the better plan is go advance into the attack, seizing ground and potentially contact with his sword to secure a solid advantage. This is a crucial principle of the system that takes courage, experience and training to execute.

Our **First Play of the Elephant,** beginning on the next page, is a useful way of illustrating the principle.

SLIPPING THE LEG
Drawn from Fiore's Fifth Play of the Zhogo Largo

In this play, the operant principles are the management of distance and the geometric laws that govern fighting at this range. Because distance is the most elementary principle employed to keep the combatant alive, we will cover it first.

Distance management has been discussed above. The geometric principle at work is the Pythagorean theorum, which discusses the relationship of Euclidian geometry between angles in a right triangle. In the play, the combatants begin at wide distance with the *compagno* in **tutta porta di ferro** or **posta di donna destra** and the *scolaro* in **tutta porta di ferro**. The *compagno* strikes downward for the *scolaro's* leg. In response, the *scolaro* steps *tornaro* with a *mezza volta*, changing his stance from one side to the other while denying (or voiding) the leg as a target. At the same time, he strikes *fendente*, trying for the opponent's head.

It sometimes happens that the combatant will end up too far away for the head to be struck. Usually, the arms or hands can be struck instead. In this case, the point is lined up already with the body following the strike to the arms—which will probably be discomfiting rather than crippling—and the point can be thrust home using an aggressive *passare* step.

This attack works because of the geometry explained by Pythagoras in his theorum. *In any right triangle, the area of the square whose side is the hypotenuse (the side of a right triangle opposite the right angle) is equal to the sum of areas of the squares whose sides are the two legs (i.e. the two sides other than the hypotenuse).* Expressed mathematically, $a^2+b^2=c^2$, where a and b are sides of a right triangle and c is the hypotenuse. Thus, the distance b will always be shorter than the distance c. From a combatants' point of view, it is shorter to attack along the high line than to strike below.

This attack is almost always successful if the distance is properly managed. It succeeds also because it occurs in *stesso tempo*—single time—which gives the opponent very little if any time to react. As the opponent's attack fails, the combatant's lands, giving little opportunity for a remedy.

If the distance is even wider, the combatant might miss entirely. In this case, the *scolaro* should collect the sword inward as he realizes he will miss, recoiling towards **posta breve** with the point aligned with his opponent's face. This attack is made in full beats—*duo tempo*—and so risks the opponent having a chance to respond. Still, it is better than making no effort to recover the initiative at all.

There is also a chance that the back leg would be struck. In this case, the *compagno* was too close, so you don't have the available distance to defend with. Instead, you should have attacked his blade using a *rebattemento*, which we'll cover in the next three plays.

SUMMARY

Scolaro & **compagno** in **tutta porta di ferro**
Compagno strikes for the leg while stepping forward
Scolaro steps *tornaro* with *mezza volta*, changing sides, and simultaneously striking *fendente* for the head.

- If the head is out of range, strike the arms or hands and follow up with a thrust to the body. Intermediates should be making the strike to the head 75-80% of the time.
- If everything is out of range, redirect your attack to **posta breve**, point online, and thrust.
- If the back leg will be struck, use a *rebattemento* instead (see **Third Play of the Elephant**).

$$A^2 + B^2 = C^2 \qquad A=58" \ B=54" \ C=79.24"$$

Here we see the Pythagorean Theorum in action. The opponent has struck, but will miss his target because the distance to the leg (expressed as C) is a hypoteneuse whereas the opponent's strike is one side of a right triangle (expressed as A). If the swords and sword-arms are of equal length, the strike to the head is shorter because the lever-arm connects at the shoulder, while a strike to the leg is further away. Fiore implores his students not to strike to the leg, unless the *scolari* has fallen.

Troubleshooting

- **Scolaro off-balance**: This is often caused by stepping back and across, or gathering the feet. The motion needed is a simple *mezza volta*, a change in sides from the right to the left, made in balance. If the feet are crossed—a common error with a *tornare* step—or gathered—a common response by experienced fencers—then the Elephant has not been maintained.

- **Scolaro strikes along a strange line or is not in position to make the follow-on thrust**: Usually this is due to the *scolaro* making a *sotano* rather than a *fendente*. The *fendente* should be made along the same jaw-knee line that is normal for a *fendente* rather than sweeping from side to side. This keeps the point available as a threat and the blade available for cover, should it be required.

- **Right leg struck**: The play began too close. In this case, the *rebattemento* in front would have been used instead. Increase the distance slightly and try again.

- **No leg struck, even had the scolaro not moved**: This is a common error made by the *compagno*, who strikes when out of distance. Until he gets a feel for the distance, he should test the distance first by stepping forward with one step and extending his blade, touching the forward leg and then stepping back into his *poste*. In this way he will be able to see how far he should be from the target.

Slipping the Leg

Slipping the Leg

DEFENDING WITH POWER
Rebattendo/Rebattemento & Redoppio/Redoppiando

As we see when the combatant is too close to avoid a strike to the leg, interposing with his own weapon is the only alternative. Whenever the blades are crossed, even for a moment, the state of *incrosa*—"in the cross"—is made and both control and information are passed between the combatants.

There seem to be two forms that making the cross takes. The first is a simple cover, what Fiore often expresses within his text as the sword "covers me"—*me coverto*—(discussed below). But a cover taken without action to immediately retrieve the intiative—a *block*—leaves the initiative in the oppnent's hands. Within Fiore's system, a cover is always accompanied with an effort to make a definitive counter-attack in order to recover the initiative. More than that, if a passive cover is transformed into an active one—a *rebattemento* or "rebating"—then the control is more strongly projected and the combatant has a much greater chance of turning the tables on an aggressive opponent. Within the Schola we don't *block*, we *attack* the opponent's weapon.

The idea of *rebattemento* is central to Fiore's theory of defense not only with the sword, but with many weapons. Using the sword in a single hand (Getty 22v.), he will set the weapon aside, following-on with a *punta*, *colpi* or *prese* of his own. He does the same with a *daga*, a *prese*, a *lanza* or an *azza*, in or out of armour, on foot or on horseback. We can see many instances illustrated and discussed in the text, and combatants striving to master the system must have a command of this central principle.

A *rebating* motion is **one that meets the opponent's weapon with power**. It can be made against a thrust, as Fiore first presents in the passage on the **tutta porta di ferro**, or it can be made against a *colpo*. It may be made on either side of the blade, front or back. In any case, you must have sufficient power to get the job done, and the amount of power necessary will depend upon whether you are attacking into the side of an attack (Play #2), the front of the attack (as in Play #3), or from the back (Play #4), as we shall see.

To attack in **front** of the blade means meeting the attack **power on power**, head-on. The German school would recognize this—possibly—as *anbinden*, or a bind in front. This circumstance will frequently happen, as we will see in the **Third Play of the Elephant** below, when you counter your opponent's *fendente mandritto* with a *fendente mandritto* of your own. Because you are countering power with power, you must begin in a *poste* that is *pulsativa* or full-powered. This limits the *poste* available for the *rebattemento* but the technique establishes solid control at the the point of crossing, the *incrosa*. If you lack power, you still try to make a passive cover.

To attack from the back or **behind** the blade requires less force but better timing. This is equivalent to establishing contact behind the blade in what the German school might recognize as *hinterbinden*. In these cases the *incrosa* is made behind the blade and its power is used against it as a direction rather than as a hard stop. A traversing step helps to set the maneuver in motion. Because less power needed is to direct the blade along a tangent, a *rebattemento* behind may be made from the center (especially **porta di ferro mezana**) or from the same side, what we call in the school a *redoppiando* ("redoubling").

To attack from the side—as against a thrust—little power is needed, although Fiore does express the principle first from the *pulsativa posta* **tutta porta di ferro**. In this case the blade is met and taken all the way to the ground, a technique he repeats in play #8 of the *zhogo largo*, the **Breaking of the Thrust**.

In all three cases the *incrosa* is made as an attack against the blade rather than as a static block. This is a critical distinction, because recapture of the initiative is key.

In the plays that follow we'll see how the *rebattemento* is done against a thrust (as Fiore first presents it in the longsword text), against a strike from the front, and against one done behind the blade. Each plays slightly differently, and taken together they give a complete set of remedies for a strong attack made against you.

REBATTEMENTO

Our term **rebattemendo** *is our term for the many variations stemming from the Italian verb* rebattere. *There are many variations in the text, as Colin Hatcher has demonstrated, including* **rebattere** *itself (Getty fol. 22r), the 3rd person form* **rebattera** *(Getty fol. 31r),* **rebatte** *(Getty fols. 23v, 24, and 31).* **Rebattendo** *is additionally found on 22r, in Fiore's description of bis basic beating motion.*

REBATTEMENTO VS PUNTA

*Drawn from Fiore's description of Tutta Porta di Ferro &
the Eighth Play of the Zhogo Largo*

*In this sequence from the Getty fol. 20v, Fiore
discusses the single-handed principle of the
rebattemento (rebattendo) against all three
different kinds of attacks, including thrusts
(as in this play), strikes (colpi, as in play
#3), and thrown weapons.*

For this play, students learn how to meet an incoming thrust and to set it aside. For the purposes of the play, we begin with the *compagni* in **porta di ferro mezana**, and the *scolari* in **tutta porta di ferro**. Initiating the attack with a *punta*, the *compagni* step forward with their attack. To meet it, the *scolari* also step forward, hammering down onto the incoming thrust with a powerful *fendente*, driving it to the ground (a *rebattemento*). This is the essential portion of the play, from which there are numerous follow-on possibilities.

For novices, the play continues when the *compagni's* sword has been driven completely to the ground. From this position, the *scolari* should have his hips recoiled, and will reply immediately with a *sotano roverso*, striking to the arm or head. Because this strike begins from a half-powered *poste*, it is likely to be discomfiting rather than final, and another telling *fendente* to the head should follow. The footwork required will depend on the exact distance between the combatants, but the usual progression uses a *passare* to accompany the initial attack on the blade, an *acresare* to make the discomifting attack, and another *passare* (forward or back) to complete it the second *fendente*.

There are weaknesses in the way this play is made. Because it is made in *duo-tempo*, the opponent has an opportunity to answer. He might answer by rising behind the blade, by stepping in for a *prese*, or he might back out.

To cover these weaknesses, intermediate students can work on refinements that work in different times in order to reduce the opponent's chance to respond. Instead of driving the blade all the way to the ground—Fiore's **Eighth play fo the Zhogo Largo**—he might instead simply move the point offline, so that his remains trained on the opponent in what amounts to the *Scambiar de la Punta*, the **Exchange of the Thrust**. In this case, immediately as the point comes on-line the combatant

must continue forward with the thrust in an unbroken forward motion. In this way his reply is now *mezzo-tempo* (half- or broken-time), and it is difficult for the opponent to reply.

Another intermediate variation will be to execute the play in *stesso tempo* (single-time), which gives even less of a chance for the opponent to reply. In this case, the *scolaro* will make an oblique step to the right such he catches the opponent's blade on his but simultaneously strikes the *compagno's* head. The two should ideally land at the same time, which makes the counter *stesso tempo*, (single time) and much more difficult to deal with.

Other possibilities include stepping onto the opponent's blade (as Fiore does in his presentation of the *zhogo largo* play, fol. 27r), extending your control further with a *prese* to the opponent's arm. This technique works with mixed weapons, such as sword against spear, or dagger against a sword thrust. But the essence of the play—*establishing absolute control over the weapon through powered contact from the side*—should be the key point developed. Novice students should not progress to working on the variations until the main portion of the play can be done perfectly and at speed.

SUMMARY

Compagno begins in porta di ferro mezana and the scolaro in tutta porta di ferro

- **Compagno steps forward with a simple *punta***
- **Scolaro steps *passare* and strikes the *mezza spada* with a hammering *fendente*, driving it to the ground.**
- **Scolaro delivers a discomfiting *sotano* to the head, followed by a fully powered *fendente*.**

Rebattemento vs punta

As Andy (in red) makes his thrust, Brian meets it with a powerful rebattemento, breaking it.

Troubleshooting

- **Leaning into the Attack:** Many times a novice *scolaro* will lean forward as he drives the opponent's weapon to the ground. The Elephant's tower must be kept straight, otherwise the head is brought closer to the opponent's array of secondary weapons (fist, etc.).

- **Struck by the Punta:** The *scolaro* fails to begin his strike in time, to step off the line, or to make the *fendente* in such a way that his sword makes cover as he strikes. Often the kinesthetic delivery of the *fendente* is at fault—a *fendente* from **tutta porta di ferro** is a fairly complex but effective maneuver that must be practiced until it can be thrown efficiently. Raising the hands is a common error: the pommel begins and remains near the belly-button throughout the strike, rather than being raised.

- **Blade arrives early:** Usually this is a function of anticipation, and the covering action is started before the thrust. As in a combat situation, the *scolaro* can try to regain contact—if there is time—by coming back with a *sotano roverso*, once more encountering the blade. Fundamentally, the *scolaro* should strive to make the attack at the right time, after the attack has begun, and not anticipate it (which is hard, in a drill!).

- **Point escapes, blade doesn't go to the floor:** The usual cause is the *scolaro's* failure to attack at the *mezza spada*, striking instead near the *punta*. Remember that it is not possible to capture at the *punta*, only at the *mezza spada* or *forteza*. In this case the *forteza* is too far away, and you'll likely be run through before your counter lands. Another cause is the *compagno's* efforts to counter. He may withdraw his blade early, recoiling towards **posta breve**. This is a natural response—and the correct remedy to the play—but it robs his companion of the opportunity to train. Don't counter until the play is working perfectly time and time again!

PLAY #3

REBATTEMENTO VS COLPO
A variant on Fiore's description of Rebattemento in the Tutta Porta di Ferro

"Anchora **rebatte** le punte a terra e sempre va cum passo e de ogni colpo ella fa coverta. E chi in quella gli dà briga grande deffese fa senza fadiga"

"Also, it **rebates** the point to the ground, going always with a *passo* and [from] every *colpo* she covers. And in which she brings great defense without fatigue."
[Getty 23v, upper left]

This is the ending point for the duo-tempo (double time) version of the rebattemento, *when the opponent's blade has been beaten down to the ground.*

Extending the technique developed in the last play, students now counter the more common *colpi* using the same technique. For purposes of the play, both *zugadori* begin in **tutta porta di ferro**, although any *posta pulsativa* will work.

The *compagni* open by stepping forward with a simple *fendente mandritto*, accompanied by the usual *passare* step, striking for the *scolari's* head. The *scolari* respond with a *fendente mandritto* of their own, striking directly for the *mezza spada*, attacking the sword, once more attempting to drive it to the ground and then finishing as they do with the last play, with a discomfiting strike accompanied with a more devastating follow-on.

Variants may be practiced from **posta di donna destra** and **posta di donna sinistra**. Further variants should be made with the *compagno* targeting other portions of the body, such as the leg (this is the case we encountered in the first play if the action begins too close—the *scolaro* must in this case attack the *compagno's* sword (or his arms) to drive the attack down).

Remember that the essence of this play is **meeting and controlling the opponent's sword through power-on-power contact.** This requires that you be in a *posta pulsativa* on the opposite side. For example, if your opponent is in **tutta porta di ferro**, then you must be either in **tutta porta di ferro** or **posta di donna destra**. If he is in **posta di donna sinistra**, then you must be in that *posta* also, since it is the only one on the correct side that has enough power.

There are a world of intermediate variants on the play, most of them found through the use of different timing. For example, a *stesso tempo* version will strike the opponent's sword and his head (or arms) at the same time,* but this usually requires an aggressive *passo a la traversa* to the right side. But as Fiore seems

to prefer *mezzi tempi* attacks, these too may be found by striking to a point that your *punta* is lined up with his upper body, throat or head; continuing the motion forward with a devastating thrust. Or, his blade or arms may be bound once the control has been established, etc. But as with all intermediate variants, they should not be worked through until the fundamental play is working.

Intermediate students should also work on experimenting with *mandritti* and *manroversi* in conjunction with the play. For example, the *compagno* begins as before in **posta di donna destra**, striking *fendente mandritto* towards your head. You find yourself in **posta di donna sinistra** (on the wrong side for the play to work), but you are *pulsativa*, so you try to strike *manroverso fendente*, and see if you can make it work. Another essential set of variants for the intermediate uses the *rebattemento* in front against the *sotani* on both sides. This is extremely effective, as gravity will assist the *scolaro* to find his mark and increases his power while the *compagno* fights against it.

The *rebattemento* in front describes a fundamental tenet of medieval swordsmanship: An over-bind, bind-above or bind in front should be done with *power*, controlling the opponent's blade and capturing it between the your weapon and something else, such as the ground, or at least clearing the center of the fight. Making and keeping this control is essential when fighting with sharp blades when fighting without armour, and the principle is well articulated in the surviving treatises.

---

* This *stesso-tempo* variant is loosely equivalent to the German play *Zornhau*, where an incoming attack is met with a "strike of wrath," to use Christian Tobler's translation.

Rebattemento vs corpo

SUMMARY

Compagno begins in tutta porta di ferro or posta di donna destra. **Scolaro** begins in porta di ferro mezana.

- **Compagno** steps forward and strikes *fendente* mandritto for the head
- **Scolaro** replies by stepping *a la traversa* behind the blade, striking *sotano*
- As the *incrosa* is made, the *compagno's* blade will be redirected to the *scolaro's* right
- While this happens, the scolaro's blade should recoil towards an abbreviated poste di donna destra
- Once recoiled, the scolaro must immediately strike *fendente*

Troubleshooting

- **Rebattemento too weak or late**: This error is caused either by the *scolaro* being late in his execution, or because he has insufficient leverage in the *incrosa*. Leverage is governed by the relative distance of the hilts from the swordsman's bodies; the point at which the cross is made on the blades; and the height of the hands. Generally, leverage can be increased by changing the center of the fight by stepping *passo a la traversa* and by keeping the hands near the center of the body, or at least between the hips. Alternatively, this can be caused if the *scolaro* began in an uncoiled *posta*, such as one that is *stabile* or an incompletely charged *guardia pulsativa*. Another cause of this error can be

passively trying to block rather than to aggressively and forcefully attacking the opponent's blade. This is a decisive action, one that hammers down upon the opponent's sword and takes command. Much *lione* is needed, supported by a strong *ellefante*.

- **Blade alignment appears to be wrong**: This often happens when the *scolaro* attempts to change the angle of the strike, or when he begins from the wrong *posta*. In the first case, a *fendente*—from jaw to knee—is the correct angle, rather than the horizontal angle that novices often attempt. In the second case, the *scolaro* may be in a *posta pulsativa*, but on the wrong side, placing him behind the blade.

REDOPPIANDO VS COLPO

A variant on Fiore's description of rebattemento and the "redoppiando" expressed in the PD colpi mezani

*These PD figures showing the incrosa have been modified so that the left-hand magistro's sword is **behind** his opponent's, the arrows showing the relative travel of each sword in coming to this point in our Play #4.*

Perhaps the favorite of the Schola plays of the Elephant is the *rebattemento*-behind, usually called the *redoppiando*. This variant on the rebating action in attacking the opponent's blade is far more elegant, requires less time and energy, and ultimately leaves the combatant in a better position to make a strong follow-on attack.

A *rebattemento*-behind or *redoppiando* works differently from the last play. Instead of meeting force with force, it **redirects the opponent's blade along a tangent** by providing an impulse of force from the *back* of the blade, rather meeting it in front.

In order to find the back of the blade, a different relationship between the combatant's *poste* is required. While the *rebattemento* in front takes place in opposing *poste* (right side vs right side, left side vs left side), a *redoppiando* or *rebattemento*-behind can be done from mirroring *poste* (right vs left, and visa versa), or better, from a stable central one, especially **porta di ferro mezana**.

If the core motion for the *rebattemento* in front is a *hammering* motion from above, the essential motion for a *redoppiando* is a *lifting* or *pushing* motion that "redoubles" the power in the original strike, redirecting it slightly out of the way. The *rebattemento* and *redoppiando* provide a symbiotic pair of actions which are essentially strikes that can be directed at the opponent's sword.

To execute the core play, the *compagni* begin in **tutta porta di ferro** (or in a variant, in **posta di donna destra**) and the *scolaro* in **porta di ferro mezana**. As the *compagno* steps forward with an aggressive *fendente mandritto* for the head, the *scolaro* also steps forward and slightly off the line, stepping behind the incoming strike (to the left, for an opponent's *fendente mandritto*) and striking the back of the blade with an ordinary *sotano*. The lifting action provides an impulse to the blade, pushing it harmlessly to the

right. The *scolaro* continues his *sotano* towards an incomplete **posta di donna destra**, striking the opponent powerfully before he can recoil and respond. If done correctly, there is a great deal of time for power to be generated by the *scolaro* because the *compagno* must first arrest his downward movement, then recoil and recharge it, finally responding.

Novice variants of the play are trained from the right and left sides, and working from the central *posta* (**porta di ferro mezana**), but also from poste on mirrored sides (**dente di zenghiaro** and **posta di donna sinestra** versus **poste di donna destra**; **tutta porta di ferro** and **posta di donna destra** versus **posta di donna sinestra**).

An adept *compagno* may notice that one available counter is to simply reply in kind as the opponent's blade lies atop his. This obsvervation is an expression of the over-binding principle discussed in the last play: if the opponent's blade is over yours, extend or maintain pressure to keep it down. If, however, you find your blade under his, as soon as the pressure abates you can redirect his blade

SUMMARY

Compagno begins in tutta porta di ferro **or** posta di donna destra. **Scolaro begins in in** porta di ferro mezana

- **Compagno steps forward and strikes** *fendente mandritto* **for the head**
- **Scolaro replies by stepping** *a la traversa* **behind the blade, striking** *sotano*.
- **As the** *incrosa* **is made, the compagno's blade will be redirected to the** *scolaro's* **right**
- **As this happens, the scolaro's blade should recoil towards an abbreviated** poste di donna destra
- **Once recoiled, the scolaro must immediately strike** *fendente*

Redoppiando
ve colpo

by stepping forward and lifting. **If above, push down; if below, lift up.** In this way, you could theoretically exchange *redoppiandi* back and forth for several exchanges, and we have in the past used this as a drill to instill the principle.

Just as *fendente-sotano* pairs form the fundamental strike-pairs that characterize blade movement in Fiore's system, so do *rebattemento-redoppiando* pairs define strikes against the blade, and they are made on the same line and using exactly the same movements.

Intermediate variations on the blade begin from the *scolaro* in **porta di ferro mezana** and working against both *mandritti* and *manroversi*, taking the attack and stepping behind it each time, accompanied with the *sotano* and finishing as usual. More difficult variations begin from an overbind (the ending point for plays two and three, with the opponent's sword on top), and from **posta breve** rather than **porta di ferro mezana**.

From **posta breve** *colpi mezani* result in the pushing motion that Fiore may have meant in his discussion of the *redoppiando* in the Pissani-Dossi discussion of the *colpo mezano*. The point drops under and behind the blade, and combined with a step behind it, it is "redoubled" and pushed harmlessly out of the way. In this case, a thrust may well be able to be found in *mezzo tempo*, rendering counters even more difficult.

An important intermediate variant on the play is to strike to the opponent's arms rather than to the sword using the same footwork and the same *sotano* bladework. From a tactical point of view, this may even be seen as superior—try to step such that you can strike the opponent's hands or arms, but if that is too dangerous, then go for the blade. Either way, you are covered and have alternative targets depending upon how the situation develops.

Troubleshooting

- **Scolaro hit with the fendente**: There are two main culprits that usually cause this. The first is being late, which is hard if a pure *sotano* is used in combination with an offline step behind the blade. One cause is often that the *scolaro* uses a circular—rather than linear—motion to intercept. The blow should be a linear *sotano* that rises from below and just happens to intercept the blade on its way towards **poste di donna**.

- **Stepping to the wrong side; not stepping; stepping back**: One common error is to step to the wrong side. The *scolaro* must step obliquely—using a *passo a la traversa*—behind the strike, not in front of it. If the combatant fails to step, he leaves himself rooted and the opponent may well take advantage. If he steps backward with the initial step, he may well miss entirely.

- **Scolaro too close to make follow-on fendente**: Distance must be managed with measure and judgment, so the steps needed that may accompany the *fendente* must vary to bring the *scolaro* to the right attack distance: this may require a *tornare* rather than a *passare* forward.

- **Follow-on fendente strikes with mezza spada or even forteza**: As with the last error, the distance between the combatants may be close, or too close. As with any close strike, the *scolaro* should strike towards his hip, keeping is hands low. This is an expression of "Striking long to **posta longa**, striking short to **posta breve**," as we say in the Schola.

- **Blade ends up on the wrong side, in front of the compagno's blade**: This will happen in combat, so the fight should continue on from this point. The *scolaro* may, as in our **Sixth Play of the Elephant**, raise his weapon to capture the opponent's blade in **posta frontale**. No matter which side of the blade the *scolaro* is on, he has excellent follow-on possibilities. Fundamentally, the problem is usually due to the *scolaro* making a circular motion with the blade rather than a linear path to intercept the back of the opponent's blade.

SOTANO TO THE HANDS

One variant on this fundamental motion, which many combatants have both used and found exasperating, are rising strikes for the hands made from **porta di ferro mezana** or from **dente di zenghiaro**.

Instead of striking to the arms, or to the sword, the rising *sotano* simply strikes directly into the hands, potentially crippling them. Some students are very quick to seize on this technique, using it remorselessly against their frustrated sparring partners.

The play works because the student has not, prior to making their *fendente*, controlled the opponent's blade. This leaves the opponent free to make the *sotano*, and the closest target are the combatant's hands, which are hard to defend. In addition, most novice and intermediate combatants allow their swords to drift too far out in the attack, resulting in a sloppy attack led with the hands. This leading suggests a strike to the hands, and some opponents are more than happy to oblige!

The best counter is to first control the blade before attacking. It can be attacked directly—with a *rebattemento*—or it can be drawn to expenditure through a feint. But if the blow has already begun, and the combatant notices the opponent making the strike (which is hard, since it is fast), he can retrieve his attack conservatively back into **posta breve** instead of **posta longa** (recoiling in the process), which should deny the hands as a target and reestablishes stability and at least some potential energy—hopefully with the point lined up for a powerful thrust.

If this continues to be an issue, have the students drill, drill and drill against *sotano* to the hands wearing very good sparring gloves or full gauntlets, and they will eventually internalize the efficiency needed.

DEFENDING WITH CONTACT

As discussed in the last section, defending with a single weapon requires that the combatant either defend himself with *distance* (through his judgment and his feet) or by *contact* with his weapon.

The last three plays looked at aggressive attacks on the blade known as *rebattemento* and *redoppiando*. These are relatively gross—but powerful—methods of attacking the blade. There are also times when an attack on the blade—front, back, or side—will not be feasible (usually because the combatant is surprised and must react quickly).

At these times, simply making cover—interposing the combatant's sword between one's self and the opponent's weapon—will be useful.

COVERING WITH THE BLADE

In order to **make cover**, the blade must intercept your opponent's attack, or his potential attack. This is the concept discussed extensively in the last chapter, when we explored *striking to cover* as an offensive action. *Making cover* is the defensive version of that principle.

If your opponent strikes first, and you cannot or do not wish to attack their blade in return, you may instead simply make cover by keeping your hilt relatively close to your body and seeking to catch the blade at the *mezza spada* or the *forteza*. A *scolaro* cannot easily catch the sword at the *punta*, where the margin for error is very small.

It is important that the combatant should turn his body with a *mezza volta*, or coil it on the same side, as he makes cover in order to allow for an immediate counterattack. This recoiling action minimizes the risk of expenditure mentioned in the last chapter. Similarly, as he gets closer to the opponent, his *guardia* should also be progressively lower, until it reaches a point at or below the groin, as Fiore shows in the illustration of **posta breve** from the Getty edition of his treatise. This is absolutely necessary, since a hilt that is high leaves the lower body exposed, defended only with the threat of an attack from above. The closer you get to your opponent, the lower your guard should be.

THE GEOMETRY OF MAKING COVER

The attacker strives to attack parallel to one side of the blade or the other, or to go under/over it. The defender strives to thwart the parallel by creating an acute angle that interposes his blade and by keeping his blade low enough that going over or under it is difficult and risky.

For the most part, the blade is kept in a *vertical* orientation, varying only thirty degrees or so in either direction except when making a *tutta volta* action.

A *horizontal* orientation of the blade defends nothing. Try placing the sword horizontally at your chest, and seeing what is covered. You will find just a little bit of your hand might be defended—everything else is exposed. The same is true when your blade is extended—you can defend only with the point and cross if you have the requisite distance.

The hilt should never be above the *punta*, as discussed in the last chapter, because this is an exceptionally weak position, not shown in the manuscript, subject to disarms and incapable of launching a powerful attack.

For the defender, these are two main components to keeping himself covered. The first is to keep his blade down, squeezing as much defense as possible from the blade's length. The second is to move the hilt conservatively from side to side in response to an attack, creating acute angles that interpose his weapon and make his cover. It is important that the tip of the sword remain trained on the opponent, and that the hilt move, rather than the tip.

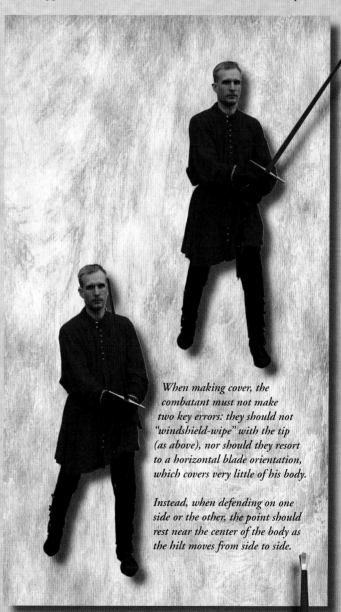

When making cover, the combatant must not make two key errors: they should not "windshield-wipe" with the tip (as above), nor should they resort to a horizontal blade orientation, which covers very little of his body.

Instead, when defending on one side or the other, the point should rest near the center of the body as the hilt moves from side to side.

EXERCISE
Making Cover from Posta breve

The *scolaro* stands in posta breve. The *compagno* attacks with successive *mandritti* and *manroversi*. The defender should move his hilt from side to side, keeping the point trained on the opponent's eyes while catching the sword at the *mezza spada*. It is as if a string held the sword-point to the ceiling, and the hilt moves from side to side under it. The tip must not move in a "windshield-wiper" motion. The *scolaro* should strive to keep the sword hilt close to his body—between the hip bones—always coiled or recoiled and ready to make a powerful thrust. As the *compagno* attacks from further away, the *scolaro's posta* can extend closer to posta longa, but he notice that as he does so, his leverage and stability decrease.

STEPPING UNDER OR BEHIND COVER

One way to increase the effectiveness of making cover is to reduce the time necessary to make it. If the sword moves at x speed towards the position it needs to cover, you can increase it only be working on the speed of the sword itself, which can be done through training. However, you can also move the body—y—as well. If you move both at the same time, you can cut the time needed to make cover by nearly half. The head or body moves away from the blow, and the sword moves towards the covering position. The result is what I call *stepping to cover*, a technique that can dramatically increase your effectiveness at making cover.

INCROSARE (EXTENDING CONROL)

Once the blades cross, even for a brief moment, they are said to be crossed, or *incrosare*. Being *crossed* means the movement towards you is not only checked, but that information now begins to flow through blade pressure (*sentimento di ferro*) between the combatants. This information can lead to substantial control if the combatant studies the *incrosa* learns to apply a few simple principles *immediately*. Most fights with swords will end up in some form on *incrosa*, and the majority of Fiore's work on the longsword in the *zhogo largo* plays are devoted to exploiting it to advantage.

One of the key aspects of the *incrosa* is that both combatants are bound or crossed, and that the information flows both ways. Because of this, the speed with which you react is crucial.

Another principle is that the quality of the cross can differ in terms of pressure. It can range from extreme binds (à la the hilt-to-hilt both-faces-in-the-closeup scenes in Errol Flynn or *Star Wars* movies) to the fleeting contact or even near-contact as

the blades "taste" the guards in **posta longa**. Reading the pressure of the bind is perhaps *the* key skill in finding success, and in the second book we will spend considerable time developing these skills. But in a nutshell, if there is little or no pressure, you drive through the bind as fast as you can. If there is a little pressure, change sides with a *mezza volta*. If there is considerable pressure, conserve momentum and allow your opponent's blade to inform your own with a *tutta volta*, striking to the other side. These are Fiore's tactics as presented in his *zhogo largo* material.

Incrosa at the mezza spada from the Getty, fol. 25v

A second aspect of the *incrosa* is *leverage*. In the bind, you would ideally like to have a leverage advantage, perhaps in addition to any other advantages you might already possess. Leverage is given by keeping your sword relatively closer to your body than to your opponent's, and by making the *incrosa* closer to your *forteza* than to your opponent's (remember, there is no leverage at the *punta*). Natural strength is also a factor; a larger opponent can generate more leverage power than can a smaller one, so for lighter combatants control over leverage is one way to help reduce a larger's opponent's advantage. Using leverage, as we will see, the point can be brought powerfully and quickly to bear.

Overall, the idea is to **extend your control to the maximum extent possible**, then to use judgement (the lynx or *cervino*) to decide what is appropriate in a given circumstance. Control with sharp weapons is first found using **distance**, then with **contact**, and finally by extending your control by **capture** with grips (*prese*) against the weapon or its user. As the combatant closes, he must also extend his control, and this is precisely what Fiore does and how he presents his ideas in both the *zhogo largo* and *zhogo stretto* sections of his treatise.

ATTACKING FROM THE INCROSA

At the novice level we focus on how to bring the weapon's most potent and lethal aspect to bear from the cross, the point. This will be the essence of the **Fifth Play of the Elephant**, *Finding the Point*. In the **Sixth Play of the Elephant**, *Capture in the Forteza*, we will look at how to advance and capture the blade at the *forteza*, which serves as the gatehouse for the *zhogo stretto* (close-play) techniques.

There are other fundamental actions which may be taken from the *incrosa*, and we'll focus in Book II on how to read and use *sentimento di ferro* in combination with the three *volte* to formulate actions against the opponent. Together, they represent a complete set of response principles applicable to just about any hand-to-hand situation, and by the end of our second book, we hope the combatant has a sense of completeness with which to approach a fight with the sword in two hands.

SEEKING THE INCROSA

Since the *incrosa* is so useful, why wait to make cover to use it? Indeed, seeking the *incrosa* is one way to secure a known position, assess the opponent's intent and reduce his options before attacking. As such, many combatants will strike first for the *incrosa*, reserving their judgement about which attack to use until they can read the pressure and intent of the bind (*sentimento di ferro*). This is why **posta breve** is such a weak place to defend from for a student of the system, since it passively offers the blade for the opponent to engage.

FINDING THE POINT
Based on Fiore's 7th play of the Zhogo Largo, Scambiar de la Punta, and effective use of the thrusting poste

Once the *incrosa* has been achieved, the quickest attack is usually a thrust. Fiore offers several interesting thrusting positions, and as we have found each has a specific place. Perhaps not surprisingly, they work very much akin to the German technique of *winden*.

Much speculation has accompanied discussion of Fiore's *poste instabile*, especially **posta di bicorno**, **posta di finestra** and **posta longa**. I would note that all are thrusting *poste*, as they emphasize the point. To this group I would add **posta breve**, and using all four together with Fiore's *Exchange of the Thrust* (*Scambiar de Punta*) we have constructed this play in order to set principles of thrusting firmly in the student's repertoire.

Novice combatants should begin in Fiore's *Second Master of the Crossed Swords*, that is, crossed at the *mezza spada*, usually with the right foot forward and with the hilts low, in the groin area. From here they will *find the point* using **posta breve**, moving the hilt to the same side as their *compagni's* sword (and moving it out of the way), while keeping the point aligned with the *compagni's* face. Gradually, the speed can be increased until the follow-on thrust is done in one smooth motion together with setting aside the opponent's opportunity. This should be practiced with the swords crossing on both the right and left.

It is of paramount importance that blade contact be held during the whole maneuver and that the hilt remain low in order to make cover. If the *scolaro's* hilt rises with the thrust, then his belly becomes exposed and his arms increasingly open to grips or *prese* (the *abrazzare*). This raising of the hilt seems to be a natural (if ill-advised) response, and combatants must strive to keep the hilt down for their own safety and success.

The next variant done by the novices is for the *compagno* to again adopt the *Second Master of the Crossed Swords*, but this time with his hilt held higher, say between the chest and ear. Now, response by the *scolaro* is to roll (or wind) up into **posta di finestra** on the same side, maintaining blade contact and stepping forward with a thrust. This action is very, very close to the German *winden* from *Pflug* to *Ochs*, but in Fiore's **posta di finestra**, the hilt remains below the *punta*, as is clearly shown in Fiore's illustration from the Pisani-Dossi. It becomes readily apparent that the *scolaro* can only roll to the same side as the *compagno's* sword, since the alternative leaves him completely and obviously exposed.

The final variant is done using **posta di bicorno**. In this case, the *compagno* softly closes the line, meaning that his blade closes the opening but does not press firmly against the *scolaro's* blade. In this case, using a *passo a la traversa*, the *scolaro* steps into **posta di bicorno**, which restores his leverage and sets the point against the *compagno's* chest. Novice *scolari* then work with their *compagni* to mix up all three, selecting the right response for the right pressure and position. With sufficient repetitions, finding the moment to make a thrust should become second-nature, blindingly fast, and extraordinarily effective.

Thrusts are one method of dealing with an *incrosa*. *Colpi* are another. Still another, covered in the next play, involves extending the *scolaro's* control still further by capturing the blade at the *forteza*.

Finding the Point

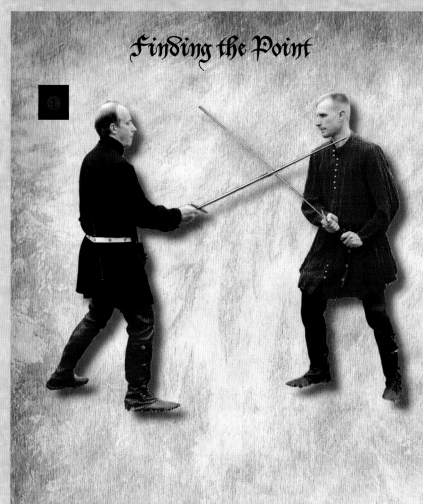

Troubleshooting

- **Scolaro hit by compagno's thrust:** This can be caused by a variety of mistakes. First, the *scolaro* may move the top of the blade, "windshield-wiping" it across instead of moving the hilt. Or, he may not have stepped *a la traversa*.

- **Double-strike (a *doppio*):** The usual cause is the *scolaro* turning his sword the wrong way, leaving the way open for his opponent to thrust. Remember that "opposition" or contact must be maintained in order to control the blade. Another reason is often a failure to step *a la traversa*, usually to the same side as the opposition.

- **Scolaro loses control of the compagno's sword:** Often this is due to selecting the wrong *posta* (especially **posta finestra**, against **posta breve**). In roughly eighty percent of the cases, **posta breve** will suffice. **Poste di finestra** is only used when the opponent's hands are relatively high (as may often happen against an opponent trained in the German system), and **posta di bicorno** when the line is softly closed.

- **Compagno drops under the guard:** This often happens in **posta di finestra** if the forward momentum is not made immediately. In the ideal, the thrust is made in *stesso tempo*—single time—as the *scolaro* rolls into *finestra*, so that the *compagno* is struck simultaneously. If the *scolaro* is in **posta breve**, then the guard was likely not low enough, allowing the *compagno* to slip underneath it.

- **Can't get posta di bicorno to work:** This is a difficult variant. If there is too much pressure by the *compagno*, or if the *compagno* has come far over, even outside the lines of his body, then it will be hard to make the **bicorno** work. Another cause is failing to step *a la traversa*, which is needed to provide a little center for the **bicorno** to settle upon.

SUMMARY

Zugadore begin crossed at the *mezza spada*
- Scolaro finds the point, pressing his hilt to move the *compagno's* weapon and thrusts, using posta breve, posta di bicorne, or posta di finestra, depending upon the placement of the *compagno's* weapon.

CAPTURE WITH THE HAND OR AT THE FORTEZA
Based on Fiore's 3rd and 6th Plays of the Zhogo Largo

Another response to the *incrosa* is to extend your control using a **capture**. Instead of attacking with the edge or point, a combatant may want to extend his control further through the use of a more solid bind, or even with a *prese* or grip. In this case he can respond by capturing the opponent's sword, either with his hand or within his castle, the *forteza*. The latter represents the gateway to the *zhogo stretto* or close play.

Our **Sixth Play of the Elephant** is done in two variants. Both begin from the *Second Master of the Crossed Swords*, that is, with the swords crossed at the *mezza spada*, right foot usually forward, and hilts near the groin, per Fiore's illustration. The *scolaro* will advance, either gripping his opponent's sword with left hand, thumb down (Fiore's *Third Play of the Zhogo Largo*). As he does so, he draws his own blade back, so the combatant cannot grab his. From here, he simply strikes as efficiently as possible. This capture is done in sparring only after the blades have been bound for at least a beat.

The second variant extends the control still further. It begins the same, but instead of extending his control to the blade using his hand, the *scolaro* now steps forward aggressively with a *passare* and raises his sword to **posta frontale**, sliding along the opponent's blade and capturing it within his own castle—the sword's *forteza*. From here, the lion's share of the *zhogo stretto* techniques are available. And in order to foster tactical thought, we usually let the *scolari* come up with their own follow-on attacks after the capture.

The most fundamental follow-on is an elbow push. Shown in Fiore's text, the hand should grasp an inch or two above the right elbow, forcefully turning the *compagno* to his right (his opponent's left). In the text, Fiore uses a kick to the groin, and this is effective; but since most combatants reading this

book will want to use this technique in a tournament context, we train this technique, but do not use it all the time in sparring. There are also several pommel-strikes available (along with my all-time favorite pommel-strike/step-and-take by the throat), many interesting disarms, and a large number of arm binds. Novices should stick with the elbow-push, kicks, and pommel-strikes.

Intermediate combatants will want to begin their play with a *fendente* or other means of coming to the *incrosa*, using the play in concert with the others to select the right one for the right circumstance. They will want to work at seizing control at both distances (capturing the sword both with their hand and with the *forteza*), working to improve their timing so that there is as little delay as possible between the capture and the follow-on attack. They will want to have their *compagno* try to make the very same play against them simultaneously, and to integrate the play with the others so that they become better at using the *tigro* to instantly notice when a blade-capture is available, seizing the opportunity at once.

In all of these cases, control of the opponent's sword has been maximized with a capture. In the first case, his sword has been grasped, which temporarily immobilizes it. In the second, control is extended by capturing his blade within the *scolaro's* castle, the extending control still further with a *prese* or grip, making the gateway to the impressive array of *zhogo stretto* techniques for which Fiore is famously known.

Capture with a Prese

❶ ❷ ❸ ❹

Troubleshooting – First variant
(stepping in to capture with **poste frontale**)

- **Grip not solid:** Often this is caused by the *scolaro* using the wrong hand, or the wrong grip. He must use the left hand (on a right-hander), thumb down, sweeping from the inside-out to keep the point from his person and achieving a solid grip at the juncture between the *punta* and *mezza spada*.

SUMMARY

Zugadori begin crossed at the *mezza spada*, right foot forward, hilts near the groin.
- **Variant 1:** After the swords have been crossed for a beat, the scolari grip the sword with their left hand, Recoiling their own and following-on with a thrust or *colpo*.
- **Variant 2:** Scolari step forward, raising their swords to posta frontale and capturing the *compagni's* with the *forteza*. Scolari follow-on with at least three different variants, each practiced for smoothness.

- **Missed grip:** Frequently this is due to taking the left hand from the *scolaro's* grip in advance, anticipating the strike. It may end in the hand being struck as it is a forward target. Less frequently, the *compagno* may not be cooperating, removing his sword before contact. Remember that to be effective, the optimal time seems to be about a heartbeat between the time of the *incrosa* and the time the grip is made.

- **Compagno grips your sword, too!:** Whenever the *compagno's* sword is controlled with the left hand, the *scolaro* must exercise caution and remove the sword from the *compagno's* reach, ideally recoiling it for a strike or thrust. It is a common thing to leave the sword at rest (even Fiore shows it!), but unless the sword is thrusting or striking simultaneously with the grip, it is a far better thing to recoil it and deny it to the opponent. This "double grab" circumstance is not shown by Fiore, but it does appear in several German manuscripts (see page 233).

Capture with Posta Frontale

Photos 2, 3 and 4 all take place from a capture in poste frontale (photo 1). Photo 2 shows a kick, photo 3 an elbow push, and photo 4-6 a double-handed pommel strike followed by a rolling of the blade that can be used to capture the opponent.

Troubleshooting – Second variant
(stepping in to capture with **poste frontale**)

- **Capture fails**: Normally this is caused by the *scolaro* failing to step forward with an aggressive *passare* as the attack is made. In this case, the step made directly towards the opponent.

- **Struck on the head**: Remember that poste frontale was also called **posta corona** by "other masters," (*Kron* in the German), which translates roughly to "coronet position." The cross of the sword must be high enough to guard the head against a downward

strike by the *compagno*, and hence the cross must be at the brow-line, where a coronet or crown would rest.

- **Indecision after the capture**: It often happens amongst novices that once the capture is made, they will pause to consider what to do next. This is normal and will recede as the students become familiar with the array of opportunities.

THE INFAMOUS DOUBLE-GRAB

Although Fiore doesn't address this case specifically, it can be a natural outcome of a *prese* against the opponent's sword if the *scolaro* fails to strike simultaneously or retrieve his sword as he makes the grab.

The "double grab" does appear in at least two German medieval manuscripts, Hans Talhoffer plate 57 (1467 version) and Paulus Kal plate 24r, shown left. Curiously, neither is accompanied with text, although the Paulus Kal does shown an odd finish on plate 25 (see *In Service of the Duke* by Christian Henry Tobler for an analysis of the German play).

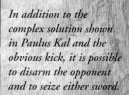

In addition to the complex solution shown in Paulus Kal and the obvious kick, it is possible to disarm the opponent and to seize either sword.

In photos 1-3, the opponent's sword is taken and he is thrown over the hip or knee.

In photos 4-6, the combatant recovers his own sword by grasping it at the *mezza spada* and turning it clockwise against the opponent's thumb.

CHAPTER TWELVE

TRAINING & SPARRING

"…the courtier must accompany his actions, gestures, habits—in short his every movement—with grace…without which all other properties are of little worth. And indeed I think that in this everyone would allow himself to be persuaded easily, since from the very force of the word, it may be said that he who has grace finds grace…But it is oftentimes a gift of nature and of heaven which, even when not thus perfect, can with care and pains be made much greater…they who have received from heaven only so much…are capable of becoming much greater through pains, industry and care. By what methods can they acquire this grace, as well as in bodily exercises?" asks the Duchess in Baldassare Castiglione's *Book of the Courtier*, Book I, f. 25.

here are many reasons and techniques available for the study of Fiore's swordsmanship. Sadly, we do not know how Fiore taught *his* students. It may be that he followed the material in the order presented in his books, or it may be that he approached it differently.

But in a modern context, the Schola's objective is to explore the original material, reconstructing it as closely as possible while simultaneously conveying something with modern value, rather than just playing with material that is centuries out of date.

Fiore's Art is essentially timeless: an efficient, integrated system as applicable to self-defense today as it was six centuries ago. The European martial arts have to some degree been eclipsed by the rapid development of effective firearms during the 16th & 17th centuries and the gradual relegation of swordsmanship to the sport halls and dueling green, but Fiore's core principles are strikingly similar to modern combatives as taught amongst special military units and elite police forces around the world. Similar joint manipulation is seen in Crav Magra, Ju-jitsu, and Aki-jitsu. Similar sword movements exist still in the Japanese arts. Fiore's set of principles works just as well unarmed as it does with a stick or an assault weapon wielded in close-quarters environments, and it is effective because it is simple, efficient, and easy to recall under the stress of a fight. If students wish, they can apply Fiore's principles to self-defense, just as they would study any other martial art.

But like other martial arts, there are many flavors and varieties. Some arts emphasize striking, kicking, grips, fighting from the feet or the ground. Some use weapons, some do not. Some systems emphasize forms, while others focus on tournament competition or street defense. Fiore's art offers all of these possibilities, and the student is free to choose a school, study group, or avenue of personal study that includes any or all of the above.

Because Fiore's system is based on a core set of principles, a student can enter into the art from the perspective of any weapon. Many schools begin with the *abrazzare*, moving next to dagger. While this book represents the Schola's basic course, entering into the system from the sword in two hands, other groups teach the principles differently, surveying a little *abrazzare*, then *daga*, followed by the sword in one and two hands. One could as easily learn the system starting with the *azza* or through the *spada en arme*, or one could perhaps start with the *lanza*.

Today's student must eventually decide where to begin, although choices about how to evolve his training can change over time. Within the Schola, we begin with the *spada a due mani*—the sword in two hands—because through it something of the romance and martial efficiency may be quickly internalized. I suspect that this is one of the main draws that brings students to our training halls.

Within the Schola, we strive to inculcate a sense of overall development, emphasizing character alongside the techniques and mental/physical aspects of their training. I believe the mental aspects of swordsmanship—rapid decision-making based on complex input streams, competing against an opponent while maintaining a sense of mutual respect, maintenance of tactical focus, the prioritization of life's stresses to free the individual while attending to committed duties—these are objectives that underlie training within the School and which will, hopefully, go with our students and instructors when they leave he training hall or tournament field and have to deal with the less interesting but more important problems of work, family, and society. Personal responsibility is a timeless virtue.

The individual student must recognize that training in medieval swordsmanship is a complex, ongoing task that carries with it a host of rich possibilities. The student must take ownership of his training, driving himself to excel, hopefully as close to perfection as possible, rather than checking a box as "completed." For the study of swordsmanship, like life, is never complete. There is always more efficiency to be gained, a deeper understanding, greater insight. And this is perhaps one of the finest gifts the study of swordsmanship offers, an appreciation for the ability of the individual to ennoble himself and those around him according to his own efforts and example by continually improving his understanding and ability.

To become a swordsman, the student must commit himself to excel regardless of the obstacles presented. He must attend to his duties, but also manage his time to allow himself to grow and develop, setting aside time for training both in and out of class. Commit to mediocrity, and you will at best become mediocre. Commit to greatness, and you have a chance to attain something more.

Modern students are as varied as grains of sand, each approaching the material with a different background and different objectives in mind. They have different modes of learning, so the instructor must develop a myriad of ways to express, demonstrate and explain a given concept.

Fortunately, modern sports sciences and kinesiology (the study of human movement) have yielded much that is of value for the modern teacher of swordsmanship. Progressive training, biomechanics, pysiological aspects of human kinesthetics; motor control, development and learning all offer key insights in helping students to develop their mind/body skills.

Within the Schola, we strive to continually improve our training regimen based on the development of new instructors and from our student base. Everyone contributes; new drills, insights and interpretations are constantly flowing. But our core structure for the development of skills has remained remarkably intact during the years and I'll present the core development strategy here.

SAFETY

Nothing is as important as safety. Not only given the modern legal climate, where everyone seems to sue for everything, but also because Fiore's whole system is based on a quest for personal security, not only within the training hall, but on the street, in a feat or arms or in war, hence perhaps his name or *nom de guerre*, Fiore dei Liberi, the "flower of freedom." Safety equates with judgement, of choosing the best course of action and weighing factors to maximize safety.

In any physical activity—and in the martial arts in particular—there is the possibility of risk to the body. Competition by its nature presses the body to extremes in the quest to control the flow of events, to establish dominance over the opponent(s). The human body is an amazing biomechanical system, but there are limits imposed by its system of joints, material strength, and mental programming.

In a martial art there may be many safety rules, but the most important one is *mutual respect*. If the combatant is more concerned about his opponent's safety than he is in scoring a point, or bolstering his ego, then it is likely that he will exercise judgement to safeguard is opponent's safety. While each combatant is responsible for themselves, certainly, they must also guard their companions from harm as much as possible.

Fiore even discusses this in his treatise: he says these arts *cannot* be practiced in safety without *concordia*—harmony—and companionship. It is for this reason that we use the terms *compagni* (companions), *scolari* (scolars) and the like. Indeed, Fiore uses the term *zugadori*—players—to talk about his students, avoiding the terms "opponent" or "enemy."[2] Students practicing martial arts *must* treat their opponents with brotherly respect. There is nothing to be won on the practice field, in a drill, or in a tournament except **renown**, but there is much that can be lost.

Always take to the field with a sense of companionship for your partner, reminding yourself of your respect for them with each salute. Do not act from fear or from a desire to prove anything to anyone. If you do, you leave yourself open to clouded judgement, and you may well make regrettable choices.

THE SALUTE

Within the Schola, we open and close any armed or martial encounter with a salute. One is given between the instructor and students at the beginning and end of class, between students when they meet in a drill or a fight, in tournaments. We have a simple "school" salute that we use entering and leaving class, but we strongly encourage students to develop one of their own for use between students or in sparring.

As I have written in the *Book of the Tournament*, there are three functions that any salute serves:

> **First**: It signals readiness. Do not salute before you are absolutely ready to engage. Make sure your mind is clear (the salute is a good tool for this), that your focus is on the task at hand, because when the salute is completed the fight has begun.[3]

> **Second**: The salute signals a willingness to adhere to the mutually understood rules of the encounter. In a drill, it means sealing a compact to stay within the bounds of the drill, to eshew "winning" the drill, and to mutually work in harmony for the development of both *zugadori*. In a sparring match, it seals an agreement between the combatants to the rules governing the fight. You are committing to a safe encounter.

> **Third**: It signals mutual respect between the combatants, and between the combatants and any judges, members of the gallery, fellow students or instructors present.

Our students are encouraged to develop their own salute for use when they engage with fellow *compagni*. The movements can be whatever the combatant chooses, but they must convey respect. If you are a student, experiment with your salute to find one that conveys strength, presence, respect and confidence.

ZUGADORI, COMPAGNI AND SCOLARI[4]

Within the School, we use the term *zugadori* to mean everyone in the class. *Compagni* refer to those who are working as the "dojo dummies," or *uke*. *Scolaro* refers to the *zugadore* who is doing the action in question, while the *compagno* sets it up with various degrees of cooperation.

All *zugadori* have the responsibility to treat others with respect and to **stay within bounds for the drill** or exercise in question.

Compagni have the responsibility to work in harmony with the *scolari*, giving feedback and helping them to learn. A good *compagno* will act as a student-instructor, helping the *scolaro* to improve his technique by communicating in a way that is not disruptive and which does not reduce the number of available repetitions. **The focus should be on the scolaro**, although at the point when the *scolaro* has the material well in hand, it is certainly permissible and advisable to *gradually* increase the difficulty presented. The *compagno* should also exercise himself by thinking about what he is seeing, how he might counter it, or how to improve his execution of his part of the exercise, rather than just being present.

Scolari work the drill, executing the techniques to be exercised. They should strive for the most perfect execution of a technique possible, working very slowly at first, only gradually increasing their speed when the technique is close to perfect before going faster. Do not rush—speed will come as a natural handmaiden of efficiency. It is better to practice good technique *slowly* than to rush and encode mistakes into the mental programming. The *Scolaro* must have the control necessary to protect their *compagno*, and should focus sharply on the exercise at hand.

All *zugadori* should avoid common errors that reduce a drill's effectiveness, such as talking instead of doing more repetitions, letting their attention wander, or trying to "win" the drill, which exposes the both *zugadori* to risk. Another common error is moving on and extending the exercise beyond what is being practiced. To counter the boredom of a repetitive practice set, infusing variability into the practice will both increase the retention of mental programming and reduce the risk of boredom.

SSG TRAINING PROGRESSION

Much work has been done in the field of motor control and learning that is directly applicable to the development of teaching pedagogy. How humans learn motion[5] is a fascinating area of study, and the Schola approach takes into account both current research and our direct experience.

In general, we present the Art with a circular model designed to gradually build skills in a progressive manner, building what is hopefully a solid foundation before moving on to the next dependent element. We go through a five-step pattern that first presents the unit, answering **why** it is important; next the movements are demonstrated, showing **what** is to be done. The students then progress through drills, where they get the idea of the movement and learn **how** to do it. Later students integrate the drill into their fighting repertoire, learning **when** to execute it. Finally, they explore it further for a deeper understanding, bringing them back to **why**.

In the **First Masters of Battle** course, the students don't do very much sparring, since they lack a tactical framework (for us, Fiore's *zhogo largo* plays), although we do encourage some free play and a fair amount of play with the *lanza* or short spear as will be discussed later in the chapter. The intent for the first module is to build positional strength and stability. This supports the split-second decision-making needed in the second module and during the integration training, the subject of the third module.[6]

PRESENTATION: *WHY*

First, the instructor or group leader should explain the purpose of the unit in question, and give an overview of what will be covered along with the historical sources. This is the "Why" phase; *why* the unit is being taught now and what it is designed to do. For modern people, this is a question of context, the logical underpinning that helps to support the vision of what the class is trying to accomplish.

It is important to avoid giving too much information, or the student's attention may be lost or they may be overwhelmed. Much of the "why" will be understood in greater detail and at greater depth over time as the circle is completed, so the instructor of group leader should not spend a great deal of time on presenting the unit's context, although the amount of information will vary according to the skill level and experience of the students.

DEMONSTRATION: *WHAT*

The movements should next be demonstrated. Fighting is an art of movement, and much can be learned through the observation of others. The instructor or leader should make an effort to demonstrate the movement slowly, and at speed, answering questions and pointing out important aspects of the movement as he understands it. Experienced instructors will have a much greater advantage because they have seen the motion performed more times and with much greater variability. The movement should be demonstrated immediately preceeding the drill or exercise phase to encourage retention.

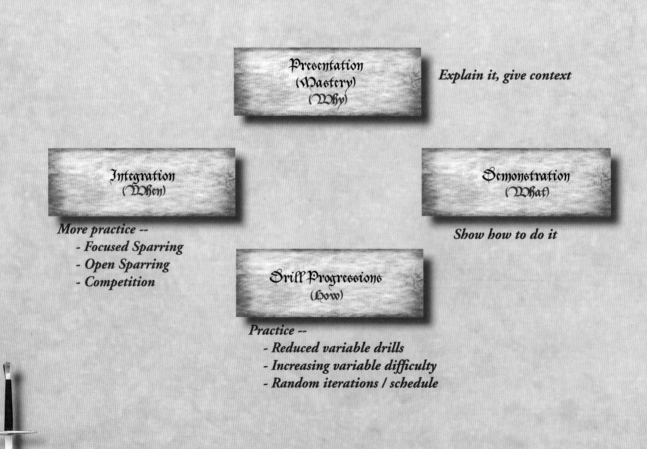

Presentation
(Mastery)
(Why)

Explain it, give context

Integration
(When)

Demonstration
(What)

More practice --
- *Focused Sparring*
- *Open Sparring*
- *Competition*

Show how to do it

Drill Progressions
(How)

Practice --
- *Reduced variable drills*
- *Increasing variable difficulty*
- *Random iterations / schedule*

DRILL & EXERCISE: *HOW*

Next comes the acquisition or practice phase, the most important element in motor learning. Here the students work through the movement, passing through stages of development as they first get acquainted with the movement, then execute it with increasing levels of discernment and skill. The goal is to get students to the point where they can self-analyze and self-correct. Drill and exercises set the mental programming for a movement, a software-like function that is precompiled and stored, ready for use.

When first presenting a movement, especially to novice students, it is extremely important not to get too detailed in the explanatory phase. Too much information not only threatens the attention span, but also damages learning. This is true also for feedback offered during practice; detail and nuance is best offered to students after they have learned the fundamentals of the motion, or when a particular mistake causes an obvious error.

To the degree that a movement is related to previously learned motions, it may be easier for the students to learn. This is there consistency within the system and a clear presentation of the foundational principles will become very important: the medieval fighting systems are not hodge-podge collections of techniques, but are merely exemplary of an underlying principle shown with a given weapon or in a given circumstance. Once the core ideas are internalized, most of the advanced techniques may be discovered by the student through the application of principle to a given tactical situation. Thus, relating one movement to others in the system is an important key.

In order for drills and exercises to be effective, they must relate directly to a useful movement. Motor learning is generally a gradual process, so repetitions of a drill are important. But at the same time, students can quickly become bored with a movement, so integrating random elements to the movement is important. Using random or serial organization[7] dramatically increases the learning value of drill progressions.

The bulk of work for first-year students within the Schola work on progressive drills to build foundational skills. Our first two modules strongly emphasize drill and exercises that increase in sophistication as the students advance. We have an evolving group of well-seasoned drills that students perform in order to practice key movements. However, a good instructor of study group leader will need to be able to create new drills and exercises tailored to a particular class or to a particular student.

INTEGRATION & FOCUSED SPARRING: *WHEN*

When the component movements and tactics have been learned, the combatant must then learn when to apply these actions in the context of an opponent. This is done by through sparring.[8] In a drill combatants practice variants of set plays. In sparring, they must analyze the tactical situation and select an appropriate response.

Sparring is complex and sometimes frustrating because it highlights the gap between *what* is known and *when* it is applied.

We have found that a combination of extreme slow work and focused sparring that gradually builds in speed and complexity helps to integrate the techniques.

MENTAL PROGRAMMING

The idea of looking the learning of movement based on an analogy with computer programming began preimaging, first expressed by Plato and other Greek philosophers, who thought it was necessary for a person to create an "image" of an act preceeding the act itself.

In 1917, Karl Lashley first coined the term "motor program," defining it as, "a generalized schemata of action which determine the sequence of specific acts."

In 1960, Miller, Galanter and Pribram proposed the idea of a "plan," which was "essentially the same as a program for a computer." Later the same year, Franklin Henry described "a neural pattern for a specific and well-coordinated motor act is controlled by a stored program that is used to direct the neuromotor details of its performance."

In 1975 Richard Schmidt proposed a less rigid model that described an abstract memory-based representation of a class of actions, with each class defined by various features.

I have long thought of the mental aspect of physical training using the computer program analogy. Using it, the goal of training and practice is to develop precompiled library functions that can be accessed with great speed when needed. In the development of computer software, programs are "compiled" to compress them and to translate them to machine code. In the same way, motor programming may create relationships between sets of neural connections providing sleek, fast-access building blocks that can be put together in various ways to make a brand new movement. This is critical in swordsmanship because very rarely will an action be repeated exactly as it was trained.

REACTION TIME & MENTAL PROGRAMMING

Scientific study has made some interesting study into the relationship between reaction time and response time. Most people equate the two, but response time is actually the total time it takes for an action to be completed from the moment of stimulus. Reaction time accounts only from the moment of stimulus to the beginning of physical motion.

It takes a baseball bat approximately 200msec (.002 sec) to complete its range of motion. This is very similar to the sword in two hansds, which may even be faster as the average weight for a bat is xxx while a sword weighs between 2.25 and 3.0lbs.

Interestingly, the response time (time between the stimulus and movement of the muscle) for a simple, discrete action is in the range of 300 and 500msec, between 1.5 and 2.5 times the time needed to actually accomplish the action. And this is for a simple, known action such as pressing a button when prompted by a light. The analysis of a movement for the sword under the stress of a fight must be considerably longer, since there is far more information to be processed before a decision can be made.

Thus, the time needed to analyze an action and select a response dwarfs the time needed to actually make the action. Training and the development of an analytical model for combat is thus of paramount importance in terms of saving precious time in combat. Fiore's system provides just such a model and students who internalize the model can apply it to a variety of contexts, not just to competition and exercise within the Western martial arts.

Slow sparring is a useful method of setting mental programming because it allows time for analysis and thought. In slow work, time cannot be accurately gauged because "slow" time is not uniform from person to person. Given this, one should never worry about "winning" the drill in slow work, but rather the combatants should work with *concordia* to achieve an exchange in which both combatants propel one another to ever-increasing levels of skill. The emphasis should be in achieving, as much as possible, perfect position and balance. As efficiency as achieved, speed comes as a natural consequence.

Focused sparring is a method used to gradually increase the complexity of the fighting environment. Focused sparring is done at full-speed, but with the choices of one or both opponents limited. At first, they are very limited, but the menu of available options is gradually increased as the partner's execution improves.

Open sparring is in the middle of the sparring spectrum, where the combatants use whatever techniques they choose.

Competition is the far end of the sparring spectrum. In a tournament, combatants meet in a formalized environment where the speed and overall maturity of their understanding challenge both technical material and mental analysis. For the Schola's perspective, it also exercises and measures the combatant's overall character through the expression of chivalric virtue.

Sparring thus follows drill and exercise, adding a critically important random element into the training. It also exercises the mental tools that are as important to the fight as the physical techniques. It bridges the gap between drill and competition.

MASTERY: *WHY*

After the techniques and analysis tools are internalized comes a deeper level of understanding. The underlying principles of the technique and forms are imprinted on the combatant's mind, tools ready to use. But there is a still deeper level of understanding where the underlying principle is understood well enough to be generalized and applied in similar or related circumstance.[9]

The goal of students should be to internalize the principles underlying the techniques well enough that they can be applied to related circumstances. At this point they can extend the system, discovering many possible and legitimate applications that could occur in a fight.

Fiore could only present a sample of possible examples in his book, but they are examples that well convey his fighting philosophy. As the student grows in skill and experience, they will find many new connections between the plays and new ways of thinking about the tactical framework.

DRILL FORMS

Drills and exercises are tools for practice used to develop physical skills. In general drills are more structured, striving to focus on specific elements by reducing the "clutter" caused by other factors. By simplifying the required motions and reducing the choices to be made by the combatant, drills should clarify and distill particular aspects of combat skill.

Exercises are generally broader structures, designed to focus on the inclusion of more variables into the practice activity. Some exercises might be done in the form of games or competitions, each carefully crafted to encourage certain practices and to discourage others. Exercises don't necessarily require more than one tactical decision per iteration, but they can expand to include several choices.

TRAINING

There are an infinite number of ways that a training schedule might be created, but all training sessions should have the following: warm-ups & stretches, review of previously covered material, new material presentation, drill & exercise, summary.

Most Schola groups train once or twice per week, although there are groups that work out three to five times per week (and their progress is commensurately faster). Most sessions are two hours, but there are groups with one-hour sessions done more often per week, and those with longer sessions once per week. Students should plan to spend at least three hours per week in class, and at least two to three additional hours outside of class.

Footwork, refining the *poste*, and *posta* transitions are training by the combatant alone, although individual elements of form may be productively practiced in a group setting. Similarly, core kinesthetics—such as the delivery of strikes and thrusts—are also things which must be drilled for many thousands of repetitions in order for a combatant to build sufficient precision.

Ideally, individual practice should be done every day, working for at least thirty minutes per session. It can also profitably be done in class from time to time or at the start of class in order to check student's progress and as a component of a warm-up regime.

PAIRED DRILL SETS

Some elements of swordsmanship cannot easily be practiced without a training partner, a *compagno*. Responses to strikes, timing refinement, and the confidence attained "in the helmet" are aspects of swordsmanship that require a training partner.

Informal training sessions may be profitably undertaken with only a single training partner who assists the scolaro by delivering blows and, critically, feedback. These sessions are often the only form of practice available (outside of solo work) for independent students, and they can be useful if they are structured and focus on only a few variables at a time.

For classes, paired drill sets are an excellent way to ensure that the students receive suitable number of repetitions and that the practice session is not hijacked by the myriad side-conversations

Sample Schola Saint George Training Content	1 hr class	2 hr class
Class Salute – Administrative notes	2-3 mins.	2-3 mins.
Stretches & Warmups – Core Kinesthetics	5 mins.	5-7 mins.
Review of key concepts from previous class	5-7 mins.	5-10 mins.
Optional repeat of key drill(s) or exercises from previous class	--	15-20 min.
Presentation of concepts for current class	5 mins.	5 min.
Drills & Exercises for current class	30 mins	60 min.
Competitive Exercise for current class	5-10 mins.	10 min.
Summary & Closing Salute	3 mins.	5 mins.

Used together, drills and exercises are an important blend. Exercises tend to maintain student interest longer while more limited drills reduce variables which can sometimes impart clarity of perception. A student's training system will be made up of a combination of training forms based on their access, dedication, and availability of teachers and fellow scholars.

INDIVIDUAL EXERCISES

There is much that can be done alone, without a *compagno* or training partner. The student should build strength, endurance and wind through a conventional exercise regimen, and some of these exercises can be married to footwork drills and *poste* transitions.

that inevitably occur. Within the Schola we conduct "onion drills" in order to ensure that combatants rotate (so as to vary their experience), working each side of a drill and in an environment that is easy for the instructor to assess performance and to provide feedback which may apply to the whole group.

Onion drills are done by creating a drill line, *compagni* on one side and *scolari* on the other. The instructor should first briefly explain and demonstrate the drill, being sure to show both parts (for example, the *compagni* may simply step and deliver a fendente, while the *scolari* respond in some way). Next, *zugadori* salute one another, signaling their readiness. The instructor calls cadence for the action, using a form such as, "reset….ready… and…1; reset…ready…and…2;" etc.). Between each repetition should be only a few seconds, just enough for the students to *briefly* confer in order to communicate mistakes and needed refinement.

Once a set has been completed—usually seven, ten or twelve repetitions—the lines rotate to the left. The last *compagno* will cross the line and become a *scolaro*, and the last *scolaro* will cross the line and become a *compagno*. By rotating through the line, each combatant has the opportunity to train with multiple partners and to execute both parts of the drill many times.

FEEDBACK & CORRECTIONS

One of the most important elements of practice is feedback. Too little feedback and the students will simply practice mistakes; too much and they will lose focus. In order to be effective, feedback should be scaled to the student's requirements.

Novice students are struggling to "get the idea of the motion." As such, only one or two of their larger mistakes should be pointed out and focused upon. Often, it helps to point out not the physical reason for the error, but rather to re-emphasize the goal of the motion, because an adult human being has already internalized many movement programs and will likely be able to leverage past knowledge if the goal is presented in the right way.

Novices frequently make gross errors in footwork, balance, and power generation. They are often too tense, nervous that they are both under perceived scrutiny and trying to perform an action they don't know well. Have them relax (breathing exercises are excellent for this)—especially their grip and shoulders—breathe deeply, and check first their core foot placement and body orientation.

As the primary goal of training is to equip the student for self-correction, assessment and improvement, the instructor should avoid creating a dependency on outside corrections. Before the training partner or instructor explains why an error is happening, they should first ask the student what they did wrong, giving them time to practice and reinforce self-analysis. This builds a most important skill, one that is clearly transferable outside of the martial art and into daily life. It also makes less work for the instructor, because at some point the students will self-correct, getting much more benefit from their limited practice time.

Intermediate students make smaller mistakes, often residual fundamental errors in stance and balance (ie., footwork), but the majority of errors relate to mistakes in timing or judgement (timing errors are themselves errors in judgement because they are really miscalculations or misperceptions). Judgement errors relate to making an inferior choice—there is often a better, "more correct" choice that will result in a higher percentage of success.

Because intermediate students have an idea about many of the core movements, they can turn their attention to refining the myriad small details that make the difference between efficiency (and thus effectiveness) and wasted movement or positional weakness. Refinement should be seen as a steady progress towards martial

grace—efficiency—working through one or two variables at a time as each small error is fixed in turn. Again, it is crucial to develop the student's abilities to self-analyze by prompting them to say what they did wrong *before* providing a correction.

EXERCISES & GAMES

While drills are useful for developing core motor skills, exercises and games are more fun and develop complimentary skill, including tactical judgement. They relieve boredom and give an opportunity for friendly competition to drive each *zugadore* to stretch their abilities. An instructor should be creative in developing exercises and games—especially with children—which are safe and which encourage sound tactical choices.

Examples of exercises are the balance competitions introduced in chapter 6 and the thrusting at the ball shown in chapter 9. Games are simply exercises where the results are tallied in a competitive environment.

WINNING A DRILL

A dangerous concept, common amongst many martial arts students of every tradition is the idea of *winning the drill*. A combatant who tries to win the drill cannot or will not set up the required movements needed for his *compagno* to learn. Instead, consciously or unconsciously, he tries to counter or to "win." In fact, both *zugadori* lose under these circumstances; safety is compromised, and neither *zugadore* learns the concept at hand.

Combatants "win" a drill when both players execute their parts to perfection. For the *compagno*, this means giving the most realistic and fluid movements possible, scaled to the skills of the *scolaro*. The *compagno* should strive, with each repetition, to refine his movements, maintain a reserve of power through coiling and recoiling, and thinking about the movements his opponent is making. He should offer his observations about mistakes in a tactful and constructive manner, avoiding being condescending. He should challenge without offending.

Scolari should approach each repetition is a chance to demonstrate perfect technique. They should focus on one variable at a time, improving their martial efficiency step by step.

CONTROL, BLOWS & RENOWN

When delivering *colpi*, *punte* or *prese* the combatants must exercise judgement. All blows should be backed by strong available power, yet the combatant should not strike harder that is necessary and must take into account the protective gear worn by his opponent.

Within the Schola we do not acknowledge "taps," or "snipes" that are insufficiently powered to do damage through a quilted fighting coat (a *zuparello* or gambeson). This means that the blows have to be properly powered, driven by the entire body, as discussed in chapter 9. How much force may be applied is a delicate but important matter: combatants who consistently strike too hard are unsafe and threaten the fabric of the group (people will eshew fighting them and may eventually leave). On the other hand, too little force allows and encourages poor technique, attacks without sufficient power to do real damage.

"I KNOW" DISEASE

A common handmaiden to "winning the drill" is what I call "I know" disease. Students showing evidence of "I know" will not easily take in new information, closing their attention by a (usually false) assumption of prior knowledge. Both "winning the drill" and "I know" disease are symptoms of a weak ego trying to compensate. In the majority of cases the student's learning is impaired, but the learning of his training *compagno* is also impaired, unfortunately. In an extreme case, safety is at risk because the student tries to compensate or to meet an exaggerated self-image by "winning" no matter what the cost and safety takes a back seat.

Study group leaders, *compagni* and instructors must take special care to deal with these issues before they become issues of morale in the group or worse, safety hazards.

This is one of the first places where a combatant's renown (or infamy) begins to develop. If his opponents do not trust or respect him, then his renown suffers. Renown is earned by demonstrating skill, knowledge, and respect for the Art and for the opponent. A quick way to lose renown is to be an ineffective training partner, to demonstrate a lack of control and respect for his *compangi*. Renown lost is hard to reacquire, and it is lost faster than it is earned.

FORCE & TRAINING WEAPONS

What constitutes reasonable applied force will depend upon the weapon trainer—with a rebated steel weapon, for example, little force should be put into the blow. With a shinai-based trainer, the blow can be more completely finished. This is the part of the problem with practicing the Art and it is why there is no perfect trainer. With a metal longsword, the potential force generated is great and is focused on a narrow edge or point. Students must thus pull their blows before they strike to avoid injury, unless both combatants are armoured. But if this is the only way a combatant practices, then they will not have experience in finishing a blow. With a more forgiving trainer, such as a shinai-based one, the blows can be finished, but the trainer doesn't quite act like a sword in terms of flight dynamics and feel in the *incrosare*. Therefore, we generally prefer that students work with both kinds of weapons. As their skills and control improves, more work is done with the metal weapons and less with the sparring trainers, although most competitions use something like the shinai-based trainers.

In general, we prefer to have students work through the plays and material in this book first with metal-based trainers. Each study group determines for itself which kind of trainer to adopt. Some use wooden wasters, but most use steel or aluminum. When students first begin striking blows as demonstrated in chapter 9, we introduce them to the shinai-based weapons or their equivalent (the carbon-fiber weapons are expected to replace the shinai), the sparring weapons are introduced as the students get used to strking and being struck at. It is at this point also that the defensive equipment is introduced, starting with the helmet and gauntlets. Blows and thrust are practiced with both kinds of weapons.

When the students begin working on the plays in chapter 11, we begin with the metal weapons and then transition to the sparring weapons so that each play can eventually be worked in a realistic sparring environment as combatants will encounter it within the practice and tournament field. As mentioned above, intermediate and advanced students transition more and more to the metal trainers, eventually using the sparring weapons only in free-play and tournament where novices and intermediates are present.

TRAINING PROBLEMS

Many scolari fail to learn because of fundamental training issues, including conflicting priorities, fear or dejection, or perhaps worst of all, poor instruction.

Conflicting priorities is perhaps the greatest challenge. Many SSG students are adults with families, careers, and sometimes competing hobbies. Students who wish to excel as swordsmen must make a personal commitment to set aside regular time for practice both in and out of class. There is simply no other way to learn, to refine the combatant's movements and judgement. As a side-benefit, many students report that the mental clarity necessary to focus on swordsmanship both relaxes them and provides an important oasis in their otherwise busy lives.

Fear and dejection are other barriers. As a novice, fear of injury, of the unknown, and of feeling ignorant or lost can be major hurdles. A good instructor should remain sensitive to these issues. Fear of injury will mostly recede as confidence is built, but students should not be pressed too fast (although they must usually be pushed out of their comfort zone), or they might react to the fear by leaving the course. Fear of the unknown is handled with a clear presentation at the start and by not presenting too much information, which risks triggering the fears of ignorance mentioned above.

Students may become dejected if during the times when they have reached a learning plateau. While curves and plateaus are natural phenomenon of human learning, long plateaus can result in both boredom and/or dejection. Skillful use of new exercises, games and even drills can break the cycle.

Worst of all is poor instruction. An instructor or study group leader has an immense influence on the quality of student learning. They can use poor teaching methods, can appear befuddled or confused, can lose control of the class. I would encourage study group leaders and young instructors to seek out works on teaching of physical arts—martial arts and sports, as well as kinesiological sources—for more study.

DEFINING WINNING

Finally, there is the issue of defining what it means to "win" in a martial art, be it in competition or in drill. In sparring, for example, one combatant "wins" by striking or being able to strike their opponent with his *compagno* being able to reply in kind. In a fight for one's life this definition certainly suffices, but what about in the training hall? One can "win" in this way but still have learned nothing, essentially wasting his time (although the ego is happier).

"Winning" during training means improvement, learning. Thus, one cannot "win" a drill unless one learns something new or refines an existing movement.

THE DREADED "DOPPIO"

A *doppio* or "double" is a double-kill, a double-fail in a Schola context. I consider it a "double-fail" because in a "real" encounter, no matter what may or may not happen to your opponent, you were struck. Similarly, if you strike your opponent but were not yourself covered (such that he could have struck you, but did not), this is only half a victory. You were essentially lucky.

Combatants should strive to resolve their fights by striking or neutralizing their opponent and demonstrating control which is as complete as possible.

10/25 FREE PLAY

We have an exercise called "10-25." In this activity, combatants strive to "spar" with one another in **very slow** motion. Exceedingly slow. It is usually done with metal trainers, each *zudadore* striving to move with perfect balance, **not worrying about the effects of time** but instead focusing on perfecting position while avoiding the *doppio* (double-kills). In this artifical slow motion world, the combatants have plenty of time to analyze and adapt, to select a viable answer to the opponent's action.[10] 10-25 is an excellent way to begin a training session or to focus on the set-up for a particular circumstance.

FOCUSED SPARRING

Next along the sparring spectrum is "focused" sparring, where the combatants work on a specific set of skills by limiting the options available to one or both combatants. Focused sparring may begin slow, gradually increasing the speed and number of options until the play resembles or is open sparring, discussed below.

The idea of focused sparring is to reduce the variables in a sparring encounter so that learning can take place. By recognizing the circumstance in which a known principle may be applied, the combatant takes an important step towards building the confidence necessary to use it in a fight. By gradually increasing both the speed and complexity, confidence is built gradually based on the experience of success (and failure!).

I strongly recommend that combatants spend at least a quarter to half of their sparring time working on focused sparring—especially when learning or integrating a new technique.

OPEN SPARRING

Open sparring (also called "free play" by other WMA instructors and "fighting practice" in combat societies) helps to exercise judgement and builds extremely valuable "helmet time." However, at the novice levels in particular, open sparring may reinforce poor judgement or bad habits by rewarding weak behavior as the equally weak opponent fails to take advantage of mistakes. For this reason it is always best to tuck one's ego away and to seek to meet the best combatants as often as possible, because they will provide a challenge that no one else can, taking full advantage of every weakness and in the process driving improvement.

In sparring, combatants may well see (but miss) an opportunity to use a technique or exercise a principle previously studied. This gap between perception of an opportunity and the execution of an action will shrink either gradually or all at once, one of those "Eureka!" moments discussed earlier. In fact, the most important discoveries are often made with an epiphany rather than with slow development, although the background development is usually prerequisite for making the leap in the first place, the realization a "breakthrough" of pent-up experience.

Sparring is extremely valuable for the development of martial judgement and the building of confidence. Nothing can replace it in this context; no amount of drill can make up for the actual experience of interacting in a combat system. I believe this is because the active intelligence arrayed against you provides both variance and checking on your decisions unavailable in drill. "Helmet time," as I have called it in my other writings, is invaluable and should be maximized.

Frequently students engaged in sparring or drill will stop and the intertia of conversation will impinge on their training time. This tendency must be countered and practice time should be paced to discourage it.

TOURNAMENTS / COMPETITION

Finally, tournaments and competition test *zudadori* in a way that not even open sparring can do. Not only are martial skills tested at a surprisingly higher level than are available in practice, but the whole spectrum of character virtues are excercised under observation by one's peers and any judges or spectators present. The result is the development of martial renown, the "coin of the tourneyer" as I wrote in *The Book of the Tournament*.

This experience cannot be duplicated and participation in properly run tournaments can be the pinnacle experience of a combatant who has long trained to build technique and judgement. Since our students will likely not be challenged in a duel, a tournament represents perhaps the most realistic exercise for his spectrum of abilities.

Of course a certain amount of trepidation can accompany a student's first exposure to a tournament. Within the Schola Saint George we use a 15th century form of challenge tournament—the *pas d'armes*—which enables each combatant to choose who and what they will fight during the course of the day. Unlike a modern elimination list, combatants are never "out," so there is little impulse to cheat. Victors are chosen for those who do the best during the course of the day and/or those who demonstrate noteworthy abilities. But as with their medieval counterparts, *compagni* earn a certain amount of valuable renown for participating, renown that rewards them for all of the invested effort. If run well, the tournament provides a stage upon which chivalric deeds can be done, a microcosm of life where the continued survival of the chivalric virtues may be proven by any combatant for all to enjoy and take strength from.[11]

-NOTES-

[1] Castiglione, Wordsworth edition, p. 33-4.

[2] Fiore does use the term enemy in the PD in a couple of instances, but the intent seems to be when these techniques and principles are used against an opponent as opposed to a training partner, with whom *concordia* must be exercised.

[3] In a competition, the fight begins even before the salute, and the salute can become an aspect of the fight itself. You want to convey confidence, surety, and respect—but you can also seize the initiative in the salute, establishing yourself as the subject of the fight to come, rather than the object.

[4] In Italian, the terms *zugadore* (players), *compagni* (companions) and *scolari* (scholars) are all masculine nouns ending in "o." Nouns that end in "o" become plural with the replacement of the "o" with an "i," hence *zugadore* (sing.) → *zugadori*; *compagno* (m. sing) → *compagni*; scolaro (m. sing) → *scolari*. Being a romance language, if the gender of the parties is unknown the masculine is assumed.

[5] Motor control and learning is a branch of kinesiology that examines how humans learn movement. Much work has been done in an effort to learn how people learn movements and how to optimize training the training regimen, prompted by U.S. military studies in the early 1940-50s.

[6] The progression of the Schola modules is the subject of the last chapter.

[7] Serial practice describes drills or exercises that are done in order, i.e., 1-2-3, and repeated, 1-2-3. A random schedule, which seems to produce equivalent or in sometimes better results, mixes the practice, 3-1-2, 1-2-3, 2-1-3, etc.. By contrast, most trainers adopt blocked practice schedules because they are easier to manage, but studies such as Schmidt (1975) and Shea & Kohl (1990, 1991) have shown that blocked practice is far less effective than the other two options.

[8] This is also referred to in the MMA communities as "open sparring," what SCA and similar groups call, "fighting practice." It is indeed practice, and it is excellent for refining both mental and physical movement. But if done without systematic training, the results are uneven—some combatants intuitively grasp or develop a system that works well, while others founder or limp along.

[9] Applying a learned motor skill to a related circumstance is known to kinesiologists as a transfer test. While both retention and transfer tests are used, I find the character of each testing type different and useful at different circumstances, and at different stages of learning. For novices, for example, a retention test will measure how well the students replicate the techniques and ideas they have practiced. But for advanced combatants, a transfer test may measure a deeper level of understanding of the principles underlying the concepts and techniques, very possibly a more mature and advanced level of comprehension.

[10] I am indebted to Paul Porter, who introduced me to this idea many years ago and who still advocates its use.

[11] I have written abou the use of tournaments in my *Book of the Tournament*, which I would, with humility, recommend for any combatant who wants to explore the structure and function of such tournaments in more detail.

CHAPTER THIRTEEN

STUDYING IN THE SCHOLA SAINT GEORGE

ne way to study Fiore's *Fior di Battaglia* is by affiliation with a Western Martial Arts group. There are many fine schools around the world, many talented interpreters, and many, many fine people associated with European swordsmanship. The community of schools, academies, and study groups makes for a vibrant mix of fellow sword-devotees.

The Schola has what we think of as a *chivalric* orientation: we use the historical arts to develop character and prowess that we hope is transferable out of the training hall and into daily life. To that end the Schola sponsors regular seminars—including our prestigious SSG International Swordsmanship Symposium—traditionally held in June, tournaments, and regular courses of study. We expect our members to develop themselves not only in the sword arts, but to polish their character as well. Many of our students also practice other martial arts, are military or police combat officers, or employ their skills within a combat society environment such as the SCA or the ECS. We encourage cross-training, and, since we don't have the "one true way," are keenly interested in the development of our scholar's analytical ability, charging all students to contribute back to the Schola's growing and changing understanding not only of Fiore, but of the European chivalric arts in general.

In choosing an organizing model for the school we have chosen to follow something like the martial arts model (as opposed to the classical fencing model) because we have found that our Art has much in common with the Asian martial arts, and we have found many kindred spirits amongst the Asian arts community. Indeed, Fiore's art is as intensive, efficient and effective as any Asian art I have seen, and it compares favorably even with the highly developed Japanese sword arts. Therefore, we have chosen to create a study and advancement system that reflects this kindred relationship while still preserving its European lineage.

As I wrote in chapter 1, one may enter into Fiore's art from any weapon. We have run courses starting with the *lanza*, the *azza*, and with the *abrazzare*, but for the most part our coursework begins with the material in this book, what I call the **First Masters of Battle** course.

The Schola curriculum is broken down into modules and units. For the most part, each module has a strategic objective, and each unit represents a block of study within a module. Schola students work through the curriculum module by module, not moving on until one has internalized a given unit. At the end of each module we administer a recognition test. If the students pass the test, they are recognized by an increase in ranking. Each rank is associated with a color in the manner of the Eastern martial arts. The ranks are as follows:

Rank Progressions

Zugadore: Not yet tested for first degree (may wear tan belt)

Compagno: , completed and tested **First Master of Battle coursework**

Scolaro Minore: Blue, completed and tested **Zhogo Largo coursework**

Scolaro Maggiore: Green, completed and tested **Four Masters of the Entry coursework**

Primo Scolaro: Red, completed and tested **Zhogo Stretto coursework**

Scrimatore: Brown, completed armoured or breadth weapon training

Magistro: choice Black or White, completed thesis or detailed curriculum

E ach level has specific requirements including coursework, reading for background and breadth, and technical skills. As the student progresses there are also equipment requirements for testing (beginning with testing for *scolaro minore*), for taking classes not taught by a Schola instructor (for breadth), and teaching lower level material. The objective is to develop students who are capable of understanding and applying Fiore's material to many different combat circumstances.

Zugadore (None or a plain tan belt): A student who has **not yet completed** the **First Masters of Battle** class and *Compagno* test.

Compagno (yellow belt): To achieve the *compagno* rank, students must work through and be tested on the **First Masters of Battle** material, which focuses on stability, the development of power, strikes, thrusts, striking to cover, and the six core plays. This is the subject of this book. The coursework should take between 10 – 25 weeks, depending upon experience and frequency of study.

Scolaro Minore (blue belt): To achieve junior scholar rank, students must learn and be tested on the tactical framework as presented in Fiore's *zhogo largo* (long play) material, which includes the *tre volte* or turns of the sword, the *tre tempi* (three times), and the eight plays we do from the *zhogo largo*. The *tre volte* and the *tre tempi* are also applied to the first six plays. Students must have their own sword, gambeson, and shoes. This level should also take between 10 – 25 weeks.

Scolaro Maggiore (green belt): To achieve senior scholar level, students must successfully complete and be tested on the on their ability to integrate the previous units into their sparring performance. This third module is built around our **Quattro Magistri d'Entrada** (four masters of the entry) course, designed to press students forward into the fight and use the **First** or **Second Masters of Battle** to quickly end the encounter according to the tactical framework presented in the *zhogo largo* section. Students are expected to spend about 50% or so of their class time sparring, the rest in drill. At this level those without significant prior experience in a combat sport or art will be focusing on the mental side of the fight, while those with experience will be striving to overcome habits. To complete this level with the sword in two hands combatants should be able to spar and be recognized as relying chiefly on the tactics and foundational elements of Fiore. The duration of this level is difficult to predict, but it can be expected to be from 20 – 75 weeks. Students test in the usual fashion but

Compagno Dan Sepham

with two additional components: Demonstration of the eight *zhogo largo* and six *ellefante* plays using a second weapon of their choice and must organize and hold a small *pas d'armes* where they act as *tenans*, or defenders.

Primo Scolaro (red belt): To be recognized as a *Primo Scolaro* (first scholar), the student must complete and have been tested on the *zhogo stretto* or close play. This material begins by going back to Fiore's grappling arts, the *abrazzare*, then progressing forward through our *daga* course, then returning to the sword in two hands, where the same principles are applied. This is a longer module than the others in terms of content, and can be expected to take a year or more.

Scrimatore (brown belt): To attain the rank of *Scrimatore* (Swordsman): The student must complete an individual course of directed study focused on a breadth element of the art, including any of the following: armoured combat, other related Italian or German material, the sword in one hand, spear, poleaxe, or mounted combat. The student must master the chosen material and be able to teach it to other interested members of the Schola. In addition, they should be qualified to teach both the *Compagno* and *Scolaro Minore* material at a minimum and must be able to demonstrate superior performance in a tournament or self-defense environment. Alternatively, they may decide to delve in detail into any of the previous material (sword in two hands, wrestling, etc.) to develop a superior understanding of Fiore's core material.

Magistro (black or white belt): The rank of *magistro* is presently the pinnacle rank within the Schola. To reach it, the candidate must produce a thesis or detailed and tested course syllabus in an area of interest to them that makes a contribution to the Western martial arts. A candidate should have two years as a brown belt or equivalent before being considered for their *magistro* rank, a level recognized only after a rigorous test conducted by the existing Schola *magistri* and invited masters from other arts.

The rank structure has been developed over time as a way of directing students into the right study material, and for setting expectations between students around the world in terms of ability and knowledge. We are in no way "about the rank," but it does help as a measure of progress.

GETTING STARTED

U nlike many schools and groups, the Schola Saint George is comprised of branches, study groups, affiliated dojos, and independent scholars. If there is no school in your area, or if you like what you have read, you are certainly invited to explore an affiliation with the Schola.

Branches

S chola branches are groups with at least twelve members and an instructor. Presently there are only two branches, one in the San Francisco Bay area (where the Schola was founded), and in the Dallas / Fort Worth area. Branches often hold special events, including seminars, tournaments, and study days. Branches run regular classes several times per week.

Study Groups

M ost SSG companions participate through a study group. A study group is formed around a group leader who administrates the insurance requirements, memberships, training schedules, and securing a place to train. Because study groups usually have no instructor, they follow a self-directed course of study based on the SSG syllabus. They advance and develop their members by studying the curriculum, working through each step before advancing to the next. Study Groups are easy to form: they need only three people, a copy of our current syllabus and a willingness to devote time to training. An application is made to the Schola Saint George, Inc., and the group is listed on the Schola website at www.scholasaintgeorge.org.

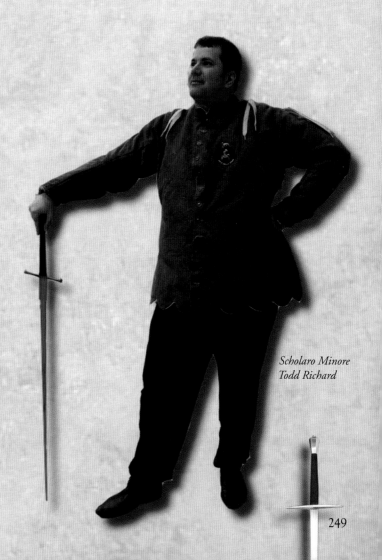

Scholaro Minore
Todd Richard

Independent Scholars

While the study of swordsmanship generally requires training partner at least some of the time, the Schola is pleased to recognize and include individuals whose careers or other responsibilities compel them along an individual path. Many of our independent scholars are also members of other schools, maintaining their Schola membership as a cross-training avenue.

Affiliated Dojos

Starting in 2006, we began to offer our curriculum to established dojos. These schools also follow the curriculum, but usually as an augmentation to their other coursework.

WEEKLY PRACTICE

Students should practice every week, preferably with two or more sessions per week. Each session should feature a salute, announcements during warm-up, and review of some aspect of the fundamentals, such as footwork. Next material from the current unit should be worked on using drills, exercises, and focused sparring. Finally, some element of the previous unit might be reviewed. The class should close with a salute. Students should study and practice the material during the week in between classes.

Measuring Progress

The students will work together to master the material. When the group has largely mastered one unit, which may take several weeks, it will be time to move on to the next. Students should actively discuss the material internally, and are encouraged to take questions to the main Yahoo! Group list, so that others may benefit from the discussion. If there are questions, ask one of the Schola instructors or post to the list. Students are encouraged to send video for critique. Finally, the group or study group leader should decide when members of the group are ready to test for rank advancement.

Advancement

Each module is tested in a combination of oral and demonstration testing. The requirements for each level are published, and while many of the questions will be asked, not all will be. Students testing remotely must cover all of the material in a video submission. Advancements in rank are marked with a ceremony, a certificate, and the right to wear a new belt color. No fee is associated with testing, but it is considered a mark of generosity to make a donation to the Schola (we are non-profit).

SCHOLA ACTIVITIES

Tournaments

Because the Schola is a sparring-oriented and tournament friendly group, we encourage local groups to hold tournaments both internally and to invite other SSG or other friendly associates in the development of a tournament circuit. Rules used in past tournaments are available.

Combatants may be qualified for tournament play after their 8th week of study with the *lanza* or short spear, and the longsword after the completion of their *compagno* testing (yellow belt). To use steel or aluminum weapons requires the completion of the *scolaro minore* (blue belt) or special recognition. To use grappling beyond an open-hand or *presa* against the weapon, they must be a *primo scolaro*.

Breadth Seminars

While the core of the Schola's instruction is the sword in two hands, we also have expertise available in the *lanza* or short spear, *azza* (poleaxe), *daga* (dagger), grappling, and in several other medieval traditions, including the Royal Armouries MS I.33 sword and buckler. Other areas are developed as students progress.

A high-point of each semester is usually the cutting day. Shown here is the Spring 2006 class in DFW.

Schola members can often provide relatively low-cost intensive modules in specific areas that might interest the students. Students must have at least 8 hours in seminars with another weapon to qualify for their blue belt, and more with each successive level. Over time, this must include study outside the Schola with other instructors in order to keep our material in synch with the WMA community.

THE SSG BOARD

The SSG has been incorporated under Texas law and has applied for non-profit status. Our Board is comprised of individuals who serve for two to four years. They are charged with managing the corporate affairs to keep the Schola moving, including registration, insurance management, and the like. The Board does not set curriculum but they do regulate things such as branch and study group recognition and disciplinary measures. Our Operating Procedures are currently in development as the Corporation and Board were founded only in early 2006.

Brian Johnson in harness. Fiore's combat techniques apply equally to armoured and unarmoured combats.

Right, Brian fights with SSG independent Scholar Aaron Shields using the azza.

BIBLIOGRAPHY

MANUSCRIPTS

Dei Liberi, Fiore.
    Fior di Battaglia. Getty MS Ludwig 13 (83.MR.183)
    Fior di Battaglia, Morgan M.0383

TRANSCRIPTIONS & FACSIMILES

Dei Liberi, Fiore
    Flos Duellatorum. Reprint of the 1902 edition, *Flos Duellatorum in arme, sine armis, equester, pedester*. Francesco Novati by Giardini Editori, Pisa.

    Il Fior di Battaglia di Fiore dei Liberi da Cividale: Il codice Ludwig XV 13 del J. Paul Getty Museum. Edited by Massimo Malipiero. Ribis, 2006.

Vadi, Filippo
De Arte Gladiatoria: 15th century swordsmanship of Master Filippo Vadi, trans. by Luca Porzio & Gregory Mele. Chivalry Bookshelf, 2002.

INTERPRETATIONS

Easton, Matt. *Fior di Battaglia, the Martial Treatise of Fiore dei Liberi (C. 1409)," in Art & Arms: Florence, City of the Medici. Proceedings of the 2003 International Arms and Armor Conference*, ed. By Christopher Dobson, 2003.

Galvani, Graziano. 1409-2002, *Flos Duellatorum: La pietra miliare della scuola marziale Italiana*. Librir del circolo, 2002.

Hand, Stephen.
    Ed. *SPADA: An Anthology of Swordsmanship in Honor of Ewarte Oakeshott*. Chivalry Bookshelf, 2002.

Hatcher, Colin. *untitled*, Seminar on the *Segno* given at the Western Martial Arts Workshop, 2006.

Mele, Gregory. *What Come Up, Must Come Down: A Walking Tour of the Fior di Battaglia of Fiore dei Liberi*. Seminar at the Western Martial Arts Workshop, 2005.

Preto, Luis. *Jogo do Pau: The Ancient Art and Modern Science of Portuguese Stick Fighting*. Chivalry Bookshelf, 2005.

Price, Brian R., ed. *Teaching & Interpreting Historical Swordsmanship*. Chivarly Bookshelf, 2005.

Rapsardi, Giovanni. *Flos duellatorum in armis, sine armis equester et pedester*. Seneca Edizione, 2005.

Rubboli, Marco & Luca Cesari. *Anonimo Bolognese, L'Arte della Spada: Tratto di scherma dell'inizio del XVI secolo*. Il Cerchio, 2005.

    Fiore di Liberi, *Flos Duellatorum: Manuale di arte del combattimento del XV secolo*. Il Cerchio, 2002.

Tobler, Christian Henry. *Fighting with the German Longsword*. Chivalry Bookshelf, 2004.

    In Service of the Duke: Paulus Kal's 15th century fighting treatise, Chivalry Bookshelf, 2006.

    Secrets of German Medieval Swordsmanship: Sigmund Ringeck's Commentaries on Master Liechtenauer's Verse. Chivalry Bookshelf, 2001.

Wagner, Paul. *Master of Defence: The Works of George Silver*. Paladin Press, 2003.

Windsor, Guy. *The Swordsmans' Companion: A Modern Training Manual for Medieval Longsword*. Chivalry Booskhelf, 2004.

ITALIAN & LATIN LANGUAGE, PALEOGRAPHY

Bischoff, Bernard. *Latin Paleography: Antiquity to the Middle Ages*, trans. Dáibhí ó Crónín & David Ganz. Cambridge University Press, 1986, reprinted 2006.

Cappelli, A. *Dizionario di Abbreviature Latine ed Italiane*, Milano, 1949.

Florio, John. *A Worlde of Wordes, or Most Copious, and exact dictionarie in Italian and English*. London, 1598. Reprinted Georg Olms, Verlag, 2004.

Derolez, Albert. *The Paleography of Gothic Manuscript Books from the Twelfth to the Early Sixteenth Century,* Cambridge, 2003.

OTHER USEFUL BOOKS

Amberger, J. Christoph. *The Secret History of the Sword: Adventures in Ancient Martial Arts*. Multi Media Books, 1998.

Ames, Winslow. *Italian Drawings from the 15th – 19th Centuries*, Shorewood Publishers, 1963.

Balestracci, Duccio. *La Festa in Armi: giostre, tornei e giochi del medioevo*, Editori Laterza, 2001.

Beaumont, C.L.. Fencing: Ancient Art and Modern Sport, A.S. Barnes & Co., 1978.

Aberdeen Beastiary, trans. by Richard Barber and published as *Bestiary: MS Bodley 764*, Boydell & Brewer, 1999.

Bascetta, Carlo. *Sport e Giuochi*, Edizione il polifilo, 1978.

Bertini, Giulio. *La Biblioteca Estense e la Cultura Ferrarese ai tempi and Duca Ercole I*. Turin, 1903.

Blair, Claude. *European Armour*, Batsford, 1972.

Boccia, L. *L'Armatura del '400 a Mantova*, Busto Arizio, 1982.

     Armi e armature Lombarde, Electra Editrice, 1980.

Cancelleria, V.. *Inventario della Biblio. E dell'Archivo della Torre in Ferrara, 1467-1512*. Pub. Unkown.

Camera, V. *Casa, Amministraz, Biblioteca, Invent., a c. VI*, 1508.

Capelli, A., "La Biblioteca Estense nella Prima Meta del Secolo XV," in *Giorn. Stor. Della Letter, Ital.*, v.XIV, 1889

Cartright, Julia. *Baldassarre Castiglione: The Perfect Courtier, His Life and Letters, 1478-1529*. E.P. Dutton & Co, 1908.

Castilgione, Baldassare. *The Book of the Courtier*, trans. by Leonard Eckstein Opdycke, Wordsworth Classics, 2000.

Collins, Arthur. *Animals and Birds Represented in English Church Architecture*, McBride & Nast, 1913.

Getty Museum, Los Angeles. *Catalog entry for Ludwig XVI 13, Fiore dei Liberi manuscript*.

Grossman, Lt. Col. Dave. *On Killing: The Psychological Cost of Learning to Kill in War and Society*. Little, Brown & Co, 1995.

Roark, Anthony Phillip. *Time in Physics IV: Aristotle's Reductionist Vision in Four Movements*. University of Washington Ph.D Dissertation, 1999.

ARMS & ARMOUR

Cosson, Baron de. & S.J. Camp. "Milanese Armourer's Marks," *Burlington Magazine for Conoissieurs*, Vol. 36, number 103, 1920.

Price, Brian R. *Techniques of Medieval Armour Reproduction*, Paladin Press, 1998.

Scalini, Mario. *The Armoury of Castle Churburg* (2 vols), including Oswald von Trapp's 1929 catalog. Magnus, 1996. Limited edition #796.

Takaiwa, Setsuo, Yoshindo Yoshihara, Leon & Hiroko Kapp. *The Art of Japanese Sword Polishing*, Kodnasha, 2006.

Williams, Alan. *The Knight and the Blast Furnace: A History of the Metallurgy of Armour in the Middle Ages & the early Renaissance*, Brill, 2003.

KNIGHTHOOD & CHIVALRY

Kaeuper, Richard & Elspeth Kennedy. *The Book of Chivalry of Geoffroi de Charny*, University of Pennsylvania Press, 1996.

Keen, Maurice. *Chivalry*, Yale University Press, 1984.

Price, Brian R. *Ramon Lull's Book of Chivalry & Knighthod*, Chivalry Bookshelf, 2001.

CONDOTTIERI & WARFARE

Deiss, Joseph Jay. *Captains of Fortune: Profiles of Six Italian Condottieri*, Cromwell, 1967.

Mallet, Michael. *Signori e Mercenari. La Guerra nell'Italia del Rinascimento*, 1983.

Monaco, Francesco Lo. *I Condottieri*, A. Barion,1941.

Rendina, Claudio. *Capitani di Ventura*, Rome, 1994.

Ricotti, Ercole. *Storia della Compagnie di Ventura in Italia*, 4 vols., 1845.

Scott, Leader. *Sir John Hawkwood: Story of a Condottiere*, Trans. by John Temple-Leader & Giuseppe Marcotti. T-Fisher Unwin, 1889.

Trease, Geoffrey. *The Condottieri*. Holt, Rinehard, Winston, 1971.

Villandon, L.J. Andrew and Donald J. Kagay, Eds. *Crusaders, Condottieri and Cannon: Medieval Warfare and Societies Around the Mediterranean*. Brill, 2003.

TOURNAMENTS & DEEDS OF ARMS

Muhlberger, Stephen. *Deeds of Arms*. Chivalry Bookshelf, 2005.

Feats of Arms: Geoffroi de Charny and the Rules for Chivalric Sport in 14th century France. Chivalry Bookshelf, 2002.

Nelson, Geoffrey. *Trial by Combat*. William Hodge & Co, 1890.

Price, Brian R. *The Book of the Tournament*, Chivalry Bookshelf, 1996.

Van der Neste, Evelyn. *Tournois, Joutes, Pas d'Armes dans les Villes de Flandre a la Fin du Moyen Age (1300-1486)*, École des Chartes, 1996.

FENCING & MARTIAL ARTS

Babin, Richard, Dr. & Bob Elder *Cutting Targets With the Japanese Sword: Practical Tameshigiri and Battodo*, Paladin Press, 2005.

Castle, Egerton. *Schools and Masters of Defence*, G. Bell & Sons, 1910.

Cohen, Richard. *By the Sword: A History of Gladiators, Musketeers, Samurai, Swashbucklers and Olympic Champions*. Random House, 2002.

Hutton, Alfred. *Old Sword Play*, 1892.

Obata, Toshishiro, *Shinkendo Tameshigiri*, International Shinkendo Federation, 2005.

Pardoel, Henk. *Fencing: A Bibliography*. Multi-MT, 2005.

Silver, George. *Paradoxes of Defense and Brief Instructions of the Sword*, Pavilion Press, 2004.

Suino, Nicholas. *Practice Drills for Japanese Swordsmanship*, Weatherhill, 1995.

Wise, Arthur. *The History of Personal Combat*, Hugh Evyln, Ltd., 1971.

ITALIAN & EUROPEAN HISTORY

Chamberlin, ER. *The Count of Virtue; Giangaleazzo Visconti, First duke of Lombardy*, Schribners, 1965.

Chronicon Estense, in L.A. Muratori, *Rerum Italicarum Scriptores XV*, Milan: 1723-1751.

Davis, Robert C., *The War of the Fists: Popular Culture and Public Violence in Late Renaissance Venice*, Oxford, 1994.

Frizzi, Antonio. *Memorie per la Storia di Ferrara*, 5 vols., 1791-1809, reprinted 1968 ed.

Froissart, Jehan, *Chronique*, Vols. 1-12, Ed. by Simeon Luce, Paris.
   trans. by Sir John Bourchier, Lord Berners. *Chronicles*. Shakespeare Head Press, 8 Vols., 1978.

Garnder, Edmund. *Dukes and Poets of Ferrara*, Haskel House, 1968.

Godefroy, Theodore. *Histoire de Messire de Jehan de Boucicaut*, Pacard, 1620.

Gori, Pietro. *Le Feste Fiorentine: Attraverso i Secoli*, R. Bemporad & Figlio, 1926.

Herald, Jacqueline. *Dress in Renaissance Italy, 1400-1500*, Humanities Press, 1981.

Kohl, Benjamin. *Padua under the Carrara, 1318-1405*, Johns Hoplins, 1998.

Lalande, Denis. *Jean II Le Meingre, Dit Boucicaut (1366-1421)*, Librarie Droz, 1988.

   Le Livre des Faites du Bon Messire Jehan le Maigre, dit Bouciquaut, Mareshal du France et Gouveneur du Jennes,Librarie Droz, 1985.

Leight, P.S. *A History of Friuli*, Ente Friuli del Mondo, 1988.

Levi-Pisetzky, Rosita. *Storia del Costume in Italia* Vols. II. Istituto Editoriale Italiano, 1964-69.

Robathan, Dorothy M., "The Catalogues of the Princely and Papal Libraries of the Italian Renaissance," *Transactions and Proceedings of the American Philological Association*, Vol. 64, 1933, pp. 138-149.

Roulx, J. Delaville. *La France en Orient au XIVe siècle*. 2 vols., Thorin, 1886.

Schele, Klaus. *Die Sforza*, Magnus Verlag, 1980.

Ulmer, Christoph & Gianni d'Affara. *The Castles of Friuli: History & Civilization*, Konemann, 1987.

Urquhart, W.M. Pollard. *Life and Times of Francesco Sforza*, Blackwell, 1852.

Valeri, Nino. *Storia d'Italia*, 5 vols., U.T.E.T, 1965.

Zanutto, Luigi. *Fiore di Premariacco ed i ludi e le feste marziali e civili in Friuli nel Medio-evo* : (studio storico) /. Del Bianco, 1907.

      Premariacco: Nella Storia Friuliese, Udine, 1906.

ART HISTORY

Hale, J.R. *Artists and Warfare of the Renaissance*, Yale University Press, 1990.

Mellini, Gian Lorenzo. "Disegni di Altichiero e della sua scuola, 1," *Critica d'Arte*, LI, May-June 1962, pp. 1-24.

      "Disegni di altichiero e della sua scuola, 2," *Critica d'Arte*, LIII-LIV, September-December 1962, pp. 9-19.

Richards, John. *Altichiero: An Artist and His Patrons of the Lateri Italian Trecento*, Cambridge University Press, 2000.

Schlosser. "Ein veronescisches Bilderbuch," *Jahrbuch der Kunsthistorischen Sammlungen des A.H. Kaiserhauses,* xvi, 1895, pp. 182, 188. 189.

RENAISSANCE DANCE

Cornanzo, Antonio. *The Book on the Art of Dancing*, trans. by Madeleine Inglehearn and Peggy Forsyth, Dance Books Limited, 1981.

Ebreo of Pesaro, Guglielmo. *De Pratica Seu Arte Tripudii* (On the Practice or Art of Dancing), Ed. Barbara Sparti, Clarendon Press, 1983.

Piacenza, Domenico di. *De Arte Saltandi & Choreas Ducendi*. ca.1450; reprint, Dante Bianchi, 1963.

Wilson, D.R. *The Steps Used in Court Dancing in Fifteenth-Century Italy*, 3rd edition, published by the author, 2003.

KINESIOLOGY

Goodwin, J.E. and H.J. Meeuwsen. "Using Bandwidth Knowledge of Results to Alter Relative Frequencies During Motor Skill Acquistition," *Research Quarterly for Exercise and Sport*, 66, 1995, pp. 99-104.

Hicks, W.E. "On the Rate of Gain of Information," *Quarterly Journal of Experimental Psychology*," 4, 1952, pp. 11-26.

Lashley, Karl. "The Accuracy of Movement in the Absence of Excitation from the Moving Organ," *American Journal of Psyiology*, 43, 169-194.

Magill, Richard A. *Motor Control & Learning*, 7th edition. McGraw Hill, 1974.

Miller, G.A., E. Galameter & K.H. Pribram. *Plans and the Structure of Behavior*. Holt, Reinholt & Winston, 1960.

Shea, C.H. & R.M. Kohl. "Specificity and Variability of Practice," *Research Quarterly for Exercise and Sport*, 62, 1990, pp. 169-177.

Schmidt, Richard A. "A Schema Theory of Discrete Motor Skill Learning Theory," *Psychological Review*, 82, 1975, pp. 225-260.

Chivalry Bookshelf

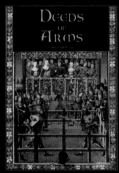

DEEDS OF ARMS

Jousts and Tournaments

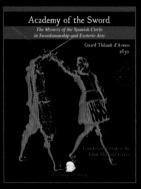

Academy of the Sword
The Mystery of the Spanish Circle in Swordsmanship and Esoteric Arts
Girard Thibault d'Anvers
1630

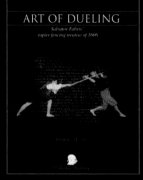

ART OF DUELING
Salvator Fabris' rapier fencing treatise of 1606

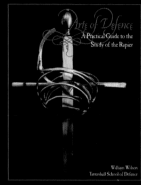

Arte of Defence
A Practical Guide to the Study of the Rapier
William Wilson
Tattershall School of Defence

The Royal Book of Horsemanship, Jousting and Knightly Combat
Dom Duarte's 15th century Bem Cavalgar

Ramon Lull's
Book of KNIGHTHOOD and Chivalry
& the Anonymous Ordene de Chevalerie

Highland Swordsmanship
Techniques of the Scottish Swordmasters
Mark Rector

Highland Broadsword
Techniques of the Scottish Regiments
Mark Rector & Paul Wagner

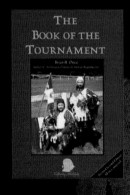

THE BOOK OF THE TOURNAMENT
Brian R. Price

SPADA
ANTHOLOGY OF SWORDSMANSHIP

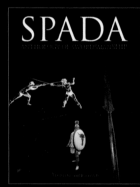

SPADA
ANTHOLOGY OF SWORDSMANSHIP

Jogo do Pau
The Ancient Art and Modern Science of Portuguese Stick Fighting
Luis Preto

The Duellist's Companion
A training manual for 17th century Italian rapier
Guy Windsor

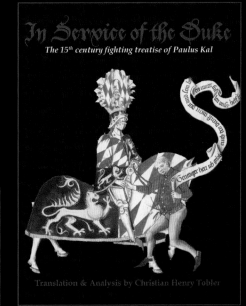

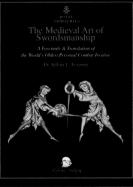
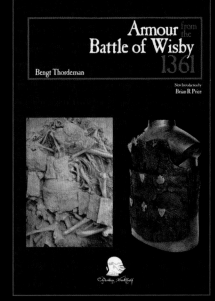

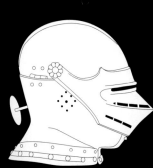

Schola Saint George

Historical Swordsmanship as a Martial Art

Like what you read?

check us out at www.scholasaintgeorge.org

Training Tips
Photos & Video
Competition Rules
Event & Seminar info
Study Groups
Independent Scholars
Affiliated Dojos
Membership

www.scholasaintgeorge.org

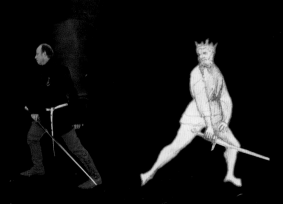